SLOWLY SLOWLY

The Old Way to Everest Base Camp

Lee Prescott

Slowly Slowly

Published by Boricua Press
Boricua Press, 411 North Woodside Road, Glasgow
G20 6NN, UK

First published by Boricua Press November 2020
1

ISBN 978-1-8382423-0-5

For Sasha, Vanessa and Hugo

Tribhuvan to Narsingh Chowk

As I stashed the guidebook in my daypack, its warning Kathmandu's Tribhuvan International Airport had been voted the third worst in the world echoed in my mind. At the sight of the terminal, I wondered where the other two lower ranked landing places were located – perhaps the deck of the USS Yorktown at Midway, the Hudson River circa 2009 or anywhere Harrison Ford happened to be flying into that day? Ahead stood a khaki brick edifice with all the charm of a 1980s-built council office.

To the rear was different – an expanse of verdant, forested foothills summitted by a massif of snowy peaks gleaming under an azure sky. Beyond those mountains was where I was headed, my aim to realise a lifetime ambition thwarted twice before – to see Mount Everest. The route I'd take was inspired by the Hillary-Norgay expedition that had summitted the mountain in 1953. I hoped to follow in their footsteps and reach Base Camp, but before I got there, I was going to have to navigate my way through that forbidding building.

This was my third visit to Nepal. My first was as a board-short-wearing callow youth in the time my children imagine life was conducted in black and white. I'd set out from Darjeeling keen for my first glimpse of Everest from a local viewpoint. Two days in, my fellow trekkers mentioned in passing the route transgressed the border. But we were fortunate and avoided any guards. What police we did encounter seemed more concerned with issuing me with a ticket based on my flagrant disregard of the Kanchenjunga district beach attire bylaws. But, alas, we reached the viewpoint to find the mountain determined to remain shrouded in cloud. Two decades later, having somehow hauled myself around the Annapurna Circuit's splendour, I tried again. After a fortnight of blue skies, Everest hid behind a wall of grey.

So, while I was patently hopeless at trying to catch a glimpse of the world's highest point, I considered myself something of an expert on how things worked in Nepal. After being ushered across the tarmac apron, I was funnelled into the throng of other passengers zigzagging through a series of disorientating corridors. It disgorged our crush into an area which would seem, to the untrained eye, a scene of untrammelled chaos. Not to my seasoned senses, though; having been through Tribhuvan before, I was unlike the 300 other excited outdoor enthusiasts. They stood confused, imploring the God of Visa Control to part the Red Sea of Immigration and let them pass into the promised land of yak milk and honey. As a veteran, I wasn't in need of such divine inspiration. I knew the score in dealing with all this apart from, of course, how the government had improved everything in the last decade by introducing automation.

Recent arrivals were taking best advantage of this streamlining of business processes. Four columns of Occidentals fanned themselves with all manner of documents on my left. They stood hopeful of completing a yet undefined transaction at what could have been a bookmaker's counter. To my right were a half-dozen lines of Westerners in front of what appeared to be the squat, enamelled blocks of a row of James Dean-era wringer washers. The landing *had* been bumpy and, while I thought it considerate of the Nepalese government to provide for the cleansing of soiled undergarments before entering the country, the number of machines seemed generous for such a task.

I stopped at a kind of polite melee where new arrivals crossed with the tail-ends of the lines, to the slight irritation of a burly Australian gentleman.

"S'cuse me mate, that's moiy place in the line," he growled, taking one step nearer to me than was strictly necessary to explain.

"Oh, I'm sorry. What queue is this?"

"It's not the one ya think you're in, mate."

"Oh, okay, thanks. I don't think I'm in a queue at the moment but would be glad to be. Where does this one start?"

"At its end." Ignoring my urge to challenge my close-up friend on the philosophical paradox of how something could start at its end, I tried to elicit further clarification.

"Where do I go for that, please?" I asked as the column shuffled forward.

"Over there." He swept his arm noncommittally towards the melee. He'd had enough of my questioning and, eager not to lose his place in line, he barged past.

"Loine's movin', mate. Heave-ho."

None the wiser for the conversation I was forced to address the trip's first dilemma. What queue to join? In the circumstances, I did what any self-respecting Britisher would do and chose to join the longest line. Queuing theory determined it would move the quickest and it came with the advantage of being furthest away from the irked Antipodean.

"Excuse me, what's this queue for?" I directed my question at a Nepali gentleman who was well camouflaged in his fleece and trekking boots within the mass of new arrivals.

"Internet visa application. You can fill in the form on the computer-machine or you can use your phone."

"You mean, there's a website that has the form? I can use my phone for that? Is that secure?"

"Website yes. Phone yes. What is secure?"

"Never mind, do you know the website's address?"

"No, but if you go to that machine there you can look." He indicated it would be fine to head to the front of the line and take down the particulars of the applicant mid process.

"Err ... okay. So once I've got the URL, the website will work fine on my phone?"

"Yes, no problem." I decided to hedge my bets and try the website from my phone while waiting in line for one of the Maytags.

"I'll give that a go, then. I don't think my phone works on a Nepali network, is there Wi-fi I could use so I can get online?"

"Yes. You can buy a Wi-fi pass for one hour."

"Great, where can I get that?"

"At the counter, at the bottom of the stairs in departures."

"Through immigration and customs?"

"Yes."

"I'm not sure that's going to work. Is there a place where I can get a Nepali SIM instead and get online that way?"

"Yes, the shop there."

"Great, so once I've filled in the form, what do I do next?"

"Take your printed form to the counter there to pay the fee." He pointed towards the other set of lines. Having forgotten to pack my

Hewlett-Packard inkjet in my hand luggage, I discounted the SIM option. Satisfied I was at least in the right place to get my visa, I resigned myself to a slow shuffle in the line towards the laundry service. As I neared our machine, it was evident by the look of despair on each face of those stepping up to the screen I'd joined the line marked 'Information Age Passed You By? Queue Here.'

It was the turn of the lady ahead. A silver braided ponytail fell from under her floral beanie to canvas trousers. She flipped up the shaded part of her John Lennon glasses, squinted through her lenses at the screen and rotated towards me. I could now see over her shoulder the form was a simple web page, with a keyboard and mouse provided to help complete the required information. It was in no way an unusual combination, but by the lady's expression, she could've been asked to solve Fermat's Theorem using hieroglyphics blindfolded. Her distress triggered the camouflaged man to lend assistance.

"You have a problem with the machine? You can use your phone to fill in the form."

"I can use my phone? Oh, that's wonderful. There's an app for everything nowadays, don't you think? Once I download the app, I can do *anything*. My granddaughter has shown me how," she opined in a genteel British accent, her face transformed.

With a pang of regret, I'd no choice but to let her down gently about the app. By the time I'd apprised her of the other pitfalls of using her phone and losing her place at the machine, her despair was complete.

"Come on, don't worry, we can help you fill the form in here. See this bit, it's asking you for your landing card number. If you give me that, I can type it in for you."

"Where do I get one of those?" Camouflage pointed to a wooden workbench littered with certificates half scribbled in blue underneath a metre-high 'Landing Cards' sign.

While she trotted off to fill in her card, I tried my own luck at the machine. As I typed in my details, my mind wandered to a realisation that it reminded me of something entirely different to a 1950s wringer washer. I now knew where Maximillian had disappeared to at the end of *The Black Hole*. Slightly disconcerted that Nepal had invested in a row of killer death robots as its solution to the automation of immigration procedures, I completed my form as quickly as its design allowed. In response, a printed A4 sheet spewed out of Maximillian's bellybutton and I was ready to join the queue with the paradoxical Aussie.

With the pony-tailed lady's return, Camouflage and I helped her complete her details, but Max must have been in a crotchety mood deciding to reboot spontaneously at the point we hit 'Submit'. Camouflage was, unlike the despairing lady, evidently at ease with this occurrence and so, he unlocked a door somewhere around Max's nether regions and disappeared into his rectum. An echoing shout requested the lady perform a Control-Alt-Delete, which I duly helped with and Max sprung back to life, ready for more input. Our second attempt was no less tortuous than our first and, as I hit 'Submit' again, the slightly unnerving feeling that we'd inadvertently programmed Max and his killer robot army for world domination came across me.

The lady was happier; she regained her cool with the flip of her glasses back up to shades mode and we moved over to the other set of lines. To test queuing theory further, we agreed I should join the longest and she the shortest of the columns shambling forwards. Their goal was a partitioned counter beneath a sign that explained we needed to ready ourselves to hand over 'Acceptable Currency for Visa Fee.'

The bank seemed happy to accept almost anything as payment in that regard; we could even pay in Danish kroner if we so desired. Unfortunately, the gentleman at the head of the lady's queue didn't and seemed bereft of the other currencies listed. He was engaged in an attempt to barter his way into the country which was falling on the deaf ears of the officials. In desperation, he offered his watch to the crowd as collateral against the loan of some US dollars. There were no takers and, as he continued to argue his case, I reached my teller first.

"How long are you going to be in Nepal, sir?"

"About 35 days."

"You need a visa for 90 days. Application form and passport please, sir."

"Here you go."

"Ah, British. You will pay in British pounds," the clerk declared, spinning a calculator around on the counter.

"Can I pay in US dollars?" The official was taken aback; he'd already gone to the inconvenience of working out the exchange rate.

He'd also thoughtfully prepared a swag bag marked 'Sterling' for receipt of my monies on the counter.

"That will be $125, sir," he stated after recomposing himself. I was prepared for this and handed over seven crisp $20 bills.

"That is $15 more than the fee, sir, too much change in dollars."

"But this *is* a bank, isn't it?"

"Yes, sir."

"But you don't have $15 to give me back?"

"No, sir."

"How about rupees? I'm happy to accept rupees if that is easier?" I enquired, resisting my inner urge to say, 'I don't mind accepting Danish kroner'.

"We only deal in non-Nepali currencies here, sir, we have no rupees."

"Are you sure? In a Nepali bank? Oh, never mind, look, I have some pounds. What about if you give me a 20 back and I give you £10 instead? Will that help?"

"That makes the necessary calculation more complicated, sir."

"Yes, but you could give me £5 back. Will that work for you?"

"No sir, but I believe you are lucky! The gentleman at the other counter has presented my colleague with payment in $5 bills. I now have the dollar currency to present you with $15."

"Great. Thanks."

I gladly took my change and receipt for the visa fee, a little conflicted. I was pleased I'd avoided the scam but at the same time insulted that the officials could think they'd be able to get one over on a seasoned vet like myself.

I waved to the genteel lady and moved along the slick conveyor of automation onto the next step in the process. Her line was still stationary behind the man who was not giving up his place until he'd pawned enough jewellery to clear his fees.

The good news at parting with such a hefty fee was I could join the express line for people who were visiting for more than 30 days. The bad news was that as I was the only person in the queue the bored immigration official decided she needed something amusing to brighten her day. This took the form of an extended interrogation based my passport's contents and the route I'd taken to Nepal.

"You came from London?"

"Yes."

"Was it raining there?"

"Yes."

"It rains a lot in London."

"Yes."

"You had a stopover in Doha?"

"Yes."

"No rain in Doha?"

"No."

"It was hot there?"

"Yes."

"It is very hot in Doha."

And so on until I'd confirmed her exhaustive knowledge of climate data. She moved on to my passport, where it was clear she had some gaps to fill.

"You are from Liverpool?"

"Yes."

"It rains a lot in Liverpool?" We moved beyond her probing of average precipitation and temperature records in North West England and onto my heritage. We were approaching a 'What is your paternal grandmother's blood type?' level of questioning regarding my credentials when I was saved by explaining this was my third visit to Nepal and, on the previous occasion, I'd trekked the Annapurna Circuit.

It turned out the area was where her family came from and her officiously surly tone disappeared. She proceeded to provide me with evidence of her own ancestry; I was presented with some family photographs at which to tut my approval. She stamped my passport and, with a toothy grin, bid me the warmest 'Welcome to Nepal' anyone could have hoped for.

This left only luggage and customs to resolve. I'd waited a full two hours for my backpack to show on my previous visit, but this time I was delighted to see it sitting there on the conveyor belt as I reached the foot of the stairs. Exiting through customs involved nothing more bizarre than passing my backpack through an x-ray machine. I stood at its far side, hoping my stash of paramilitary gear missed at Gatwick airport wouldn't be spotted. A second later, the bag rolled to a stop below me. The guard waved me on and, with glee, I realised I was in!

As I strolled out of the control zone, I noticed something that *was* an improvement from my previous visit. A new arrival could now call a regulated taxi to take them to town. Ten years earlier, I'd agreed to take a taxi via a tout. I made it safely to a decent hotel, but the cost was to be pursued by him for the next two days trying to sell me a trekking trip. He was the variety of hawker who would've still been trying to broker a deal as I crossed the Thorung La pass at 5,400 metres. So, for this trip I'd arranged with my hotel to be picked up from the airport, to spare myself a similar experience.

Outside, the seething mass of speculators I'd expected, trying to relieve me of my 'Acceptable Currency', was curiously absent. The young man in a leather jacket holding up a sign saying 'Mr Prescoll' was easy enough to spot, though, and the spelling was close enough so I wandered over.

"Namaste."

"Namaste. Mr Prescoll?" I wasn't going to quibble, thinking it unlikely there was also a 'Mr Preschool' on the same plane as me.

"Yes." He bid me follow him over to a waiting taxi parked next to a motorcycle.

"Please sir. Get in." He zipped up his leathers, clipped on his Ray-Bans and straddled the bike.

"Aren't you coming with us?"

"No, I will escort you." I was suitably impressed and at once anxious. It was nice to be driven into town in such a way but I wondered what threat could be abroad requiring us to be guarded by Kathmandu's version of the Terminator.

There was a dearth of traffic as we pulled out of the airport. As I surveyed the surroundings from the back of the cab, a broad and uncontrollable grin spread across my face. The picture was how I'd remembered Asia, the source of my smile the realisation I was finally back. The afternoon was warm, the atmosphere dusty and the buildings ramshackle, but it was the smell that brought home I was back in Kathmandu. It was the tang of life being lived on the street.

"First time in Nepal, sir?"

"No, I was here 10 years ago. Kathmandu isn't as busy as I remember. The traffic was much worse then. Has something happened? Traffic zoning?"

"No, sir, traffic in Kathmandu is much worse than 10 years ago."

"It doesn't look it at the moment. Where is everyone today?"

"Tomorrow is Tihar, sir, festival time. People gone home to their villages, so not much traffic today and tomorrow."

"Tihar? Is that the same as Diwali? The festival of lights?"

"Yes sir, Indian people name is Diwali. Nepal people name is Tihar. Biggest festival for Hindu people in Nepal."

"Ah, that explains it. So, how about you? You aren't going to your village?"

"No sir, I am home. I am born in Kathmandu. Everyone from mountains come to see me. I make big Tihar party for all family!"

"That sounds good. What does that involve, a feast?"

"Yes, sir, lots of fooding and drinking. Durbar Whisky!"

"Can't argue with that."

"Yes, sir, we have good time. Sir, may I ask why you wait 10 years to visit Nepal? Is it not very beautiful?"

"Yes, it is beautiful. I don't know why I didn't come back earlier. There was always an excuse with work or whatever meaning I never organised it."

"Yes, I agree working is very hard, sir. Work is very hard for taxi driver in Nepal. The earthquake very bad for taxi business. Now I am happy you come to my country and I welcome you to Nepal."

"Thank you. Dhanyabad."

"Ah, your Nepali is very good. You are making trek?"

"Yes. Base Camp."

"Mount Everest. The top of the world! Khumbu is beautiful; I will go one day." I didn't have time to enquire why he'd never made it there but expected he'd give something akin to the same excuses I'd been using for the last decade.

He squeezed the taxi down a narrow alley and pulled over opposite a tented display blocking the way to where the K-Terminator dismounted his bike. 'Come with me if you want to live', his expression seemed to say. I bid the cabbie a happy Tihar and followed my cyborg guardian down an even narrower pedestrianised alleyway. Three hours after landing at Tribhuvan International Airport I was back in Thamel, I'd arrived.

Narsingh Chowk to Paryatan Marg

I had made my reservation at the Hotel Potala on the basis that I'd hoped I'd stayed there in the last few days before I'd left Kathmandu on my previous trip. The lack of precision in my recollection assuredly nothing to do with the amount of beer consumed in celebration of the Annapurna Circuit's completion and more to do with how hoteliers choose to label their accommodation in the city.

It is as if the Kathmandu city burghers have stipulated the name of any commercial lodging must contain at least one of the following words – Everest, Annapurna, Mustang, Tibet, Potala, Kathmandu, Garden or Peace. The most popular is the famous Kathmandu Guest House. It is booked up months in advance. The city's hoteliers are nothing if not a canny bunch and so for those unlucky travellers who aren't sure of its name the city's Thamel district offers the Kathmandu Garden House, Kathmandu Peace Home and Kathmandu Peace Guest House as alternatives. To make things even more challenging for potential (repeat) customers, establishments also periodically change their names. The institution that had always worn the moniker of the Kathmandu Guest House was now known as the Kathmandu Madhuban Guest House. If that wasn't confusing enough, some family-run places opt to move their location taking their name with them.

So, the Hotel Potala I was arrogantly striding towards *could* have been the same one at which I'd spent a few enjoyable days a decade earlier. The thoroughfare through which I hastened seemed familiar with its neon gaudiness of supermarket signs, trinket stalls and watering holes. In my excitement to confirm that I had the hotel right, I'd bustled past and left the K-Terminator for dead somewhere behind. A cybernetic concern echoed along the alleyway.

"Sir, please follow me. I will show you to the hotel."

"Don't worry, I've been here before. I know the way."

"Sir, the entrance to the hotel is difficult to find."

"I know where it is." I darted into a narrow alley that had been constrained further by rows of discarded motorcycles, delighted to see I was going to be staying at the same hotel. It had the same strange entrance via a dingy blue-lit workshop whose business I could never discern. One day it seemed to be the repair of clockwork fob-watches, the next arc-welding of mobile phones.

I skipped up the stairs past the De La Soul Bar on the first floor, a place whose merits seemed to be lost on the trekking populace. The last time I was in town, its lack of custom had intrigued me and I'd tried to get a drink there. But I'd failed as the place's only occupant ever seemed to be the piped hip-hop music. I hazarded at the time a better name would've been the Not A Soul Bar. I was surprised to see it had survived and determined to pop in later to see if there was anyone to ask whether there had been anyone in since my last visit.

I reached the hotel reception on the next floor and was struck with doubt that I was, after all, in the same place, despite all the indications otherwise. This was not how I remembered it. As I stood there confused K-Terminator, or KTM as I'd now come to think of him, squeezed past me to take his place at the counter opposite. He ceremoniously took off his helmet and unhurriedly unzipped his leathers, emphasising I shouldn't have been in such a rush.

"Welcome to the Hotel Potala, sir, how may I help you?"

"I've got a room booked for two nights; the name is Prescott."

"Very well, sir. I will see if I can find the receptionist to confirm your reservation." It seemed strange KTM would ask me these stock questions given he'd escorted me to Thamel. It was almost as if he was following some sort of computer programme. I was also confused why he couldn't confirm my reservation and check me in himself as he seemed in charge. He headed upstairs and returned shortly afterwards with a smartly dressed young lady who took up residence behind the counter.

"Welcome to the Hotel Potala, sir, how may I help you?"

"I've got a room booked for two nights; the name is Prescott." I was appreciative she didn't respond with a statement about the need to find her under-receptionist to confirm my reservation. For a second, I had a vision of being stuck in a never ending Russian doll series of ever more junior receptionists repeating the same questions over and over again for eternity. As it was, she efficiently found my reservation email and showed me to my room.

The room was functional. Its most arresting features were a portable television with neither power cable nor aerial, and the view afforded by the window. I was at the hotel's rear overlooking flat roofs onto a brick-built alleyway. All the scene needed was the graffitied tube of a D-Train rumbling by and I could've been in a less salubrious part of Brooklyn. But I was unperturbed by this, I'd chosen to stay at the Potala largely because of fond memories of its cosy terrace overlooking the street, rather than its rooms. From there, with a drink in hand, I'd watched the world go by on many occasions, and was keen to do the same again to celebrate my arrival. So I was disappointed when the receptionist told me it had closed years ago and to head up to the rooftop bar if I wanted a drink.

I wasn't sure why I was expecting the rooftop bar's furniture arrangement to be something approximating my memories, but in my mind's eye that was what I was heading towards as I climbed the stairs. So it was a shock to find the place remodelled on a London chill-out zone circa the year 2000. It was nice enough in its way, although I'm not sure what the interior designer was trying to achieve with the artificial turf wallpapering. It wasn't for me. There were even fewer signs of life in the joint than at the De La Soul. I'd have to venture out onto the street and take my chances there if I wanted a beer.

It was marvellous to see the Northfield Café still thriving. It was doing a brisk trade in the evening light, its clientele comprising groups of freshly scrubbed Westerners. I ordered a bottle of Everest lager, keen to soak up the atmosphere. I overheard genial conversations detailing how the travails encountered in completing various treks had been overcome. By my second beer, I was struggling with a battle of my own. The alcohol's influence on top of 30 hours without sleep was making me drowsy.

Nepal is five-and-three-quarter hours ahead of GMT. The curiosity of the 45-minute offset is designed as a very public statement from the Nepalese government to say 'Look, we are *not* India! To prove it we even have our own time zone.' My plan to deal with the time difference had been to reject sleep on the flights from London and stay awake until around 8pm local time. Hopefully, I'd then sleep through to the next morning. As I drained the Everest's last drop, the plan approached completion – I was 90 minutes short of my target.

I'd managed it through a combination of caffeine and the in-flight movie service. It triggers something deeply avaricious inside of me when presented with a choice of 'free' airline entertainment. I'm compelled to organise my viewing so a second isn't wasted where I'm not glued to the paperback-sized screen. This, although it's designed in such a way that at whatever angle it is set, it achieves maximum reflective glare.

A victory in this regard is retiring the use of the headphones against a set of closing credits truncated by the opening of the cabin doors. Usually this involves a mixture of content no sane person would ever consider watching, the only rationale for its selection a calculation that the subtitled Magyar for 'Best Boy' on the Hungarian spinnaker mockumentary would roll by as the final descent is called. I also like the added frisson of excitement when coming into land; air stewards can be overzealous in their safety procedures and blank the last five minutes of a movie. I'm not sure what this achieves regarding security and remain slightly miffed I still don't know what happens at the end of *Titanic*.

I'd managed a personal best of five full-length features on the flight over. This included the latest Tarantino, which I reckoned excellent, even viewed with a squint. I'd also watched a critically acclaimed movie about the Glasgow rave scene in the nineties. That was only tolerable because it was necessary to stay awake and the kindly stewardess had plied me with a bucket full of coffee. But now my cinematic exploits were in danger of catching up with me. Dozing off in the café, I reckoned it best I retire to my room and listen to music until my allotted bedtime. I unpacked my Nano and played the *Bellybutton* album by Jellyfish from its start. An hour later, I collapsed into sleep; it was 8pm.

I slept the sleep of the dead and was disoriented on waking. After regaining my senses, I was delighted the plan to combat jetlag had worked. It was mid-morning, so I could enjoy a leisurely breakfast before completing my tasks for the day. I had money to change, a bus trip to sort out and trekking permits to secure. KTM acknowledged me from behind reception as I passed by on the way to the first of my chores. As a veteran with two Himalayan tours completed, I was fully prepared to outwit the bureaucratic pulling of teeth that was changing money in a Nepali bank. I had a bundle of freshly ironed £10 notes, a visa-stamped passport, driver's licence, proof of address, utility bill from the last three months and the multiple passport photos that every administrative task seemed to require on my last visit.

I hoped the Himalayan Bank was still a 10-minute stroll away and I headed out on the street in the direction I recalled. The Thamel that met me was at once familiar and changed. I couldn't point out in an identity parade which stores had been committed to memory since my last visit, but there was something different to the place. At the Narsingh Chowk, it dawned on me that the streets had been sinicized. Where a decade earlier the neon boards proclaimed noodles and rice in English, now their preponderance was Chinese.

My stroll to the bank was uneventful apart from the attentions of a persistent taxi driver who was insistent I was better off experiencing the 100-metre journey in his jalopy rather than on foot. It pleased me the bank was in the same spot and hadn't suffered the fate of many of its UK cousins in being converted into the brand of cavernous drinking emporium populated by hordes of youths at odds with the Victorian décor. It was still reassuringly engaged in matters of fiscal transaction; a shotgun armed guard outside confirmed the fact. Either that, or the Fire and Ice Pizzeria opposite had become so rough over the last decade the bouncer now needed to pack some heat.

Although the bank was still in the same place, there had been a development in the intervening decade. A sentinel of Maximillian's robot overlord invasion force now guarded the stairs leading to the tellers. A Scandinavian-looking gentleman in a drab Buddhist monk robe had lost his cool and was remonstrating with the machine in an un-lama like way. Whatever he'd tried to do had evidently not met with success and so he treated the unit's pedestal to his best kung-fu, muttered a Viking curse, turned on his heels and marched past me swearing in English. It was clearly worth investigating what had frustrated him so much.

The sentinel had cleverly disguised itself by adopting an almost perfect local camouflage. If it hadn't given itself away by the blue 'ATM' sticker plastered to its side, I'd never have guessed it was a cash machine; all other symbology was in Nepali script. I thought it worth a go to see whether I could do better than the vexed Scandi-monk and wring some cash from it. Anything was better than two hours upstairs explaining to the teller why I looked so much younger in my passport photo.

My first challenge was to convince the machine to display in Roman script. In response, I did what all self-respecting science graduates do and broke the problem down into a logical sequence of steps, testing each hypothesis as I went. To an outside observer, this may have appeared as a random, manic pressing of buttons, but it irrefutably was not; this was attested to by my empirical approach successfully bearing fruit and the presentation of a menu in English.

My next challenge was to calculate the maximum amount of cash I could extract without exceeding my three attempts at doing so and having the machine revert to the Nepali menu. My opening gambit of four million rupees was met with an unwillingness on the machine's behalf to dispense such an amount. I typed in 45,000 which should've been fine, the equivalent of £300, but the machine baulked. I changed tack and chose one of the default options, which was 30,000. I was rewarded by a whirring of cogs and a screen that reverted to Nepali presenting a Hobson's choice of an unreadable hieroglyphic or unintelligible squiggle. I selected the squiggle, hoping I hadn't agreed to an exchange rate of one rupee to a pound. The machine agreed I'd done something right, my reward the robot sentinel's trouser pocket opening to reveal a breeze block of notes making me feel minted and paranoid at the same time.

I squirrelled away the hoard of rupees as best anyone can do without a suitcase and decided to take breakfast across the foyer. The waiter at the Fire and Ice remarked it was unusual to see a codpiece worn in such a pronounced manner at that time of year and took my order for an expansive breakfast. The bill for the food was as elevated as its quality. Perhaps they'd seen me coming but Rs.800 for eggs, toast and a coffee was more expensive than at my local greasy spoon. I didn't mind, though – newly flush with untold wealth, I peeled off a Rs.1,000 bill, dropped it on the table with disdain and swaggered out, keen to complete my next task.

I was headed to the Tourist Service Centre to obtain my Trekkers Information Management System card. The Nepali government dictates a TIMS card is required by all trekkers, in theory to keep them safe by tracking their whereabouts in the mountains. Having seen how the system operated on the ground, in reality it was just another mangle to put trekkers through to press a few more dollars from their pockets.

As I neared, I couldn't help but think the same architect had been employed in the centre's design as at the airport. But, in its case, a more enlightened town planner had negated the need to view its façade until one was upon it by thoughtfully locating it in a large hole. It was dark, humid and busy inside. The queuing mechanism was analogous to the one in the airport. Its footprint formed a NATO flag – the circle was the tussle of a central scrum zone; the arms of the cross were lines leading in and out.

I'd equipped myself with the same paraphernalia needed for the bank transaction, prepared to have my application processed in the speediest possible way. Even so, I still expected an inexplicably long wait at the centre before the stamping and handing out of papers. That was confirmed, because before I could get in line, a sign directed me to fill in a form that, to my mind, asked a lot of pointless questions to which nobody would know the answers. I don't believe even the most ardent of plane spotters can remember their inbound flight number. Knowing the score, that this was bureaucratic detail for bureaucracy's sake, I falsified that information as convincingly as I could and joined the back of the longest queue.

"What's this queue for, please?" I directed my question to a blond behemoth of a man, his bronzed Charles Atlas-dimensioned arm muscles bulging out from a Victoria Bitter singlet.

"This is for yer TIMS card, mate."

"Great, thanks. Where are you guys headed?"

"The Annapurna Circuit."

"Shouldn't you be in the queue over there for the Annapurna permit, then?"

"Nah mate. Robbo and Jonesy, our mates, are over in that line. We're double teamin' it. If they get to the front of their line first, we'll all pile over and get those tickets. If we get there first, they'll pile over here."

"That sounds like a good way to do it."

"Yer, it would be, 'cept there's no-one workin' over on the Annapurna counter. Tihar holiday or somethin'. They're waitin', hopin' someone will turn up."

"At least it looks like there's someone working at the end of this line. You'll love the Annapurna Circuit; I was there 10 years ago. It's fantastic. Are you guys from Australia?"

"Yer mate."

"Whereabouts?"

"Surfers, mate."

"Cool, what do you do in Surfers?"

"Surfers."

"Yes, but what do you do in Surfers?"

"Surfers." He was laughing now.

"You mean you're surfers in Surfers Paradise?"

"Yer, sorry for messin' with ya mate, it's good value that one. We're all instructors."

"You make a living at that, being a surfer?"

"Yer, not bad money n'all, mate. We're goin' back to Surfers after the trek for the summer." I was unsure why, but I hadn't considered people actually surfed in Surfers Paradise and even less so that someone would make a living from teaching them. Those wetsuits bobbing on top of the waves were part of the furniture.

"That doesn't sound a bad thing to have to go back to."

"Yer mate, it's cool. We work the summer then go travellin' in the winter. It's too cold for surfin' so there's no work. We were in India for three months before this."

"Goa?"

"Yer and Pondicherry. Where you goin', mate?"

"Everest Base Camp, I'm going to walk in via the same route as Hillary and Norgay did when they climbed Everest."

"Cool man." Robbo came to join us, the Annapurna queue going nowhere. We chatted for an hour about their trek as the TIMS line gradually shuffled along. He swapped with Jonesy and half an hour later they had their TIMS cards stamped. It was my turn. A flustered, smallish lady indicated I needed to hand over my paperwork. She examined it through half-rim glasses.

"Namaste. Everest Region sir? Start at Shivalaya?"

"Namaste. Yes, that's right."

"You trek with a group, sir?"

"No, I'm an independent trekker"

"You have a guide?"

"No."

"You trek with a porter?"

"No."

"This is not possible. Individual trekking in Nepal is now forbidden. Unfortunately, sir, I cannot issue you with a permit."

"Why? Last time I was here I trekked alone. It was no problem."

"You are experienced in trekking in Nepal, sir?"

"Yes."

"May I ask where you trekked, sir?"

"I walked the Annapurna Circuit."

"Good! As you have expertise, I can allow you a permit. This is only possible if you agree to accept the risks of individual trekking, sir. Do you agree?"

"Yes, where do I sign?"

"There is no need to sign, sir. Just say you accept, please."

"I agree to take on the risks of trekking alone."

"Good! $20 please, sir."

"But the Australian guys only paid $10?"

"Yes, sir, they are trekking in a group."

"So, the fee is $20 for individual trekking, which is forbidden, but $10 if you are a member of a group?"

"Yes, sir, individual trekking is not officially allowed but there are no checks in the mountains. I can make you a permit for that as no-one will ask you for it. The fee is $20." I resignedly handed over the money but, overall, was relieved she'd granted me the paperwork. The 10 extra bucks were significantly less than if I'd needed a porter. She seemed equally relieved to be free of a potentially troublesome customer as her demeanour changed from agitated public employee to cheery smiling grandmother. She palmed the cash, stapled photos to my shiny green card and stamped it with the force of an Anthony Joshua jab.

"Thank you sir, which colour would you like?" She pointed to a thali tray of powder on the table to her side.

"The red one, please." She daubed her thumb in the powder, left a firm imprint in the centre of my forehead and incanted something in my direction. She told me my trek had now been officially blessed.

"Please sir, it is Tihar festival today. Please take a Nepali sweet." She pointed to a sugary coagulation perspiring on her desk. I chose a sticky chocolate toffee and left the office thrilled to have acquired my permit and, a minute later, a significant concern over the integrity of my dental work.

Next on my list was a bus ticket to Shivalaya, where I was going to start the trek. Ratna Park bus station was a short stroll away over a metal footbridge. I entered it through a battered tin gate where fume-spewing buses loaded to the gills and more were rattling out onto Durbar Marg. If there is ever a clichéd image of the chaos of urban Asia requiring filming, send the drone to Ratna Park. The scene was one of such an unrestrained disorganisation of industry, I'd wandered through its entire length before my senses could take it in.

On my first pass, I spotted nowhere conspicuous to purchase my ticket and so turned back in the direction from which I'd entered. On my second survey, I fared no better, doubting I was in the right place. The map in my guidebook had the bus station across Durbar Marg and so I reckoned I'd missed the entrance to an alternate bus station. I exited the way I'd arrived and re-crossed the iron bridge to stroll the street's length without luck, so thought it was possible there was an entrance around the next corner. This did bring me to another bus station, with a helpful sign saying 'Buses to Bhaktapur' at its entrance. A friendly bus driver confirmed I was in the wrong place for the Shivalaya bus and that I wanted the bus station back across the metal footbridge.

I trudged back to Ratna but a third scouting of the station left me none the wiser, the locals unable to help with where I should buy my fare. So I decided my search would be better served by returning when the place was less manic the following morning. It was possible I had to buy my ticket on the bus and now, at least I knew its departure point.

I grabbed lunch at a small café in Thamel and spent the rest of the afternoon preparing for the mountains. I allowed a taciturn young Nepali gentleman to strip my mobile phone down to its bare metal and weld an N-cell SIM into its innards, was invited to navigate four internet pages to activate it and pay £20 for the privilege. I hoped it worked better than on my previous visit where the claims of coverage in the mountains had been dashed as soon as I'd left greater Kathmandu.

I bought some essentials for the bus journey: bottled water, a ciabatta from the excellent Hot Breads bakery and a tin of tuna. I bought a head torch and pottered around the shops until dinner time.

Unadventurous in my choice, I ate at the Northfield again with largely the same results. There were lots of groups of self-contained trekkers but no-one with whom I gauged I could strike up a conversation. As an older individual traveller, it seemed I was of little interest to them. I was something of a ghost, invisible to their eyes. It made for a lonely evening but, overall, I was content with that. It afforded me the luxury of being left in peace and allowed me to pick my company. I knew I could always present myself to one of the groups if I needed.

On this occasion, I didn't and so returned to my room to try out my new Kindle. My reading *The Sparrow* by Mary Dorrell Russell. After an hour, I followed with some music, starting *Get Up* by Ben Harper and Charlie Musselwhite at track six. An hour later, despite jetlag, I was ready to try for sleep; it was 10.40pm.

Booking the Potala had been relatively painless. It took a web form so state-of-the-art it forwent the need to attach two recent passport photos. Half a dozen chaser emails later, I neared the confirmation of my booking, learning in the process that at festival time Nepal is automatically disconnected from the internet. My email correspondent had warned me the Hotel Potala could be rowdy. He also suggested he could offer me alternative lodging with a degree of serenity more in keeping with a gentleman of my advanced years. If I took the tranquillity option, it would incur a marginal surcharge merely doubling the price of my stay.

I'd opted not to take the correspondent up on the invitation – not so much based on cost, more on my desire to revisit old memories. Besides, I wanted to be at the centre of everything, to hang out with all the young (surfer) dudes. I thought I could still party and so a little noise wouldn't bother me. So, I was irritated with myself to discover that, as I took my headphones off, ready for the land of nod, the musical volume seemed to increase.

I use the term music in its loosest sense. There was a shrieking of guitars coming from the bar next door that would've benefitted from some prior scale practice and the removal of mittens. The guitars were drowned out a couple of minutes later by a loud explosive bang and the screeches of rockets. Either the Indians had finally had enough of that quarter of an hour time-zone insult and had taken the opportunity afforded by the Tihar festival internet blackout to invade, or there was a pyrotechnic display going on. Despite my tiredness, I had to see that, so repaired to the rooftop to get a view.

I found the upstairs chill-out zone mobbed, but decidedly not chilled. It appeared Dionysus was in town and had chosen the terrace as his centre of operations. Every slouch couch was crowded with Nepali revellers who sat around knee-high tables cluttered with bottles of Old Durbar whisky, gin, and strange liqueurs in various stages of drainage. A barrage of stars burst overhead, accompanied by the popping of crumpling air. I'd arrived as the display was increasing in intensity. I joined the party-goers as they migrated towards the railing to watch the show.

"What're the fireworks for, Tihar?" I enquired of a particularly friendly roisterer who'd gripped my shoulder to steady himself from falling into the invisible whirling pit on my left.

"Yes, Tihar festival. Big party tonight."

"I thought the party would've been last night and folks sleeping it off today?"

"Yes, we party last night. Sleep this afternoon and party again tonight." I'd no cause to doubt him but anticipated his partying for the evening would soon be over. More rockets streaked into the air, invoking the terrace to a cacophony of cheering and the volume of the rooftop chill-out soundtrack increased in response. The Nepali interpretation of chill being some form of local reggae-reggaeton mash-up.

Beneath us, a parade of djembe drummers marched through the alleyway, their pounding echoing upwards and commingling with the soundtrack. My new friend invited me to his table, and I couldn't help but think I had lousy timing. I was at the Nepali version of Hogmanay and had to be up in five hours to catch a bus, so I politely declined my new drinking buddy's offer of a shot of Old Durbar. He took it gracefully, simply happy to have found solid ground as I dropped him on his chair. The aerial display was now over, and I no longer had a reason to be there; this wasn't my festival, after all. As the fervour of the drinkers approached the tipping point between boisterous merriment and uncontrollable drunkenness, I judged it was time to leave, jealous of the folks who seemed to be having such a good time.

My room was situated for optimal amplification of the reggae-reggaeton music down its narrow corridors. It was as if my email correspondent had put me there as an 'I told you so.' I was going to get no sleep until the festivities ended, so I opened the Kindle again. Nepal is an early-to-bed nation, so the party couldn't go on much longer, I hoped. At 2.30am, the music stopped. I buried my head back in my pillow thinking, if I were lucky, I'd get three hours' sleep.

There was the scuffle of a befuddled attempt at the padlock of the door opposite, accompanied by the exaggerated laughter of a woman. A couple were trying to gain entry. A stumble and a collision of shin on wood announced that they were in. I hoped if they were going to get jiggy, they'd get it over with quickly. More voices, perhaps four or five, echoed down the corridor. I thought my email correspondent had surpassed himself. That 'I told you so' included for my listening pleasure the assorted grunting of the local chapter of the Kathmandu Swingers Association.

There was giggling before something unexpected and marvellous happened. Silence. A minute later it was broken by an operatic lament. I'd no idea what the lady was singing about, but the way she did it was something special in a kind of undulating warbling. She sang unaccompanied for a quintet of songs prior to duetting with a male singer. They continued for a half-dozen more ballads before it was time for everyone to join in. It sounded like they'd used the time when the more talented members of their ensemble had been entertaining us to finish whatever booze they had left. The result was what had started off as a throat-sung version of *Nessun Dorma* ended up as the local equivalent of a bawdy version of *I've Got a Lovely Bunch of Coconuts*. They gave up at 4am.

There was no point in sleeping for an hour, so I used it to read, gathered my gear, and headed downstairs to check out. Tihar had taken its toll on KTM, who was recharging his auxiliary power unit on a couch by reception. He had company; his miniature version slumbered beside him. After a period of exaggerated stomping of boots and general noise-making, the smaller unit woke up. Mini-KTM couldn't have been more than 18 and had enjoyed a good Tihar, judging by his uncertain movements. He composed himself enough to conduct a small disagreement over the tariff, which we settled amicably, and I headed off towards the bus station.

The alleyway below was busier than it had been when I'd been out shopping the previous afternoon, bands of youths stumbling in zigzags across the road. There were plenty of friendly greetings, attempted hugs, and invitations as I dodged through the throng. The fast food places were taking full advantage of the bevvy-induced hunger and there were queues out onto the street. It reminded me of chucking-out time at the clubs in Glasgow without the undercurrent of menace that can sometimes pervade. The crowds didn't abate until the right turn on to Kantipath, although even there I was able to tailgate a group through the darkness all the way to the entrance to the bus park.

Ratna, by comparison, was empty. There were a handful of buses standing in isolation and some groups of young men smoking in groups, but it felt like the place hadn't been invited to the party. In a way I was pleased – the dearth of activity narrowed down the choice of buses that could be going to Shivalaya and so less chance of missing it. I reasoned that by asking each driver I'd find the right one quickly.

"Namaste. Shivalaya bus?"

"No. No Shivalaya bus." I was hopeful it would be the next one.

"Namaste. Shivalaya bus?"

"No. No Shivalaya bus." There were three more to go.

"Namaste. Shivalaya bus?"

"No. No Shivalaya bus." I was about to head off and try my luck on the next one when the driver remonstrated.

"No Shivalaya bus today. Tihar festival. No bus go outside Kathmandu."

"No buses? What about all these?"

"Take Tihar people home in Kathmandu." It then dawned on me that this post-Tihar morning, the station was exclusively dedicated to the provision of drunk buses. As we were talking, an inquisitive man who had more headwear than teeth came to join us.

"Where you go?"

"Shivalaya."

"No Shivalaya bus."

"Yes, I gathered that."

"Go tomorrow. I sell ticket. Come." The topi-hatted man led me to a wooden booth at the station's edge. I realised how I'd previously missed it; a person of middling stature easily obscured it. The man opened a hatch and took up station behind a chicken wire grille.

"Where you go?"

"Shivalaya."

"When you go?"

"You said there's a bus tomorrow?"

"Yes. When you go?"

"Tomorrow, then." He nodded and, after completing a series of obtuse mathematical calculations requiring a colleague to be called over for verification, he presented me with a ticket for the princely sum of Rs.757. He told me to be back at Ratna at 5.45 sharp the next day. It didn't register until I was outside Ratna's gates that it was strange for a ticket-seller to be there at that time and I might have been scammed.

Disappointed not to be on my way to the hills, I made my way back to Paryatan Marg. Finding somewhere to accommodate me before 7am post-Tihar festival was going to be a challenge, so I opted to check back in to my room at the Potala before KTM had recharged. Mini-KTM didn't look surprised to see me. He mentioned something about expecting me back before waving me back towards my room. Ninety minutes after leaving on my failed attempt to reach Shivalaya, I'd arrived.

Paryatan Marg to Ratna

I was disappointed not to be rattling towards the mountains but less so to be returning to bed. Another night without sleeping had reactivated my jetlag, my body clock telling me it was two in the morning. I slept until 11 and headed towards the Northfield for brunch. With an unplanned day in Kathmandu at my disposal, I opted to revisit Swayambhunath, thinking it would give me a chance to improve on the quality of pictures of the monkey temple I'd taken on my last visit. I could also see how the repairs on the stupa were proceeding after the earthquake. A bonus would be the opportunity for an internalised Clouseau or two, a childish 'Do yew 'ave a leesonce fur yur minky?' aimed at anyone foolish enough to be feeding one.

The stroll up to the hill was shorter than I'd remembered it, but the stairs to the stupa complex seemed steeper. It appeared the monkeys had been in a cycle of reproductive frenzy in the past decade. The numbers thronging the steps were more an army than a troop. Inside, it was pleasing to see the eye of the stupa restored and most of the complex's centre intact, but disheartening that some peripheral buildings had been so damaged to need buttress support. I sauntered around enough time to think I'd got my money's worth and headed back over the Bagmati river to Durbar Square.

The rest of the afternoon was an ambled tour of the old town's dusty streets. I spent some time with a fishmonger learning how he used a fearsome-looking contraption to slice his fish. It was a cast iron doorstop surmounted by a trident of razor-sharp spears. His technique appeared to be to toss his catch in its general direction. But, with every throw, he manufactured two perfect fillets of fish and a set of bones that would grace any episode of Tom and Jerry.

I wasn't hungry at dinner-time and so reverted to the option of fast food. Crazy Burger included a beer with my burger and chips for Rs.400. I figured I'd hit gold dust and conducted with the owner my longest conversation since arrival. Business in Thamel wasn't great, apparently, which I couldn't understand with the bargain fare on offer. Our chat exhausted itself so I settled on trying to get an early night. I finished *The Sparrow*, which I thought superb – the premise of a religion-led space race particularly intriguing – and moved on to music to send me off to sleep. I started *Plastic Beach* by Gorillaz at track 10 and an hour later, I was ready for sleep; it was 9.30pm.

My hopes of rest were thwarted at around 9.31. Rather than a repeat of the soundtrack to the Tihar-induced Bacchanalian revelry of the previous evening, this noise contamination came from below. The floor juddered to the oscillations of a dense thud, courtesy of the Purple Haze's cover band. Above was an impassioned or pained screaming. A yowling lead guitar filled in any residual sonic void, leaving the audience in no doubt the band's amplifiers did indeed go all the way to 11.

At middle-aged, middle class dinner parties when the subject of musical taste arises, my preferences will be politely settled on as eclectic or wide-ranging. The same debate with my teenage children will result in an agreement, at least on their part, that my taste is as obsolete as those antiquated shiny silver disc things I insist monopolise all the living room shelf space. This is usually followed by what seems to be a preternatural activation of Post Malone, AJ Tracey or The Weeknd on the Sonos music system at Walls of Jericho-crumbling amplification. This is designed to educate me in what good music sounds like now, not 'the olden days'. This demonstration of my superannuated lack of musical appreciation usually follows with some form of grave pronouncement. I only like the music of dead rock stars, or at least ones who *should* be dead by now. Occasionally they let the posturing slip, though, and the Sonos will fire up, blaring *Call Me* by Blondie or some other outdated Eighties band that are somehow not pushing up daisies and have crept back into fashion.

Armed with my Jurassic era knowledge of music and no choice in the matter, the challenge of identifying each tune with the band's opaque audio clues kept me captivated. The ensemble weren't trying to match the previous night's acapella Nepali folk music or chill-out zone reggae-reggaeton. The repertoire centred on Nineties indie rock with a smattering of its Seventies rock precedents. The tunes identifiable were *Boulevard of Broken Dreams* by Green Day, *Smells Like Teen Spirit* by Nirvana and *Highway to Hell* by AC/DC. There could've also been a Hendrix or Kravitz track mixed in, as it seems a traveller universe constant at least one of these is included on the setlist of bands recruited to play in this archetype of backpacker rock-bar.

Apart from the easily identifiable tracks from Nirvana *et al.*, the band left me guessing. In this, I was aided by another ready reckoner about the bands that seem to circuit this variety of venue. 'Santana's Law' was born on a trip through Mexico in 1991. For some reason, that trip seemed to involve visiting a lot of cantinas. Each one seemed to employ the same band, playing *Oye Como Va* all night. In New Zealand, there had been no hint of *Black Magic Woman*, musically or otherwise. So the law was not hard to deduce. It states that the number of Santana guitar solos in the set of any backpacker bar band is inversely proportional to the distance from Playa del Carmen.

I'm still baffled the scientific community hasn't yet confirmed the universality of this law and it isn't common usage in the same way as $E=mc^2$. I'm similarly disappointed my other breakthroughs concerning backpacker bar-dynamics have never been called to light by the famous Norwegian committee. The lack of recognition for 2001's 'Hindu Om Theorem' and 1996's 'Null Dart Proof' is particularly galling. The former postulates that there will be at any finite point in space-time at least one braceleted backpacker sporting a Hindu tattoo in the bar. The latter confirms mathematically that the position chosen for a bar's dartboard will correspond *exactly* to a location where there is zero probability of finding a single arrow.

Kathmandu's Thamel district is almost at the furthest longitude from the Yucatan. So it seemed safe to assume that, after they'd dispensed with what sounded like *Corazon Espinado*, that was it for Carlos. Guns 'N' Roses would take over. As it transpired, the band were maybe a Thin Lizzyesque dual lead guitar outfit. The set covered *The Boys are Back in Town* along with *Welcome to the Jungle*.

This mix seemed to be well received by the audience. At the completion of each number, there was a respectable degree of cheering and applause followed by some mostly indiscernible stage-led banter. This was presumably about the next song, presumably in English. I associated this appreciation with a young crowd but had no rationale for this preconception. By the level of noise, the audience equally could've been a bus-load of karaoke-starved drunken Japanese Sararimen out to celebrate the completion of their corporate team-building trekking exercise to Everest Base Camp, or two mildly excited Mid-Westerners whispering about how great it was to be on their first trip outside the States.

Playing *Name That Tune* through the wall until around midnight was entertaining but, with a start at five in the morning, by one o'clock I was becoming agitated the band were still cranking it. By two o'clock, I was cheesed off and by five past two annoyed with myself for becoming so. It was my own fault that, due to my arrogant insistence on staying at the Potala again, I was still awake. When the band finished their set and Chad and Todd from Kansas City called it a night around 2.30, I wasn't in the slightest relaxed. The remainder of the small hours were a lost battle against wakefulness.

Five in the morning came as my body had decided it was time to slumber. At the alarm, I awoke in that semi-dazed state resulting from being roused at the point where the body is trying to catch up on lost rest and wastes no time in telling you it hasn't. My backpack was mostly arranged, so in my stupor it was only a matter of making best use of the shower to stir myself and squeeze my damp travel towel into one of the pack's outside pockets before I left. I fleeced up, wiggled into my waterproof trousers, tightened the macarena of backpack straps, took its weight and donned the Powercap. The bus was leaving Ratna Park at 6.15 and the toothless ticket-seller had briefed me to be there for 5.45. How correspondent this instruction was going to be with the actual departure timing was anyone's guess, but I thought it better to be safe than sorry.

Travel anxiety means I too easily default into what my children call 'Airport Dad' mode. I like to think of this as where I enter a polite but assertive, single-minded and purposeful frame of mind to focus on ensuring everyone is sitting comfortably in the departure lounge a solid three hours ahead of the gate being called for the flight. This is, of course, for a short-hop flight carrying only hand luggage. Needless to say, my children have a different view of my behaviour while in this mode and haven't been afraid in letting me know their opinion. After a flight I'm often left reflecting that, for teenagers, they seem to have a remarkable recall of all the major figures in the Third Reich's history.

The prior morning's inadvertent dry run had told me the walk from the hotel to the bus was 20 minutes. But my conclusion from navigating the chaos that was the bus station the previous day was that timetables would operate more around guidance rather than a stipulation-based code. That meant, on leaving my room at 5.15, thoughts of missing the bus and having to spend another day in the city swirled around my head, even though I knew I'd ample time to get to Ratna. But here I was unencumbered by family criticism. So I comfortably slipped into 'Airport Dad' mode, determined to be first on that bus, sitting patiently for its departure even if it left at noon.

Mini-KTM was flat-out on the couch in reception. I dropped the key on the desk as agreed and proceeded to the iron gate he'd left open for me. Left open to a degree more suited to a person of his own dimensions, which meant I scraped and scuffed as I squeezed my pack through. There was no movement on the couch. I found myself inadvertently checking to see if the boy was still breathing as he hadn't stirred in spite of the racket. His chest was moving, so I took my leave safe in the knowledge there was no immediate medical emergency to attend to. I was both impressed with the Mini-KTM's relaxed attitude to customer service, but also faintly disappointed he wasn't consciously present to wish me good luck on my travels. Perhaps he was expecting me back soon.

Without the illuminating effect of Tihar-celebrating crowds, downtown Thamel dissipated from a Times Square neon-clad dazzle to a London Blitz-level blackout on a Himalayan gradient. Tridevi Marg formed a transition zone where the pavement was shop-front illuminated by a low-slung parade of upmarket boutiques.

During the daylight hours, this quarter bristled with activity. At the gear shops, lead guides wrestled sheening new kit bags into mini-vans gaudily daubed with the names of adventure expedition companies. Assertive congregations of cabbies sucked in particulates from their idling battered jalopies. The bookstores saw erudite, emaciated bean poles laden with copies of *The Snow Leopard* and cultural histories of Manang gormlessly step into the thoroughfare. Stalls were clogged with un-Hipster bearded, sandal-clad climbers seeking pashminas for their loved ones. Portly, topi-topped merchants amiably grinned their takings to the Himalayan Bank. Assortments of veteran Ghurkhas, Tibetan tour touts and carved flute-sellers made up the melee. An orchestra-without -conductor of tuk-tuk horns, a straining putt-putt thrum of un-serviced Suzukis, the rip of gleaming, overpowered Kawasakis and the babel of commerce provided the accompanying soundscape.

Before dawn, Tridevi Marg bristled with a different kind of activity. Under the arcade's penumbra slumbered those invisible in the sunlight. A dozen taupe rucks spilled from the pavement into the road, the focus of their bicuspid guards a score of canvas sacks. The unseen were sheathed in sleeping bags secured by clenched steel teeth. Those less fortunate double-wrapped around themselves to layer out the cold. Hill-woven woollens and synthetics crested with Premier League badges were pulled down tight over grubby wraith faces. Hands entangled the cords of their sacks. I imagined these to contain the entirety of their possessions.

Although I didn't know the origin of their plight, I wondered how these poor folks had come to this. Nepal seems almost benevolently tribal in its adherence to its mores; extended family first and village second. Conversations with Nepalis frequently arrive at what they'll be doing at festival time. For the rural folks, the stock answer is to follow the tradition of honouring it in their village. An entire village's diaspora may be confined within the municipal boundaries of Kathmandu but, for its members, celebrating in that tumultuous urban turmoil of a town isn't an option. The respectable thing to do is to return to your place of origin to spend time with rural kinfolk. There everyone is provided for, the social fabric of Nepali woven so kith and kin look after each other. How had the threads of the lives of those prone on the pavement become so broken? How did they fall through this cultural safety net to become so detached from their clan?

It was only as I looked back the shame at my lack of empathy for their sorry circumstance surfaced. I'd experienced no upwelling of sadness or pity for them. No anger rose at how any society in the new millennium's age of plenty could disappoint with tolerance of this sub-class as a norm. Instead, my initial reaction was one of only a slightly detached disquiet. Nothing more. This was supplanted by a resigned disappointment at this being the way of the world. After all, this was to be expected in Asia, in one of the poorest countries on Earth. Not I nor any other affluent passing Westerner would be able to change it. My pre-programmed anti-guilt mechanism had kicked in, justification for my lack of compassion at the disarray, an easy get-out for the continuation of my self-indulgent 'living like the locals' holiday with a minimum of self-reproach. I moved past with a deliberate, despondent, heavy exhalation. My conscience anaesthetised, back in 'Airport Dad' mode, I resumed my rushed scuttle towards Ratna Park.

I was stalled again 50 metres further on, at the cusp of the last finger of illumination. Swept into a circle of school compass precision was a pitcher's mound of convenience store detritus. Shuffling around the midden of deflated Dasani bottles, crushed Surya Luxury King boxes and chilli sauce-smeared greaseproof paper was a group of perhaps a dozen silently intent foragers. The men were clad in a drab disrepair of loose-fitting trousers, knee-length padded jackets and city footwear. The women wore shapeless, muted checked skirts, olive fleeces and flip-flops. Heavy-duty black plastic bags were gripped underarm. They wordlessly padded around the rubbish hump like Big Five predators stalking at a Maasai Mara water-hole. Espying their prey, their arms would dart into the dust heap and withdraw a deformed, muck-covered bottle, inspect it according to some invisible specification and squirrel it away into their hoard. They'd resume their place in the pride and continue the hunt.

There was no perceptible aggression displayed from the others at an individual's success, more a disinterested, momentary acknowledgement that left the rhythm of their search uninterrupted. I assumed these folks were making a living somehow by scavenging the plastic for recycling purposes. A bottle of water in the tourist markets in Thamel sells for Rs.20, the equivalent of 15 UK pence. The plastic bottle's cost is only a composite part of that. How these people could eke a living from what they were doing was beyond me.

Already ignobly inured from my encounter 30 seconds earlier, I moved on wondering about the relationship and relative social positions of the two groups I'd passed. Could they all be of one group, with some members designated for refuse mining each day, allowing the others their uneasy rest? If they were two groups, were the scroungers deemed higher in the social strata than the sleepers? They at least had the opportunity to obtain some paltry income by selling their recycling. Or was it the other way around, with the sleepers able to rest – however uncomfortably – while the accumulators had to work?

As I was about to step out of the last of the light, a sky-blue painted refuse truck emerged from the night in the other direction. It reminded me of the 1970s Renault 2CV truck the *Chef Inspecteur* had driven relentlessly into a Cote d'Azur swimming pool in the *Pink*

Panther movies. Except it was far less mechanically robust. The paintwork was scraped to bare metal on the lateral bins to the rear of the driver's cab. As it slowed to a halt, two wiry athletes sprung out bearing wide-panned shovels. The gatherers stepped back from the garbage hummock, their movement almost synchronised as in some form of soundless Strip the Willow. They dissolved away with their caches into the darkness as the two council workers fiercely scraped away the hillock into the bins. It seemed the meagre opportunity for the foragers to make money was time bound and dawn signalled their time was up.

I reached the corner of Tridevi Marg and Kantipath, thinking that, without a homebound group of Tihar revellers to tailgate, I'd have to navigate the darkness alone. I left the relative reassurance of the arcade's faint corona behind me and ventured into the unlit avenue. I'd angled the Powercap's light downwards to avoid any trek-ending missteps courtesy of the uneven sidewalk. Despite the assurance my safe return from the same excursion the previous morning should've given me, an autonomous tensing of muscles was my reaction against a sense of vulnerability. Although I was alone and the street was ill-lit, it wasn't a primal fear enveloping me, rather a paranoia based on the threat posed by others.

The logical part of me reasoned that the chances of an early-bird mugger camping out overnight on this particular stretch of Kathmandu real estate at 5.30 were slim. Most travellers weren't foolhardy enough to strike out on their own and the odds unfavourable for group robberies. There was no serious crime problem in Nepal, despite the poverty I'd witnessed, and so all the indicators pointed to an inherent lack of danger. But when it is dark, the logical part of me is a poor adversary for its irrational survivalist opponent. Ahead I imagined shiv-armed assailants coiled in every doorway between the turn into the inky blackness of Kantipath and the bus park.

Beyond the corner, I focussed on not falling into any fresh voids constructed at the perimeter of the new bank's building site. I pussyfooted across the ubiquitous cambers of ski-jump graded cement ramps at the entries to the businesses along the way. Five minutes into the dark, I met my murderous thugs. Clearly, their tactic was to bolt from their Tartarean hiding hole, cause panic with their high-pitched shrieking and wailing and to rush at me, their killing daggers arcing ahead of them. I'd be slashed and left for dead, having been looted of everything of value. I knotted every sinew, ready to run, put up an insipid pretence of fighting back or, at worst, meekly handing over everything in my possession.

My death-dealers emerged from the murk. A rotund, middle-aged harpy berated her presumed husband, who was twirling his outstretched umbrella in a manner as absent as his expression. I thought it was pretty early in the day to have already done *that* much wrong to deserve such a dressing-down. They passed me without a second glance, giving me the impression this route was the couple's daily commute. In a Kathmandu October, coming across a trekker at dawn was about as thrilling as watching the final of the Paknajol rice-boiling championship.

I crossed over the six lanes of Kantipath, heading for the psychological safety of the speckle of light affirming the location of a sentry box. At about a third of the way across the boulevard, I realised my timing couldn't have been more amiss. Looking left, the thoroughfare which had been a mill-pond of emptiness two minutes earlier was now a surging tsunami of growling yellow beacons. My scurry across the four lanes avoided death by tuk-tuk. But I was out of breath by the time I passed the overweight, khaki-clad sentinel nonchalantly sharing a first-of-the-day cigarette with a hawker. I greeted them with my first 'Namaste' of the day. The hawker responded in kind, but the soldier didn't; I presumed not wanting to let his guard down.

I skirted by the attendant of a mini-submarine-shaped public WC complex as he swilled the previous day's overflow into the street. I crossed the junction with Bagh Bazar with a minor heart flutter; a local blindfolded Barry Sheen swerved past me under the footbridge, his leathers abrading on the tarmacadam. A larger complex of toilets welcomed me through Ratna's Pungenty Gates with a gag-reflex-inducing tang of urine. At 5.35, 20 minutes after leaving the Potala, I'd arrived.

Ratna to Shivalaya

As the muddy dawn patchily disassembled the night, the bus park revealed itself. Its threshold marked a step change in activity from the unpeopled streets outside. The station wasn't yet bubbling over with the stew of chaos evident when I sought out my ticket, but the pot was on the hob with the gas lit.

Pods of skinny twentysomethings in even skinnier jeans mulled, lit up and passed around, enjoying a joke at their bosses' expense as they toked on sullied Surya brand cigarettes. Septuagenarian be-skirted village elders serenely leaned on stout walking staffs; tree-pose relaxed. Assuredly, the bus would come to them. Lines of ladies in colourless saris waited their turn in sedately British order to exchange their rupees for citrus, tomatoes and mangoes. These would be expertly packed in carriers resembling funfair gold-fish bags at the driftwood-inspired fruiterers' shack. Mothers crabbed over strollers and placated their toddlers, down-swaddled to resemble puffed-up starfish, half-drowsing but awake enough to vent their irritability at being roused to beyond all four corners of the station.

"Aaaaaaaaammmmmmmmmmmmmmmaaaaaaa..........." The drawn-out screech of complaint from a somnolent rug-rat targeted at their mum didn't need 'Hey Siri' to translate.

Tardis taxis disgorged a dozen or more passengers, each extended family commencing to spin in Brownian motion across the square, searching for their longer distance conveyance. They'd hit and ricochet off each bus, the clan breaking up like video arcade Asteroids on their first fruitless collision.

"Chai-na, chai-na, chai-na, chai-na." Their disappointment was hollered and hollered again, their lead taken from the Purple Haze's band, vocal amplifiers turned all the way to 11. They curved, arced and bellowed.

"Cha! Cha! Cha!"

Dance completed, they'd coalesce again as one of their troupe signalled their conductor had been found. Patriarchs lumped duffels of gas cylinders, vehicle spares and TV sets towards their bus. Matriarchs effortlessly ported coal sack-sized carriers of microwaves, school fare and 12 score towers of Ra-Ra noodles, a hugging infant resting on each hip. Primary school age children gripped mercilessly on grungy, stuffing-starved teddies, grime-blonde barbies and rainbow-flanked moulded pink unicorns. Their older siblings dawdled behind, focussed on their temporary sedative of milk chocolate treats oblivious to the Minoan trails of Lego spilling from their unfastened Sponge Bob Square Pants rucksacks. Uncles, aunts, cousins first, second and third flanked, took point or tail-gun Charlie for each clan, heaving their riches of global industrial manufacture – those destined to be hawked, traded or ingeniously installed at higher altitudes.

Navigating the throng and securing my seat on my bus before it departed would be my trip's first real test. From my research in the guidebook and advice from the ticket-seller, I knew with a reasonable degree of certainty there was only one bus to my destination that morning. Unfortunately, in my mind, a reasonable degree of certainty transposes itself into a Mariana Trench of paranoia at the first sign I may have misunderstood, whispering in my ear that I *would* suffer the ignominy of missing the bus, even though in decades of travel I never have. I think this fear is the root cause of my 'Airport Dad' conduct. No matter if getting from A to B is via land, sea or air, the fretting is the same, but my children have decided 'Ferry Terminal, Train/Bus station or Airport Dad' doesn't have the same ring.

I had honed my language skills in anticipation of this first trial. As I approached the first coach, I was ready to impress the three young men who were sitting in the stairwell with my knowledge of the vernacular. They were chatting mutedly, all their focus on taking their first nicotine of the day in those long, sucking breaths requiring the inhaler to roll back their torso with each draw.

"Shivalaya bus?" I enquired, unfortunate my fluency in Nepalese not being demonstrable to a greater extent, as the local word for 'bus' is 'bus'. But the men clearly recognised my superlative linguistic ability. Wanting to show off their own, they politely reciprocated with an answer in English. Each word found itself as a uniquely defined sentence, the end of each word-sentence a softened drift into an undiscernible draught.

"Noohhh......"

"Ahhhh......"

"Fronthhh......"

"Ovffhaaahhh......"

"Thaaahhhh................."

An arm was thrust out in slow motion inside the coach and I found myself thinking I wasn't so sure it was only tobacco in those cigarettes. The arm's vague indication was towards the park's opposite end via a 45 degree angle through the bus's skylight. This was the signal I'd been dismissed and the group purposefully went back to the tarring of their lungs.

I nodded a 'Dhanyabad' in gratitude.

In addition to confirming my Nepalese diction was perfect, I'd learned two things from the encounter. The first was probably that was definitely not my bus. The second was my bus was possibly one of the mass of vehicles between the one occupied by the smoking trio and all the others at the end of the station. Armed with this MI5-level strategic intelligence, I ventured in that general direction, not attempting the suggested skylight route. Instead, I managed four steps or thereabouts at ground level.

"Excuse me, where are you going, good sir?"

On hearing such perfect Queen's English, I swivelled towards the voice's source, expecting to see a gramophone record-educated gentleman from the days of the Raj, hair slicked back with Brilliantine, clad in a Duke of Windsor double-breasted suit and sporting a monocle. Instead, I could have sworn it was one of the stairwell smokers who presented himself.

My inquirer was attired in the uniform of the under-30s Nepalese man about town. Joining the corps as an urban private requires the donning of a lived-in T-shirt, jeans of a bygone Western fashion and trainers of dubious brand authenticity. Higher ranks add fake Supreme or Stone Island hoodies and faux leather jackets. Generals accessorise with a Shenzen-sourced Rolex or a Himalayan-practical diver's watch. White cotton surgical facemasks are optional, depending upon airborne combat conditions in the capital. Style dictates these are worn in bank-robbing Spaghetti-Western villain fashion while riding motor vehicles. The command for foot soldiers is that straps must dangle loosely from the ears and the mask flap at chin level, handily acting as a comprehensive spittle catcher.

My questioner was a private, first class, although how he passed the couture army's height requirement I'd never know. Bisecting aretes of starched creases in my inquisitor's stone-washed denims declared his clothes very recently laundered and, without any shadow of a doubt, pressed with the zealous motherly love attributed to an only son. His bangs were immaculately Brylcreem coiffed in tribute to the bands of the Madchester era. His smell of a fresh lime soap scrubbing almost masked the heavy stink of the toilet block to my left. I was impressed by the gentleman's bearing, given the hour.

"Err ... hi, sorry, I mean good morning. I'm going to Shivalaya." My bearing was marginally less assured, embarrassed at being called 'Sir'. I don't think I'll ever get used to that. Does anyone not brought up with their target monocle selected at birth?

"Then you will kindly need to convey your good self on the Shivalaya bus. That is the Jiri bus."

"Dhanyabad, thank you very much, but isn't Shivalaya the stop after Jiri?"

"Indeed, that is the ordering of the transportation, good sir."

"Great, so I need to take the Shivalaya bus?"

"Yes, good sir, that is the Jiri bus."

"Thank you ... err ... sir. So, the Jiri bus is the Shivalaya bus?" I had, with Turing-like code-breaking skills and at lightning speed, cracked my advisor's cypher.

"Could you please show me which bus is the one to Jiri?"

"You mean the Shivalaya bus, kind sir?"

"Yes. Thank you."

"Sir, I don't know which bus that is."

Good grief.

"Oh ... okay, well, thanks for your help."

"You are very welcome, most gracious sir. May I take this truly fortunate opportunity to introduce you to my mother's superior teahouse trekking lodge establishment?"

"Yes, of course, is it on the trek from Shivalaya to Everest Base Camp?"

"No, kind gentleman sir, it is in most beautiful region of Nepal. Mustang region. It is most secret, forbidden and unseeing hidden kingdom. To visiting is to see the true Nepal, like in India Jones moving picture, Raiders of Lost Ark. It is stirring film. Most excitable part is when the not estimable gentleman like yourself eyes are falling out."

Double good grief. It was now 5.40. Five minutes before the scheduled check-in time and Airport Dad was whispering in my ear the bus was going without me.

"Okay, thanks very much, but Mustang is a very long way from where I'm going."

"Perhaps, good sir, you will now change your plans and have most pleasuresome visit to Shangri-La of Nepal. Please take business card of most estimable establishment. Please to visit Facebook page 'Gates of Forbidden Kingdom Tea House and Trekking Lodge' and give like."

I thought 'That must have cost a fortune for the sign' and, triple good grief, how was I going to get out of this conversation before I was left stranded? I was caught between my mounting Airport Dad stress and the type of British social conditioning that says it would be rude to interrupt your ISIS executioner in the midst of his frothing pre-beheading rantings to his internet audience, unless of course it was to let him know politely the webcam light wasn't on and therefore he was achieving less than the optimal video stream.

"Thank you for the card. I'll be sure to look it up, but excuse me, I must find my bus."

"Wonderful, you are most kind, sir. Perhaps you are needing eatings for the bus? It is very long time."

"I thought you didn't know which bus I needed or anything about the journey?"

"All bussings are very long in Nepal, most kindly sir. My mother's fruitings are over there. There are many superior fresh fruitings and cold bottle water. Price is best in Ratna. Best price for first customer of day. I will agree with her you are first fruitings customer."

"Your mother is selling fruit over there? I thought your mother had a teahouse in Mustang?"

"Yes, very kind gentleman, sir. Fruitings is other mother. My brother mother."

Quadruple good grief.

"Okay ... thank you for the offer, but I really must find my bus. Perhaps after I've found my bus I can come back and get some fruit for the trip?"

"That is most agreeable, gentlemanly sir. Please, I will now kindly be directioning you to your bus."

Quadruple good grief is my limit, if only because I don't know the word for five times something. My patience significantly frayed, I moved off without a further word, back in the direction indicated by the arm-wafting tobacco chimneys. The one seated on the lowest step dispensed with a crumpled packet, adding to the carpet of crushed debris on the station's ground. The scuffle of mini-shuffling steps was unmistakable in their pursuit.

"Please sir, mother's fruitings are this way. On way to bus."

My good grief limit had been exceeded and triggered the Defcon Four version of Airport Dad behaviour. I stopped and faced my tormentor.

"Look, I know you're only trying to help, but could you leave it please? You said you didn't know which bus it was to Shivalaya or Jiri, so how do you know if your mum's stall is on the way, especially if she's in blummin' Mustang?!"

I knew instantly losing my cool and making this retort was a mistake. The only relatively painless way out of this situation and making my bus on time, unencumbered by half a metric tonne of mangoes and a booking for a three-night mini-break at the 'Gates of Forbidden Kingdom Tea House and Trekking Lodge', would've been to ignore any further conversation and make for the bus, wherever that was.

"Most kind sir, it only takes minute for all your eloquent shoppings of all type of fruitings. Best morning price for you."

"Again, no thank you," I muttered between gritted teeth.

Head down and grimacing, I turned to make strides again to anywhere but where my gently polite and dogged fruit and lodging Torquemada lay in wait. I was instantly stopped in my tracks, with no going forward. I stood like a wildlife enthusiast on safari awaiting the passing of a parade of elephants. The herd was headed by a bundled Sherpa lady leading her family in a line across my path, each member toting baggage of at least twice their own body weight. I was now helpless, like a becalmed shipwreck survivor, drifting in the Pacific among a circle of great whites, waiting for any part of my body to slip overboard. The hawkers had smelled my blood.

"Snaak ... snaak. Delis snaak ..." A lithe pedlar brandishing a wicker basket topped by a slag heap of Day-Glo coloured packs of crisps materialised to blast his sales pitch a metre from my left ear.

"No thank you."

"Snaak ... snaak. Delis snaak ..." His yell tailed off and with its declining note, he vanished as efficiently as he'd appeared.

"You have ticke'? You wan' ticke'? Where you go? I take you to ticke'. I get you ticke'. You give me money for ticke'." A miniature bespectacled Jawaharlal Nehru purveyed his travel agent services.

"No thank you."

"You need ticke'. Bus go now. Need ticke' quick. I help."

"I have a ticket, thank you."

"I help you, upgrade."

"I have a Super Deluxe ticket already."

"I get you best seat on bus."

"Thank you but I've been on many buses in Nepal and all the seats are the same."

"No sir, seat near driver is best, for when bus is crashing. Most easy to get out bus. Also best music soundings."

"Thanks, but I'll take my chances, I'm fine, thank you."

"Snaak ... snaak. Delis snaak ..." Somehow, he had appeared to my left again. Who was this guy, I thought, David Blaine's love child?

"You wan' chai, you wan' tea? Best quality Nepali tea, from mountain region. Ilam tea. Delis and refresh. Better than Darjeeling tea. Nepal Ilam tea best in world. India tea no as good. India people no good." This soft sell was delivered in a steely whisper by a great-grandmother donning a head wrap that saw and raised double Erykah Badu's ante.

"No, thank you, but I really don't have the time."

"Bus no go. What bus you go? You take chai and I tell driver he wait."

"No, really thank you, I'd rather just get on the bus."

"Bus, plenty of time. You take tea now."

The first battered diesel behemoth roused itself into life to my right. Its engine booming and spluttering black muck into the air, it lurched across the hardcore. I knew deep in my heart of hearts, that *must* be my bus, I'd missed it. I was paralysed while forlornly watching it go.

"Sir, I tell you want best Ilam tea?"

My inner voice told me it was only 5.44, it can't have been my bus. I was sure nothing ever left early. The ticket-seller had said the departure was 6.15, but doubt needled me with the possibility the bus had been full and the driver had decided one more passenger wasn't going to fit.

"No, most definitely, no thank you very much."

"Very cheap. Better than India tea. India tea no good. India people no good. No make good tea. Morning early best price ..."

The littlest member of the battalion of trunk carriers passed. The five-year-old's load looked like it could contain a Trident submarine's nuclear generator. I made a breakout from the rolling maul of higglers and hucksters surrounding me with only one indefatigable tackler still in pursuit.

"Sir, still time to buy best quality fruitings."

It was 5.45. Airport Dad Defcon Three.

"Will you *please* leave it, mate? I said I don't want to buy any of your sodding melons. I don't want any tangerines or mangosteens or whatever else is being flogged over there. So, leave me alone and stop bloody following me, will you?!"

"There is no need to be having very most ruding attitude, most kind sir."

He was right, but it was going to take a while for things to de-escalate from Airport Dad Defcon Three. The shame of losing my cool and being untowardly priapic to my newfound companion hadn't yet set in. Like everyone else trying to flog their wares, I knew he was only trying to make a commission, but I was going to be unsympathetic to that for a while.

Something defensive and combative is embedded in my reaction to touts. This is compounded when I perceive I'm being seen as an easy target, a dollar cow to be endlessly milked. This is in spite of the sums involved being so trivial to anyone who's able to afford a trip to Nepal. After many trips to Asia, I've still failed to master the fight or flight reaction that touts trigger and always seem to end up doing both rather than going with the flow. I stormed off towards the candidate buses indicated by the baccy smokestacks earlier. I sensed he was still in my slipstream.

"Which bus you want?"

My new questioner was a serious-looking, pot-bellied man. If he'd been pregnant, old wives would've predicted it was a girl. Most of his middle-aged girth pointed passive-aggressively at me.

It was 5.50. Defcon Two.

"Shivalaya."

"That is Jiri bus."

"I have already told the most estimable gentleman of this fact."

This was a dangerous escalation by the fruit tout. Defcon Two barely holding, the silo hatch was sliding back on the verbal nukes. Dual keys had been inserted into launch controls by shovel-jawed military buzz-cuts. All I was awaiting was the correct code phrase ...

"But Shivalaya is *after* Jiri, isn't it?"

"I am bus driver. I know way. We change bus destination to Shivalaya after Jiri."

"Do I have to change buses at Jiri, then?"

"No, same bus. Bus go to Jiri first."

Confused, I tried to make sense of that, guessing the logic was biggest regional town first, other destinations next. It was different from the European approach but I was just relieved to have found my driver. At that, Mr Gleaming White Nikes admitted defeat on the fruit front. He slipped away, seeking the next round of Vitamin C-deficient trekkers on the seven o'clock buses.

"You have ticket?"

"Yes, here it is." I shuddered through a momentary spike of angst as I feared I'd lost my papers, even though I'd checked, double-checked, zipped my inside pocket and patted it down 20 times before I left the hotel room. I reached in and showed him my 'Supper Deluxe' ticket. The relief brought de-escalation to Defcon Three.

"Bus leave by 6.15. Thirty minute. Why you here so much early?"

Airport Dad declared victory.

"Err ... the guy at the ticket counter told me. Could you take me to the bus please, so I can get my seat?"

"First give ticket. Come. Follow."

I handed over my pink slip and he examined it, fingers first. Seemingly satisfied, we marched off towards the huddle of buses obliquely indicated by the smoking crew.

"Wait!" he ordered, still grasping my ticket.

We were 10 metres from the nearest bus. Without warning, he darted off like a rotund Usain Bolt towards the ticket shack and dread rose. It told me I'd fallen for the oldest trick in the book, the 'sell a bogus ticket to a hapless tourist, steal it back in the morning and sell it on again to the next hapless mark the following day' ruse. But before I could take stock, he'd sprinted back and, without offering any further explanation, returned my paperwork. As I wondered how he'd got such a big rolling belly if he could do the 200 metres in 19.2 seconds, we resumed our walk to the bus.

"This my bus."

"Great, can I get on?"

"You wan' buy fruit? Jiri is very long bus."

His bus wasn't very long. Dimension wise, it was as if a National Express coach had been sawn in half and crushed height-ways by about 20 per cent while retaining its girth. There was an open door about a third of the way up the driver's side. The driver sat atop a rusty wheel arch where a muddied tyre had landed in one of Ratna Park's many turbid, detritus strewn puddles. The rear wheels were doubled up. The windows could have been stolen from a pre-war commuter train serving the Brighton to London Bridge line. They weren't spared the splodges of dried muck and veneer of dust coating the rest of the bodywork. A climbing frame of metalwork crowned the roof and laddered down the driver's side.

Full-length mirrors proudly protruded at each side of the full-width windshield, an orange and black Devanagari declaration stuck to the interior. My written skills in Sanskrit were no match for my verbal proficiencies in Nepali, and although I was sure it decreed something deep and karmic, deep down I couldn't unthink it spelled out 'Trev' and 'Sharon'. I wondered if Nepali visitors to the UK think the bannering of couples in the windows of pimped-up Year 2K Volkswagen Polos proclaims some profound Christian truism?

The bus's paintwork was muted in a singular periwinkle blue, punctuated by depressions of bare metal where the bodywork had been battered and pitted by the road. I reckoned the bus's skin had more contusions than a fast food-loving pubescent suffering the height of an acne attack.

"No, thank you, I'll just take my place, please."

Usain Bloat showed me to my seat. I was expecting him to ask for my backpack and was prepared to hang out from the door frame to keep an eye on him stowing it on the roof. I wanted to make sure it was lashed down properly and no-one made off with it before we left the bus park. I was happily surprised when he insisted he stashed the bag under the seat in front, even leaving space for my legs. 'Supper Deluxe indeed!' The driver disappeared and left me sitting there in the semi-darkness, astonished to be the first passenger embarked.

Reaching my seat had discharged my anxieties and I sat there alone. I relaxed, incredibly pleased with myself in overcoming my first challenge. It hadn't exactly been the equivalent of chucking that magic ring into the volcano, but I'd take it. My elevated position allowed me to view smugly the bedlam outside from which I'd escaped. I was a bug who'd escaped the petri dish and become a scientist observing sibling microbes through the lens of a microscope. I could now make out whirls and patterns; there *was* a choreography to the randomness at ground level. The trick was to filter out the noise and focus on those family groups. The program was: taxi disgorge, break and seek, squawk, retry, coalesce on success, fruit, water, snacks and tea, wait at the foot of the bus's stairwell *en masse*. Loop.

The first couple of family groups had completed that routine and were good-naturedly waiting at the bus door. Apparently, one of the paterfamiliases had made a mistake only a man could make and required berating by a bevy of female relatives. I got the impression he wasn't going to be able to go back and turn the television off/lock the back door/put the bins out. There was nothing to be done about it, but the ladies were determined not to let him forget it for the next nine hours. The other family group were doing the much of nothing all families with small children do when waiting for boarding. The parents stood head down slyly eying their charges waiting for them to run off at the slightest hint of anything less boring than their parents, which, of course, was anything.

Six o'clock chimed. Dawn had broken and with the first warming of the sun the day felt fresher. By now, the families had been joined by a dignified elderly couple but there had been no further sign of the driver. A lance-corporal in the Nepali urban uniform had been left in charge and manoeuvred into the assembled throng to bark an order. The patriarchs dipped in to and patted pocket after pocket in alarm, their partners tensed to pounce with a verbal mauling should they not have been able to do that one simple thing asked of them that morning. There was a palpable look of relief as they flapped their tickets in the air in the victorious fashion of Neville Chamberlain and Peace in Our Time.

The venerable senior male dexterously reached into a hidden recess in his dress and produced his tickets without batting an eyelid. I'm sure I detected a faint smile at the corner of his lips and a satisfied micro-glance at his wife as he presented them to the lance-corporal with feline grace. The carnets were inspected with a gentle banter and all seemed in order as boarding began. The lance-corporal showed the passengers the open door and stood back. His duties discharged, one chevron proceeded to light up and, with the cigarette in his mouth, he was the double of one of the trio of smokers from earlier.

It was 6.10. The first of the other passengers, the chastised dad, momentarily stopped at the top of the stairwell and meerkat-stared at his options for seating. Usain had shown me each ticket had an equivalent number, so no matter where he *wanted* to sit, he was going to have to locate his family on their designated seats. His disappointed frown became an impish grin as he realised his allocation. It included a seat next to the weird guy who'd been sitting alone in the dark for the last half-hour. His revenge for his earlier chastisement was to sit his wife and one-year-old next to him.

"Namaste."

"Namaste. Where you go?"

"Shivalaya."

"Good. This bus go to Jiri."

I knew better by now and said nothing to his wife, who handed me her baby without a by-your-leave. She'd brought with her a bag-for-life stuffed full of nappies, bottles, wet wipes and all the other childcare needs a Sloane Square nanny would be proud to carry while pushing an heir presumptive around Hyde Park. This was all stuffed under the seat in front. Next, her husband passed her a woven basket containing a glowing lava stream of luminescent corn snack packets sliding over the edge, a stapled multi-pack of gummy sweets and an urn-sized thermos flask. This she balanced on the bag's lip squashed under the seat.

The smiling husband handed over a schoolbook-sized backpack. This was forced, opening first, into the sliver of space afforded between my hip and hers. My personal space had been restricted by 25 per cent, but my British conditioning meant I murmured not a word. Besides, I'd been skilfully taken out of the game by the handing over of the toddler. It was hard to mount a defence of my bum space while trying not to drop a baby who was looking at me as if I'd just landed from the far side of Alpha Centauri. I could tell the father was laughing silently as he settled back into his seat.

Six-fifteen came. The older statesman seemed to have found an escalator in the stairwell and majestically glided up the stairs and into his seat. The gentleman was how Neo in *The Matrix* would move if he were 90. All his experience showed in not having to suffer the faffing of the families taking their stations. He'd timed his embarking of the bus to perfection, so he hadn't been bumped or hassled.

Despite my newly allocated cramped conditions, I was happy. There were only 10 people on the bus and one of them was cooler than an Arctic cucumber; it was obvious he wasn't going to bother anybody. Three seats each meant the Wifey next to me and her toddler could move away to sit with her family. I could luxuriate in stretching out for the nine-hour trip ahead. I wondered why the bus wasn't on its way but there had been no sign of Usain coming to do the driving, so I thought: 'Not to worry, nothing leaves on time in Asia.'

Six-twenty-five arrived and four other trekkers boarded. I was mildly annoyed at the sight of them. They were all fit-looking 20-odd year-olds and were dressed in top-of-the-range fleeces and muscle-hugging Lycra tights. The reason for my vexation was what I perceived as their lack of respect for the culture they'd chosen to visit. The Nepali norm is to be conservative in one's dress. Bare skin is frowned upon and, in certain cases, considered offensive. While the youngsters' spray-on Lycra tights weren't nude shade, they did the job of accentuating all the body parts they nominally covered and so I thought they may as well have been.

I'd read Nepalis are offended by this but hadn't yet had an opportunity to discuss it. Given the brazen persistence of the bus park's pushers, it was hard to believe the average Nepali would be way too polite to mention their unease, but I understood that to be the case. The Northern European ruleset for the limits of acceptability around invasion of personal space and the moral line between fair bargaining and swindling salesmanship aren't drawn in the same places in Nepal. Ditto for Nepalis not being comfortable with the odd bare calf and how that contrasts with the European tuning out of millions of pallid, overfed bodies exposed to self-fry on the Mediterranean beaches each summer. But I could tell by the turning away of heads from the centre aisle as the four moved through the bus the local folks found the new passengers' attire distasteful. They parked themselves out of the way on the back seat to chatter excitedly in French or Quebecois.

"Putain, ces collants m'écrasent les couilles."

Six-thirty-five came with the return of Usain, full of energy. He must have fuelled up by demolishing a double dhal baat for breakfast. He swiftly scaled the stairs, jumped into his seat and revved the engine in one seamless movement. His tummy seemed to self-suck in over the wheel and spread back out when he settled. He shouted something out of the open window to the lance-corporal who'd been toking away in the centre of a formless group about 20 metres away, resulting in the start of a stampede of sorts.

I was crushed, not only physically, knowing straight away these were going to be my companions for the next nine hours. Lance easily summitted the bus and noisily beckoned for the heavy-duty luggage to go on the roof. Western health and safety regulations would dictate that the items hoisted would need a team of four men or a small crane to complete the job without danger of injury. These were passed up with apparent ease by the scrawniest granny of each family.

By 6.45, every seat had been taken, some occupied by two-and-a-half passengers. Mothers with one toddler on their lap and one bum cheek of another split between theirs and their aunts'. There were sacks of travel comforts and items too valuable to be trusted to the roof arranged in every available nook and cranny. The aisle had become about as navigable as the upper reaches of the Bhoti Kosi river. I considered myself lucky, though, only to have the two near companions. My Wifey neighbour hadn't uttered a word since her confirmation that this was the bus to Jiri and was staring passively at the headrest in front of her. She hadn't even motioned to ask for her child back.

He hadn't made a sound or broken his stare. I was beginning to feel more and more uncomfortable, like someone who is being very deliberately psychologically deconstructed. I wondered whether the boy was some sort of infant idiot savant who'd revived a long-buried KGB thought-control experiment and was conducting it on me. The spell was broken when his mum opened a bag of lurid corn snacks and started to champ away vigorously. He wanted back to join the nosebag and kicked out. Wifey made to receive him and I passed him over, glad to oblige and relieve myself of those interrogative, unblinking eyes.

By 6.50, Usain had completed his pre-flight checks, confirming without any shadow of a doubt that the engine revved. The sugar rush from his hearty breakfast must have worn off as he decamped from his seat, flew down the stairwell and took off across the station. My stopwatch recorded he'd made the 100 metres in 9.3. He returned with a samosa stuck between his teeth and was back at the wheel in less than 30 seconds. It was enough time for a goose feather-swaddled babushka to have taken her chance to sneak off to the fruiterers and buy another bag of tangerines; her time for the 100 metres registering in at 9.3 minutes.

At seven o'clock, Usain revved and revved again and finally found gear. Lance ran alongside the bus and swung himself into the stairwell via the door's stanchion as we crept forward. It was designed to look cool, but the nonagenarian Neo's expression gave away he wasn't remotely impressed; he could do that without touching the jamb. But I thought it a defining moment – we were on our way!

Seven-ten passed and Usain's Supper Deluxe had run straight into the backlog of buses funnelling their way out of the station. Lance had alighted and was negotiating with a colleague of equivalent rank about the order of their buses for the next exit. The negotiations seemed to involve the intensive bargaining of nicotine which needed extensive sampling before being accepted as part of the trade. A crumpled packet later, an accord had been reached. Lance wolf-whistled loudly out of the door, double thumped the bus's side panel, gave two more wolf whistles and followed with another double thump. As I was thinking he was attached to the signals corps, Usain's shoulders tensed for a moment and he crunched back into gear. At 7.15, the Tata's front wheels crossed the bus park's threshold.

The sky had turned a flawless blue as we turned right into the four lanes of Durbar Marg. Through the grimy window, I saw a handful of local taekwondo enthusiasts sweeping their limbs through their katas in a graceful slowed motion. They had sited themselves on a small hummock in the Tundikhel parade ground, pulling aside a chicken-wire fence to allow them access to their morning stage. At the tump's base, morning ablutions were in progress. A dozen men apparelled in white T-shirts covering pot bellies rivalling, but not exceeding, Usain's were either leant at right angles over red plastic buckets, their locks lathered into an ivory foam, or zigzag lined up and awaiting their turn. They smiled and waved lazily as we passed.

The rush-hour traffic was unexpectedly sparse, and we were soon out of Kathmandu's tourist centre and on a raised stretch of urban motorway cutting through the banking district. The guidebook indicated this was the Kathmandu Super Highway but I couldn't help but think it should've been named 'Supper'. From this vantage, the city's scale and density were discernible. Every 50 metres, a 90-degree potholed thoroughfare dwindled its lopsided construction into the smoggy haze.

The motorway's four lanes were soon busied out; commuter vehicles ground out fumes past the multi-storey buildings banked on either side. At first glance, they seemed solid and modern, but as we rattled past more and more of them, I realised there were only a few ultra-modern concrete and glass erections.

Most of the property was reconstituted traditional brick structures of four or so floors, their antiquity masked by imposing signs and billboards publicising the wares of their occupants. A 10-metre Mo Salah in mid sprint, his pharaonic afro pushed back against his forward velocity, adorned the Standard Chartered Bank. It left me thinking Usain could do the 200 to the Panipuri barrow boy in 19 seconds, but doubting he could then put one in the top right-hand corner at the same time as noshing down his snack.

It was good to see a reference to Liverpool Football Club and the comfort of home in such an unexpected setting. I'd a confirmed trip with my son and some friends to see Liverpool thrash Crystal Palace on their way, hopefully, to taking the Premier League title the following March.

The warm glow of the reminder subsided as I wondered about how the decision to erect such a prominent image of Mo in that place had been made. The time difference means a 4pm Super Sunday kick-off match starts at 9.45pm in Nepal. Nepalis are in bed by 10pm, except, I'd learned, during Tihar, when bedtime reverts to 10am. There's only so much Mo can do in 15 minutes; probably a perfect hat-trick followed by a rabona from the halfway line into the top bins against Crystal Palace but there wouldn't be much of an audience to see it.

While Liverpool FC are undoubtedly the greatest ever English football club and Anfield sits in a fine Georgian city on the banks of the serene River Mersey, the cost of a flight to the UK, triple that for the train from London to Liverpool, hotel and hospitality ticket, meant I doubted even the most ardent of Nepali LFC fans would ever make it there. So, I wondered, what relevance and pulling power had Mo to make people in the country go and open that current account?

The best I could come up with was it was not important enough to figure discretely on the agenda in one of the bank's routine executive sales meetings. The decision was *de facto* made by the grey-suited senior management team without any concept of its relevance in the Federal Democratic Republic of Nepal. I knew football was a poor relation to cricket in that part of the world. If they had, instead, selected Jos Buttler from Lancashire County Cricket Club, undoubtedly the best in England, they'd have generated a lot more recognition and interest.

I realised had been taking my passive acknowledgement of the effects of globalisation for granted. I hadn't recollected seeing any Premier League images on my previous trip to Nepal and, while spotting the image of Mo was a surprise, the image wasn't. I'd seen the same in the UK countless times over the last couple of years. They'd become filtered-out background noise in the same way as one doesn't take note of a lamppost or supermarket car park, which I imagined wasn't the intent of their designer, but I'd challenge anyone to recall all their exact details.

My musings over the billboard took me back to my inner motivation to experience some of the planet's wonders as a 'traveller' rather than a tourist. At the end of the Pleistocene, before my first round-the-world backpacking trip, a friend's mother, aghast that I'd given up my job and decided to travel, asked me why I wanted to do such an imbecilic thing. She told me I was a squandering my life and was unable to fathom why I wasn't taking an opportunity to start accountancy training in Harrogate, like her son. Gap year travelling wasn't much of a thing then, so I understood her thinking to a certain extent. Her internal program for what constituted a successful life was so ingrained that going on a reckless wastrel adventure to Australia simply didn't compute.

For my part, I reasoned the alternative she had in mind for her son was a waste, so terminally dull. I wanted to take a risk and bypass the slow, cloying feeling of an unsatisfied decay into a suburban death. The sensation of numbed encasement in Laura Ashley wallpaper and curtain-twitching from the living room out onto rows of colour-coded Audio Quatros, regimented across the close, was not going to be my next 50 years.

So, I chose my response to her in what I believed a measured way. I craved to meet the world before it became homogenised into the same drive down a Texan highway. I told her I anticipated everyplace was going to end up carved into eight-lane freeways. A world of adverts for outlets selling stuff we don't need posted on 10-metre billboards every half kilometre. Exxon gas, McDonalds and Taco Bell available at each exit. My friend told me the next morning his mother hadn't appreciated my answer and was on the verge of kicking me off her property; my impure thoughts polluting the atmosphere and risking her son's exciting journey into the arms of Ernst and Young. She was determined in her thinking I'd be back in three months and, after realising my folly, I'd be straight into a career in actuary. As a side note, apparently, she'd also never heard of Taco Bell, which was fair enough; I still don't think they have one in Yorkshire.

As we sped past Mo, it wasn't with any degree of satisfaction that I recognised my clairvoyant image of homogenised dystopia had already taken shape. I was about to fall into the resigned dejection of being helpless against the march of such progress when my spirits were raised by the next sign along the road.

'Welcome to Anti-Virus Café'

'Have some of *that,* globalisation!' Whatever the mega-corporations' marketing machines could come up with could never compete with the subcontinent's interpretations of English in my book. I'd easily forget that image of Mo Salah – sorry Mo, no offence – but I don't think I'll ever forget the image of the Anti-Virus Café sign. I'd no idea what the proprietors were thinking when they settled on the name, but I thought it wonderful.

If the owners wanted to stimulate business via a debate on the meaning of their title they had me in an instant. Did the sign mean come in, have some bara and aloo and your influenza will be gone by the time you've paid the bill? How about immunity to herpes with every lassi? If so, there would be a queue around the block. The place could be offering geeks a free malware scan of their laptop with a julebi or a Window's Defender tutorial with their momos. I speculated the place was originally an internet café and had suffered an issue with infected computers. The owners had rebranded once they were able to publicly demonstrate the viruses had been removed and that their clientele had stopped receiving emails about unclaimed inheritances from their long-lost millionaire uncles in Nigeria.

The Supper Highway widened into six lanes after an hour or so and we drew up to a green sign indicating we'd reached Bhaktapur. Bhaktapur is often cited as one of the sights to see in Nepal – an unspoiled medieval gem of a city reflective of a long-lost epoch. This may have been so when Nepal was first opened to Western visitors, but the citadel was now well camouflaged by the same densely packed, heterogeneous brick and concrete sprawl through which we'd driven for the last 60 minutes.

The Supper transposed itself into the Araniko Highway as it unfolded through this negligence of town planning. Across the traffic was a military zone demarked by wire fencing interspersed with warning signs and sentry boxes posted every 100 metres. Our coach slowed next to a bus stop opposite, inconveniently occupied by a convoy of pickups idling blue smoke. Phalanxes of young urban workers clambered into their open cargo spaces. They were wearing the uniform and I was tempted to don my snow-glasses in response to the reflected Adidas sneaker dazzle. Usain decided to park the bus on the motorway's inside lane, adeptly blocking in the convoy and starting a tailback.

Why were we stopping? Bhaktapur was an hour from Thamel. I'd learned searching for Ratna that there was a dedicated bus park less than a block away serving passengers who wanted to commute between the two. Why would anyone take a slower, less frequent Ratna bus and get off here? No-one looked like they were about to disembark, although Nonagenarian Neo's movements were so imperceptibly fluid he could've debussed and been enjoying a cup of chai at home before Usain had had time to put the bus into neutral.

There hadn't been any sign of the yawing associated with a puncture, the thud of an exhaust collapsing, or luggage having been jettisoned onto the tarmac, so I was nonplussed what was going on.

'Once you eliminate the impossible, whatever remains, no matter how improbable, must be the truth.'

I wondered whether Conan Doyle had ever visited Nepal? I'd eliminated the impossible; that is, there was no chance whatsoever a single additional passenger could be jammed into the already overfilled bus. So, I'd deduced some other unlikely event was happening. It would be improbable but not impossible Usain was a fully paid-up shop steward in the National Union of Nepali Omnibus Drivers and Conductors. He'd only stopped here to remind those pickup drivers forcefully the bus stop they'd chosen to occupy, in direct contradiction to any act of socialist solidarity and comradeship, had been demarcated for the sole use of union members. As Lance guided up the stairwell a genteel-looking lady carrying what appeared to be the immaculately laundered whites of the Bhaktapur cricket team, I realised that in Nepal, Sherlock would've been defeated more often than not.

The refined lady was followed by another woman porting an infant wrapped into her side. She hopped Louis Vuitton wheelie-luggage up the stairs by its extended handle. Three robust Sherpa gentlemen in well-worn grubby padded jackets carrying assorted duffels buffeted their luggage up into the main cabin. Where were they all going to sit? Usain could suck in his belly for the next eight hours and the lady from the sports pavilion could squat in lap-dance fashion between him and the steering wheel, but what about the other four or five seats needed?

I'd seen folks riding on the roofs of buses in Nepal, but this one was fully laden with all manner of electrical goods. Surely mother and child astride a Zanussi at 60 kilometres an hour was a bit much, even for Nepal? The answer soon revealed itself: sitting was unnecessary. The men moved to the back of the bus and stood, shying their faces away from the French 'Paquets au Linford Christie'. The ladies made the best of their lot, crouching on the flotsam and jetsam washed up in the aisle.

After a short altercation between the lance-corporal and a scabrous ute driver who'd taken up the challenge of completing a 784-point turn to edge his way out into the highway, we were off again. The traffic was mercifully light in front of us. Usain knew what he'd been doing in backing up all those vehicles.

The conglomeration soon thinned out and we ascended. As the houses improved into grand-turreted, three-storey structures plumped out in their own stucco-walled compounds, they became less frequent. At the same time, the highway narrowed to a single lane in each direction. As Usain picked up some speed, we crossed an invisible cultural boundary that meant the use of the bus's horn was now possible.

It was evident the use of the horn was tolerated in only a few highly selective situations, similar to the code of practice for the discharge of firearms by the British police. These eventualities narrowed down to the handful of occasions when Usain was crossing another bus coming in the other direction, spotted a bus of the same mark or make, was overtaking on the wrong side of the road at a blind summit, was hurrying a cow to the side of the way or saw a friend toiling in a field. A double note signalled to a samosa vendor the bus was slowing slightly for Usain to buy a quick starchy something to keep him going.

The horn was standard fare: a quadruple blast emulating an old-fashioned, rubber-pumped bicycle air-horn amped through a Marshall stack. Trees backed 100 metres away from the highway shed an autumn of leaves at the shock wave from the klaxon.

We blared through the countryside on the ever steeper highway. Overladen buses like our own, dilapidated trucks piled with spoil heaps of aggregate and tarpaulined blocks of imports from China blurred past us every few seconds, sometimes even on their own side of the road. Overloaded pickups conveying construction crews, spotless four-by-fours, rusted Toyota mini-vans and three generations of family saloons attempted to overtake. The odd ancient Hindustan taxi, horizontal leaning BSA motorcycles and weaving mopeds fought to occupy an invisible middle lane.

Usain had settled into a rhythm of dodging the oncoming stream while balancing the bus's passenger side wheels at a 50 per cent overhang on the 200-metre precipice unguarded to our left. Despite my scientific training telling me, according to Newton's first law, the inertia associated with the other 95 per cent of the mass of the bus meant there was no possibility we'd topple into the void, my inner voice told me we were already goners. I wished I'd taken up that offer in Ratna to be positioned in the best seat for crashings.

I looked to Usain for reassurance, determining that if his face was grim-set in concentration on the road, I'd relax a little. Unfortunately, he was plainly bored and was guiding the wheel with one hand, his other busily searching through a carry-case of CDs. But I was thankful he hadn't decided to watch a Bollywood blockbuster at the same time on the dashboard mounted television. When it arrived, the music from his selection took me by surprise. His initial choice was, I think, an anthology of 1950s and 1960s duets from romantic musical comedies. I vaguely recognised a number of the songs, but the one to which I knew more than a smattering of the words was *How Do You Like Your Eggs in the Morning?* by Dean Martin and Helen O'Connell. Nonagenarian Neo's cool was momentarily broken by some head-bobbing to the swing of the beat, but no-one among the other passengers seemed to take much notice.

At the end of the duet CD, Usain took advantage of the opportunity to switch discs while taking a call. He must have grappled the wheel with his paunch and been steering by that method. 'No matter', I thought, the precipice had reduced to 50 metres and our drop would be cushioned by the houses in the village below, so we were covered for any false move. Usain finished his call, happy with the outcome. He chose to switch the music up a gear and selected what I'd describe as Now That's What I Call Nepali Reggaeton for our next hour of listening pleasure. It had a great beat and there was a lot of bobbing of heads by the more fresh-faced voyagers. The music would have graced Old San Juan. I wondered what a Himalayan J Balvin would go by: T Treakin?

My mind wandered on the subject matter for the songs, thinking this would need crafting differently to Puerto Rican gangsta lyrics for the context to be relevant in Nepal. The lack of prevalence of violent crime in Nepal, even in the cities, meant 'puttin' a cap in ya ass' wouldn't reflect daily life. But 'I am remaining cool, calm and collected until such point as you really wind me up and then lose it, go to my Gurkha uncle's house, come back and split you from head to toe with his khukuri' didn't lend itself to much of a rhyming couplet.

I guessed poverty, inequality, police and government corruption, environmental destruction, pollution and lack of social mobility were some things that would make young Nepalis angry. Whether the lyrics belting out at me were saying anything about those issues or were an ode to grandmother's cheese momos I had no clue.

Three hours in and the Wifey and her Midwich Cuckoo had demolished their mound of corn snacks, leaving a spoil heap of packets pyramided in the splinter of space between us.

"You Jeewan."

I hoped not. His mother handed him to me before licking the orange coloured coating from her fingers. The consumption of a surfeit of E-numbers had flipped the switch on Jeewan's snot fountain of a nose from 'Off' to 'On'. On the plus side, I was spared the soul-boring stare. Try not to blink while a gushing river of bogies cascades over your top lip. On the minus side, my trousers were being flooded with phlegm faster than if I'd attended a gobbing competition at a convention of bronchial punks.

"Excuse me, do you have a tissue, please? Jeewan has a runny nose."

"You tissue."

I assumed she meant I must use my own tissue to wipe her son's nose, rather than to use myself as a human handkerchief to stem Jeewan's gush.

"Err ... sorry, I don't have any, mine are in my bag. It's squashed under the seat."

"Pradip!" The Wifey rattled out a phrase towards her husband with a scowl. Her mate looked up as Jeewan was clutched from my grasp and hurled towards him. Pradip's catch was to clasp Jeewan by his forearm and swing him into his midriff. It wasn't as cushioned as Usain's but there was ample padding and so Jeewan was spared a collision with the window opposite.

I didn't see it, but I'm sure Nonagenarian Neo had it covered. If needed, he would've plucked Jeewan out of the air a fraction before he hit the glass and only pulled back his arm once the nipper was secure in his dad's pouch. Mrs Pradip had found a packet of tissues in the inverted backpack and handed them over to Pradip. These had been used up within five minutes, Jeewan's mucus production as relentless as his stare.

Three-and-a-half hours in and we'd broken out from the lush shadow of the valley and our charabanc had become hot from the mid-morning sun. I'd taken the opportunity of Jeewan's repose with his dad to shed the Rab. Wifey had taken the opportunity to break open some fruity gobstoppers. She blow-piped foamy red pips onto the floor with the regularity of an oak floor fitter's nail gun.

I'd already started to slow roast an hour before, but my cowardice had prevented me from daring to peel off. I knew one false elbow that disturbed the Wifey or Jeewan's chomping of the corn snacks would mean I'd have to hold little Chucky. Having seized my moment the Rab was semi-balled in my lap, ready for stuffing into the gap between my hip and the window.

"Pradip!" An order was barked again from between blood-red lips and Pradip flung Jeewan back towards his mother. It was as well I'd my jacket to hand, as Wifey had decided to dummy Pradip's pass as she rummaged for more tissues and left me to do the catching. I managed to pluck him out of the air and clutch him into the folded material of the coat just before he concussed himself on and broke my window.

"Excuse me! What the hell?"

Pradip let rip at Wifey with something augmented by pointing fingers. Wifey retorted with a look conveying disbelief. How could anyone be so stupid to pass the child while they could plainly see she was busy looking for tissues? While they were arguing, Jeewan looked up at me, impassively, from my catcher's mitt and a growing heat spot started to bleach the back of my corneas. Wifey located a multi-pack of tissues and gesticulated at Pradip with them while continuing to berate his actions. Her head swivelled and, with a glazed stare only surpassed by her firstborn, nipped at me.

"Give."

I gratefully passed Jeewan over and Wifey passed him back to Pradip in a single move. Pradip didn't want him and passed him back to Wifey, but Wifey was having none of that and Jeewan went back across the aisle to his father. Neither was going to accept defeat and the exchange increased in speed. Soon Jeewan was being moved between the two like a Gilbert being spun by the All-Blacks' backline. A Jeewan knock-on was only saved by Usain jerking the bus to a halt on an incline in the middle of the highway. There had been no need to use the horn to signal that.

We had halted in a nondescript place, the road cutting through a steep wooded slope. To our right there was a tangle of trees, uninterrupted up and across the hill. To our left was more open, the same trees broken by a gap afforded by a rocky cliff. I was relieved Usain had chosen not to dangle the bus over the edge, instead straddling it across both lanes.

A slight commotion behind me resulted in an old lady pushing past the Sherpa gentlemen and making her way over the sacks of goodies towards Lance. He took her hand gently and waltzed her down the stairwell like a stone-washed Gene Kelly. It was plain she was charmed. Lance clambered up the side of the bus and what looked like a medium-sized white plastic coffin was passed down to the old lady who received it with a palpable grunt. Lance was smarter than he looked if it contained the remains of her husband. As she buckled under its weight, the crown of a head grew larger at the cliff's edge. The crown became a full head, torso and finally a fully-fledged young man. He wasn't wearing the urban uniform, rather a more rural outfit of flip-flops and loosely fitted skirt wrapped beneath his holey T-shirt. With the old lady at one end of the coffin, he took the other and together they disappeared via an unseen set of steps down the escarpment. All I could think was 'What timing!'

I was braced for an onslaught of Jeewan tossing but *détente* had broken out between his parents. Wifey must have finished all the fruity gobstoppers because the gummy sweets had been offered in the peace accord. They were now being sucked on. Lance did his signal corps routine at the foot of the stairwell. I was unsure who he was calling but Usain seemed satisfied he wasn't missing out on any new fare-paying customers. With a toot of the horn, we moved off into the vortex of leaves that ensued.

Ten minutes later, Usain pulled up again across the dividing lines. Another couple of older ladies from the back of the bus nudged the Sherpa gentlemen aside and Lance Astaire swished them off the bus. I wondered if the bus doubled as the dial-your-local morgue drop-off service? The two old ladies were first off, followed by the rest of the women on the bus. As I was deciding whether the Kathmandu valley was undergoing a spate of spousal homicide, all the men alighted. Except me. Lance stuck his head through the doorway.

"Pee."

"Excuse me?" This must have been a sophisticated conjunction of the subjunctive tense I hadn't reached yet in my advanced Nepali language studies.

"Pee. Your dick."

Or perhaps?

"Pee. You're dick."

"Ah, thanks, I see."

"Bus go, five minutes."

I didn't need to go, but reasoned I'd better take my chance to squeeze something out as the itinerary for stops hadn't been made clear on the detailed schedule. It had said leave Kathmandu at 6.15, arrive in Shivalaya somewhere around nine hours later. I dropped onto the tarmac and scanned the terrain.

I'm an inveterate Victorian when it comes to my toilet etiquette and shudder at the thought of those moulded trifold pissoirs common in Amsterdam. I have a deep-rooted fear of being caught short and having to use one of these conveniences, be unzipped and hear something along the lines of: 'Hey, Englesman. From what I can shee, looksh like your countrymen aren't only schort in your veticalsh height! Ha! You should drink more Heinekenshs. You'd get a stronger flow like ush cheeshe headshs and stop drippingsh on your bootsh so much. Tot ziens!'

The line of men sloped down behind the bus in various states of a leant back, hips forward, fire-hosing stance. Confident in their handless tobacco puffing, they watered a crop of calf-length grass. I could see there was no room to go there undisturbed by prying eyes but uphill, forward slightly to my right, seemed an empty quarter. There were a couple of well-foliated shrubs so I calculated I'd head that way, find a covering bush and complete my business unperturbed. I rounded the shrubs and was greeted by what could have been mistaken for a set of equidistantly spaced, Home Counties-crocheted loo roll toppers. The only fear greater than public exposure while peeing is being found doing it in the ladies.

"Sorry, so sorry, err ... excuse me, terribly sorry." I apologised in my best Hugh Grant.

I made for the bus's rear and the possibility of going against a tree across the road, but Usain's positioning of the vehicle had resulted in a fleet of suburban commuter vehicles dammed behind a nervous driver. He was struggling to navigate the gap between the bus and the stone drainage channel-cum-moat at the camber's edge. I wasn't going to give his mother in the passenger seat an eyeful so surmised that was a dead-end.

Half of my co-travellers had now made their way back onto the bus, the net result of which was my latent fear of getting duffilled, as it's defined in *The Great Railway Bazaar,* emerging. I could hear the swish as Lance Astaire placed the rest of his partners at the top of the stairwell. My only remaining option was to head to the end of the line beyond the last male irrigator, out of sight of their inquisitive stares. All except Jeewan, of course, who no doubt could stare around corners at a range of 100 metres.

"Fast! Bus go now!" Lance ordered.

Airport Dad trumped Victorian embarrassment and all I could manage was a few dribbles onto the asphalt before I was back in my seat. Fifteen minutes later, Usain returned with what could have been a couple of pickled eggs. He rested them on the dashboard and gunned the engine. After he shouted through another phone call and unwrapped his dairy produce with the care of a top-end jeweller unbinding a dubiously-sourced cache of diamonds, we moved off.

The highway skirted the same inclines as earlier in the morning and we gradually climbed above the hills defining the central valley before plummeting down to a raging Sun Khosi river. An orange-segment-shaped metal bridge led us into a small settlement, possibly Dolalghat. The junction in the village was too narrow for Usain to navigate in one movement without toppling any kerbside houses. So, after some triceps-building wheeling to get the Tata around, he had us straining up the slope across the river. The vegetation here was dense montane jungle and we switch-backed through a shadow of mature trees, the river's bate showing itself in diminishing snippets as we gained height.

The road deteriorated. My online research into the Araniko Highway's history stated that it originated from a yak track. As we drove on, I wondered when, for this stretch, there was going to be any road construction on top of that. At first, the asphalt cracked in the same way as arrow-straight Death Valley freeways are depicted in drone-captured vistas at the start of a myriad of Hollywood blockbusters. As we hairpinned up, next came ochre sandbanks of rutted dirt washed up over one lane. The hillsides abutting were ruptured with landslides, the vegetation's vivid green scarred by giant tiger claws of oranges and browns.

We climbed further to where copper fingers of a gritted fudge mixed with splintered flora poured down from the slope into rubbly impediments of pediment; the road's width at best halved. Another switch-back and the corniche had become a corrugated iron sheet of umber rills interrupted by ever shrinking islands of tarmac. Usain had taken off his overshirt. He fought the wheel hard, arms braced against every misdirection thrown up by the surface, and the Tata's chassis complained as it decapitated crusty mushroom heads of sediment.

We reached a precarious cutting through the hillside. Usain navigated through wrecked tramp steamers of asphalt cross-section that lay half-beached against its upward shore. The road became thirded where muddy streamlets had caused the surface texture to become softer. I was glad Usain had built up his strength; he now wrestled the Tata through a semi-quagmire of pre-eroded vehicle ruts at the edge of a ledge. A bump and the near side wheels dived into a tyre track half a metre deep, and we lurched to the left. The lean held momentarily while gravity decided which way we'd pivot. The offside wheels mercifully took our weight as the bus settled. Usain reversed and rocked the Tata, had another run at the rut and the bus reeled to the right before righting itself as we crested out.

The corrugations, potholes and ruts continued. Although Usain's helmsmanship was superb, my fear increased at every totter, thinking sooner or later, he was likely to misjudge the camber and we'd topple.

Our route cut around a bend making cliffs above and downslope of the road. It brought us to face a Tata idling behind a rocky avalanche that narrowed the way to, at best, our Tata's axle-width. Downhill, there was another landslip that had vomited over the bluff's edge and felled a forest swathe 200 metres below where the gradient was easier. If Usain made any misjudgement traversing the next 30 metres, we'd be over the edge.

A narrow triangular dune of undisturbed sand glistened on the constriction's lip. No other heavy traffic had risked the obstruction. We'd passed a lot of vehicles travelling in the opposite direction that morning, so that didn't make sense. I realised the earthfall must have happened within the last hour or so. The other Tata driver wasn't idling out of a noble adherence to the Araniko code of the road; he was sizing up whether to risk taking his bus through the choke point or wait for a bulldozer to make its way up to clear it. Usain was either more coolly calculating, reckless or impatient. The stick was forced into first and he encouraged the bus forward.

The bus's nose at first stood proud before dipping into a hollow at the avalanche's base. Usain floored it for the incline and made it two thirds of the way before the driver's-side wheel slipped on the untouched bank of sand at the fall's edge. The view from my window was uncluttered by anything between the end of the bodywork and the broken trees below. I gasped, but no air seemed to enter my lungs. I checked for reassurance from my companions but the other passengers were also looking on concerned. We were in a more perilous situation than I'd thought if the Nepalis were worried. Strangely, this sharing of dread did something to calm me and my breathing settled.

Usain grappled the front wheel to an angle where he'd checked the slip. We'd stopped but weren't going forward from where we were. Lance was told to take stock of the situation, forgetting his ballroom elan on disembarking. He confirmed something with Usain from the front of the bus, rotated his arm and Usain followed with the wheel. The bus rocked backwards into the hollow.

Lance stood midway up the pediment as Usain tried the incline again, revving the engine to its maximum and we bumped over the avalanche's lip escaping the chasm below. Only then did Usain realise he'd miscalculated, and I was jolted forward into the headrest in front as he stopped us dead. The Tatas were overlapping.

My window view now led directly down into the forest canopy. I stole a look at the ashen Frenchman who'd the same view from his side window as well as the abyss at the bus's rear with which to contend.

Usain leaned out of the window, shouted to his counterpart in the other Tata and both wing mirrors rolled in. We rocked back again before Usain whirled the steering wheel around, dervish fashion, to squeeze past the other bus centimetres apart. He guided our vehicle into a more central position, stopped and pushed out a long, deliberate breath of relief as he waited for Lance to rejoin us. Numbed, I realised we'd made it through.

The bus ground on through the sandy bypass for the next 40 minutes at the pace of a limping packhorse. The road surface didn't improve much, but neither was there a repeat of anything as perilous as the pediment. My heart rate calmed to normal as Usain topped us out of the bush into high country farmland where the road was coherent again. Verdant fields were dotted with smoky hamlets on either side. I found myself grinning at the first real sight of the Himalaya proper and being alive to enjoy it. Over Pradip's shoulder, a ridge of blue, snow-topped mountains smeared a panorama across the field of vision.

I needed to share with someone, needed to blurt out a euphoric 'Wow, look at that', but my immediate options were nil. I could tell this vista was nothing of interest as far as the local folks were concerned. It meriting the same level of excitement as spotting a Little Chef on a trip from Welwyn Garden City to Peterborough. I looked for support at the back of the bus and was reassured the French spandex models were equally thrilled, having tipped themselves into the one seat nearest the far side window to gesticulate and argue impassionedly. I fancied I could smell the faint trace of friction burning elastane as one of the men wrestled his lunch box over his companions to get a perfect shot with an expensive-looking camera.

The arable landscape gradually gave way to a craggier terrain, reminiscent of upland Scottish sheep farming regions, and we reached a narrow saddle, the mountains now horseshoeing around us. Usain expertly chicaned the bus through boulder fields clawing at the edges of the ever more constrained road. As he oversteered out of a corner, he was met with a truck laden with stone coming in the other direction. The truck was the same model of Tata as the bus, the passenger cabin substituted for a flatbed. It had exited a quarry where excavation was vigorously underway by dozens of people and it became evident that the top of this ridge was being scooped out, the mountain being relegated in front of us.

Usain and the truck driver exchanged increasingly complex horn salvos for the next two or three minutes. When their symphonic duelling was complete, the truck driver backed into the quarry so a victorious Usain could take us to the next double bend. The road headed downwards again into a bowl, back into an area of cropping villages. The bus heaved itself up the far side incline. I imagined if a vehicle could be sweating and red-faced, the Tata would've been drenched and deep scarlet by now. Usain decided to take pity on his poor beast and pulled into one of the two parking bays outside a solitary building.

It was 11.30am. Lance broadcast something in Nepali, to nods of agreement.

"Lunch. Eat. Thirty minute," he directed towards the Europeans. He lit up, smoked half a tab and ball-roomed down the stairs into the roadside restaurant in five seconds flat. He was second in the lunch queue behind Usain.

Everyone else had decamped by the time I'd sorted my day pack. I bypassed the general *alfresco* mulling and smoking and had a gander inside the restaurant, hoping for a nice cup of tea. The orderly lunch queue started by Usain and Lance had now evolved into a set of familial clumps to the left of a skinny lady standing authoritatively behind several steaming tin tureens. Her face was deeply lined, each crease and crenulation concertinaing with every careful rotation of the heavy ladle she brandished. She was engaged in a tennis match of conversation with the hungry passengers. I challenged myself to decipher the system from the apparent chaos.

"Chai. Dhal baat?" The skinny lunch lady opened serve.

Returned by a perceptible nod and right-hand signal with a number of fingers.

Returned by a nod of acknowledgement.

New service. "Chai. Dhal baat?"

Returned by perceptible nod and right-hand signal with a number of fingers.

Returned by perceptible nod of acknowledgement.

New service. "Chai. Dhal baat?"

Returned by perceptible nod and right-hand signal with a number of fingers.

I thought I'd spotted something of a pattern. I waited through a couple more rallies, hoping for a local wag to order a sourdough salmon and cream cheese bagel and full fat soya latte, but it didn't happen. The passengers settled down on plastic chairs around moulded tables as the skinny lady passed them shiny tin plates of piping hot rice and lentils. It looked like serving was going to go on for the full 30 minutes, so I lost patience with waiting for a chance to order a cup of tea and wandered outside to enjoy my lunch.

The restaurant was located in the timber runoff of the sawmill next door. Drumlins of chopped wood lay two metres high beside the parking bays. I settled down on a log and took out my repast. The ciabatta I'd bought two days earlier was flattened, but plumped up again nicely with a bit of persuasion. I opened another of my provisions, a tin of tuna, with the mild trepidation that comes with taking the risk of eating tinned seafood in a mountainous, land-locked country 1,000 kilometres from the sea.

I managed to balance the tin on my knee, avoided stabbing myself and had pierced and prised the can open in only a few minutes. I expertly balanced the bisected ciabatta on the other knee and spooned the tuna onto the bread with the penknife to complete my sandwich. Luckily, my trousers were so caked with Jeewan's dried bogies and the collateral spattering of red-foamed gobstoppers, that the half a tin of spilled sunflower oil that ended up in my lap was hardly noticeable.

"Excusez-moi. Vous etes Français?"

"Non, mais je parle un petit peu de Français." Oh no I didn't.

"Is possible I borrow ze knife, please? For make san'weesh."

"Sure, it needs a bit of a wipe, but here you go. You probably want to use your own trousers to do that."

"Merci."

"You're welcome. De rien."

The other three members of Spandex Beret had joined us.

"Alors, vous parlez le Français très bien." Oh no I couldn't.

"Err ... Où habitez-vous? Where are you guys from?"

"I am from St. Etienne and zey are from Clermont-Ferrand. Ze centre of France."

I'd never been to either, so couldn't start a conversation from there.

"And you, monsieur, where are you from?"

"Je suis Anglais mais j'habite en Écosse."

"Ah ... she 'as good whiskey in Écosse. I 'ave been to Edimbourg for ze festival. Do you 'ave any butter for make san'weesh?"

"Sorry, I'm afraid I don't." 'Unfortunately, I'm also out of camembert and saucisson, and have just finished the last drop of my Beaujolais,' I grouched silently.

"No problem, we make san'weesh with joost ze cheese." At that, I thought they were living high on the hog, as I'd seen imported cheese was the steepest marked-up item in the Thamel tourist supermarkets. It was within my budget, but I was far too mean to pay twice the price I would at home for a piece of rubbery cheddar that's sweated under the delicatessen section fluorescents for three months.

"Yeah, sorry, it wouldn't be worth it to carry butter. Are you all together? Where are you heading?"

"Yes. We are friend, from ze university. We go to Shivalaya."

"Cool, me too. This bus goes to Jiri."

"But Shivalaya, she is ze village after Jiri."

"Yes, I know. We get to Jiri and then we change to Shivalaya."

"So, we change bus at Jiri?"

"No, it's the same bus." When in Rome ...

It confounded me that my new friend hadn't had to go through the same rigmarole I'd been put through earlier, reckoning he must have lived something of a charmed life. It was also possible all that Lycra acted as a strategic deterrent against bus park pests. It must be hard to try to peddle rip-off rate tangerines when your potential customer looks like he has a couple already stashed at groin level.

He handed me back the penknife with a puzzled look on his face. The conversation had taken a downturn and the Spandex silently tucked into their fromage baguettes. I let them know I wanted to go and have a look at the sawmill and headed off. Fifty metres up the hill, I peered over a low wooden fence to see tonnes of weather-darkened tree stumps, trunks and branches heaped on a football pitch-sized space. The volume and disorder of wood reminded me of black-and-white photos of the Tunguska event.

I'd read of Nepal's deforestation problems and interpreted the source of it as the surge in population and, so, demand from hillside villagers collecting their daily firewood. Naively, I hadn't expected industrial exploitation on this scale and, equally naively, hadn't expected to be as shocked by the sight of it. I supposed my mind could conveniently choose not to equate the need for a bed, table and chairs for every home in each one of Kathmandu' slap-dash constructed apartment block-strewn districts with the cost laid out before me. Disappointed with myself for not making the connection, and a sad resignation to environmental ruination returning to my thoughts, I returned down the hill.

Another bus pulled into the bay next to the Tata. It disgorged its passengers and they headed through what estate agents would describe as a 'feature void' allowing the restaurant to claim a sort of *al fresco* dining. The skinny lady started her next dhal baat serve-and-volley match as Usain waddled out of the restaurant, looking sated, having finished his seconds first. He ambled over to his driving counterpart and they examined the contents of a shared pack of cigarettes. They enjoyed a brief chat over a toke and parted ways.

Usain shouted something over to Lance, who was looking discernibly upset he'd missed out on a smoke, and beckoned to us that lunch was over, and we should re-embark. Airport Dad was first in the sprint to the front of the bus and around its corner, but a rapid ascent up the Tata's stairs was prevented by Usain, whose girth seemed lodged between the two buses.

"Dhal baat."

This was the first time I'd heard the phrase used as an apology. After some gentle nudging we were back on the bus. The late morning sun had greenhoused the interior and I opened the top hatch of the window as Wifey took her seat beside me in the humid heat. She won the minor bum scuffle with the rucksack again, but I was willing to concede as Pradip had boarded, cradling Jeewan who'd collapsed into a post sugar-rush slumber. His head nestled on his father's shoulder and his chest bellowed heavily in that manner small children adopt in sleep when they feel safe and comforted.

Lance paso dobled a couple of the straddlers up onto the bus. We were off again, after what sounded like a smattering of cursing from Usain at the expense of the other driver for parking too close. I wasn't sure what the problem was; it was only the small matter of a 40-point turn back onto the highway.

We undulated with the terrain reaching the town of Charikot an hour or so later. The events at the pediment had reinforced a gratitude in me that the ride had been pleasantly non-eventful. We'd motored through rusty, ramshackle villages. Their greys and blues contrasted with the riotously green terraces that fed them. In the distance and paralleling our progress were the incomparable, snow-topped Himalaya.

After an hour or two of such picture-perfect, postcard scenery my elation at their first sighting had been reduced to a Sherpa's nonchalance. I'd heard psychologists state that humans currently only use 10 per cent of our brains and our capacity for learning is infinite. So I wondered why do we seem to reach a certain point of saturation with natural beauty?

Jeewan had slept the satisfied sleep of those who know they've numbed their dad's arm to the point where its amputation would go unnoticed. As Usain parked the bus in Charikot's main street with maximum traffic-calming measures in mind, Wifey stirred herself into making some pleasantries.

"What your name?"

"My name is Lee."

"My name is Sangeet."

Introductions completed, Sangeet signalled to Pradip and he hoisted his charge. She gathered her emptier baskets and they both disembarked, leaving me hoping my next cultural exchange would be a bit more involved. I wondered whether she wanted to let me know who she was so I could look her up next time I was in town, or maybe she was just keen to inform me where to send the cleaning bill.

Charikot bustled with the unmistakable air of market town prosperity. The high street contoured a ridge and the town's brown high rises draped themselves over the hillsides on either side. Hotels boasted their exemplar status in yellows and reds from five storeys up. Open-air stalls strung necklaces of corn snacks from their battered metal porticos. Bunches of mini bananas defied European Union measurement standards above tables of equally intransigent vegetables. Plastic milk cartons served to offer a potato pick-and-mix. All manner of unnaturally coloured carbonated drinks were offered in dusted bottles. There was the incessant hum of exchange and commerce. I liked it straight away.

The blocks of flats cut into the hillsides and the ambience of success reminded me, bizarrely, of Monte Carlo. It was strange as there was no marina-side setting or the remotest comparison in terms of opulence. There was, nevertheless, something about the confidence in the place's wealth exuded by its denizens that shone through. Fancying a look round, I signalled to Lance the question of stretching my legs for a while.

"Leave not possible. Bus leaving, five minutes."

He sashayed down the stairwell and troubled his lighter again. That seemed the signal for circa 40 per cent of the passengers to disembark. I was sad to see Nonagenarian Neo float down the stairwell, sadder still to see Nonagenarian Trinity hadn't fared so well over the years; she struggled down the flight with an arthritic difficulty.

I was disappointed Lance had forbidden me from at least joining them to stretch for a few minutes. I thought the journey over the disintegrated road had jarred an old ski injury. I imagined my coccyx had shattered again and shards of bone were needling my lower back and buttocks. I had a numbed pain in that region and needed to move around to relieve some of the discomfort. I half-crouched, half-stood in the aisle and saw a parade of white goods being manhandled onto the pavement. I sensed the Tata ease on its springs as a disproportionate part of its cargo was unloaded. A source of the town's relative affluence, it seemed.

Those who'd finished their journey in Charikot weren't replaced in kind with others travelling further. A few people embarked, but the bus was now only half full. Lance beckoned me back into my seat and, true to his word, five minutes on, we left town.

The highway's condition from Charikot onwards was much better. With the bus now lightened, Usain picked up the pace and the next couple of hours consisted of a skilful negotiation of uphill hairpins followed by prolonged acceleration downhill. Where the road was clear, he'd let the Tata freewheel like Eddy Merckx bombing down from the Col d'Izoard. He made it obvious he was enjoying it and I imagined this must be Usain's reason to come to work.

Cresting another ridge unveiled the first vista of the Jiri district. The literature described this area as 'The Switzerland of Nepal'. I found it hard to find fault with this comparison. Fatted cows munched long-stemmed grasses in emerald Alpine meadows. Shallow, stony rivers meandered pacifically through wide valleys, no hint given of the downstream anger vented at Dolalghat. Lightly terraced fields of harvest-ready rice were hemmed in by gentle slopes of expertly managed pine forest, their stands thinning out as they scrambled up to the snow line.

The standard for the farmhouses was two storeys of four or five windows set in smooth plaster under sturdy, slatted roofs. I reckoned that, with a wooden balustrade or two, they could be taken for St Moritz ski chalets. Ridges were dappled with snow and above it all was the exultation of the snow-capped Himalaya. It was stunning simply to pass through it.

As the Tata coasted to the end of a long straight, we had our first sight of what I speculated was the town of Jiri. If anything, this part of the valley complex spoke of even greater affluence. Usain stopped the bus at a junction of a minor road running to the right where an expectant gaggle of elders fronted a pristine, shining Range Rover parked unsympathetically on a verge. A sign declared this was ranching country and I wouldn't have blinked if it had offered an invitation to a fondue party or a triangular chocolate-making tour.

The car's owners, presumably, were the ranchers. A couple of our cohort were welcomed off the bus with hugs by their family. The Tata was unburdened of a couple of metal rivetted trunks and a duct tape-reinforced microwave box. Usain had decided these were the people to impress in this neck of the woods and so, after a 10-minute discourse with the eldest of the elders, he moved the bus on with a vigorous farewell.

Another 10 minutes further on, we reached Jiri and I was thrilled to be able to see the place that had a particular resonance for my trip; this was where the Hillary-Norgay expedition had started in earnest 70 years past. They had walked all the way from Kathmandu. I'd got this far by a much less arduous route and in a lot less time, but that didn't prevent my spirits rising. Although my trip was incomparable to the scale of their adventure, it was exciting to think I was retracing their steps a little.

We drove through the bazaar part of town and arrived, in the late afternoon sun, to a broad skidpan of asphalt. Scanning my surroundings, I was slightly disappointed the façade to my left was without a mechanical clock tower cuckooing four o'clock. This quarter was quiet by any standards. I could've been mistaken but thought the only person who'd crossed the square was a pin-striped, bespectacled gentleman struggling to carry a rare Vermeer over to the bank in the corner. The bank must have been doing well, judging by the number of Hindu symbols indicating prosperity and good luck adorning its entrance.

This part of town looked on to a vista broadcasting more agrarian abundance beyond a structure sunk into the ground. I hadn't expected to find an underground Victorian gentlemen's public convenience at the terminus. There were two figures grooming themselves down in the shadows where I could make out black combs tickling tresses backwards. And then they were up the steps; the Jiri Suavecitos were upon us.

The duo were barely forgotten of their teens but had fixed an attitudinal swagger matching the arrogance of their pomade. I was unsure if they'd adopted their Latino James Dean expecting their sweethearts to fall into their arms off the bus, to rival Lance for the favours of a well-to-do village matriarch or to impress a couple of female Swedish trekkers. They were disappointed on all fronts. After paying Lance a fare, one came to sit beside me. Ten hours on the bus and my central nervous system had had enough of the relentless buffeting. I was only able to move my buttocks a quarter of a cheek at a time back into my seat from where I'd spread out.

"Sorry. I'm a bit stiff from the trip."

"You go to Shivalaya, yes?"

"Yes."

"Now we change bus."

Before I could object, I saw what he meant. Usain removed a tachometer from behind the 36-inch TV on the dashboard and welcomed his relief driver. The new man's low body mass index betrayed he was new to the job. As he greeted Usain, even I could spot his rookie mistake before he took the driver's seat. He'd boarded without a fortifying samosa and seemed to have left his pickled dairy products behind.

The majority of the passengers had left the bus at Jiri but Usain II drove those of us remaining carefully. The road now resembled a trip through shadowed Devonshire walled lanes, incongruously coupled with dripping, broad-leaved jungle. It broke out into early evening sunshine at bridges crossing once again angry rivers and turned onto immaculately curated cobbles. This stretch gave thought to a driveway of a British stately home cutting through expensively sustained botanical gardens. The area was remarkably beautiful, and I became transfixed by the sedation of lightly bobbing leaves and crystal rivulets of emergent springs. My meditative state only broken by the slight rumbling of the wheels to a skidded stop.

"Shivalaya."

It was barely a raised voice; it didn't need to be anything more. Usain II looked over his shoulder to the few who'd survived the journey, indicating that, 11 hours after leaving Ratna, we'd arrived.

Shivalaya to Bhandar

The sweet-smelling smoke emanating from the front of the bus told me the Suavecitos were enjoying a rest break with Lance. The two Usains had also disembarked. I tried to stand up and was met with reluctance on the lower part of my body; my legs joining my rear in losing all sensation. Movement gradually returned with pins and needles prickling down to my boots from my numbed buttocks. A sharp pain stabbed where my coccyx used to be intact as I tried to extract my backpack from the seat in front, where it envisaged it had settled in for the night. It had wedged itself underneath and behind the metalwork with the trip's turbulence but, eventually, I managed to extricate it with the insistence of a dentist's removal of a rotten tooth.

I disembarked, body insensate, lugging a backpack torn and smeared with the red juice of Sangeet's discarded fruit pips but with that inane grin spread across my face again.

"Thank you, sir. Good trip?" Usains I and II disembarked me with the salutes of a couple of stewardesses at the end of a transatlantic flight.

"Yes, thank you. Dhanyabad."

"You trek now?"

"In the morning."

"EBC trek?"

"Yes. What about you, do you stay in Shivalaya now?"

"No. Eat dhal baat. Go back after."

"What? To Kathmandu?" I had a vision of an exhausted Usain toppling the Tata over the ledge at the pediment in a midnight accident. The loss of lives would be spoken of as a human tragedy in the Himalayan Times. The report moving on to cite this as another example of the government's incompetence in repairing the highway; the same report cut and pasted almost in its entirety when it appeared again the following week. The stoicism and dignity the Nepalis adopt towards this saddened me. It shouldn't just be karma to accept the number of lives lost on the highland highways. I was baffled that a simple government regulation to ban bus traffic after dark in certain areas, which would decrease the death toll markedly, hadn't been put in place.

"Jiri."

"Ah, okay, that makes sense. Dhanyabad again. Drive safe."

"Goodbye, sir."

Ahead, the gravelly high street of Shivalaya descended forgivingly to an unseen but audibly rushing river. The 'one horse dorp' uttered by Sir John Mills in the film version of *The Thirty-nine Steps* came to mind. This notion dissolved into an image of Clint Eastwood's Man with No Name unhurriedly arriving at a dusty, one-street pueblo in *A Fistful of Dollars*. Subconsciously, I assumed my inner Clint and stirred my uncooperative lower half into movement, striding purposefully into the village. In *A Fistful*, this would be because the Man would be looking out for shooters, not because his butt cheeks were welded into his chaps and the muscles in his groin were struggling to rebound from 11 hours perched on his ride.

I stopped about 50 metres down with a decision to make. Shivalaya's main drag was a parade of meticulously painted lodges. My research indicated those by the river were a shade better but there didn't seem to be any distinction after the first couple at the bus stop, which admittedly did look more down-at-heel. My dilemma was should I follow the guidebook, provide my custom and help perpetuate the mix of guest house standards in the town? Should I be more adventurous and try elsewhere, spreading a little wealth?

Ovine-like, I followed the guidebook, wanting the soothing sound of flowing water as background music for my first night's sleep in the hills. I sauntered down to the bridge at the end of town. At the river, a guest house was competing with its immediate neighbour, the KalaPatthar Hotel and Restaurant, on the strength of their paint jobs. Both were pristine in whites, oranges and primary colours. I opted for the guest house because it was right on the riverbank and had a robust concrete patio protected by a wrought iron fence where I fancied taking late afternoon tea.

A lady was awaiting my arrival with a warm smile and palms steepled in a namaste of greeting. She was perhaps my age, her hair bound in a headscarf knotted tightly under her chin. She wore a padded blue jacket, an ankle-length skirt and flip-flops.

"Namaste. Do you have a room, please?" I greeted her. There was a faint trace of a nod, followed by a sweeping motion of her left hand welcoming me onto the patio. She was silent as she disappeared into the guest house. As she moved, I was only then able to tell that from the back of her bustle, waist up, she was stooped forward. A minute later, an arrestingly beautiful younger version of her mother emerged, the older lady in tow. She wore the same garb as her mum and stood erect, her stance yet unbroken by years of hard manual labour.

"Yes, we have a room."

"Can I have a look, please?"

"Yes, of course. This way." Her diction was perfect. I followed her up the exterior staircase towards the rooms. At the top, my young hostess paused.

"The toilets are over there. The 'Western style' is on the left, the 'Nepali style' is on the right. The shower room and sink next door. I'm sorry, there is no hot water today, so we can only offer a cold shower. Please take a look."

I was unsurprised the facilities failed to meet the same exacting standards displayed at the public WC in Jiri. The three stalls were typical of what I'd encountered on my previous trek in Nepal and so decided everything was good on first inspection. We moved towards room number one where a hefty, unlocked padlock hooked over a sturdy bolt was removed.

"Here is the room."

The room was a whitewashed wooden box containing two cots, its linoleum floor patterned in a 1970s motif. There was a window with a set of functioning curtains and the bonus of what could serve as an indoor washing line. It was better than expected.

"This is great, I'll take it, please."

"Very well. Would you like my father to bring up your bag?"

"No, no. I can manage, thank you very much." I wasn't going to ask her dad, who in my mind was a feeble, stooped old man, to struggle to lump my rucksack up a flight of stairs. But this was as unimaginative as it was ungenerous. No doubt her dad could port me and my bag up the stairwell in one trip.

"Would it be possible to have some tea, please?"

"Yes, of course. Would you like a cup, a small pot or large pot?" I'd had a long trip, so opted for the small pot.

"I'll drop my bag and be right down. Could I take my tea outside?"

"Certainly, you may. Would you like something to eat with your tea? We have very nice home-made cakes."

"No, thank you. Just the tea, please. A menu for dinner would be great, though."

"Certainly. Could I ask that you order when taking your tea, please? It is getting late and we'd like to close the kitchen before it gets dark. I will bring you the menu. Also, if you'd like the internet, I'll bring you the code."

I nodded and was down at the patio five minutes after stashing my bag. I was stretching the numbness out of my back and legs in a form of yet-to-be discovered Pilates when my tea arrived.

The sophisticated demeanour of my host and her perfect English had lulled me into expecting the service was going to be of the silver kind afforded to a brigade of blue-rinsed *grandes dames* in an olde worlde tearoom in Harrogate. The small pot to be of the best Wedgewood. This would be presented along with floral, delicate-handled china cups and saucers. The GiantThermoCool brand thermos and built-to-last glass cup brought me back to reality. I'd estimated I'd asked for a couple of cups of tea at most; the reality was I'd ordered a full litre. I laughed inwardly at my cultural *faux pas*, thinking no harm done. The full litre wouldn't go to waste – I *am* British, after all.

My hostess brought me the menu. It was an A4 laminate, double printed with a wide selection of options and after a respectful wait, she inquired.

"What may I get you, please?"

I chose the Chinese noodles.

"Would you like more tea to go with that?"

"No thanks, I think I have plenty. Where did you learn your English, it is excellent?"

"No, no, no it's not. My English is very poor."

"No, really, it's faultless. Where did you learn it?"

"I spent two years at university in Canada. Toronto."

"That must have been different?" She ignored my inanity.

"Yes, it was. Canada is different to Nepal ... *we* don't have Mounties."

"Ha-ha. What did you study?"

"I studied business management. If you will excuse me, please, I'll go to help my mother with your order."

"Of course." I wondered for a moment at how a business management graduate from a Canadian university was in Shivalaya having to suffer my fatuous small talk. But it was a foolish question. Shivalaya may have been restricted to one street but it was in a heavenly spot. Wanting to take in more of the place, I took my tea a few steps to inspect the view from the suspension bridge.

From the span's centre, the view upstream was idyllic. The last of the evening sun dappled the pine trees covering both banks before bowing down to kiss the water cascading through a shallow gorge. A fisherman had balanced himself on a mid-stream boulder and was casting his rod, hopeful of a catch before it was too late to serve for dinner. Back through the village, the rice terraces arranged in circles above were seeing the last of the light and silhouettes of workers could be seen making their way back home. There was the odd cymbal crash now and again of something metal being dropped in a lodge but, overall, the river's soothing rush dominated.

Arcadian as it was, I could see it was a hard life there. I knew I'd the luxury of deeming Shivalaya a rural idyll because I was only passing through. I guessed it wouldn't seem that way to the residents wanting a better standard of living, healthcare and improved literacy. It seemed to me the young lady had brought her experience back from Canada to help realise all that. The sacrifices her parents must have made to send their daughter to North America to achieve her business degree would hopefully be repaid many-fold in her home village.

I returned to my spot on the patio and refilled my teacup as the proprietor returned bearing a plate mounded with steaming noodles. I spotted the Usains coming out of a restaurant at the edge of town, pleased to see, by the look of contentment on his face, Usain II had completed the advanced dhal baat speed-eating module of his driver training course. They skipped to the bus, fired it up, one-eightied and sped off in a cloud of biscuit-coloured dust. I was sad to see them go, somehow feeling abandoned.

"Thank you very much. Looks delicious." And it was. The noodles were complemented by egg and vegetables in a sticky black sauce. I wolfed it down and was supping another cup of tea when the young lady returned.

"How long have you been back from Canada?"

"I returned after the earthquake in 2015."

"I saw the pictures of that at the time. It looked awful. Was Shivalaya affected?"

"Yes. Shivalaya was damaged very badly. We were near the earthquake's epicentre. All the lodges on that side of the street collapsed. Some Shivalaya people died."

"Oh. I'm sorry." I didn't want to press further on the tragedy and thought I'd try to say something positive.

"You could never tell from how the village looks there was an earthquake – everything looks brand new now."

"Nepali people are very resilient. Shivalaya people are very resourceful. We had no choice but to rebuild our homes and businesses." Her mood had darkened, the conversation had hit a nerve. The young lady was humouring me only from the politeness offered a guest. I changed tack.

"Has business recovered?"

"No, business is very bad for the Shivalaya area now, but the earthquake was only one reason for that. The main problem now is that all trekkers fly to Lukla and start their treks there, not in Jiri anymore. The guidebooks say the trek from Jiri to Lukla is very hard, so people don't want to come this way. Now, we have only five or 10 per cent of the trekkers from before the guidebooks said that."

"Oh ... that's not so good. That's a shame."

"May I take your plate, please?"

"Sorry, yes, of course." With that, my plate disappeared along with the young lady into the lodge, leaving me alone, uncomfortable I'd inadvertently upset her. The best I could come up with was 'that's a shame' when her village had been destroyed, people's lives had been lost and local business hadn't been able to recover because of a few lines in a guidebook. What an idiot.

As I was trying to think of something to say to recover in the eyes of my host, one of Spandex Beret, who'd made the KalaPatthar their choice of lodging, headed over in my direction.

"Bonsoir, monsieur, do you know where I make ze permeet?"

"I guess you have your TIMS for the Everest region. Do you mean the permit for the national park?"

"What is TIMS?"

"TIMS is the Trekkers Information Management System. You need it to trek in Nepal. You got that in Kathmandu, right?"

"No. I don't know I 'ave to make permeet in Kathmandu."

"Oh, in theory then, you shouldn't be trekking. You might be able to get one here in Shivalaya, but I don't know. It needs two passport-sized photos. Do you have two?"

"No, I 'ave no photo. 'E is possible, no, to make photo 'ere?" I thought his chances of finding a passport-sized photo booth in town weren't too high.

"Maybe you could take one with your camera and ask for a local to print it out if they have a printer. Or ask a local to take and print it for you."

"D'accord. Ze ozher permeet need photo also? Maybe I can make in ze office. 'E is where?"

"I'm not sure, but I'd get a couple of extra pictures if you can, just in case. The trek starts at the other end of town. So I guess there'll be an office up there somewhere. I haven't checked, to be honest."

"Do you know how much monae is for zeeze permeets?"

"I think it is Rs.3,000 for the entry to Gaurishankar conservation area project. The TIMS is about Rs.2,000," I replied as I broke the halfway mark on my thermos.

"I must pay Rs.5,000? Zat is a lot of monae, no? Do you know where ze bank is? I need to make change." No butter, no permit, no photos, no money; I wondered what could be next.

"Do you 'ave ze card?"

"You mean the permit?"

"No, ze card for game?"

"Oh, playing cards. Yes, give me a moment, I'll get them for you."

"Merci. I look if I buy some in ze village and if not possible, I come back." He spun on his heels and headed off. Shadows had now immersed the valley in twilight and the evening now merited taking some more tea to warm up.

"Too cold, cold. Go inside." A man leading a solitary mule with dual conical wicker panniers offered me some local advice before sedately strolling up the main street, tying the donkey to a railing and entering an uptown lodge. I half-followed his advice and took the thermos up to the balcony. As the last of the light collapsed into night, I started on the last third of my tea. With the unclouded night I became fascinated by the different perspective on the stars. They seemed more lucid in the clarity of the mountain air and I wondered why the Big Dipper wasn't where it usually was, was it?

As I finished the last of the tea half an hour later, I could see the profiles of Spandex through the KalaPatthar's upstairs window. They'd found some cards and they were engaged in a game, one of the advantages of group travel, I supposed. It had been an early start, so I decided to turn in. I unpacked my bag, made a washing line in the corner and aired my soiled clothes. I completed my toilet, relaxed into my sleeping bag and powered up the Nano for some music before bedtime. *Come Find Yourself* by Fun Lovin' Criminals, starting at track five seemed apt given the days to come. An hour later, I was relaxed enough for bed; it was 8.45pm.

At 9pm, the first of the excess tea needed removing from my system. A dam had been burst and it was only by 11.30 the reservoir had been emptied. It was a few hours before the call of the middle-aged prostate made itself heard. At 5am, a disagreement with the pre-war tin of tuna from lunch surfaced and again at seven. It left me thinking I'd have been better off asking the rate for spending the night in the Western Style lavatory.

I left the loo to start the day. No warmth had yet spread through the valley, so I chose to take my breakfast inside. The dining area was made of the same whitewashed planks as my room and a photograph of the young lady with her parents in traditional dress decorated one of the walls, surrounded by framed certificates of proficiency in hotel management and hospitality.

Visible through a door at the end of the room was the old lady's back as she stirred something while humming a pleasant tune. I sat and waited to the end of her symphony's third movement. The lady had given no indication she'd noticed me and I wrestled with what was the best way to deal with this situation. Was it rude to waltz into the kitchen and ask for a menu, or was that the expected behaviour? Would my hosts be offended if I sat there silently and waited to be served, or should I shout up? Was the former showing respect for their establishment or a lack of appreciation by being unfriendly and vice versa? Not knowing the local custom, I dithered, doing nothing apart from fretting.

"Why are you waiting, sir?" The young hostess had entered from the outside to resolve my etiquette dilemma. Looking across to the KalaPatthar, I suspected the members of Spandex hadn't neurotically navel-gazed in the same way and were by now midway through the hot buttered croissants they'd insisted were made to order.

"You would like breakfast." It was a gentle nudge of a command rather than a question. I nodded in response.

"I will get you a menu."

I ordered scrambled eggs to calm my stomach, Tibetan bread and a cup of tea; a small pot would've meant delaying the trek's start until around lunchtime. My food was served in a fine china bowl portraying painted roses; this was placed on a Delft blue plate atop a place mat depicting a cornucopia of fruit in a fuzzy green. The rich yellowness of the eggs completed the colour-scape. They were full flavoured, and their excellence brought home to me the blandness of the mass-produced food we eat in the West. These were real eggs laid by the real chickens scratching around at the village edge. The Tibetan bread was too sweet for my taste, more of a sugary cross between a chapati and a pancake, but even so, happily replete, I asked for my bill to be totted up.

"Five hundred rupees for the room ..." The young lady smiled as she read out my bill. The room rate came as a shock and there was a separate charge for the internet code but at least the food and tea were as priced on the menu. I realised that I had mistakenly anticipated my look of seasoned trekker would mean all parties would settle at the price point for the room quoted in the guide. That was Rs.300 lower.

I debated whether I should accept the rip-off as a learning lesson, or argue the point. Rs.300 was £2, or half a pint of beer in real money, so I opted to accept the sharp business practice; it was nothing and they needed the money more than me. But I couldn't help feeling that slight twinge of resentment at being the dupe. Unlike my comments about the earthquake, that was a shame. It had sullied a fine night's stay and marvellous start to my time in the hills.

So, I paid my dues and gathered my freshly aired gear. After paying one more visit to the Western Style I was on my way with a dhanyabad and a goodbye. Spandex emerged from their accommodation as I was tightening my straps at a wooden board-cum-map of the Numbur Chuli cheese circuit. They'd broken out their trekking poles and, with a wave, they rapidly disappeared up the gradient, the eight low-slung bowling balls of their buttocks reciprocally rotating left and right.

What they lacked in preparation and organisation, it looked like they'd make up for with trekking prowess. As they motored up the high street, the tortoise and the hare came to mind. They may be faster, but I'd overtake them again at the conservation area checkpoint as they tried to barter four photos in exchange for all their residual Roquefort. I didn't rate their chances, given we were in cheese country. I sucked in my stomach and clasped my waist strap, determined to catch them up. This was it, the start of the trek.

I wondered what this spot must have been like when the 1953 expedition passed through. I'd read the forward party consisted of 150 porters, the latter 200 and they carried with them 50 tonnes of equipment. Like Ratna but with less smoking, I thought, the expedition rationed to a mere 15,000 cigarettes.

My start suffered from legs still leaden from the bus trip. Lack of sleep and repeated visits to the Western Style had also taken their toll. By the time I reached the conservation area checkpoint, I was already ready for a rest, thinking it was going to be a *very* long trip to Base Camp if I needed to stop every 100 metres or so.

The checkpoint sat at the top of a set of concrete steps, an open shop-front wallpapered by dog-eared maps. Two gentlemen were sitting beyond a stout desk, the morning sun reflecting back off its veneer. The older man wore a long shirt over trousers and sported a gaberdine topi; the younger a hand-me-down overcoat and jeans. The younger roused himself to accost me in the street. With the sun blinding me, it felt as if an interrogation was about to commence.

"Gaurishankar conservation area project permit."

I don't know why I was disappointed not to be met by an armed guard in army fatigues and an officious-looking bureaucrat in a brass-buttoned tunic at the checkpoint, but the sight of two nondescript geezers unnerved me. I was anxious about being fleeced again after my experience at the guest house but knew there was a permit to be bought, so reasoned it better to show I knew what I was about. I went with what the guidebook had stated was the fee.

"The permit is Rs.2,000," I stated with a questioning nod.

"Cost is Rs.3,000." The guidebook was four years old, so the price may have gone up, I thought, but I doubted the Shivalayan economy had been ravaged in the interim by such Weimar Republic levels of hyperinflation. After all, my room at the guest house hadn't been wallpapered with Rs.50 notes. Rs.3,000 seemed steep, especially since the EBC trail only passed through the conservation area for a few hours.

"Are you sure? The guidebook says it is 2,000."

"Guidebook is old price. Price change in 2018. See." The elder beckoned me over to an encyclopaedia-sized ledger to examine the evidence supporting his case. Lines of neatly inked payments next to names and passport numbers ran down half the page. The fee marked Rs.3,000 in each case. Whether this was an elaborate ruse forged for my benefit, every other trekker had been hoodwinked into paying Rs.1,000 over the odds, or the price had gone up, remained to be seen. The evidence wasn't conclusive, but the two gentlemen at the checkpoint were judge, jury and executioner.

Perhaps I was being cynical, but I'd have been more trusting if the officials had been attired as per my expectations. I knew this made no sense, as corruption knows no uniform, but the fact the men looked like chancers only served to fuel my suspicions. I handed over the cash anyway, thinking Rs.1,000 was the price of a couple of pints, but that wasn't the point.

The payment broke the tension in the air, the younger officer breaking into a beaming rictus of broken pegs; I could tell his ill-gotten gains weren't being blown on dentist bills but was unsure whether or not to be pleased about that. The ledger was spun around, and I was asked to make my own entry as the older, also oral-hygienically challenged, grinning man examined my passport. I wondered whether he was happy to have made some extra money that day, or was my passport photo really *that* hilarious?

"Mr Lee?"

"Yes."

"UK?"

"Yes."

"EBC trek?"

"Yes." I was in no mood to expand the small talk with my potential cheats and wanted to be on my way. He returned my passport as I finished the ledger entry, noticing there were no French-looking names immediately above mine. Spandex must've detoured around the checkpoint. Either that, or the two gentlemen before me were ardent disciples of Shivalaya's New Romantic movement.

I re-donned my pack and plodded up to where the trek proper started. There was no announcement to the trailhead which lay beyond a concrete apron surrounding a house at the village edge. The sit-down at the checkpoint revived me and, combined with the excitement of starting my first climb, meant I was undaunted by the vertical staircase ahead.

Ten minutes later I was bent over sucking in air with the enthusiasm of Lance grabbing his first smoke at Charikot. The staircase was just that – a melee of broken slabs of rock forming the up-steps, with clawing mud in between. The stairs jumbled up the crag-side in a series of tight hairpins. It was a brutal start to the day, but it had done a sterling job of banishing the numbness in my legs and lower back. From my first vantage point, I looked down on Shivalaya. The village looked higgledy-piggledy from above, but this didn't despoil its setting. The half of the village nearest the trail was still shadowed, while the river side basked in the light of day. On the Khimti Khola's far bank, stands of pine relaxed in the warming sun.

I climbed to reach a dirt road. In the absence of signage, logic dictated that I followed it upwards. I was rewarded by shouts of encouragement from a young man at a blue house clutching the roadside.

"Up. Up. Deurali. Up," he implored. There was nowhere to go up directly and so I let my confusion sit, plodding around a corner to where his instructions became clear. There was a muddy gully cut in the road's uphill side which was freshly made trail. It broke out onto the road again and I followed the same pattern. This time my navigational aid came from above, an old lady crowing at me from atop the steep cliff the road had cut into the hill.

"Up. Up. Chai." She paralleled my steps while pointing down to where the entrance to another gully had been cut into the cliff, in the opposite direction to the road. I'd have missed it unaided.

The gully broke out onto a tiny lodge which greeted me behind the old lady's sympathetic smile, and I could see what the lodge lacked in size, it made up for in design. I sat at the single table in the midst of a sunken patio, its flooring a crazy paving of the same angular slabs of rock I'd clambered up. The downhill-side patio wall was planted with mature marigold bushes that merged imperceptibly into the field beyond the patio's boundary. The plants in a glory of maximal bloom.

"Here is Sagbanda?" I asked. The lady nodded and launched into her sales pitch.

"You wan' chai? I have best Nepali tea, is Ilam tea. Drink delicious after trek. Nepali Ilam tea better than India Darjeeling tea. I bring you tea." Instantly, I imagined I may have met the lady's cousin at Ratna and so nodded tiredly my agreement.

The lady's grandchildren slipped through the door as she made her way inside with my order. The oldest must have been around six, the youngest two or three. As they spun into the patio, their energy gave away they were going to be the most engaging of tearaway urchins. They made straight for my backpack lying inclined against the patio wall. The soft toy tied to its back was the obvious source of their fascination and desire.

It held a special place in my heart. The Raving Rabbid had been my company on the Annapurna Circuit trek 10 years earlier. My then nursery-age daughter had insisted I take it with me and, ever since, it had become the family's official trekking mascot. This time, the Rabbid was coming to EBC, with the aim that we'd take a joint photo like the one we had from the pass at Thorung La. So, I was loath to lose him — but if I hadn't fastened him securely, I'm sure he'd have been raving for evermore in the Ramechhap region.

"Can I have this, sir?" The older child piped up.

"Sorry, I can't give it to you. I'm carrying him for my daughter. She gave him to me." Undeterred by my explanation, she gave me her cutest tearful kitten eyes and begged me again.

"Please sir, give to me."

Her smiling granny reappeared with a tray of tea to break the girl's bewitchment before the spell had done its work and I'd handed her the Rabbid. I hadn't specified how much tea I wanted so was relieved to see that small pot wasn't taken as the *de facto* order. I was presented with a single glass, silver sugar bowl and spoon.

As she lowered the tray, the granny's initial amusement at the children's pawing of the Rabbid turned to a frown. She became impatient as they continued to implore her, grasping and pointing at the toy. A threshold was breached, and a reprimand was given. It did the trick as the youngsters gave up and returned to the table where the eldest took the opportunity to practise her English lessons.

"How old are you, sir?"

"Have a guess."

Her furrowed brow revealed this was an answer not yet covered in class. As she looked lost, I took the initiative.

"How old are you?"

"I am six years old."

"Very good. How old am I?" I pointed towards myself and she nodded her understanding.

"You have ..." She grabbed her hair and signalled my colouring was the same as her grandmother's.

" ... and you have ..." She pointed towards my stubbly chin.

"A beard."

"Sir, you are 80 years old," she announced with the certainty only a six-year-old can muster.

"Thank you very much." I laughed, thinking the morning's walk must have taken more out of me than I'd gauged.

"I am not yet 80 years old," I continued. She managed to nod sagely and grin simultaneously.

"What is your name?"

"My name is Jenny."

"Nice to meet you, Jenny. What is your brother's name?"

"My brother's name is Rock and Roll."

"That's a nice name." I knew an enquiry how Rock had come by such an unusual name was going to be fruitless.

"What is your name?"

"Lee."

"Nice to meet you, Lee." This concluded the lesson; Jenny whirled around, grabbed her brother under her arm and they made off laughing.

I drank the tea, which lived up to the first part of its marketing. Beyond the patio marigolds, the terraces were laid out like a giant's equivalent of my path of labours that morning. Amongst the verdure, isolated farmhouses blew wisps of blue smoke into the air and, below, I could see the Khimti Khola speeding through the valley. I'd hoped to catch one last view of Shivalaya but all I could see was the river on which it nestled. I sat listening to the birdsong, my legs becoming dangerously relaxed. The tea had been so refreshing and I was so contented, I was at risk of becoming the latest Sagbanda lotus-eater. Drowsily, I roused myself from my repose by asking for the bill.

"Rs.100." The old lady's grin betrayed nothing of her daylight robbery. The going rate was 20 and I realised I'd done it again and not agreed a fixed price where it wasn't written down. But I didn't blame her for wanting to make a killing; I was most likely going to be her only and without doubt her last customer today. I paid up and left, disappointed with myself, and resolved to learn my lesson and make sure I wasn't a sucker at the next stop. This was a necessity; if I didn't mend my ways, with all the sharks in the hills, I calculated I'd be washing dishes in exchange for board and lodging by day five.

I checked the Rabbid hadn't met with an unfortunate unattachment incident and said my goodbyes. Fast-Buck Granny, Jenny from the marigold block and Rock and Roll were soon left behind and the pathway passed through another gully, this one between rich forest. The floor was a semi-scree of ruler-length jagged rocks. It wasn't a pavement yet but was being trodden down to form one. The area had suffered from storm damage and I found myself clambering over a primary forest's fallen boles and branches.

The gully emerged into a welcome view of much flatter going, a beaten earth trail passing through terraced farmland. I was ascending the valley of the Chaja Khola, a tributary of the Khimti Khola. The waterway itself couldn't be seen; instead, newly tilled fields comprising of terraces two or three metres wide and one metre deep dominated. I couldn't tell whether harvesting was complete, and they awaited a new crop for planting, or these terraces were freshly hewn from the hill.

The gradient continued to be kind and I found a rhythm. The path broke into a loose gravel through young stands of bamboo. I could have been taking a Sunday afternoon stroll through Kew gardens.

The relative ease of this section allowed me to take in the farmhouse design. A jumble of outbuildings and outhouses would be scattered within a 20-metre radius of the main structure, typically two-storey and brick-made. Its favoured finish was whitewash, although on some houses a stucco of whites and pinks was preferred. Blue or black painted solid wooden doors centred on the ground floor, usually ajar with a mandala patterned curtain keeping draughts at bay. A quartet of windows in the same blue and black lit the upper storey under the vaulted roof's exposed eaves. A stone slab patio, low-slung wall and simple wooden bench catered for resting outside in the sun. Some of these courtyards were abutted by stone water fountains, inscribed with Sanskrit and the footway often merged. I ambled by nosing into empty living-rooms-cum kitchens.

I came upon a farmhouse which, at first sight, looked like it benefited from all mod cons. Equilaterally spaced rectangular boxes of white extruded from a pink stucco on the upper level. My immediate thought was that it was an impressive feat of porterage to haul a couple of ugly, US-style air-conditioning units up that punishing staircase from Shivalaya as the units gave off a low hum. I was surprised to discover the buzzing's source wasn't electrical, but from hundreds of drones flitting in and out of two hives cemented into the first floor.

I guessed having beehives as part of the furniture made maintenance and honey harvesting easier. I wondered if Hillary had been there to persuade the inhabitants the positives of at-hand bees for crop pollination outweighed the negatives of potential swarming. After all, he was an apiarist and climbing up to the honey wouldn't have seemed out of character. It was a brave harmonisation with nature but not something with which I could be comfortable, as verified by my reaction to the insects increasingly finding my ears of interest. It appeared I was on the main flightpath to the nectar below, so I stopped dawdling.

The bee-house marked the easy going's end and the earthen path ended abruptly at a fork. To the left was a stone staircase, to the right a more beaten path. A wasp-coloured sign seemed to grow out of a tree trunk. 'Way to Deurali' it pointed non-committedly. As upwards had served me thus far I reasoned I'd continue that way, the trail becoming progressively steeper and the forest more broken as I climbed. Each break in the woods disclosed more terraces and lonely farmhouses scattered on the hillside. It was strange the fields were devoid of labourers, no matter where I cast my eyes.

My view now took in two tributary valleys, while the trail had become exposed to a sun directly overhead. It had become a warm enough day for the few locals who I did pass to be out and about in single layers. I did my best to emulate them by stripping down to my T-shirt. As I unwrapped, I counted my blessings I hadn't caught up with Spandex, thinking that with their sartorial sensibilities, they'd have already been down to their Speedos.

Ascending slowly on the rocky way the acclivity started to take its toll. Every 100 metres, I found myself breathless and needing rest. The heat, coupled with my exertions, meant I also needed to cool down. The Nepalis had clearly contemplated that and, as I rounded another rock-stair hairpin, I came across a shelter that catered for sweaty, pink-faced trekkers. It was a well-cared for, open-sided shed, its blue tin roof providing much-needed shade. I plonked myself on the wooden bench furthest from the trail, my shoulders thanking me when I dropped my pack.

The shed was situated in a grand spot. As I was idly enjoying the vista and rehydrating, I was joined by a well-groomed gentleman in his 40s who was finding the going considerably easier than I was. He was wearing dark blue jeans, tasselled loafers and an Arsenal shirt adorned with the number nine. He carried a small black backpack, a computer case in one hand and a large plastic bag in the other.

"Hello, how are you, sir? It is a fine day."

"Yes, it's a beautiful day. It's a bit warm to be walking uphill, though." He laughed but not in an unkind way.

"I do not think it is fair to call this a hill, sir. Are you heading towards Namche? If that is your direction, there will be real hills to climb on the way there."

"Yes, I'm heading to Namche. I hope I'm still on the right trail?"

"Well, I can tell you, sir, that you have at least started from the right place. Where are you going today?"

"Today I hope to get to Bhandar."

"I myself am going to Chamur. It is beyond Bhandar so we will share the same path. May we walk together for a while?"

Truthfully, I wanted to rest longer, but it wasn't polite to refuse. We started back into the heat of the uphill ascent, my backpack seeming 50 per cent heavier

"Do you like the Arsenal?" I managed to get a question out between laboured breaths.

"Yes, I like Arsenal very much."

"What do you think of Lacazette?" This was met with a blank stare at the end of my new acquaintance's uphill stride. I tried again.

"What about Mesut Ozil? Do you think he deserves all the bad press?" Another vacant gaze ensued. Speculating I was barking up the wrong tree with my questioning I changed tack. Perhaps he was a fan of the halcyon days?

"What about Thierry Henry? He was some player?" Silence.

"That forward line with Dennis Bergkamp?" Again, he was Jeewan impassive. I was getting desperate to kick-start some dialogue.

"How about Arsene Wenger?" His face gave away no sense of recognition and so I was at a loss what to ask next.

"What *do* you like about the Arsenal, then?"

"The colour of the shirt."

I managed a gasping chuckle. Well, at least he wasn't going to be disappointed in that, unlike the rest of the Arsenal faithful were going to be with their season.

"Are you trekking the Shivalaya to Everest Base Camp route?"

"Yes."

"Alone?"

"Yes."

"Why, because you don't have any friends?" I gasp-chuckled again. My new friend had a wry sense of humour.

"That's right. Where's Chamur, where you're going?"

"It is about an hour and a half, maybe two hours further on from Bhandar."

"Why are you going there?"

"I am a teacher. I travel across the region to the schools to give special lessons. I have in my briefcase a computer. In my backpack I have audio-visual equipment to make a presentation and in this other bag I have all the things to join everything up."

That impressed me. He showed me the contents of his carrier, revealing a krait's nest of black cables and adaptors. We kept our pace, he sauntering casually while I traipsed breathlessly.

"What do you teach?"

"Well, sir. I am in demand! It depends on where I am asked to teach, but mostly I teach computing skills."

"Really? I work in computing. What do you teach the kids, sorry children?"

"I teach how to use the internet. How to make an email. Word and Excel. For older children we teach some programming."

It encouraged me, thinking that if the children in the villages were learning these skills on top of basic literacy, that could only be good for the region.

"All that with one laptop?"

"Yes."

"All by yourself?"

"Yes."

"Why, because you don't have any friends?"

As he chuckled, his casual, deceptive strolling belied a relentless pace I couldn't match.

"Sorry, but I need to take a rest. Catch my breath."

"Would you like me to stay with you ... to be your friend?" This he said with a twinkle in his eye. He made me want to chortle again but my chest was heaving.

"No. Thank you, it's very kind, but I wouldn't want to hold you up from your students."

"Are you sure, sir? You look not too well in the face, if I may say." I must have been lobster-coloured.

"Thank you for your offer, but I walk slowly and don't want to hold you up."

"In Nepal we have a saying, sir. It is to always walk slowly so you reach your destination safely. For short, we say 'slowly slowly'."

"Thank you, I heard that before on my last trip to Nepal."

"Very good, sir. Before I leave, may I ask your name, please?"

"It's Lee. And yours?"

"My name is Rajendra. Raj. I am very pleased to have met you, Lee. Please have a safe trek to Everest. Enjoy our beautiful country."

"Thank you."

"And remember ..."

"Yes?"

"Slow Lee, slow Lee."

Beaming and with a nod, he resumed his lolloping gait uphill. We'd stopped where the forest had closed in again against the sides of a ravine, so I was able to take some water and cool down in the shade.

I was wary of false summits but it was getting near midday so I figured even at my pensioner's pace, I should be nearing the top. The guidebook had said three to four hours from Shivalaya to Bhandar and I'd been going for practically four. Slogging my way upwards again I was a little disheartened when passed by a young boy and his grandmother carrying bundles of clothes. It didn't last long as my fears around false summits proved unfounded and, five minutes after my stop, the trail exited the forest onto a broad meadow. With advertising.

' *You are heartily welcome to us*
HIGHLAND SHERPA
Guest House and Restaurant
Earthquake Resistant Building'

I reflected on what my young host had told me the previous day about the earthquake and reacted to my queries about that time. It was saddening to think earthquake resistance was a differentiator to be used to attract potential customers.

I came to a circular mani forming Deurali's centre a minute later. The Highland Sherpa stood to my left where an elevated sun terrace topped white glazed brickwork. A 'No Parking' sign had been etched in blue on its wall. Blissfully, I realised I hadn't seen a vehicle all day and thought the owner must possess either visionary forward planning skills or was a real optimist. Lacking a road, I wondered whether the local town planning department contrived a future vision of the circular mani doubling up as the Ramechhap district's first roundabout.

The guest house itself was in a Tibetan style and decorated with fearsome dragons, presumably intended to enforce the no parking message. Park here and your virginal daughter may end up locked in a tower somewhere nearby for the next 30 years. Chalked on a blackboard were the day's specials of apple pie, cheese pie, organic potato chip (singular), organic juice and more. The owners had made it clear that if you wanted it, it could be rustled up as a special. I was, surprisingly, not hungry after the four-hour ascent so decided to try to make it to Bhandar for lunch.

I followed the guide's advice and avoided the mistake of not taking the steep stone steps out the hamlet's other end, thinking that if the stair depth was awkward at my height, it must be near impassable for the locals. At their end, there were two possible routes. EBC was indicated with another non-committal sign; it could've been pointing left, down a steep gully, or right, curving onto a flatter gradient. There was nothing for it but to wait and ask a passer-by the right way.

Five minutes later, what appeared to be an off-duty extra from a World War I film laboured up the defile on the left. His head was bandaged around his ears upwards, the wrapping leaving only a pineapple leaf of mousey hair to poke up from the trekker's crown. The bandage was soiled, and a red blotch stretched from his left eyebrow to his ear. His clothes looked equally grimy and wounded: his shorts were spotted with dried mud and ripped at the front. The extended walking poles he speared into the ground in front of him appeared the only undamaged part of his aspect.

"Namaste."

He greeted this with a nod.

"English?"

A head shake.

"Français?"

Same again.

"Español?"

And again.

"Nederlands?"

No change. I was almost out of options. I *was* out of options for any meaningful communication unless this smashed individual was as fluent as myself in advanced Nepali.

"Russkiy?"

"Da."

He offered nothing else. My Russian was limited to hello, no, red dog, red cat, bless you (post-sneeze), cheers, thank you, goodbye, beer, vodka and baby is crying. As our discourse had passed the hello stage, I surmised that, unless he'd been bitten in the head by a red dog, clawed by a red cat or fancied a line of Stoli shots at the Highland's bar, my phrases were going to be of limited use. I reverted to sign language and pointed down the ravine he'd emerged from.

"Bhandar?"

"Da," he confirmed.

"Spasibo."

"You velkom, Ingleesh. Dasvidaniya." He sounded more like a Bond villain now, rather than First World War movie extra, so I was down the ravine before he could decide he needed to do something with a laser to my unmentionables.

The path broke onto another dirt road, the last section steep and unstable. The construction blasted through the hillsides had obliterated the route of the traditional pedestrian-cum-donkey trail. But I could see the locals weren't to be denied their direct routes and a new walking trail was being cut along the fresh cliffs abutting the road.

Mini avalanches of grey rock paralleled my tentative descent. I could see a fall here would be directly onto the road – not likely fatal, but a serious injury would ensue. The new path highlighted the ineptness of my skills in the hills as compared to the Nepalis. I reached the road, glad to have made it, shaking not only from the exertion, whereas a post Deurali shopping trip Raj tootled down the same treacherously unstable, avalanche-initiating chute carrying both bags in one hand and scanning the horizon for a mobile phone signal.

"Slow Lee, slow Lee." He chuckled to himself as he disappeared with a thumbs-up down another fresh trough teased from the forest across the road. He was going to dine out on that one for a long time. I was grateful to him that he'd shown me the way; I'd have missed the unmarked hollow at the roadside that was its entry point.

The weather had turned, and lead-grey clouds had swept down from the ridge, the temperature becoming similar to that before daybreak in Shivalaya. As I redonned my fleece, I considered it a good warning about the changeability of the mountain weather. Dressing afforded me the luxury of taking in for the first time the scenery beyond the saddle at Deurali. The Likhu Khola's broad valley unfurled itself. Verdant hilltops merged into an enveloping mist in the distance and the outlines of whitewashed village buildings softened in the diminished light. The hills were clad in pine forest, chopped cleanly at the edge of pastures and arable land. I'd travelled 7,000 kilometres to get a view of Perthshire! It wasn't quite – the rolling hills thrust up at a grander scale than in Scotland – but under the gunmetal skies I fancied I could've been a 90-minute drive from home.

The new trail was the site of my first fall. The surface had seemed relatively solid compared to what I'd just traversed but something had given way underneath me and I was tipped backwards to a cushioned landing of sorts on the backpack, my feet splayed in front. My lower back cracked on a rock. Either my coccyx was broken again, or the tumble had pushed the pieces disassembled on the trip from Kathmandu back together. In the circumstances, and with the familiarity of the Scotland-like landscape, I reckoned my spill merited some proper Alban cursing in mitigation of the pain.

"Argh. Ya fookin' pure fanny ya!"

This was met with the disinterested continuation of the chirping birds in the forest. After the brief bludgeon of pain in my lower back had subsided, I cautiously got to my feet. It was an undignified rise as I levered myself up, using branches and rocks to steady myself. Physically, I'd suffered only minor damage, but the fall had dented my confidence. I deflected the blame on to my new boots, rather than my lack of aptitude. I was worried I'd selected the wrong type of sole for the conditions and, with much more challenging and dangerous terrain ahead of me, I was going to seriously hurt or kill myself. I took a few deep breaths and put the worry aside – it wasn't going to help.

The trough broke out into a zigzag that was better worn, and this section of the traditional path soon snaked out into pastures. I was well met by a few shaggy cows chewing the cud. They weren't too far away from being the Highland coos associated with home. The main difference the even longer horns sported by my incurious spectators.

The pasture gave way to terraces where the track became sodden and passed between low drystone walls defining hectare plots of grazing and crops. The lea had been harvested and three-metre-tall gatherings of drying grasses collected. The haystacks reminded me of Cousin Itt in the 60s version of *The Adams Family*, their shape a circumcised penis.

The trail dropped down through more terraces of haycocks and I entered a flatter area where I met two children playing on a Nepali swing. It was of a typical manufacture, made with four slender timber poles sunk into the ground at each corner. Each diagonally opposing and side pair of poles was tied off against each other and the side pairs secured to a cross beam. A rope loop dangled from the cross beam, where friction was prevented by thatches of lashed straw. To my mind, built to last.

The children giggled and pointed when they saw me. The one in motion decamped on the upswing and they ran over to take a closer look. The giggling and pointing continued as I walked by and I realised the Rabbid was the source of their fascination.

"Bhandar?" I asked and in response they pointed horizontally across a terrace before running back to their swing. It didn't look much of a trail, just a dried terrace of patchy grass, but I followed their advice. The track gave way to a muddy pony trail bordered by broad swards of four-metre-high bamboo. I passed a farmer yanking at an intransigent cow by a rope fastened to its nose ring, reckoning he looked too busy to be troubled with a request for directions.

Fatigued and hungry, I realised the decision not to take lunch at Deurali was another mistake I shouldn't repeat. I heaved myself up after a short break and continued, to be rewarded a few minutes later by my first sight, in the distance, of Bhandar's twin chortens. I was at once delighted and deflated to see my destination. Delighted, because

I had a fixed point for navigation purposes. Deflated, because it still seemed such a long way off.

I trudged on, my legs wobblier, stopping frequently on the side of drystone walls to recover some strength and to drink. My path meant the chortens didn't seem to grow any closer. I footslogged down alleys of stone parallel to the monastery before right-angling towards them, only to have to parallel again. My progress was as assured as one of those metal balls in a wooden maze puzzle where the player has to twist the frame so it finds the right route. I was beginning to feel despondent my slow-motion ricocheting was getting me nowhere when another farmer caught me up.

"Namaste. Bhandar. Bhandar. Come! Come!" he blared, and motioned me onwards with an irresistible overarm bowling action. I smiled wearily, got to my feet and followed, tracking his lower half, not paying attention to the surroundings, trying to keep up. I was in danger of falling so far behind he'd be lost out of sight when he jolted to a stop.

"Bhandar. Bhandar." He spread his arms downwards to splayed fingers, bowed and left me at the monastery entrance before I could thank him. The two chortens stood on a lower terrace beneath a red square temple. The gold of the chortens' Buddha eyes matched that of baying deer above the temple's portico. I was pleased to be there, but too tired to appreciate it. I told myself I'd return after finding a place to stay, getting something to eat and resting. There was no obvious indication there was a lodge nearby, so I took a few selfies in case accommodation was miles away and sombrely continued.

Another village spread out in the distance where I could see a couple of larger structures which looked like they could be lodges, so I headed in that direction. I tramped down a couple of terraces, guided by another low-slung wall, to find hidden from above, and nestled in a hollow, was an imposing-looking building in two shades of blue. Its signage declared it 'The Shobha Lodge and Restuarant [sic], Chyangma, Bhandar'. The guidebook had indicated Bhandar was a three to four-hour trek for day one. Six hours after leaving Shivalaya, I'd arrived.

Bhandar to Chhimbu

I found myself wearing that vacuous grin again. Resigned to accept another half an hour of tremulous trudging to the village below, coming upon the Shobha's stealthy positioning was a welcome surprise. I'd landed on a cricket-square sized flagstone courtyard, reminiscent of those cobbled spaces found in old English coaching houses. This formed both the approach to the lodge and a dry crossing to the barn, byre or stables adjacent. For such a large tea house, it was remarkably well hidden.

The lodge itself had the appearance of a two-stage assembly. The third on the left-hand side could originally have been a farmhouse, with the other, fatter two thirds added later as the lodge. The building's top half was clad in a navy-blue corrugated iron, which it shared with the roof. Its window spaces were painted in the same black and white I'd seen on the trail the day before. They contained a more intricate display of five or six smaller windows, backed with what appeared to be a set of low-rent French shutters. There were five doors from which to choose entry; I thought my best bet was to try the leftmost of the two open.

I called my greeting at the doorjamb and was met by a lady of about 30 with two children hiding behind her skirts. She returned my greeting with a beatific smile, nodded and waited. I was determined not to be hill-sharked yet again at this establishment so, despite my fatigue, attempted to fix a reasonable price.

"Do you have a room, please?"

"Yes."

"One hundred rupees?" My premeditated strategy would be to open negotiations with an offer of a price so risible it would show I knew how to play the game. But, by the proprietor's reaction, I could see I'd overdone it; her exalted smile was replaced by pursed lips and an over-excited metronome of finger wagging. She feinted to stomp off, posturing offence before halting to think better of it.

"No, no, no. Room more money." Game on, but how much should I proffer for the counter?

"Two hundred." Her expression returned to triptych-painted Catholic saint.

"Welcome." That was too easy, I thought, there must be a catch. I wasn't going to be finagled on the second part of the deal and end up sleeping in the byre, so determined to ensure the accommodations were up to snuff before sealing the deal.

"Please can I see the room?"

"Follow." She took me through the dining area to a wooden staircase at the back. Initially, the stairs were wide and ceiling high, but they narrowed into a svelte, pygmy-sized crawlspace that necessitated squeezing to reach the landing. This had clearly been designed with bargaining in mind. After agreeing a price, a negotiant was lulled into a trap: whatever the number settled on in relation to the room's condition, they weren't going to take the trouble to squash themselves through that space again after a long day's trekking.

Never having been described as a pygmy and with even fewer references to being called svelte, my progress was difficult. I forced myself up the stairs, my knee joints popping at every step. My pack caught on the handrail and as I tried to wiggle it free, I managed to smack my forehead on the joist. I emerged at the top stair and, a little dazed, was shown the room.

"Okay. This is fine." And it was, more than. My host, evidently impressed by my display of bargaining with veteran hill-shark finesse, had given me the best suite in the place. The Milne, with an upgrade to Winnie the Pooh-motif under-sheets thrown in for free. The lady having departed, I dropped my pack and took out my sleeping bag, looking forward to spending the night with Tigger.

As I removed my boots, tiredness got the better of me. Horizontal on the cot, I could do little more than stare at the ceiling imagining a squashed Eeyore giving my aching legs a run for their money in their grousing. An hour later, I was sufficiently recovered to exert myself to examine the room in more detail. It could have been a compressed version of the one in Shivalaya, the bedding the only real difference.

Four o'clock was approaching, time for afternoon tea. My legs had stiffened to the extent that I descended the stairs like the 80-year-old identified by Jenny. I took a better look at the dining area and a sense of something vaguely ecclesiastical came to mind. Polished dark wood tables pushed out from cushioned benches at the foot of the stairs and windows. I eased myself onto the nearest settle. Opposite sat a man of about 50 with five small mounds spread on the table in front of him.

"Namaste. Are you making chai?"

"Namaste, sir. Yes. I make black tea." I was gratefully spared the Ilam tea refrain.

"How do you make it?" He motioned me come and I limped over.

"This is leaf. Take other off." He took from the green pile and showed me how he removed the young leaves from the stems. He chucked the stem onto a second pile.

"Roll leaf." He took the leaves between his palms and did just that. The leaves darkened and the result went onto the third pile.

"Come." He swept the third pile into a tea towel and I hobbled behind him to a storage room where he dumped the rolled leaves onto a shelf.

"Three day. Wait. Then like this." He used the tea towel to carry a withered pile of leaves back to the table and added them to the fourth pile.

"Make small." He took a handful of the fourth pile and crumbled the leaves into smaller bits.

"That's something. I didn't realise it was such a lot of work to make a cuppa. Do you grow the tea yourself?"

"Yes. Outside." He pointed out the doorway.

"Can you show me?"

"Come." We crossed the courtyard to the side of the barn/byre/stables opposite.

"What's this?" I pointed to the building.

"For animal. Look."

He pointed over to some bushes. Confident my tour was over, he returned inside to continue his painstaking labours and I had a quick look at the bushes. With my authoritative knowledge of sub-Alpine zone horticulture, I could've been examining a gooseberry bush, for all I knew. They fronted onto a view I did know, however. The weather had closed in and a mist had cast a dark brooding over the valley and the hills beyond. All that was needed to complete the Caledonian ambience was the drone of bagpipes, an idea I thought would never spring forth into my mind.

There was a washing area piled with pewter plates at the byre side. A table battered from blue to its white undercoat stood to one side. As I crossed back to the main lodge, I noticed I'd missed an upturned circular tin bathtub atop a yellow tarpaulin lying on the ground, with maize kernels drying all around. I wondered how I'd also missed the absence of a 'No Parking' sign, thinking the owners were not planning for the new road to pass by, as at Deurali, or had already developed an avid dislike of parking attendants.

As I re-entered the lodge, I was enthusiastically met by an older lady. She was bundled in the conventional dress I was becoming used to seeing – flip-flops, bustled skirt, padded jacket and babushka headscarf. She was a heavier version of the lady with whom I'd haggled earlier, which led me to presume she was her mother.

"You like our tea?"

"Yes. It's fascinating to see it made."

"You like drink our tea?"

"Yes please." I'd almost forgotten that was why I'd come down in the first place.

"I make. Big pot?"

"No thanks. Just a small pot will do."

"I make big pot. I share with you." Her manner betrayed she wasn't going to take no for an answer, and I was glad I'd met her daughter, not her, in the price negotiations. She barked a command at the tea-sorting man who looked up with a slight grimace that said he knew better than to argue. He slouched into the kitchen.

"Where you from?"

"The UK."

"UK good people. Where in UK?"

"Glasgow, Scotland."

"Ahh. I have daughter in Scotland ... in London."

"Scotland isn't in London." Hoping to help, I mistakenly took the default approach to broaching this geographic technicality, but my advice fell on deaf ears.

"Yes, she live in very nice place. I visit. In Edinburgh, in London." I was unsure whether to press home my point and risk being considered rude, but also didn't want her to continue to think the whole of Scotland was in London. Unless she planned to stand as a Tory Member of Parliament for any of the home counties, that view wasn't going to serve her well.

"What time in London now?"

"It's what? About quarter to five here, so it's about 11.30 in the morning," I replied.

"We call daughter later. When work finish. She like I have Scotland man stay." I'd leave it to later, then, and let her daughter explain the geography. The tea came and we all shared a cup justifying the preceding effort in the subtlety of its taste. I complimented them on it and the man returned a satisfied nod.

"You welcome. I like you like *my* tea."

That was met with a rebuke and I wondered whether he'd made a mistake in using the singular possessive or had done it on purpose to get a reaction. Repentant or fulfilled, he decided he'd finished his work and left towards the byre.

"You have wife?"

"Yes." I'd decided from the outset I was going to reply yes to this at the start of a conversation. It wasn't going to be worth the effort and potential confusion to try to explain to the Nepali folks the cultural differences in marriage values. At least at first, anyway – if the conversation subsequently went the way of how families are made up in Europe, I'd broach it then.

"You have children?"

"Yes. Two. A girl and a boy."

"You show me picture now!" The lady had a way of making a friendly request sound like she'd taken elocution lessons from Frau Farbissina. I scrambled for my phone and pulled up a couple of pictures.

"Beautiful. Beautiful nice children. Now show wife picture." I swiped to a picture of myself and my partner.

"Too young! TOO YOUNG!!" she cried.

My partner is biologically nine years younger than me and very much looks it, but I've never felt in our relative looks we resembled Michael Douglas and Catherine Zeta-Jones. From the matriarch's instinctive emotional reaction, she clearly did. I was beginning to come round to Jenny's 80-year-old assessment of my appearance when the matriarch snatched my phone and stomped off to the kitchen.

"WIFE *TOO YOUNG*! WIFE *TOO YOUNG*!!" she bellowed laughingly.

She returned a couple of minutes with her daughter and I was examined up and down. The younger lady agreed with the assessment in a much more subdued voice. The matriarch returned my phone with a wry smile that appeared sympathetic.

"You too old. You should be marry to lady like me." I wasn't sure whether this was a proposal and became worried I'd stumbled into one of those Nepali districts where the women can take four husbands. She'd struck me as a lady who wouldn't be denied something once she had set her mind on it, so I said nothing lest I found myself being measured for a morning suit. She seemed disappointed I hadn't responded.

"What you want to eat?" This was perhaps another ruse to convince me of the marriage proposal's attractiveness. The saying 'The way to a man's heart is through his stomach' must be the same in Nepali, I thought.

"I make Sherpa stew. It take two hours to make Sherpa stew. I eating it so you eating it. We share!" Once again, this wasn't a suggestion and I dutifully nodded my acquiescence. Besides, Sherpa stew was going to be a new experience for me, so I was pleased she'd made the selection. She returned to the kitchen, leaving me alone to enjoy another cup from the big pot. The silence was a cue for the two youngsters I'd seen on my arrival to reappear from a hidden recess.

The cabinet at the entry end of the dining room supported a 30-inch flat screen TV. The older child grabbed two remote controls from a shelf and push-buttoned the television into life. She'd selected a Bollywood dance show that was a multitude of colours spinning at full tilt. Couples performed routines redolent of the Golden Age of Hollywood musicals. They were backed by massed ranks of dancing girls in saris performing synchronised Kathaks at double speed to a subcontinental twist on contemporary disco. It would've got my toes tapping if I could have moved them. I made do with a nodding of the head instead.

The booming beat coming from the TV was the prompt for an excited step-for-step imitation of each dance by the older girl for the next 30 minutes. To my untrained eye, the exactness of her moves to the on-screen choreography was staggering. She ended her show with a curtsy.

"Whoooo, that was great." I cheered in my best Anton du Beke. She twirled around into a head-level crouch across my table, one hand clutching a remote and on the other, her fingers thrust in a Churchillian victory sign.

She was around reading age, dressed in black with a red pashmina beanie. She danced in flip-flops. The toddler was in a pink dotted onesie, green Thomas the Tank Engine wellies and a multicoloured knitted bonnet.

"Do you speak English?" I asked, pausing for effect between the words.

"Yes. I learn English at school." The fluency of her reply put my condescension to shame.

"What's your name?"

"Sondiya."

"Nice to meet you, Sondiya. How old are you?"

"I am six years old."

"Is that your sister?" I pointed to the other girl, whose nose was attempting to break Jeewan's district record for an hour's worth of mucus production.

"Yes. It is my sister."

"What's your sister's name?"

"I no tell you."

"Ah, is it a secret?" This was met with folded arms and a petulant teenager's frown which I guessed said, 'We haven't done that lesson yet, stupid old man'. Being used to dealing with that sort of approach, I tried a different tack.

"How old is your sister?"

"My sister is two years old."

"Excellent! What's your sister's name?" But she was finished with the conversation. The remote was re-pointed at the TV and she flipped through 100 channels of satellite dross before settling on a dance show that was a facsimile of the first. Sondiya twirled into action again, her replication of the moves uncanny. Her sister had plucked up the courage to join in from a distance and was spinning and falling at the back of the dining area. I drank my tea and enjoyed the spectacle, and the show ended half an hour later. In one movement, Sondiya completed a whirl, grabbed the remote and flipped through the channels to Indian MTV.

The next 30 minutes were choreographed to Bengali garage house. I hadn't been exposed before to the Indian take on rap. The music had a great beat and the lyrics sung interspersed with English phrases made me wonder what the songs could be about. Mostly pomaded bad boy meets sweetheart across a Montague and Capulet divide, it seemed from the videos. And lots of motorcycles roaring away into the night. I found these unintentionally funny, the take on the gang culture of Chiraq or South-Central Los Angeles not convincing at all. Muscled Bollywood heartthrobs and beautiful Indian ladies posing moodily in leather jackets and boob-tubes didn't convince me they'd lived on a diet of MacDonald's and crack cocaine – more like straight out of Kolkata than Compton.

I'd been taking for granted the surfeit of dance and music shows across hundreds of satellite channels before it struck me how incredible it was to be viewing them here at all. But to my mind, the glossy dance shows and other offerings on the high-definition channels through which Sondiya flicked seemed incongruous with the surroundings of the dining room. The room was more than comfortable but incomparable to the images of luxurious villas with swimming pools being beamed into it. I wondered what the local folks made of all that. Did they think the images of suburbia portrayed in the US shows were something to aspire to, irrelevant or something else?

Sondiya evidently took the sensory bombardment in her stride and I could see the lure of junk food being pitched between shows hadn't yet fully taken hold. From the energy she was able to expend on her dancing, it was clear she hadn't succumbed to the couch-potato lifestyle of so many Western kids. Her enjoyment of what was on offer was evocative of my own experience of TV at that age. It was an exciting enhancement to life enjoyed after spending all day outside on my bike or playing games with the other kids in the street.

Her choice of content was selective: only music to which she could dance. I imagined she got as much pleasure from the traditional swing I'd passed earlier as from her time in front of the TV. I guessed the post-school day would be filled with chores around the farm and in scrubbing pots and pans for the lodge at the concrete sink outside. That seemed a healthy balance to me.

The young lady returned, and the children were ushered towards the kitchen. Sondiya's allocation of TV time had come to an end. She blanked the TV with the remote, and so had mine. Anticipating two hours until Sherpa stew, I figured a wash before dinner would be a good idea.

"Do you have a shower, please?" I enquired.

"Cold s'ower? Hot s'ower?" Stupidly, I hadn't considered to qualify my request.

"Hot shower, please."

"Yes. I show you hot s'ower." I'd seen many place names with double h's on the map of Nepal; was it because the first one is silent?

She led me via the corridor from the dining room to a rotted wooden door. It was squashed into a space two thirds average human height by a large concrete step and a nose-level lintel. She pushed the door open and we crossed the step-over into a cold, concrete wet-room. In the nearest corner sat a red propane cylinder. Curiously, it wasn't linked to the power-shower unit affixed to the wall opposite. The tubes running from its top led somewhere else. The shower unit was linked by a rubber hose to a metal pipe on the wall, the flow of water from outside regulated by a pressure control valve appearing to have been recycled from a German U-boat. Another hose stretched from the unit to the shower head, which was strung from a hook in the ceiling by shoelaces. A thick, insulated cable ran taped to the first hose, broke out into a couple of smaller wires and terminated in the shower unit.

My host went over to the unit and fiddled with the controls with no discernible result before trying the submarine wheel. The shower head spurted out water in a thin, powerful stream which rapidly pooled on the floor. It was obvious the drain wasn't working properly but I was anxious to make the best of the flow, so I tested the water. I shook my head as it was freezing. The lady ran her hand through the jet and concurred. She went across to the propane cylinder and turned the gas on. I couldn't see how that was going to make any difference as it didn't seem linked to the shower, but who was I to argue?

My host went back to the shower unit and fiddled with the knobs again. I was beginning to think our chances of not being gassed, blown up, electrocuted or drowned before exposure set in were negligible when I heard the unmistakable sound of a pilot light igniting. There must have been a gas pipe linking the shower to the cylinder through the wall.

She smiled and tried the stream again, but it was still cold. She tutted and twisted and turned the dials on the unit in all manner of combinations and we waited a while in silence, helplessly willing the stream to warm. The chamber whispered if I were a proper man, I'd whip out an adjustable spanner and have it all working in a jiffy, not stand there shivering like a Christmas tourist admiring the Mannequin Pis. She ran her hand through the jet again and her face lit up.

"Hot s'ower. You s'ower now. Water cold soon." But I'd foolishly not prepared for the welcome invitation. I knew she was thinking it would be a quick dash upstairs to fetch my travel towel and clean undies, but the reality of my seized legs meant I was going to return at the pace of an also-ran in a Zimmer-frame race. The number of complex combinations of dial rotations, buttons pushes and wheel half-turns the lady had mastered to get that warm flow was a feat akin to the completion of a moon landing. How could I ask her to wait for five minutes and start again? I had to break it to her gently and apologise profusely, which was the cue to adopt my hapless English fop routine once again.

"Dhanyabad. Sorry, sorry, I'm terribly sorry, but I need to get my towel." I pointed upstairs towards my room. 'She looked daggers' didn't describe her expression. It was more like, 'She looked khukuris'.

"I really am most awfully sorry," I apologised, thinking I could detect a trace of a plummy Notting Hill accent in my voice.

"Really, I *do* apologise. I'll be back as soon as I can." She already had the water off. Ten minutes later, I returned clutching my towel, a fresh pair of underpants and a clean T-shirt. She'd been practising on the advanced gas-cooled reactor while I'd been away and, with one turn of a dial, the water was back on. The khukuris were sheathed with a grin as she pointed to the hot stream. As she dipped through the door space, she bid me a kindly: "You welcome."

I followed her and tried to lock the door using the pretence at a wooden latch with nowhere to catch onto. If I jammed it, the best the door was going to afford me in terms of privacy was five seconds to scream an objection to entry. So, I decided a song would warn the shower room was occupied; my singing able to deter anyone from proceeding without caution. I managed to jam the door tight, at the expense of peep-show width triangular gaps at the lintel and bottom of the door, and cleared my throat, readied for my best rendition of *Happy Birthday*.

The reason for the chill was an open window at the end of the room. It afforded a fine view onto the yard. Reciprocally, the yard had a fine view into the shower room. Wanting to spare any passers-by the embarrassment of accidentally stumbling upon a scene of soaped-up eroticism, I looked at what modesty could be provided by the curtain. Unfortunately, it reached across only one pane and so I had a delicate choice to make. Did I use the curtain to conceal my modesty at the front or back, so to speak? I judged the lesser of the two evils was to expose my bum to any potential onlookers.

It had only been a day on the bus and a day's trekking but, nevertheless, the cleansing tingle of the hot water was marvellous, and I lathered all over to remove the grime. That was when the shower unit first fluttered, and a cold firehose burst of water hit me. I'd no time to react to the shock before it was followed by a scalding blast, equally rapidly returning to something less than Venusian temperature. I hadn't earlier identified being flayed alive as one of the hazards, but recognised I needed to get a move on if I wanted to avoid that fate.

It was only when my legs were calf-deep in soapy water I realised the drain wasn't partially blocked, it wasn't draining at all. In my estimation, at the rate the basin was filling, the level of the concrete step at the door would be breached in a couple of minutes and so I rinsed myself down and turned the shower off. I was clean, standing in a scummy bath of soap, dirt and my own dead skin.

There was a grid on the elevated area up by the gas cylinder with a white bucket standing next to it; it appeared such an inundation had been anticipated. I couldn't leave the water sitting there, so I started naked bailing into the grid and 10 minutes later I stood shivering on a cold, damp floor. As I walked back through the dining area, my host greeted me with a straight face.

"Did you like hot s'ower?"

"Yes, it was very good, thank you. Dhanyabad."

I dropped my dirty clothes and towel back in the room and returned to the big pot for some warming tea. Sondiya had finished her chores and/or dinner in the kitchen and was back giving it *Saturday Night Fever* in front of the box, her sister boogying unsteadily behind her. Her grandmother came out of the kitchen and ended the spectacle as I sat down.

"Good s'ower? Now you are clean man. Sherpa stew. Ten minute." I nodded. Sondiya didn't object as the TV was shut down and came over to the table.

"Play game."

"Sure, what do you have to play?" I looked towards the cabinet for cards or something else suitable, but the shelves were empty of anything resembling Snakes and Ladders.

"Play game."

"Okay. Do you know Rock, Paper, Scissors?" This was met with a look of bemusement. I started with the three downward arcs of my arm, which Sondiya emulated. I showed the scissors hand symbol.

"Scissors, Sondiya." I made the cutting motion and she followed suit. I followed the next three arcs with the flat, horizontal hand for paper.

"Paper, Sondiya." She imitated my motion with the exactness of her dance moves. Rock followed, with the same explanation and mimicry. The next bit was going to be tricky.

"Let's do one-two-three." She misunderstood the first time but followed my lead. I finished with a scissors and she copied. By the second attempt she had it down pat.

"Now you make scissors, Sonidya." After a little hesitation, she understood. I made the paper gesture, and reached over to her scissors and showed her how to cut the paper.

"Scissors cut paper. That is one to you. Yay." She looked confused.

"Let's try again." The result was the same.

"Two to you. Now we choose. Scissors, rock or paper." We went again and I rocked her scissors.

"Yay. That's one to me. Two to you." She looked upset.

"You can choose any of the three. That's the game, Sondiya. Try to guess." She nodded.

"One-two-three. Scissors." It was a draw and I knew I hadn't explained things properly.

"Sherpa stew ready. Come take." My musing on how to explain things differently to Sondiya so she'd understand she could choose the other two were interrupted.

The matriarch showed me to the kitchen stove. I was encouraged to self-serve into a glazed bowl before returning to the table where Sondiya was still one-two-three-scissoring. We played another few rounds while I ate, Sondiya coming out the winner 10 to one by maintaining her nerve with scissors. I was suckered into choosing paper every time by thinking she was going to change her mind to rock. She was delighted with her win and, with a squeal, she took off out the front door.

"Sherpa stew good? You take more. When finish call daughter in Scotland." I judged the Sherpa stew excellent, a glutinous soup of dough and vegetables with a starchy texture offset and complemented by an underlying hint of curry, so wasn't displeased to do as I was told. When I returned to the table, Sondiya presented me with two purple thistle flowers. I was touched and as I bid her my thanks, nodded to her grandmother. I needed to take some of her parenting skills home with me.

It had become cold in the room at twilight and the matriarch closed the doors. As I was washing down my dinner with what I vowed was my last cup of tea of the day, there was the grumble of a vehicle pulling up outside. I was taken aback as I hadn't considered the path to the lodge was driveable. There was a loud series of bangs, a lot of shouting and an exterior door was flung open. A tall, handsome Nepali man, a coal-black bandeau keeping his equally Stygian, shoulder-length tresses partially in check, announced his entrance in Shakespearean fashion.

"Bonsoir, monsieur," he bade me and, dropping his satchel to the floor, went to hug the matriarch. After an extended period of envelopment, which left me wondering if the new man was possibly husband number two, she went to fetch tea.

"Bonsoir. Hello."

"English?"

"Yes."

"It is cold, no? I am happy to arrive. My name is Matthieu," he announced, leaving me doubting it was his given name.

"Yes, it's starting to get chilly. I'm Lee. Nice to meet you, Matthieu. How are you doing? Have you got here in a jeep?"

"No, we have come on the bus from Kathmandu. The bus is there." He pointed out to the yard.

"No way. I didn't think the bus came all the way to Bhandar?"

"Yes. There is one each day. We left at six this morning."

"Ouch. Thirteen-and-a-half hours. That is some trip."

"Yes. There is a bad landslide at Charikot. We had to wait for two hours to pass it." That made me think of Usain and how lucky I'd been that he was able to bypass it with his impressive driving skills.

"Yes, I passed through that yesterday. I've come from Shivalaya today. Are you trekking alone?"

"No, I am with a group. I am the tour leader guide. My guests are behind," he replied. As if a cue for an announcement, a thin lady of a similar vintage to myself entered the room, followed by two ladies of about post-graduate age. The older lady asked for the toilet. Three smaller Nepalis schlepping plastic duffels trooped through the entrance, laid them down centrally and went to fetch some more.

"Bonsoir." One of the younger ladies greeted me and I replied in kind. Matthieu indicated to the big pot the matriarch had plonked on the table nearest him and told his guest in French there was tea if she'd like it. The older lady, who I took as the mother of the other two, had returned and we exchanged introductions. They were from Marseille. The group's porters had now finished toting the remainder of their load and a pile of bags now dominated the room. A sweating porter asked the French ladies if they wanted their bags taken to their room and, with their approval, they headed upstairs together. I was surprised because, without reason, I hadn't expected the porters to be fluent in French. Ironically, I expected everyone to use English as their *lingua franca*.

"Do all your group speak French, Matthieu?" I continued in English.

"Yes, of course. Everyone in my group speaks fluent French. We learn English at school as our first foreign language. Those who become guides or porters with my company must know at least one other language too. It is the same for all the good tour companies. If the tour is for trekkers from Italy, it will have a guide and porters who speak Italian. The most popular language companies want guides to speak now is Chinese." The episode, and Matthieu's explanation, had done a great job of revealing to myself something of a latent Anglo-Saxon prejudice. I determined to try to learn something from that, but not knowing what it was yet.

"Is Matthieu the name you use when guiding?"

"Yes. The name started as a joke with a group many years ago and has stuck. I think it is easier for French people. When they book a tour and learn Matthieu is the name of their guide, they are more comfortable. Nepali people use my Nepali name."

"So, should I call you Matthieu or do you prefer your Nepali name?"

"Matthieu."

"Okay. Have all the Nepali folks in your team taken French names?"

"No, just me." The porters and other trekkers returned, and we shared another cup of tea. The matriarch re-entered, handed out menus and queried in English: "What you eat for dinner?"

I recommended the Sherpa stew, not too put out they'd been given the option of making their own selection. The matriarch made to head back to the kitchen.

"Are we going to call your daughter, in Scotland?"

"*NOT NOW, NOT NOW. TOO BUSY! TOO BUSY!*"

She beetled back into the kitchen waving her arms and I took this as a natural break point to bid everyone good night. I was shattered and wanted to rest my weary body. I hugged the rail as I hauled myself up the stairs again and eventually back in the Milne, I snuggled into my sleeping bag and powered up the Nano. I chose *The Very Best of Chic* by Chic as my soundtrack to take me to sleep. Sondiya was the best exponent of track two Nile Rodgers could've ever wished for. I listened to the music for a while becoming relaxed enough to slumber. It was 9pm.

I dozed for a while but was awakened by the curse of the big pot and gingerly made my way to the toilet. It was downstairs through the dining room, next to the shower room. The continual splosh of water revealed the contraption was being used. As I rinsed the lavatory clean, I heard a high-pitched squeal of pain, followed by a tumult of Gallic swear words; the hydrothermal vent temperature shift.

Only the porters remained in the dining room, slouched on the benches, elbows hoisted to compare amiably the glowing images on their mobile phones. I crawled back up the stairs to bed and was out like a light. I was awakened by the noise of unpacking and arrangement of luggage from the room next door.

Do da diddle ai do da. Do da diddle ai do da. "Hallo." I'd decided years previously only a dedicated misanthrope could end up working in the cadre of people responsible for selecting pre-programmed mobile phone ringtones. There was a short conversation followed by the creaking of cots as the guests settled in for the night.

Do da diddle ai do da. Do da diddle ai do da. "Hallo." After that, the words became indistinct. The dialogue's tone was clear, though. The called party started the conversation in a calm, measured manner, became increasingly irritated and hung up. I interpreted that to mean he must have received a cold call from the UK asking about his recent automobile accident. I checked the time and found it was 12.30am. Not too late, I thought and closed my eyes again.

Do da diddle ai do da. Do da diddle ai do da. "Hallo." Five minutes later, the argument repeated itself and was followed by some commentary relayed to the room's other occupant. I was becoming fed up, thinking that if the marketeers had his number, he should turn his phone off. If it was a personal call, he should take it once and finish it.

Do da diddle ai do da. Do da diddle ai do da. "Hallo." Off he went again; this time the quarrel was extended for 10 minutes. It was one in the morning and becoming irksome.

"Excuse me, can you finish your call, please? People are trying to get to sleep here." The latest exchange ended abruptly. There was no hint of an apology.

Do da diddle ai do da. Do da diddle ai do da. "Hallo." Whoever owned the phone had forgotten the request in the intervening 60 seconds. My fist banged on the thin layer of wood between us.

"Turn your phone off or take your call outside, mate, it's gone one o'clock." My request was ignored, and my annoyance built by the minute as I waited for him to finish his squabble. The chat ended as abruptly as the others and I tried to relax again, but my adrenaline had been stirred. A 10-minute hiatus ensued.

Do da diddle ai do da. Do da diddle ai do da. "Hal ..." I was out of the sleeping bag and at the neighbouring door before he could mutter the end of his greeting. The door rattled on its hinges as I thumped it.

"Come on, mate. Enough is enough." My pounding had woken the rest of the landing, resulting in groans and curses in French and Nepali. There was muted rushed talk on the phone followed by silence and I waited outside for the next reprise. After what I estimated to have been the customary interval between rings, I returned to Eeyore and Tigger to get some sleep. Three hours later, I was still wide awake.

I waited for 30 minutes after first light and headed downstairs in anticipation of breakfast. I hoped this was enough time for the proprietors to rise and have their morning meal before I bothered them. If it weren't, I'm sure the matriarch would've sent me back to bed like a naughty schoolboy until she was ready to receive me. I hadn't slept a wink since Deepthroat had finished his last call in the Shobhagate affair and the few stairs down to the dining room had been taken with legs seized like a rusted piston. I stopped by the WC; the Sherpa stew hadn't agreed with me and so I wasn't in the best of spirits as I sat down in the diner. At least I needn't have worried about being first up. The matriarch greeted me with a look that said, 'Did you enjoy your lie-in?' as she handed me the menu.

"Breakfast?" I wasn't going to be let out to play without a good meal inside me. I selected the banana porridge and black tea and the matriarch left me alone to ponder how she'd managed to obtain the bananas. They were a lower altitude crop and so I reckoned they'd possibly come with the bus from Kathmandu. I was cheered by the porridge; it would've satisfied Goldilocks.

Matthieu's group appeared as I was finishing my tea, one of the porters looking especially sheepish. I decided to make a start of it, gathered my things, returned to the dining room and hailed the young lady in the kitchen.

"Can I pay, please?" She beckoned me in to the sound-proofing of her pots and pans.

"Room 200. Big pot black tea, Sherpa stew, porridge, cup tea." All priced as indicated.

" ... s'ower 200."

"Shower is extra? I thought it was included with the room?"

"Hot s'ower 200." The beatific smile was back, and I realised I'd done it again and allowed myself to be hill-sharked. I felt like the Monopoly player who habitually lands on the Income Tax square straight after they've collected their 200 for passing Go. 'Never mind,' I thought as I thanked her and paid up.

The rest of Matthieu's group was now gathered in the diner and I bid them adieu as they were placing their orders. I hefted my pack and stepped out into the chill of the shadowed courtyard. I stretched out the rust from my legs, took my first steps and reached the byre's corner where the day exploded before me in technicolour. The cowshed's shade had been conquered by a harsh brightness. Yesterday's cloud had shrunk to a bench of horizontal, hoary mist caressing the gentle slope ahead and faraway farmhouses rose from the brume, their outlines miraged by the morning sun. In the distance, the green of the lush hills rose to meet the powder blue sky. I took a lungful of air realising that a minute ago, the morning weighed cold and damp; now, it tasted crisp and invigorating.

I'd been looking forward to this section – the guidebook said it was all downhill for the morning – but I'd awoken tired and crotchety. The banana porridge and the morning's vista had lifted my mood considerably. As I was about to take my first step into the haze, Sondiya and her sister came racing after me. They stopped short and waved, giggling excitedly, and my spirits were lifted further. I waved back as they disappeared inside the lodge, ready for another day at the disco.

I headed down the hill contentedly. The sun burnt off the mist to reveal the walled pastures beneath. I crossed a wooden plank bridge which brought me to a farmhouse, and I rounded its corner to meet a family outside at their morning repast. The spread was made up of eggs and porridge. A teenage boy stood aside, the sun glinting off a hand square of mirror. He was fixing his hair into a style fashionable 6,000 miles away. He reminded me of my own son, the backdrop different but not the actions, and I wondered what had instigated the dominance of Suavecito fashion in this region. My best guess was the same bus that had brought the bananas had carried a bellyful of Brilliantine as ballast on its way up to Bhandar. The local market for male grooming products had been created and flooded at once.

Cogitating on the relative merits of professional styling surf paste versus wet-look hair gel, I crossed over dashing streams and dropped down through more fertile meadows. The trail disappeared across pasture and I looked down on a forested gully, realising Bhandar was set on something of a plateau.

Below was a footbridge intercepting the enthusiastic splash of a waterfall and I could see on its other side, the trail widened and ascended. The guidebook ventured this was a four-wheel- drive track and I thought, if so, it appeared unused and poorly maintained, the track ruts covered with a skin of broken rocks. A drive along this road would've been hairy by any standards. It was barely more than a Cadillac wide and it easily met the Nepali highways department's minimum requirement of a 200-metre sheer drop on the downhill side.

For a pedestrian, though, it was a pleasant stroll in the early morning sunshine with numerous stops to watch basking geckos squirting themselves into narrow cracks in the rock wall to my left. I moved on and met what could have been a derelict house advertising organic tea. The marketing proclaimed Rs.150 for 100 grams or Rs.1,500 for a kilo. So much for the bulk discount.

I continued with the road's undulations and came across the day's first obstacle. The road ascended to a crest before a sharp turn. Immediately before the crest, in a crook in the road, there had been a rock avalanche that tipped over the trail into the vertical ravine below. The local folk had cut a sinuous, single-file path through the loose rock, paying no heed to the precipitous drop. The previous day's fall had dented any confidence in both my boots and balance, and I fretted about how I was going to make it across. There was no other option, though; I wasn't about to turn back at the first, admittedly petrifying, bump in the road.

As I strode towards the 100-metre approach to the defile, images of my broken body smashed on the rocks played in my mind. As I met the rockfall, I sucked in a deep, fortifying mouth of air, dropped my head to focus on the placement of each footstep and headed across the 50 metres of disruption. At the end of the narrowness at the crest, I was forced to scramble, my knuckles ahead, chimpanzee style. On my knees, I hauled myself over to the security of the upside cliff. I rested my backpack on the rock wall as I shook in the sun.

It took some time to calm my galloping pulse. I drank some water and was heartened by the view ahead as I regained my feet. The road looked unbroken and so I carried on, slowly regaining my tempo. Ten minutes later, I heard a commotion from below and was able to summon the courage to peek over the road's shoulder. My view was met by a gang of semaphoring adolescents.

"Wrong way, mister!" They signalled I should backtrack, dread returning as I conceived I'd crossed the avalanche for nought and would have to navigate it again to join the right path.

"Follow man." They pointed at a bandanaed head that had disappeared down the cliff side and I expelled a deep breath in relief, realising I wouldn't have to risk the crossing again.

The head reappeared below with an accompanying torso, its owner tobogganing down the hill at a rate that laughed at my slow, rolling progress. To my eyes, he looked a *bona fide* mountain dude, carrying off the black paisley bandana and lime green blouson look through his sheer proficiency. I stopped and watched him, hoping to garner some trail knowledge by observing the coils of the path he weaved through broad-leaved shrubs. His dual walking poles gave his position away more frequently than the camouflage of his headscarf and top, seeming to emerge from the undergrowth with a hitch-kick into the air. I duplicated his lead over the cliff, and it was there I suffered my second fall.

I'd slipped on friable rock again. The path had given way with the weight of my downslope boot and, fortunately, I'd fallen onto my uphill elbow and side. If I'd tumbled the other way, I'd have crashed two or three metres down a dusty rock slope onto a terrace, but my curse betrayed no gratitude for that. I dragged myself up to my feet and carefully stepped down to flatter ground, checking for damage. I was relieved that, apart from a miner's coating of white dust, I was physically unscathed, but my self-esteem was another matter.

The path I'd seen the mountaineer follow was now easier, becoming a narrow hopscotch over broken flagstones set atop the lip of the terraces, and turning sharply downhill through winding chutes. The terraces were narrow and steep here. The chutes interconnected the yards of drystone houses reminiscent of those found in the English Lake District and I found myself many times greeting folks at their daily household labours. I found it peculiar that, in this valley, everyone seemed to be wearing the same brand and colour of Wellington boots, rather than the flip-flops I'd seen folks sporting elsewhere, and I wondered if that Brilliantine-carting bus had also contained a job lot of Hunters.

The trail was dissected by fast-flowing streams disappearing into lush clumps of green. Terrace-end waterfalls seemed to signpost every change in direction to downslope. All manner of flowering climbers, stands of marigolds and cardamom plants burst vibrantly from the trailside. As I rested in the shade of a small copse of mandarin trees, the older lady in Matthieu's group passed me with her porter. They stopped for a quick chat before racing down the hill. Walking again, the lack of sleep now started to catch up with me. The path became ambiguous and I found myself on a steep grassy slope that contoured above a road. I could see a settlement in the distance which looked big enough to be Kenja, my planned lunch spot.

The path had now disappeared, but the slope resembled those I'd walked many times in Scotland. My traverse would be a gradual zigzag down to meet the road in the distance but, 100 metres from the convergence with the road, I realised I'd made a mistake. The road had been freshly excavated from the hillside and my only way forward was to skirt the top of the cut via what was an intermittent animal track of sorts.

Ten metres from my goal, I was on my shoulder and side-skidding down to an uncontrolled meeting with the road. I broke my fall by grabbing a gorse-like bush growing before the final drop of two or three metres. I skidded down from there to the road on my behind. Hoisting myself to my feet, I surveyed the damage which was restricted to a few grazes on my hands and a rip in my trousers – and no belief in my boots. Confidence dented in my hillwalking abilities, my mood darkened.

There was no shade along the road, and I trudged on wearily under the mid-morning sun. An aggregate truck headed down the valley with a construction crew packed into its open cargo space. The remainder of Matthieu's tour trooped past me at the confluence of two rivers marking the village boundary. Kenja was at first a hodgepodge of dwellings along the new road, but the trail guided me into an alleyway between lodges. I elected for one on the right, with a shaded outdoor patio, as my lunch spot.

A man of about 30 sat at ease, his feet horizontal across a chair pulled up opposite. He was drawing in a lungful of tobacco smoke. To his side, brown walking poles lay parked against a top-of-the-range backpack. I bid him hello and was met with a nod when I signalled if I could take the table next to him. After our initial greeting, I asked where he was headed and was met with an embarrassed look of non-comprehension. I tried my luck with the various flavours of Pidgin I knew and got a match with my second guess, Spanish. He was Alexis, a Pyrenean mountain guide who hailed from Teruel. With the knowledge of his day job, I felt better at being unable to match his hiking speed or skills downhill and, overall, a little less sullen. Having succeeded in communicating the most rudimentary of questions and answers, I decided it was time to expand the conversation by giving my lack of Castilian vocabulary and coherent grammar an outing.

"Of where you go, today?"

"I'mgoingtoGoyembuthavehurtmyfootsomayhavetostopearlier." He machine gunned his response. My opening-line salvo of ineptitude hadn't warned him I had no clue as to his language's finer points.

"Sorry. My Spanish is bad. More slow, please."

"I...am...heading...to...Goyem...but...I...have...hurt...my...foot...so...I...may...have...to...stop...earlier."

"You is goes Goyem? Yours feets are pain? Stop must feet pains?"

"Yes."

"What is you problem with feets ills?" He pulled his nearest leg off the chair and took off his sock to unveil a deep red blister sore running from his big toe to the ball of his foot.

"My god! How are able you to been walking with that? Is a big problem, no? Much pains?"

"Yes. It is painful to walk."

"I have ... errrr ... things." I pointed towards the sore and broke the top straps on my bag. A minute later, my table was strewn with underpants and T-shirts as I unzipped my first aid kit. I passed him a tube of antiseptic.

"Do you want your laundry done along with some food?" The lodge proprietor had joined us and, with a smile begging sympathy, I asked him for a minute.

"Wash your hands. Power this cream on ill. Ills breathing one hour. Next blister plaster." I'd learned the word for blister plaster on walking the Camino in northern Spain.

"Thank you, I already have Compeed. They work well. I think it is time for me to leave now if I want to reach Goyem." He took the lodge owner's appearance as the cue to relieve his ears from the butchery of his mother tongue and request his bill. He chose not to dress his wound, but redonned his bandana and acid green windcheater and was on his way with a friendly thank you.

"I'd like the dhal baat and a black tea, please." Every guidebook I'd read told the same story that this was the only meal that could combat tiredness and provide enough energy for trekking in the hills. The dhal baat arrived minutes later on a circular tin thali plate, the rice forming a perfect white hummock. The lodger owner poured the dhal onto the plate from an iron jug and indicated I should say 'when' as he twisted the jug's handle. The meal came with a side dish of spinach and another of curried pickles.

It surpassed any dhal baat I'd experienced before in Nepal. The dhal was the right consistency and had an undercurrent of spice keeping it from blandness but not overpowering the taste buds. I cleared the plate and the owner returned to ask if I wanted a re-fill, which I gladly accepted. The second dish was all that I could handle, and I sat replete, hands on belly waiting for some space for my tea.

"Would you like some more dhal baat, sir?"

"No thanks, that was delicious. The best dhal baat I've had."

"Thank you. Where are you from, sir?"

"The UK."

"Ah, which part? I was based in Aldershot for a while."

"I'm from Liverpool but live in Scotland. Were you a Gurkha?"

"Yes. Twenty years. I served mainly in the Singapore police."

"That must have been something, how was it?"

"I was very proud to finish my service, sir, but now I'm here." His tone had turned wistful and his very presence seemed to have shrunk.

"You don't sound too happy about that?"

"Things could be better, sir."

"Things don't look too bad to me. Kenja is a beautiful place, the sun is shining."

"Yes, but there is no business here, sir."

"How come? Your lodge is great, and the food is fantastic."

"There are only 10 or 20 trekkers a day at peak season. That is between all the lodges you see in town."

"Because all the trekkers fly to Lukla?" He nodded.

"And because of the guidebooks. Most trekkers follow them and only stay in the villages they say are stopover places. It means hardly anyone ever stays in Kenja."

"I didn't realise that. I'm sorry." And it dawned on me that, although the lady in Shivalaya had said her business had been impacted because the guidebook stated this trek was tough, this gentleman had been hit harder. It seemed whatever residual trekkers existed were actively advised to ignore this place.

"It is worse now than when I finished my service. Twenty years ago, there was business. Not all tourists had the same guidebook and some trekkers stayed in Kenja. Also, porters stayed here, but now there are too many donkeys."

"The donkey trains have replaced porters?"

"Yes, a lot." It seemed obvious when I thought about it, but it hadn't even registered. I was trekking blinkered.

"When I returned from Singapore, I took out a loan with the bank and bought this lodge. The interest is very high and today there are so few customers every year is difficult." He looked so forlorn as he told me this I wasn't sure of the right thing to say. He sounded resigned to his existence without much hope of improving his lot.

"Is the government doing anything to help with tourism?" His head shake told me otherwise.

"How about the new road from Jiri to Lukla. Will it pass by here? What about the two rivers? They look like they could be great for white water rafting or canoeing."

"Some Swiss people came last year with canoes. The only time we have had foreign people on the rivers." His explanation was interrupted by the arrival of half a dozen dust-caked men. One gentleman was clad in a tan sheepskin-lined coat and was puffing on a cigar. I instantly decided he must be the local black marketeer, though what a World War II Cockney spiv was doing selling nylons in Kenja was beyond me.

My maudlin friend's mood seemed to lift and, with a smile he greeted them. They settled themselves in the restaurant's interior. He pulled a bamboo tube cylinder from the shelf and served them small glasses of clear liquid.

"Do you want to try rokha?"

"What's that?"

"Local whisky, it's very good, Gurkha strong."

"No thanks, it's a bit early for me." It was 11.54am.

"Very well."

"Do these guys come here for a drink every day?"

"Yes. They are working on the new hydro-electric scheme in the valley. They like rokha very much. I recommend you take some with them." Images of half-cut dynamiters blowing themselves up at the dam that afternoon flooded my mind. I decided to make a break for it in case they'd brought the odd stick with them and the racketeer's cigar sent the place up.

"No thank you, just the bill."

Another round of the spirit was demanded as I paid, and the sad restaurateur returned inside to join his friends for a drink. I set off, my leg muscles having tightened during the rest, and it took until the end of town to ease the stiffness out. Ahead loomed an intimidating stone staircase unconcerned with twists or turns. I dealt with the initial 100 metres adequately and stopped to admire a score or so rhesus monkeys scampering across the steps towards lunch in the trees.

The staircase now steepened, the trail a punishing switchback climb towards the midday sun. I was forced to take a break every 40 or 50 steps to catch my breath and take on fluid. An hour later, I came across a two-tone terracotta-coloured house where thousands of what could have been borlotti beans were drying on the patio.

I trudged higher, my legs and lungs suffering. The fatigue of earlier had returned, the brutal haul's relentlessness becoming an ordeal. I persisted, stopping every 20 or 30 steps to catch my breath and, eventually, Kenja came into view along the valley to my rear. The clouds rolled in, but away in the distance I suspected I caught a glimpse of Bhandar through a break in the grey.

I rested near a bank of cardamom. The terraces in the area spoke of agricultural decay or abandonment. Broken hitch posts and unrepaired fences sagged in the middle of overgrown fields where wooden tools lay with the randomness of piles of toothpicks. I'd stopped at an unremarkable twist in the trail where, detergent rotting its insides, a long-planked cylinder and plunger stood sentinel over the valley. It was a beautifully inconvenient place to do one's laundry.

I heard someone puffing their way up the trail and lazily awaited them, appreciating the extra time to convalesce. A young man in his early 20s came puffing into view. He wore an olive polyester shirt, its wicking working overtime, and the image of a wolf centred on a red flag flapped from the hip-belt of his backpack. His demeanour showed he was having an equally tough time overcoming this route and I took some solace in the fact.

"Hi. It's tough going, isn't it?"

"Yes, this is too much, man." He came to a stop beside me.

"I'm finding it really hard as well. Where are you heading?"

"I have come from Deurali. I am going to Goyem tonight. Did you see a Spanish guy? I am travelling with him."

"Alexis? Yes, I ate lunch with him."

"Yes, Alexis."

"He's probably a couple of hours ahead by now, but he has a problem with his foot. He said he may stop earlier than Goyem, depending on how it feels."

"Thank you. Where are you headed for?"

"Sete. I think it's another two hours, but I'm tired, so may stop somewhere before if I find anywhere. I will see."

"Two more hours to Sete? Che cazzo!"

"Ah ... you aren't Spanish, then? You're Italian?"

"Yes, Antonio. From Roma."

"Well, I don't think your ancestors built their roads this way, mate."

"No. This is too hard, man."

"I'm from Liverpool, did you see the Champions League semi-finals?" This was met with a good-natured harrumph.

"You were lucky. We will win next year." He mopped his brow again and we proceeded uphill together for a while. Thirty minutes later, I bid him good luck as we separated. His pace had proven faster as he needed to rest less frequently; in the heat of mid-afternoon, I was now stopping every dozen steps. I dragged my way upwards, exhausted as the path rose mercilessly once again to a construction crew building a new house on a ridge. It flattened out around the nose of a ridge of rice terraces coming to a broken staircase disappearing into a shadowed copse of trees. Head down, determined to reach another rest point across the wood I almost missed the sign. It declared a couple of structures gathered around a stone courtyard as the 'Top Himalayan Guest House'. A young girl came out to meet me as I caught my breath on the bench outside.

"Sete?" I enquired.

"No, Chhimbu," she replied.

I was unconcerned by her answer. It was three in the afternoon and I was beat. The guidebook said it was a five-hour trek from Bhandar to Sete. Seven hours after leaving, I hadn't reached my destination, but I'd arrived.

Chhimbu to Goyem

T he lodge was a two-storey, L-shaped building painted in the same whites and blues of the Shobha. I wondered if that had evolved over the years, the soothing blue subconsciously inviting to potential guests? The foot of the L faced a smaller building separated by a flight of steep stone steps leading downwards to a shack marked as the toilet facilities, 50 metres away. The property was in keeping with the air of abandonment that had pervaded on its approach. A lonely beer bottle had been discarded, along with a scattering of chewing tobacco wrapping paper, on the cracked paint of a window ledge. The bench beneath was decorated with the remains of marigolds and child's solitary rubber boot. Ears of corn flopped over the balcony above.

The young girl looked at me with a bemused stare. My chest was heaving from the exertion and that didn't figure – I could've only walked up from Kenja. I caught my breath to order a small pot and, with the arrival of the tea, the girl came to join me. As we shared the first cup, I opened the price negotiations, determined not to be hoodwinked in any way this time.

"Do you have a room please?"

"Yes. All rooms 100 rupees." That concluded matters – I'd have paid Rs.100 to sleep on the bench. In a way, I was almost disappointed; but at the same time slightly suspicious, waiting for the catch. We headed into the main lodge and through a storeroom where heaps of potatoes and maize were drying. A conversation along the lines of 'bill is 100 rupees and four hours shucking corn' at checkout time sprung to mind.

We climbed a ladder to a landing where musical instruments adorned the walls and passed through a door frame covered by a traditional curtain, its pattern a yellow cross on a background of snooker-baize green. Inside was a whitewashed timber box with dual wooden cots. Although I was slightly disappointed the linens were floral rather than Piglet-themed, I was also pleased to learn I'd be sleeping in a bed of roses. The window was set at cot height and, if a guest were so inclined, they could clamber through and enjoy the view from the balcony. I tested the mattress; it had been well used but was more than adequate for my needs.

Ignoring the dank, rotted-wood smell permeating the chamber, I nodded my acceptance and my new host departed. I dropped my pack, took immeasurable pleasure in removing my boots and hobbled back down the ladder stairs to the bench. My legs had seized again as I cooled down and I eased myself into a sitting position with no grace. I was taking my second cup of tea when my host popped her head out the door of the smaller building and, Pocahontas pigtails flying, she ran over to join me. She was dressed in a green jumper and pinstripe trousers befitting an Edwardian stockbroker. I put her at around 14.

"Where you come from today?" she asked, chewing gum spinning in her mouth at the speed of a tumble dryer on its final cycle.

"Bhandar."

"Ah ... very slow. You go to Lukla. Trek?"

"Yes, that's right. What's your name?"

"My name Dolmo."

"Nice to meet you, Dolmo. My name is Lee."

"Nice to meet you, Lee."

"Are you here alone?"

"Yes. Work lodge alone."

"What about your parents?"

"In field."

"Growing potatoes, like in the storeroom inside?"

"Yes. Father grow potato, rice, maize, vegetable. Little brother help."

"Little brother? How old is he, Dolmo?" I queried, confused, as my expectation was a younger brother would've been at school, not toiling in the fields.

"He 17."

"Your *little* brother is 17, Dolmo?"

"Yes, I 21." Twenty-one! It appeared I was as competent as Jenny in the age-guessing department.

"What about your mum, is she helping them with the potatoes as well?"

"Sometime. Now mother grow fruit. You see." She showed me over to the side of the smaller building and pointed towards a garden where vigorous bushes of chilli and what may have been vanilla pods were growing.

"Are those apple trees?"

"Yes, apple. What you grow in your country?"

"A lot of things – wheat, oats, barley. We have a lot of cows and pigs. Lots of chickens. We grow apples and things like strawberries. No rice, though, it's too cold," I answered.

"We have chicken. See." At the head of the stair between the buildings was a muscly bird tied to an upturned wicker basket. Half a dozen downy chicks pecked around her.

"You'll have good eggs in the morning."

"Good egg, yes. You have picture your chicken?"

"Err ... sorry, no, I don't have any chickens."

"You say you grow chicken in your country, you no have chicken? Have cow picture?"

"Sorry, I don't have any cows, either."

"Have pig?"

"Sorry, no."

"You have *some* picture animal?"

"No, sorry, no animals. I have some pictures of home and of the trek which I can show you instead?"

"I see?" I took out my phone and flicked through a select few pictures in the gallery.

"Give!" I was beginning to worry that I'd inadvertently made a gift of the phone to Dolmo. She seemed keen to hang on to it after completing her forensic examination of every photograph and detailed history of its back story, but after an hour she handed it back. Tea finished, Dolmo headed back to the kitchen and I fancied relaxing by reading before dinner. Five minutes after returning to my floral chamber, I'd nodded off on my bed.

I was awakened by melodious singing coming from the room to my left. It was accompanied by the strings of a mandolin or lute. The primary vocal was sung in a deep, gruff baritone with the harmonies a couple of octaves higher. The main vocal broke out of the harmony at the verse, with the emphasis on the last word, which was extended. The lute didn't follow the harmony, rather filled in the gaps in the singing. It wasn't like anything I'd heard before – perhaps akin to Portuguese fado, but an analogy with that style wouldn't do it justice.

Curious to see who was serenading, I stepped out onto the landing and saw the curtain next door was drawn to one side, revealing my neighbours were in a sort of dormitory-cum-utility room. The walls were oak wood coloured panels with cushioned benches squared around. It could sleep six or so. A low table crowded with duffel bags, instruments and their cases dominated the floor. I exchanged greetings with the dozen men who were preparing for their next tune and stood in the door frame for the next hour as they continued their practice. Rehearsal finished when Dolmo escorted another guest to the room on my right.

The new guest was a pretty lady who could've been in her early 20s, properly attired for the mountains in a fleece, waterproof trousers and sturdy boots. She was an early adopter of eco high-tech; a solar panel collector was strapped to her huge pack, a wire lacing its way to the mobile phone charging in a pocket. The floor complained at the weight of her gear as she dropped it by the door. I was impressed she'd managed to haul everything up from Kenja.

"Do you know where the bathroom is, please?"

'What do you need that for? It looks like you've brought your own Western Style,' I failed to say out loud.

"Yes, if you go down the ladder and out the door, there's a gap between this block and the other building. Go down the steps and the toilets are 50 metres away. I think there'll be a sink in there. You can't miss them." As she thanked me, I realised that since leaving Bhandar I hadn't needed to visit the restroom once. I'd filled my LifeStraw water bottle four or five times at the waterfalls and streams *en route*. Along with the tea, I must have drunk five litres during the day. The walk had made me perspire more than I'd realised; I was dehydrated without having been aware and I made a mental note to drink water throughout the day, even if I didn't feel thirsty.

There was a knock on my door as I was optimising my sock arrangement for aeration among the flora on my room's second cot.

"Excuse me." It was my new neighbour, looking flustered.

"Hi."

"Did you hear anyone go into my room while I was away?"

"No, I don't think so. I think there were some people moving around on the landing but, to be honest, I wasn't really paying too much attention. Has someone broken into your room or something?"

"Not broken in. I didn't put my lock on the door when I went to the bathroom, but I can tell that someone has been in the room. My things aren't where I left them."

"You're kidding! Has anything been taken?"

"I don't know yet, but my backpack isn't where I put it and some of my under-things have been moved from where they were on the bed."

"You'd better check if something has been stolen. If your money or passport has gone we need to tell Dolmo now. I'm not sure what she can do to help, but if there's a thief about I'm sure the lodge owners would want to know. I don't know where the nearest police would be." She returned to her room and was back five minutes later.

"It doesn't look like anything has been stolen."

"That's a bit of a relief."

"Yes, but it's horrible to think someone has gone through my things. Are you sure you didn't hear anything?"

"I thought I saw a shadow cross the window earlier, but I put it down to a cloud going past. It could've been someone on the balcony, I suppose, but I don't remember hearing anything. I wasn't really paying attention, so might have been imagining it. What do you want to do about it? I think it's a good idea to let Dolmo know. If there's a dodgy character around, it's best she knows."

"Yes, I agree. I'm going to tell the lodge people now."

"Okay. Do you want me to watch your room? Do you have a padlock?"

"Yes, I'll lock the room. If you could listen out for anything I won't worry about someone going through my things again."

"Sure." She left me standing guard on the landing. Five minutes later, she returned with Dolmo and a man who I took to be her father. He stormed into the dorm room where voices were raised for a few minutes.

"You have no problem now. I make sure," the father reported. My neighbour nodded, satisfied with the assurance, and he bundled himself down the stairs. Dolmo trailed behind, looking sheepish.

"Are you okay?"

"Yes, I think so, but I don't feel good about this, though. If I wasn't so tired, I'd go to the next village."

"I can't say I'd blame you. At least nothing has been taken."

"Yes, but the thought of someone's hands on my underwear ..."

"Yeah. Not good. At least you're only here one night, so you won't have to think about it too much tomorrow. I'm going to eat in about half an hour, shall I give you a knock and we can go together?"

"Okay."

Thirty minutes later, we were sitting in the kitchen-cum-dining area, my friend seeming slightly recovered from the unwelcome intrusion. Dolmo, her father and a lady I assumed was her mother were busy attending to pots and pans. The older lady was laughing heartily as we arrived. She sported loose, blue-flowered trousers I initially mistook for a skirt, a thick grey fleece, flip-flops and a headscarf deviating from the usual babushka fashion. It was a thick white bandana that merged into a loose turban, with a fringe of ribbons sprouting from each side. Dolmo's father came to the sawhorse width bench doubling as our table.

"Dinner?"

"Yes please."

"My wife make Sherpa curry. You want Sherpa curry?"

"What's in it?" I enquired. He brought over a large pea-green fruit resembling a horse-chestnut seed-pod, only five times the size.

"Is it spicy?"

"Spice. As you like. We grow many chillies. You like spicy?"

"Not too much, please." He nodded. I'd no idea what the fruit was, or the relative meaning of spicy in Chhimbu compared to UK curry houses, but decided to give it a go. My friend opted for a more conservative noodle soup.

The kitchen occupied three walls. On the left wall, a tin trough serviced by a single tap constituted the sink. A two-ring gas hob was supplied by a dark propane cylinder perched next to it on a wooden table. The back wall was devoted to shelves of thermoses and tin crockery. In the nearest corner was a grey, moulded earthenware stove.

The dining space ran along opposing walls where narrow benches served as both seats and tables. At the opposite end to the cooking area stood a more substantial table covered in a knitted blue tablecloth. Dolmo had peeled and chipped a mountain of potatoes and continued to add to them as my new companion and I settled into small talk.

"Where are you heading, Everest Base Camp?" I asked.

"Yes, I'm going to do it as part of the Three Passes trek. Gokyo."

"Sounds great. Do you have a lot of time for your trip, then?"

"Yes. I finished my studies in psychology in July and left Belgium for India. I was there until last week."

"Four months in India? That sounds like a proper trip, where did you go?"

"Goa, Varanasi, the usual places."

"I was there nearly 30 years ago. I'd love to go back to see how it's changed. Back then, I spent two days on a steam train going from Delhi to Kolkata."

"Steam train? What is that?" I was amused my explanation didn't translate across the generations. By the end of attempted charades of coal shovelling and whistle tooting, she looked flummoxed, so I chose to steer things back to the original topic of conversation.

"So how much time have you got in Nepal?"

"I will trek until Christmas. I have a flight home to Brussels on Christmas Day, it's the cheapest day of the year to fly. I will spend Christmas with my family and then go to my new job in Ghent in January. How about you?"

"I got to Nepal a few days ago. I'm trekking, trying for Base Camp. I'm Lee, by the way. Are you trekking the Three Passes by yourself or going to get a porter? Your bag looks really heavy."

"Yes! It is too heavy, the climb from Kenja was really hard. The problem is I have a lot of things I bought in India and clothes for warm weather. Were you in India for the monsoon?"

"Yes, I caught the tail end of it."

"The monsoon in India is *so* hot, no? Very horrible."

"Yeah." I nodded.

"For Nepal, I have big coat, gloves and the other things for the mountains. I don't have money for a porter, so trek alone."

"I'm also trekking solo. I can't get out of my head this stupid, macho idea that you haven't really done the trek unless you carry all your own stuff."

"This thought is not just for men; I understand this too. I'm sorry, you asked me my name. I am Hélène."

"Nice to meet you, Hélène. The other stupid thing I can't shake off is that, because I studied geography, I wouldn't feel I'd done it unless I'd found my own way."

"I have downloaded all the trekking maps. If you can use a phone, you can find your way."

"Yeah, I don't even think you need that – I just ask folks along the way if I'm pointing in the right direction. I did the Annapurna Circuit 10 years ago and managed, so am hoping I can still do it the same way for EBC. If I find it is too much, I'll try to hire a porter. I found today really hard going as well, so maybe I'll get a porter sooner rather than la ... what?" The room was now lit only by the dim firelight from the stove. There was a curse accompanying the thump of knee on wood before a torch illuminated the darkness.

"Power cut. No problem," briefed the father as he sat down opposite me.

"Does this happen often?" I politely enquired, in the manner of small talk over canapés at a suburban dinner party.

"Most day. Many people live in valley. Power come last up hill. If all Kenja people want power, no in Chhimbu. No problem. We used. You take flashlight."

"I've got my own, thanks." I added to the torchlight by flicking on my Powercap. This was evidently something of a novelty and quickly became the centre of attention. Dolmo desisted from her slicing of potatoes and, with a slight nod of her head, indicated she wanted to give my headgear a try.

She donned the millinery and cat-walked up and down the kitchen, the tips of her pigtails swinging with every exaggerated swish of her hips. Mum was next. She double turbaned, with the Powercap search-lighting the ceiling as she sashayed down the room, arms akimbo in a mock Victoria's Secret model's stance. Dad was invited next to give it his best David Gandy pout and slouched flat cap pose but was saved by the reillumination of the lights. He returned the Powercap, laughing with the rest of us as he did so.

Supermodel Mum built up the fire on the open stove. I was fascinated by her casual skill. A groove in the moulding cleverly directed the air supply to feed the fire. She first nurtured kindling twigs into a flame before adding a bundle of medium-sized branches that were rotated in the air stream until they blazed. Branches followed, the result an intense heat that made best use of the fuel. It seemed incongruous when she placed a charred but modern-looking pressure-cooker above the flame.

The power failed again. In the firelight I talked amicably with Hélène about travelling, trekking and Christmas traditions in Belgium versus the UK, pleased the incident in her room seemed behind her. Her noodles and my Sherpa curry arrived. The giant horse-chestnut fruit had the same consistency of under-ripe pear cores. I found the taste equally bland, but the rest of the curry made up for that. It was the same delicious, starchy taste the matriarch in Bhandar had gently persuaded me to try.

The lights stuttered to life as the men who were staying in the room next to me meandered into the kitchen and took up station at the benches opposite. Two wiry boys followed them and sat at the big table. It was the signal for Dolmo's dad to come over.

"Finish? Good? Want more?"

"No thanks, it was good, yes. Are those boys part of your family?"

"Yes, nephew."

"How old?"

"Him 10, him nine. Come from village for dhal baat. Very hungry boy." The boys sat there placidly in huge, oversized knitted jumpers waiting for their dinner. Supermodel Mum brought them plates with rice and lentils piled Matterhorn high and they tucked in without ceremony.

"They must be hungry!"

"Very hungry boy, yes!"

"What about the other guys across the room, are they part of your family as well?"

"No, they music group. Play at Tihar festival. In valley. Go home now." I surmised, from his demeanour, that the bandleader didn't look one to get the party started. He sat scowling underneath a tea cosy of a hat. I guessed he'd been the one admonished and tried not to think too much about what he'd been doing in Hélène's room. I hoped she wasn't thinking the same things.

"You want try hot rokha? I make now. Help stomach after dinner."

"Maybe. How are you going to make it?"

"Take maize mash. Add yak butter and mix three time. I show you." He went over to the gas hob, pulled down a stewing pot and poured a plastic bottle of clear liquid into it. He lit the gas and added the yak butter, stirring for five minutes. It was clearly a labour of love. He turned off the gas and sat back down with us.

"Now wait go cold. Do again. Two more time." It was going to be another hour until the moonshine was drinkable, so Hélène decided to call it a night and I stayed to chat some more with dad. He sometimes worked as a guide in between farming and helping with the tea house. Dolmo's brother returned from the fields and helped himself to another Swiss peak of dhal baat before the liquor was ready. A minute later, dad brought me a glass and I found it wasn't the firewater I was expecting. The flavour was similar to a delicate schnapps but with a slightly grainy texture. There was a small burning as it hit my stomach, but it hadn't stripped away the lining of all my internal organs on its way there.

"Ha, ha! Very good, eh? Wait."

He shared around a tray with the boys in the band. Tea Cosy shouted something that I took as a countdown and they slammed their drained glasses on the benches in front. To a man, they voiced their approval and banged their glasses in demand of a second round. At that, I supposed the band may get boisterous and was thankful the Top Himalayan boasted no colour TVs or swimming pool.

"Good, eh? More?"

"No thanks, I think I'll call it a night. Goodnight."

I stepped into the courtyard and took in the night sky. The stars pulsated and I thought that, although the local folks were unlucky in material things, they were fortunate still to have a wonder like this, uncontaminated by light pollution, upon which to gaze. This was followed quickly by regret; I'd slipped into Western patronisation again. I shambled through the under-croft musing on my need to justify enjoyment of a thing by the use of comparators rather than just being able to enjoy the beauty of the constellations.

My thoughts wandered to our relative behaviour when presented with such a celestial opportunity; how mundanity breeds apathy. I was alone in the courtyard craning my neck to the skies, while the locals were busily getting shit-faced in the kitchen. We exhibited a lot in common there, I thought: if I counted up the number of times I'd ventured outside the city to take advantage of the excellent hillwalking in the Scottish countryside compared to the number of times I'd got steamboats in the pubs in Glasgow, there would be no comparison.

I reached my door and twiddled the combination on my padlock to find the first dial was stuck between numbers. I squeezed the lock into its catch and tried again, with the result that the lower three dials rotated. I could feel they were in the right position to release, but not the uppermost. I tried rotating the dials again and again, twisting with brute force, but the mechanism held firm. The door had been well made – there were no hinge or lock screws to undo – so there was nothing for it but to ask my host to break out the tools and bust the lock open. The party was bubbling along nicely when I returned to the kitchen. I felt bad interrupting Dolmo's dad in his roistering; he seemed to have a certain flair for it.

"Ah. You come for more rokha?!"

"No thanks. I've a problem with the lock on my door. Could you come and help me, please?"

"What is problem?"

"My padlock is broken. It will need to be broken off, I think."

"Ah. No problem. I help. Come." He swilled down his drink and we headed to the room, accompanied by the band. He repeated all the measures I'd tried and achieved the same results.

"Ah. I need to break. Wait." He headed back down the stairwell and returned with a pair of pliers. He broke into a sweat as he attacked the lock's loop, twisting this way and that while I stood impassively along with the band members observing his progress. Another equivalence in cultural comparators, I thought: there are always at least three men supervising another's work when any manual labour takes place. Hélène's head popped out from around her door, curious at all the commotion, and I figured I'd try my hand as dad's face had turned crimson.

"Let me have a go." My attempts only resulted in a second red face on the landing. Tea Cosy took my vermillion flush as the signal to offer his services, the net result being three scarlet faces. The lute player repeated his boss's efforts, but the other two band members weren't going to lose their cool and made no offer of help. It was back to dad's turn and he grimaced and uttered something as he twisted the lock. It cracked, the lock's body slipping from the loop, and he was able to twist it free from the door hoop. We cheered rather more than the occasion deserved and dad held up lock's broken pieces with the stance of a victorious gladiator.

"Dhanyabad. That deserves a drink, I think!" We decamped and celebrated with a round back in the kitchen. It was the signal for the carousing to take off. I bid my workmates goodnight once more and, back in my room, I nestled into my sleeping bag to contemplate what would make an appropriate soundtrack to end the day. There was only one choice I was going to make, starting at track eight of *Back in Black* by AC/DC. Forty-five minutes later, it was time for sleep; it was 9.30pm.

The morning broke bright through my window. I'd slept well compared to the previous two nights and I made my way to the toilet shack in good form. A Western Style option was absent, so I chose the nearest stall. My stomach was no more settled than the day before. I washed and made about 20 metres from the latrine towards the kitchen before feeling the urge to return. The result was the consistency of whipped cream. I cleansed again and this time made the kitchen door before stomach cramps forced me back again, with even less pleasant consequences.

As I held court in the khazi for a good half-hour, I contemplated that, if this continued, I'd have no strength for the trek and would need to take something for it. I resolved to track my daily motions and decide in the next couple of days on whether to medicate. On my eventual return to my room, I scribbled my morning's tally in my notebook; the *Diarrhoea Diaries* had been born.

After greeting Supermodel Mum with a namaste, I ordered an omelette and chapati for breakfast, anticipating something bland would calm my insides, but finished neither. Nausea and a numbing weakness beset me as I sipped on my milk tea. I decided I'd rest for an hour before setting off in the morning. I retired to the patio bench, hoping the combination of fresh air, sucrose and caffeine would revive me. Hélène surfaced, took her breakfast, returned fully laden and was bidding me farewell before I'd finished my cup. We arranged to meet at Goyem that evening. She checked where she was going on the app on her phone, re-holstered it in her side pocket and set off determinedly.

"Wrong way, Hélène, it's around that way out of the lodge."

The delay in the courtyard did me good and I made to pay my bill. There was no attempt at any hill-sharking as Supermodel Mum calculated my debts; she'd been fair in all her charges. I was delighted the first glass of dad's *rokha* had also been thrown in gratis. It topped a lovely stay at the lodge. There had been a lot more in the family's treatment of me than the conduct of a commercial transaction; I'd been welcomed as an honoured guest.

The air smelled of freshly mowed grass as I plodded uphill under the blue sky and somehow, the rocking movement from foot to foot settled my nausea. The way was gentler than the day before; the terraces had become more field-like in their breadth and width. Gentle eddies rippled their way across crops of a wheaten gold and tethered cows chewed the cud lazily in meadows terminating abruptly at imagined chasms. I was appreciative of the slow incline – it allowed me to ease out the knots in my thigh muscles gradually and my breathing to keep pace with the rise.

The rhythm was a lullaby into a meditative state, unworried by the potential travails of the trail or earlier biliousness. All I was focussed on was the next step as I steadily climbed the trail that wound around spurs in the charmed countryside. I raised my head from the bobbing of my boots to find I'd reached a cluster of large wooden buildings standing above the trail. I took these for the lodges at Sete, but the path passed through the woods beneath them and curled around the next hillside.

The way opened onto a broad hillside of terraces and across a flat traverse around a spur. As I rounded it, I was met with a small flight of stairs leading to a duo of imposing-looking stone buildings. The edifice explained itself as being a lodge in the village of Sete, Solukhumbu. As I was in no rush, I elected to take some early-morning tea to fortify myself for the next stretch.

I dropped my pack at the English beer garden-style table centred on the stone terrace between the two structures, thinking suntanned Italians sipping cappuccinos in their Ray-Bans and Fendi jackets wouldn't have looked out of place. The view could equally have been from the foothills of the Italian Alps.

The last vestiges of the early-morning chill had been burned off and I was able to strip down to my T-shirt to enjoy some sun while awaiting the collection of my order. A man was finishing off some washing-up in the building to my left, so I waited. He was taking his time, so I waited some more, slipping on my own sunglasses to enjoy the warmth on my face.

The man had finished his washing-up and was now hosing down the inside of his kitchen. Completing his deep clean, he turned to the stove to scrub an unseen stain. The service was in danger of becoming worse than in the Italian Alps. So I popped my head into the doorway, made my namaste greeting and asked for some black tea. The man came to the door and, with a gummy smile, reconfirmed my order. He disappeared around flank of the building which made me think maybe he *was* Italian, off to put in his Armani dentures and gather his fashionista friends to come around to have a laugh at my non-designer brand sunglasses. Ten minutes later, a lady with a toddler nipping at her heels bowled around the lodge's side.

"My father said you would like tea?"

"Yes please."

"We have very good coffee also. Espresso or café latte, if you like." Why wasn't I surprised by that?

"No, thank you, just some black tea please. A small pot." It was such a gorgeous spot, I'd decided to stay awhile. She returned shortly afterwards with a thermos and a cup and saucer in a delicate china. She gathered the hose from the kitchen and sang to her child as she watered the flowers in the concrete planters along the terrace wall. Birdsong and a rustling of the trees were the only sounds above the intermittent gush of water from the pipe. It was another spot where it would have been easy to idle away the entire day. My compromise was to spend an hour there before heading on.

The sun was high in the sky as I trudged up the steep ascent from Sete. The route passed through fields that progressively became ever narrower terraces. Without shade or the fast-flowing streams of the descent from Bhandar to replenish the LifeStraw I was wary of the previous day's dehydration. I was glad I'd consumed the entire small pot and, for a change, my bladder wasn't complaining about it.

I came across an isolated farmhouse where the trail was badly eroded into a narrow slit. Fiercely patrolling this cruddy gully was a dark brown bull which seemed disinclined to grant me right of way. I sat down; being in no rush, I could wait until the animal was on its way. The bull had other ideas and came roaring down at me. Before I could react, it had turned 90 degrees, pointing its hindquarters directly at face level and I decided that, if I'd had more time, I'd have taught Bully how to wipe. Satisfied my olfactory organs had been duly incensed, the bovine muck-spreader charged off in the direction of the farmhouse.

Beyond cow-dung canyon the trail narrowed between hedges of chest-high, bracken-like bushes. The day was windless and, in the late-morning sun, my walking technique became a crabbing dash between the dappled shade provided by solitary trees. Locals bemused by the sight of a stubbly European squatting in the centre of the thoroughfare skipped by, heading downhill on their daily business.

As I sat down on a ledge to rest, a violent rustling and loud growl from the foliage behind me warned me not to come any closer or risk attack. The snarl wasn't canine; the closest I could imagine was that of an enraged mountain lion. I scrambled across the path and looked to see what I'd disturbed. There was nothing in the hedge, but its leaves were somehow moving. Fear spurred me into action, and I ran upwards as far as I could before doubling over to catch my breath. On surveying my surroundings, I found I'd stopped in a gully where the path had been cut through a large hummock, the perfect spot for an animal ambush from above.

I raced out of the cleft to a flatter area with a better field of vision and saw the bracken tops move; something was stalking beneath. Breathless, I couldn't run again. I'd have to defend myself. I twisted my backpack to my front – I'd throw it at whatever came my way or use it to shield me from claws – retrieved my penknife and pulled out its blade. I knew it would be useless against anything bigger than a Singapura, but it made me feel better.

I saw no movement in the undergrowth. Whatever I'd irritated, or had foiled in its predation, had given the impression it had gone away, but there was no way to be sure. I caught my breath and, with an eerie calmness, padded up the trail in what my subconscious told me was the correct way to back away from big game, my practical experience in that discipline restricted to the viewing of a number of David Attenborough documentaries. I gripped the knife out in front of me and only retracted it once I'd reached cultivated fields. In direct contradiction to my trekking style, I didn't stop until Dagchu.

Dagchu was a lonesome lodge sitting atop a ridge approached via a score of steps. On reaching the place, I was glad to see the owner had provided a shaded area on its broad stone patio. Three terracotta circular table-and-chair combos sat underneath pristine yellow parasols bearing the Highland Ice Cream brand logo. The investment in plastic beach furniture seemed incongruous at practically 3,000 metres but as I collapsed, panting, at the middle table I was pleased it had been made. I was alone outside but I reckoned a group of porters was somewhere nearby, judging by the half-dozen wrapped bundles laying discarded on the terrace wall.

It took so long, with a deliberate effort, to calm my breathing that the owner had loped over to take my order of Ra-Ra Noodle soup before I'd fully recovered. I guessed he must have had the same dentist as the gentlemen at Sete but, in his case, was defiantly holding onto the one green-black incisor at the centre of his top gum.

I was still shaken by my encounter with the animal when the soup arrived. It was a spicy concoction of spinach and celery topped with a mass of perfectly steamed noodles. It was so good I made my way inside the lodge to order seconds and found that the porters were watching a quiz show on satellite TV. They seemed to know a lot of the answers and cat-called and gesticulated frustratedly when the contestants got it wrong. I settled back outside and waited for my second bowl, which arrived with fast-food-joint immediacy.

"Do you have wild animals here?"

"Many cow."

"No, I mean like tigers or leopards, raaar, raaar?" I made the motion of a clawing beast which was met by a low chuckle emanating from his one-peg smile.

"No tiger. No leopard," he explained and I felt stupid for asking, thinking of course there weren't going to be big predators in such a well populated and cultivated area but, on the other hand, I had been scared by something.

"Bear in forest. In valley." I doubted it was a bear from the sound I'd heard, but, bizarrely, given I was going to be solo-trekking for the next couple of weeks, it made me feel better to know there were things lurking in the foliage.

The game show must have finished as the porters trooped out of the lodge and lit up at the far table. They were a half-dozen 20-year-olds, hill-folk garbed in a motley of Premier League football shirts and skinny jeans. Their footwear was a mix-and-match of designer trainers and flip-flops. As they smoked, a couple of die-hard Chelsea fans shared an earpiece each from one of their phones and bounced in musical appreciation. They were still bopping when I started my second cup of post-noodle tea and the first Frank Lampard wandered by.

"What are you listening to?"

"Budi. Nepal music. V-e-r-y cool." I wasn't sure if Budi was the name of the artist or the genre.

"Can I listen?" He handed me over his phone, his face contorted into a dismissive smirk that said this old fossil isn't going to get it. I pulled the Nano and its earphones out from my pack.

"What's that?" He pointed at the Nano.

"It's like your phone, but only for music. It's old technology now but still works. It's great for the mountains coz it doesn't weigh anything. Have a try." I handed it over and he chortled as he tested the weight in the palm of his hand. I jacked in my earpieces and hit play on Budi. It was a light rap over a plucked ukulele providing the beat, with a bowed violin in counterpoint. The closest artist to whom I could relate the sound was Manu Chao, in some of his slower songs, but the beat and style were evocative of Puerto Rican Reggaeton. I found it beyond catchy and was singing along to the chorus in Nepali by the third time it came around.

"That's really good. Is all Budi's stuff like this?" Frankie's guffaw said it all. He'd spotted this relic wasn't hip from a mile away.

"*Budi* is song. Singer is Nepali man. V-e-r-y cool Nepali man. Five Five Five."

"Five Five Five?"

"Five Five Five is man name. V-e-r-y cool. Look." He showed me the artist on the screen. It read 5:55.

"Ah. Five Fifty-Five or do you say it Five to Six?"

"Five Five Five. Real name Chirag Khadka. V-e-r-y cool man. Nepali rap man."

"I think it's cool as well. You like rap music?"

"Yeah, man. Me an' ma' hommies hang to da gangsta!" He laughed again as he slouched his language into a perfect imitation of Dr. Dre. The dual hand signals came with it for good measure.

"If you like rap, I have some stuff on the Nano that you might like. Stuff from all over. Let me select it for you." He plugged his headphones in, and I started with what I estimated was safe ground.

"V-e-r-y cool. Famous man in Nepal. Gangsta man." His head bobbed to *California Love* by 2Pac.

"Mmmm ... no know this. I like. Cool, man." I'd switched to *Regulate* by Warren G. and reckoned it time to mix it up.

"No sing English. What?"

"French."

"V-e-r-y nice, cool man. I like dance." He tapped his toes to *Je Danse le Mia* by IAM. I moved it on.

"French?"

"This one is Spanish."

"No like. Slow, like old man." It was *A Lo Cubano* by Orishas.

"Okay. What about something more upbeat? This guy is the most popular rapper in the UK at the moment."

"Urghh ... bad. No cool. UK rap no good." A pithy assessment of a blast of *Big for Your Boots* by Stormzy.

"You don't like Stormzy? I guess Grime hasn't crossed over to Nepal yet?"

"No like Stormzy Grime. I show friend Nano?"

"Sure. I have some other rap stuff if you want to listen with your friend? I can put on some Puerto Rican reggaeton on if you like?"

"Reggaeton?" He looked at me quizzically.

"Yeah. You know Daddy Yankee?" He shook his head.

"It's a bit like Five Five Five but in Spanish. Want to give it a go?"

"Yeah. Dat be cool, man." Dre was back and I set him up with some Tego Calderon, but it didn't meet with his approval.

"*Budi* better, more cool."

"Fair enough. What about some other rap then? Do you like Snoop Dogg?"

"Yeah. Cool. Snoopy Dogg." He took the Nano over to Lamps Number Two and the rest of the entourage of soccer pin-ups. The Nano was evidently cool, but the music had a mixed reception. I gathered the crew must have been using an obscure version of Newari because, even with my advanced knowledge of Nepali, I couldn't make out the details of the dialogue. Their conversational drift wasn't hard to discern, though – it was the friendly dismissal of each other's musical tastes between good mates.

"Snoopy Dogg is rubbish," stated Sergio Aguero.

"He's better than Biggie Smalls and the rest of that East Coast rubbish you listen to," countered Frank Lampard Number Two.

"They're both crap. The original stuff like NWA is the best," interjected Steven Gerrard.

"Come on. You can't dance to rap. It's all garbage, that stuff. Now funk, that is real music. Check out Prince," suggested Romelu Lukaku.

"It's all derivative. It all came from the Beatles and the Stones. In turn, their influences were the blues inspired artists of the fifties, like Chuck Berry and Muddy Waters, who in turn plagiarised their licks from the pre-war delta and Chicago blues. Can't you appreciate the *oeuvre* of Son House or Robert Johnson? For real music, you need to look at the creative heyday of the late sixties. Sergeant Pepper, now there's a paragon of musical excellence written by artists at the peak of their powers, played on real instruments and recorded in one take. Halcyon days," posited Harry Kane.

"Shut up ..." It went on until Frankie L. Number One returned the Nano. Lunchtime was up, and it was time to heft their loads.

"Thank you. Where are you headed to?"

"We are going to Bhandar. Carry trekker gear from Lukla. Climber shoes."

"That is a heavy load, by the looks of it. How much are you porting?"

"Forty-five kilo."

"Wow! You're kidding? That's too much."

"No, is load for porter. We strong."

"I believe it. Well, watch out down there. As I came up there was some kind of animal in the bushes."

He didn't believe me, but nodded and gave me another Compton Crib sign before heading back to his workmates. Cigarettes were stubbed out and, in quick succession, they secured the loads around their foreheads and disappeared down the steps. I could still hear the music banter reverberating up the hillside five minutes later and gauged it was time to move on myself.

The trail followed the top of a wall extending from the patio, five minutes later spilling out onto a dirt road seeming to start as the forecourt of a small lodge that looked abandoned. I was confused because the guidebook hadn't mentioned a road on this section. It took me a few seconds to spot the blue painted arrow across the road, pointing up into a rhododendron forest at the dead centre of the slope. It signalled the road construction was newer than my guidebook.

The way through the forest became more difficult as the path wound further inside. A number of trees had been felled or disturbed by the road-building and blocked the path. It became hard going, clambering over the fallen logs and through and under semi-collapsed trees. Thirty minutes after entering the trees, the trail became a vertical climb of 10 metres which topped out back onto the road. It had switch-backed up and around the hill to meet the more direct pedestrian route.

I crossed the road and sat on another blue painted rock indicating a steep climb back into the woods. The rock climbing had taken its toll and I sat there panting like a greyhound at the end of a race, estimating I must now have reached 3,000 metres, the start of the altitude sickness zone. I adjudged the construction was going to prove a gentler walk up to Goyem, if the trail through the forest was going to be a repeat of the previous section, so I ignored the blue arrow and set off up the road.

I hadn't seen anyone since leaving Dagchu. The only sounds above the bird calls became my breathing and the shuffle of my boots. Mentally, I was resigned to another hard slog to reach my destination but, somehow, the negative thoughts about chest pains and fatigue disappeared. My progress became autonomic, as if my conscious told to take a backseat and my senses to grab the wheel. Goose-bumps prickled with the momentary chill of a breeze running down my exposed forearms. Powder dusted my tongue with every unambiguous breath. The fetid rot of fallen boles oozed from the forest. A hundred plumed birds chattered and whooped in the branches. My boots scrunched fresh gravel and skittered dislodged pebbles. Everything was lucid, but without a thought.

I'd have continued upwards in my meditative state but something residual in my programming told me to take stock. I'd reached the next blue arrow without stopping, not conscious of resting. Part of the reason I'd wanted to do the trek was to experience that subconscious state where I could cast off my neuroses from back home, any worry about the trail ahead, and enjoy what I was doing in that moment. I looked back down the road that had butchered its way through the forest and thought it ironic my first taste of that sensation had been on such a mechanically excavated part of the trek. One which I hadn't known to exist or expected to take. I'd happily take it, though.

I hadn't considered I'd dawdled at Sete and Dagchu, as I'd enjoyed my time at both for different reasons, but it meant the hour was getting late. I took the blue arrow through the forest, thinking it would be a quicker route to Goyem. The forest was primal now, the way snaking between ancient trees draped in mosses. The sunshine of the road was replaced with a grey murk and, beyond the deep greens of the immediate, only shadows of the trees ahead could be seen.

I broke out of the gloom onto the hillside. In a crag-side recess were the first people I'd seen since Dagchu; a mother and her infant daughter, clad in rags, standing ahead of a pitiful clapboard shanty half collapsed. There was nowhere for crops to grow at this altitude and the forest had been mutilated, so I couldn't comprehend how they were able to eke out a living in this place. They looked shocked to see me, bidding me a namaste as I passed them. It was the first time I'd received the greeting without the intonation rising at the end. It made me realise how cheerful the greeting was in its usual form, not uttered in the forlorn way by these poor folks.

I felt the same frustration as I had at the Tridevi Marg arcade; the sight was pitiful but what was I to do? This wasn't my destination; my tourist rupees would go to the lodge owner further up the hill. Grappling with the reality I couldn't help everyone along the way, I carried on trying to dispel my unease at probably reinforcing the inequalities in the area.

The murk I'd first encountered in the forest had now become a low cloud that spread across the entire mountainside. For the first time since leaving Shivalaya I donned the Rab. The path widened out and I was back on a section of newly cut road. I trudged into the white mist, the silhouette of an abandoned bulldozer leaning into several mounds of gravel gradually emerging. I climbed a small hillock and beyond the machine, the shrouded outline of a building emerged.

I descended, squeezing between the machine's side and the slippery gravel where my boots hit much firmer ground. I was on a tennis-court sized patio; a drystone building was to my left and a long wooden cabin ahead of me. Confusingly, the drystone's signage declared it as 'The Tashi Delek Restaurant and Lodge Goyom'; the cabin as a cheese shop and 'The Lamjura Pass Himalayan Lodge and Restaurant'. I was worried that, if I was at the latter, I'd overshot my rendezvous with Hélène, so I hobbled towards the former, determined to find out. The guidebook had indicated Goyem was around a three-hour trek from my start point. Four-and-a-half hours after leaving Chhimbu, I'd possibly arrived.

Goyem to Junbesi

I headed to the clapboard cabin's open door on finding the Tashi Delek locked. Three thousand metres lower, I'd have assumed it made from driftwood. The roof was a monochrome of two-by-fours nailed from its apex. It was as if a blindfolded cyclops had played a giant Steinway keyboard with hammers. A man in a charcoal grey fleece, puckered black fez and matching face-wrap greeted me at the door. The rhythmic half folding of his pink flip-flops against the sooty floorboards spoiled his otherwise sinister appearance. He slipped down his mask to reveal a middle-aged man who'd evidently tried several false starts at a goatee beard.

"Room?" he queried. A fair price was agreed in a matter of seconds as he seemed disinclined to bother with haggling. A lady garbed in traditional Sherpa clothing was summoned from the dark inside to show me the facilities. We walked back across the plaza to the drystone building, her stooped gait express compared to mine. I caught her up at the entry to the lodging area, where 'Room' was daubed in white on the lintel. The door was the shade of Rajasthan blue that decorated the lodges, complete with white panels and a flag with prominent hammer and sickle sharpied black on one of the squares. An industrial padlock secured it. It appeared the sense of collective didn't extend to unfettered access for the local proles, then.

Inside, there was a sense of money having been well spent and the sleeping quarters being well cared for. Several sturdy, solid wood doors led to rooms off a central corridor. I was thankful to see each came with a padlock dangling from a hoop. The smell of fresh sawdust gave away the recently completed repairs to the balustrade leading up to the first floor. The proffered room's air held a faint tang of what I guessed was nail polish. Its construction was in the same fashion as the corridor, the oak-coloured wood panelling's polish mirroring the light from a single bulb.

"This is great. Can I take some tea now?" She nodded, so I dropped my bag, secured the room and accompanied her back to the cabin. The man with the tassel-lacking fez still lounged in the doorway. He sprang back as the lady bustled back into the restaurant, issuing him a sharp rebuke as she passed. I offered him an apologetic smile as I dipped my head through the door. The mountain air's sharpness was replaced by the smoky charcoal fragrance of incense diffusing the humidity of overboiled rice.

The cabin's interior was split into three parts. To my right was a hearth that dominated the end of the wall. It constituted part of the cooking equipment, complemented to its right by a two-ring gas plate. Framing a copper sink were shelves of cups and saucers, pots and pans and tin plates stacked with an obsessive-compulsive precision and, above, charred, cast iron pans which chandeliered out from hooks and nails. The arrangement had the perfection any aspirant rustic kitchen designer would hope to emulate.

The afternoon light shone amber through bottles of oil on a shelf bisecting the window. On a battered table next to a mortar of freshly ground cumin glinted rows of spice jars marshalled by height. The more I took in the clearer it became the lady liked to keep her galley ship-shape. The room's middle third led from a table across from the hearth, the dining area. A low wooden counter cordoned off the last third, which had the makings of an Old West General Store. Four powdery characters cradled Everest Beers facing the entrance.

"Namaste," I called to them. The greeting and steepled hand signal were returned, followed by the raising of beers. I took the table nearest the hearth and addressed the man in the fez.

"Is this the Tashi Delek Restaurant or the Lamjura Pass Himalayan Lodge, please? There are two signs outside."

"It is the Tashi Delek. Lamjura is at the pass. You want a drink?" A tin cup dangled from his hand as he headed over to the gas stove to refill it from the pan.

"Rokha?"

"You know rokha? I have the best rokha here." He beamed.

"Yes, I tried it in Chhimbu. Not now, thanks, just some tea, please." At that, he shot a line of Nepali over at the lady. Her rebuke filled the air before he started his next sentence. She fixed him with a stare that said she already had it covered, how could he even think to ask such an imbecilic question and how dare he talk to her like that. They were clearly man and wife.

"Where did you come from today?"

"Chhimbu."

"Only Chhimbu? You walk very slowly." His face told me he was genuinely taken aback by my lack of progress before he took a first sip from his cup and grimace-smiled.

"Yes. I know. I'm in no rush, so it's no problem. Has a young Belgian girl made it here yet? I was supposed to meet her here."

"No Belgian girl today. Many Germans."

"Oh, okay, thanks. Is this the only lodge at Goyem?"

"Yes. Next lodge is at Lamjura La. Another 200 metres high." He swallowed a gulp this time. I thought Hélène must have decided to carry on. I wouldn't have missed her at any of the teahouses along the trail and, at my ponderous speed, I couldn't have overtaken her, so she must have been ahead. It was only 2.30pm so there was plenty of trekking daylight left. She could've decided to make for the pass or even head to Junbesi. 'Ah well, not the first time I've been stood up for a date,' I thought.

"Are you guys staying here?" I attempted to start some small talk with the four beer-sippers but was only met by blank stares.

"No English. They don't stay here. They work on the road building. I am boss."

"Is the bulldozer outside being used to make the road?"

"Yes. Has flat tyre. We are fixing it now." He swigged the last of his cup and half raised it in congratulation. The gang of four saluted him back and took their own slurps of beer. The communist symbology wasn't a legacy reminder of the civil war, then. It was a statement of the ideology being aggressively pursued by the local proletariat reflected in their work ethic. I imagined Fez as the crew boss reporting on the day's progress to the local politruk at the Congress of People's Deputies in Kathmandu.

'Report, comrade Fez!'

'We are on plan to complete the primary objective of the People's Supreme Soviet, comrade commissar! I am proud to have been given the honour of leading the Goyem brigade in the pinnacle of achievement for our glorious leader's five-year plan. I can report as of today we are broadly on schedule to complete the road to Lukla on time, comrade commissar!'

'*Broadly* on time, comrade Fez? You have reported you have been *broadly* on time for the last three weeks but have only completed 100 metres of road!'

'Yes, but what a road we have made, comrade! It will live in the memory of the people for a thousand generations.'

'Quite. Report on the dimensions of the road completed today!'

'Regrettably, comrade commissar, I must report today's progress stalled. The inferior imperialist machine foisted upon us by those central office apparatchiks has suffered yet another breakdown. Comrade crew are toiling with the utmost haste to repair the latest deficiencies we have found with the earth-mover's capitalist design.'

'Yes, I appreciate the Japanese engineering is sub-standard. Your daily reports of mechanical failure have been reported to the congress and will be addressed. Report on time to repair, comrade Fez?'

'As soon as possible, comrade. Unfortunately, a bourgeois interloper has arrived. He insists we take refreshment with him, hampering progress. As you are aware, comrade commissar, we are obliged to follow supreme soviet diktat number one. All Nepali socialist workers must ensure maximum capitalist dollars are secured from the western bourgeoisie trekkers to fund the next stage of our glorious Bolshevik revolution. We must carry out this duty, no matter how distasteful the task may be for our acclaimed workers.'

'Of course, comrade Fez, carry on. I look forward to your report tomorrow.'

My tea arrived and I elected to leave Fez and the Marxist construction crew to their own devices inside, taking my small pot onto the terrace. The air was brisk, but I was warm enough under my coat. As I cooled down properly from the trek, I began to feel the effects of altitude. My exertion was no more than lifting the steaming cup of excellent tea, but required taking in longer breaths.

I wanted to find out how much more air I needed in my lungs to feel comfortable at this altitude and what was the best technique to achieve that, so experimented with my breathing. Longer breaths and deeper breaths alternated with longer and deeper breaths. Within the silence of the clouds that shrouded the hill, I was soon focused on nothing more than the appearance of the vapour I expelled, entering a daydream-like state.

An hour passed before my reverie was interrupted by a dog that came bounding out from the cabin. He wasn't a pedigree breed but was magnificent compared to the other raw-boned specimens I'd encountered in the villages along the way. His mix was something between a Tibetan Mastiff, Bernese and wolf. Fez flip-flopped across the patio, called him over and chained him to the wall to keep lookout. A smirk of unreasonable satisfaction spread across my face; in my mind that translated to Fez being worried about me doing a runner.

It was barely four o'clock, a couple of hours until dinner. I didn't fancy getting involved with the drinking in the lodge, so I made my apologies to everyone when I returned the drained small pot. Back in my room, my breath condensed on the windows as I wiggled to get warm within my sleeping bag and my attention was drawn to the choice of posters selected to keep me company. One appeared to be an advert for skin cream in which, chosen as its exemplar, was a lady from the subcontinent who was a young Phoebe Cates' doppelganger. The other was of a cascade of over-fluffed toy bunny rabbits in various unnatural hues. From a point in the distance, they hopped along a yellow brick road and congregated around the bases of purple trees. I wondered what was going through the owner's mind when she settled on this surreal combination for the interior décor, coming up with the theory she wanted to convey a subliminal environmental message which said this is what happens to lab animals when they've been used to test Phoebe's skin cream.

My jiggling under the gaze of psychedelic cottontails caused the zip to burst on my sleeping bag. The next hour was spent in failed attempts to try to get the slider's jaws aligned with the bottom teeth on the chain and to bend the bottom stop back into position to keep the mechanism in place. I reached that state where each fruitless effort comes with an increased return in frustration and settled on living with the problem for one night. But I was going to have a lot of cold nights if I couldn't fasten my bag, so I decided that, as Junbesi was my next stop and a much bigger settlement, I'd try to find some sort of tailoring skills there and have the zip repaired.

I wrapped the Ajungilak around me, trapping the broken seal underneath and balancing the Kindle against the wall. I was a recent convert to the device, having always resisted its lure, adopting the stance of a technological Luddite. The look and feel of a real book was better – you could smell it, bend it and even spill a small pot on it, and it would recover. My argument extended to the eye strain being unbearable compared to real paper and if real books were good enough for Shakespeare, they were good enough for me, and so on.

My previous long-distance walks, though, had taught me one thing over all others: the primacy of weight reduction, including that of the trekker as well as the pack. Having failed miserably in any reduction in my own BMI in preparing for the trek, the weight of my burden was pre-eminent. The five or six novels I would potentially read over five weeks were going to add a lot of unnecessary kilos to my load. My 'TOO YOUNG' partner had thoughtfully pre-empted this problem by buying me the Kindle as a birthday present. It also gave her an opportunity to force me to admit I'd been wrong all along and my clinging adherence to Gutenbergian technology was as flawed as my loyalty to my CDs and the Nano.

My reading matter was *Oryx and Crake* by Margaret Atwood. I'd never read any of her novels so wasn't sure what to expect. An hour-and-a-half later, I'd been so engrossed in the book that I was only made aware sunset had passed by the light being extinguished. I could've read on by the Kindle's light, I wryly discovered, but the power cut reminded me of the time – I was 30 minutes late for dinner.

As I pulled on my coat, the Powercap illuminated a Mephistophelean grin on Phoebe's face. The drop in temperature outside and the dog's slobbered barking as he strained against the chain hurried me across the courtyard. I entered the doorway to the lodge to see Fez lying flat on his back under a blanket on the bench opposite, his eyes closed. On my first step inside, he rose with the smoothness of a Swiss Army knife unlocking to a right angle and opened his eyes. I was reminded of a vampire an unwitting pathologist had on a gurney behind him ahead of an autopsy.

"Good evening," he greeted me. I was grateful he didn't pronounce it in a Christopher Lee accent.

"Namaste. Sorry I'm late," I replied, doubly grateful he chose to spare me 'We were expecting you'. His Leninist crew had departed, so our company was completed by his wife and daughter. Preternaturally pretty, she was dressed in much more contemporary clothing than her parents. Black sweater, black jeans and black boots completed her look of bloodsucker in training or a Sherpa Goth.

"Would you like something to eat?"

"Yes please. Sorry I'm late. I'll have what you're having, please." As long as it wasn't Type O negative, I hoped. The fire in the hearth was roaring and I could see a dark mass of lentils bubbling in the pot over its heart.

"Dhal baat curry. You want spicy pickle?" I did. I nodded, and Fez offered me the place by the hearth. I was incredibly grateful, not only because I was cold but also because I understood this an honour in Nepali culture. I sat myself near the fire, pleased I'd done it with considerably more ease than at my last couple of dinner dates. My legs were stiff but not seized; they were becoming accustomed to what was being asked of them.

The dhal baat curry was quick in arriving. The curry element had been achieved by the addition of chilli-spiced potatoes as a side dish. I polished off my first plate and was offered more, as per the custom, my hosts seeming more than confident I wouldn't be able to break the restaurant's unlimited refills policy. They were correct in that; in the end, I could only manage three helpings of lentils and two each of rice and potatoes. As the food digested, I started to feel bloated so asked for a mint tea to wash things down and settle my stomach. Fez passed me over my drink.

"You trek alone?" Fez seemed none the worse for his afternoon session with the Trotskyite crew.

"Yes. I was planning on meeting someone here tonight and trekking together tomorrow, but she must have gone by."

"Not good to trek alone. Anything can happen to you and no-one would know."

"I've trekked alone before and it was fine."

"But what if you have a problem? If you get sick who will bring you down the mountain?"

"I'm hoping not to get so sick that I can't bring myself down."

"What if you fall down cliff from the trail? If you have guide or porter, they can help you." My tumbles came to mind.

"Yes, that's a good point. I'd hope that, if I'd an accident, people would hear me calling and would come help."

"What if you fall and hurt head very bad? Can't talk? No-one knows you are there? Easy to die."

"Yes. I hope I don't fall, then."

"What if bad man steals from you? No-one can help stop him."

"Yes, but Nepal is a safe country. I know some people have been mugged and some killed but it is really rare that anything happens."

"Yes, but he can kill you."

"There are bad people everywhere, I guess."

"Lots of Germans here. Last night camp at Lamjura pass. Twenty people. They have guide and porters. Go to EBC. You catch guide and ask to trek with them. They help you if have a problem."

"Okay, I will," I replied, anxious to end the lecture, but it was a white lie. I'd no intention of trekking with a big group. I was aware of the risks pointed out by Fez before I chose to trek solo. And, as the day had brought my first trance-like experience of the trip, which I knew would be harder to fall into within the confines of group-trekking, I wasn't going to give that up.

I changed the subject to the excellence of his wife's cooking and how good the mint tea was, followed by a conversation about the new road he was working on. He was pleased with the immediate work it provided for himself and his gang. He was also encouraged by the prospect of future economic development for the area.

"Road will bring trekkers. Many trekkers will come from Kathmandu and Lukla and stay on new road. Too much travel from Kathmandu for one day, so bring good business. Trekker stay here or at Phaplu, spend a lot money. Can bring many big things on truck, wash machine."

"Yes, but won't you lose trekkers like me from Jiri or Shivalaya who want to walk on the old trails? Nobody wants to walk on dirt roads all the way from Jiri."

"There is not lot trekker now. You only guest today. Yesterday Germans stay at Lamjura, no-one here. Day before, no-one stay. Not much money. New road best for local people. If many trekker use road, government make road from Kathmandu better all way."

"I guess so. The road to Jiri was pretty bad."

"Road wash away in monsoon. Charikot road very bad. Lot buses fall every year. Many people die. Concrete road best. Not many bus fall from concrete road." I understood his point of view and it was hard to argue with it. Although I'd taken advantage of the lesser gradient of the road earlier, I hoped it wouldn't obliterate the ancient trail's entire route in the same way it had hacked its way through the forest below Goyem. From what Fez had said, though, I wasn't optimistic the Nepali government and the locals could realise the benefits of both the new road and of retaining something of the ancient ways so trekkers like myself would keep coming.

The conversation moved on to the differences between Nepal and the UK in terms of living standards, food and what I did for a living. After an hour, the subjects for discussion became less obvious and the chat petered out, so it was time for bed. I thanked my hosts and bid them a good night.

Given the outside temperature, I was thankful the drystone lodge had an integral toilet room. It lay at the corridor's end, unusual in that its door led to a space building's full width. It was about a metre-and-a-half wide with half-length windows fitted at each end. It seemed the space was mainly used for the storage of potatoes, semi-rusted double-handled saws and other tree-felling equipment.

The privy itself was situated a step down in a half hexagon of polished wood and glass. It wasn't Western Style. A concrete square had been designed to have four grooves running from each corner to the aperture in the middle. Unfortunately, it was easy to distinguish the relevant blueprints hadn't been followed to the letter during construction; two grooves actually ran uphill to the hole from their respective corners. The place spoke of the user needing to do their business in a conservatory where the chances of hitting the target were no better than 50-50.

I was happy the odds had tipped in my favour on my first visit and thinking 'Beginner's luck', I returned to my room, braved the chill in my smalls and wrapped the sleeping bag under me. As I warmed up, I mused on the evening's musical choice. I'd been inspired by the meeting with the Gangsta porters at Dagchu, so I chose *Alliance Ethnik, Le Best of* to listen to. The power failed again; no matter, I reckoned, I'd listen in the dark and played the album from track one. The mix of styles and multilingualism echoed what I'd heard by 5:55 and an hour later, it was time for sleep; it was 10pm.

I'd hardly had time to wrap the headphones around the Nano when I heard a heavy vehicle's gearbox being thrashed. A vehicle skidded to a halt on gravel, doors were slammed, footsteps skittered, calls whooped, and a greeting screamed from the cabin in response. There was shuffling followed by the unmistakable report of a glass bottle smashed on stone. The dog responded with an aggressive bark. I wondered who could have come visiting. The lodge was an unlikely place for a frat party.

A torchlight beam momentarily swept in through the window, partly illuminating Phoebe's diabolic smirk. It was followed swiftly by another before the silhouette of the torch's bearer was briefly at the pane. The lodge's front door rattled open, there were footsteps and the slap of flat palms on the wooden panelling outside my door, accompanied by a shrieking which transformed my initial bemusement into alarm. The picture of drunken frat boys I'd formed in my mind had been replaced by a collage of every murderous horror-movie freak I'd ever seen. The image shifted to a pickup having rolled up and out of the flat back had jumped the Nepali version of the hillbillies from *Deliverance*. There would be no reason for anyone to be here other than to rob me or do worse.

I told myself I was being paranoid and tried to calm down, the rational side of my brain telling me I was safe here. Trekking and trekkers were the lifeblood of this lodge. There may be some quick money to be made by the theft and murder of one solo trekker, but the damage to the area's reputation would be unrecoverable. Logic said it was better to keep a steady trade going, but I figured desperate people didn't think logically.

The irrational side told me Fez had dispatched his crew downhill in the afternoon to sober up and gather what they needed to do me in when they returned after dark. They had shared a bottle of rot-gut whisky to provide the Dutch courage for the job before cutting the power. They'd briefly confirmed their victim was where they wanted him before their next task of fetching the dismemberment equipment from the storeroom. And they had all angles covered – if I escaped, they'd let loose the vicious hellhound from its chain to track me down. Fez's words from earlier reverberated repeatedly in my head.

'*Anything* can happen to you and *no-one* would know.'

The door at the corridor's end slammed. I was now standing by my door, listening intently for their next move. Footsteps marched along the hall and the front door was slammed shut. Reason told me it was a drunk emptying his bladder; irrationality told me Leatherface had gathered a corroded double handled-saw and was carting it to the cabin to sharpen its rip teeth.

There was a second of high-spirited yelling at the front door before a diminishing hubbub. It sounded like the murderous band had retreated to the cabin. I knew my wild imagination needed checking and calmed myself. It was Fez's crapulous construction crew returning uphill with a crate of something to finish their afternoon drinking session. He'd told them they could all crash in the lodge; there was only one guest so there was plenty of room. They'd even tried to encourage the party-pooper out of his cold room and over to the warm cabin to have a schwally or two. The power had gone out again so what was he doing in the dark anyway?

My shivering told me I needed to return to the sleeping bag's warmth, where I sat bolt upright, uneasy at what had happened. My thoughts focussed on that I was alone and no-one knew I was here. I'd told my family I'd send a message home every couple of days or so because contact would be erratic in the foothills. So, if I disappeared, it would be likely a week would pass without any action being taken. An unfamiliar sense of vulnerability now nagged at me.

My earlier statements to Fez weren't bravado; I'd never factored wilful harm-doers into my thinking about the trek. Now my head was fully occupied with exactly that. Much had been made at home of the trip being an adventure, but I'd never considered I'd ever be in real peril, certainly not from the hill people. My Annapurna trek had taught me I was hiking through some of the most civilised countryside on Earth and I'd run far more risk of harm if I ventured into some of Glasgow's rougher parts. On the other hand, that relative safety rested entirely on the mores of the country I was walking through. If the local folks suddenly decided *en masse* trekkers were fair game, I wouldn't stand a chance.

My ruminations didn't quell the disquiet and I recognised sleep wasn't coming anytime soon. I couldn't risk the Nano as I wouldn't hear Jigsaw coming and so concluded that, if I was going to become a victim I should at least be a well-read one. I opened the Kindle again and returned to the story. Its premise was based on the last man standing on Earth. He's exhausted, lonely and feels exposed by his circumstances. He's among beings with whom he can only communicate to a limited extent. I couldn't help thinking it strange that from all the books on the Kindle, I'd chosen that one, then.

There was nothing more than the occasional muted yell from the cabin to disturb me as I took in the story, reading until one in the morning. Whatever the band of villains had been doing in the cabin was over and I heard the slow scuffle of footsteps on stone drawing nearer. The dog vented its disapproval at whoever was on the courtyard before the front door banged back on its hinges and I knew they were outside in the corridor. There was the stomp of boots climbing stairs, more doors slamming, silence and snoring from across the lobby. The party-goers had burned themselves out and, after the assurance of 30 minutes of drunken stertor, I gauged I could rest.

I had, at best, a night of broken sleep. I awakened several times before I could descend into the deep sleep of dreams. The light of morning came through the window both too soon and not soon enough. I knew I wouldn't shake off any more of the tiredness from lying in my sleeping bag so decided to make a start to the day. I was bloated and had stomach cramps, so needed to visit the toilet. Once again, I was pleased to manage the uphill camber. I recorded an entry in the *Diaries* that read a Type Six on the Bristol stool chart. If things didn't improve by the same time tomorrow I'd take some medication.

Outside revealed the night to have been colder than I'd thought, the patio table and chairs coated with a thin layer of rime glistening in the morning sun. The verglas crunched satisfyingly as I left a line of boot-prints up to the cabin door and, inside, I found Mrs Fez busy tending the fire on her own. I hadn't eaten rice pudding for years, but it was on the menu, so I opted to have that for my breakfast. The sugary, milky, glutinous mess brought back fond memories; it was always a battle to skim some more of that special treat into my bowl at my grandmother's house when I was a boy. Mrs Fez's recipe was a rival for that, and I particularly enjoyed the burnt skin

My stomach didn't receive the meal as well as my taste buds. I forced myself to finish despite the cramps, hoping in vain the rice would solidify and ease the pain. After settling my more than fair bill, I hot-heeled it back to the crazy-golf hole WC. My second visit of the day registered a Type Seven in the *Diaries* and also recorded a six over par with the five buckets of water it needed to coax everything uphill into the hole.

I did feel better afterwards and started the trek. Fez's crew had the bulldozer jacked up and a wheel off, the machine tilted at a 45-degree angle.

"Morning, namaste."

"Morning, sir, did you sleep well?" Fez responded.

"It wasn't my best night's sleep, it sounded like there was a bit of a party going on last night," I replied but the comment didn't seem to register. The punctured wheel was propped up against the gravel mounds and I figured, by its size, it must have taken the entire crew to manhandle it off. There was no sign of a replacement.

"That looks like it would've been hard work to get off. Where's the other tyre?" Fez pointed to a ute stranded at the intersection with the road.

"Well, good luck. Thanks for the stay. Dhanyabad." He returned a namaste and I squeezed between him and the jack precariously balancing the earth-mover. The crew was now heaving the replacement wheel over the lip of the pickup that was rocking violently and I scuttled past, eager to avoid any chance of being pinned between it and the gravel mound.

There was no sign of anything apart from the fulvous road forming the trail, so I followed it upwards. A minute later, I was brought to a halt in eyeshot of the crew by an uncontrollable coughing which hacked up a puddle of white phlegm. I took this as the clean air gouging out the last of the crud from my lungs accrued in Kathmandu's smog.

The way up the road was gentle but, even with my newly scoured bronchus, I could feel the effects of being at over 3,000 metres. I told myself the first hour of the day was always the hardest, reasoning once everything warmed up and I fell into a rhythm the rest of the day would be easier.

The road skirted right before crossing back to the ridge's left. The morning was clear, and I got my first close-up view of snow-capped mountains between the trees to the left, the peaks looming beyond a forested cordillera striated by deep ravines. The road's powdery orange and grey dust had been cemented by the night's frost and I revelled with a schoolboy's glee, crushing the upstanding edges of caterpillar tracks between my boots where the hoar melted in the sun.

My game was interrupted by the drone of an engine heard over my left shoulder. I instinctively looked up but there was nothing where it should've been. My eye caught a movement on the horizontal – it was a twin-prop aircraft and I imagined the passengers could see me clearly through its portholes. The plane disappeared along the valley, followed by its thrum. The only sounds remaining were those of my crunching of the tyre tracks and the continuous orchestral warm-up of trills and chirrups from the forest.

The road rose above the tree-line into the full sun, where the frost had melted, and my game was over. Ahead was a straight section leading up to a cluster of buildings set in a hollow to the left. There was what appeared to be a lodge, with its bright blue painted roof just visible above the other structures. Three bungalows with the same piano-scape driftwood roofs as the cabin sat before it, their stonework plastered in orange. A small brick outhouse and a polythene-tented hothouse completed the complex.

I heard an engine behind me, this time deeper and less consistent. As I passed the heavily advertised Lamjura Pass Himalayan Lodge, I could see a bulldozer emerge from behind the corner where I'd stopped to let the aeroplane passengers take a good look at me. I walked on, wondering whether the road was going to take me all the way over and down the pass. My guidebook was only five years old but was already dated, with no mention of the road, and so I was anxious to confirm its directions of a steep descent down through forest weren't equally archaic.

The road ended shortly after the lodge in a turning circle and as I stepped onto a flagstone causeway, I could see Fez behind me. It appeared he was doing his morning rounds, one of his crew riding side-saddle against the cab. The machine's trunnions were fully elevated, the bucket angled horizontally and crammed with 30kg sacks. I could just make out an orange printed 'sugar' on one of them. As he drew up towards the lodge, a Sherpa lady came out to meet them, the bucket was lowered, and the crew member hefted the sacks over to the lodge. Fez and the lady enjoyed the contents of the small pot she'd brought over and balanced on the bulldozer's engine housing. I could see Fez was beginning to shrug off his socialist leanings and embrace the road's commercial opportunities; his local version of Amazon already doing very nice business.

The flagstones led through heather-like shrubs up to a bothy, a small, squarish mani and a chorten bedecked in prayer flags. I could just make out a figurine of Buddha reclining in the aperture in the Vase Filled with Treasure section above me. The whitewash of the stupa was weathered and down to bare brick in places, but the gold of the Umbrella of Protection and Heart-Mind shone brightly in the sun. I was pleased to have made the climb to the pass in such good time but was confused the path seemed to offer no way downwards.

The trail became more difficult after the chorten. The flagstone path was shaded, and my boots returned once again to crunching on frost. Its route was intercepted by diagonal thrusts of slippery rock which required a clamber across, with hands supporting uphill. It was then back into a jumble of a rock field. This messy arrangement didn't last long, and the path reappeared between a scrubby ribbon of rhododendrons, the trees half shading the beaten earth trail.

The soil was still frozen in the shadows but, above, my torso was in full sun and I resumed my sixth form pleasure of crunching the hoar beneath my tread while basking in the warmth above. The muscles in my legs moved fluidly. My breathing had regulated due to the gentle acclivity, the only other sound the slow swish of the rhododendrons swaying in the breeze. I was at 3,500 metres, in every sense and figuratively near heaven.

A tea house sat in a hollow immediately beneath what I now saw was the pass. The proprietor greeted me warmly but frowned when I declined his offer of a cuppa. Even with my sensibilities in that regard, it was too early to stop for tea. He told me I was the first to make the pass this morning and asked me if there were many trekkers following me up the trail. His frown became a grimace when I told him I hadn't met any Westerners since Chhimbu.

I scrambled up to the apex of the pass, which was decorated with a sign in both Sanskrit and English. The English version read 'Thanks for visit Likhu Peak Rural Municipality'. The Sanskrit version topped and tailed it in double the number of words. I'd no idea if it was equivalent or a local ordinance forbidding photography involving stuffed animals. I was confused by the new reference to Likhu Peak. Where was that?

Deciding to ignore any local bylaws, I unchained the Rabbid. Sliding on ice and with prayer flags cords whipping around we posed for selfies. I reattached the Rabbid and descended a narrow chute between two bothies into the forest across the pass.

The path corkscrewed through fragrant evergreens unlike those before the pass, the undisturbed specimens distributed in an ancient pattern. The track was steep and rough, with loose rubble making an ankle twist a hazard with every step, but the forest had insulated its floor from the worst of the frost. Only in deep shade lurked yet unthawed puddles and pockets of rime.

Fallen trunks and branches were common. I found myself straddled across blocking boles, clambering over and squeezing under collapsed trunks and cutting through matted gates of newly horizontal branches. My muscles fought against the uneven camber to maintain an even descent while keeping my backpack balanced and knees intact.

A mule skinner and his charges heading uphill were my first fellow trail-users of the day. As I sat on a grassy bank and let them by, I counted 15 donkeys carrying sacks similar to the ones that had been delivered by Fez lashed to their backs. I jumped to my feet as the last animal's tail passed by and my feet gave way. I grazed my arm as I tumbled before being stopped by the next twist in the corkscrew. I explored uphill for a cause while uttering the requisite number of profanities. I'd tipped a conglomerate of loose pebbles over and the underlying substrate had avalanched beneath it.

I laboriously unpacked my backpack to reach my first aid kit taking a mental note to keep it at the top from now on. My best at cleaning the wound was a gulp of water from the LifeStraw regurgitated onto my arm. I slathered on antiseptic cream to counter any nasties I'd spread in the process. After gathering myself, a little disconsolate, I carried on, vowing to wash the wound properly at the first running water I met.

My second trail-user encounter of the morning was also heading uphill. He wore a black and white flowered bandana above his wraparounds and extensive white whiskers, his one patch of exposed face crimson red and filmed with sweat. He was puffing like an Old West steam train as he dug his walking poles into the ground forcing himself up. He responded to my greeting with a namaste in a north American accent. He was in no mood to stop and chat and we crossed without a further word. I understood his reticence – struggling as he was, he wanted to maintain what momentum he had.

I stopped at a waterfall much lower down to bathe and disinfect my graze, finding myself in another perfect woodland setting. From a two-metre-high cliff, the falls dropped into a shaded pool, the source of a brook that careened its way between mossy boulders and twisted a splashing swirl through the trees. Cleaned, I climbed a small incline to the wood line's edge, marked by the ruins of a house. At least, I thought it had been a house – it could equally have been a byre or barn. It was hard to tell as only one wall had been left standing; purlins, chords and the battens of a roof lay scattered among the stones of the other collapsed walls. The place must have been one of the earthquake's unfortunate victims. Seeing it up close brought home to me the reality of that event; no-one could've gotten out alive.

Beyond the ruins, the valley broadened to a much happier view and the track now became a series of short stone steps between sections of laid flat rocks. A drystone wall bounded rich fields of long-stemmed grasses where cows were serenely grazing, and an occasional bovine would be hurried along the path to fresh pasture by its female owner. The houses were made of the same drystone construction as at Goyem but were much larger here. I passed through a clutch of dwellings centred around a massive boulder which was painted with mantras and where the trail split to either side.

I stopped at the village's water supply to refill my bottle, a wooden half-pipe issuing a steady stream of ice-cold water, and gazed back to where I'd come from. The view was similar to those I'd seen from the Number Four campsite in Yosemite; massive vertical cliffs led up from the forest directly to the pass. I was amazed by how far I'd already travelled that day and was glad I was tackling the trail from the direction of Shivalaya. The approach to the pass from this orientation was brutal.

I reached the outskirts of Tragdobuk by late morning, dhal baat time by the local clock, so decided to stop for some lunch. The walking had taken my mind off the stomach cramps from earlier but, as I sat down at a simple tea house, they resurfaced. I knew it had been a mistake on the first day not to eat at Deurali, but on this occasion reckoned my stomach wouldn't have been able to take anything. So I reasoned it better to take tea, calculating Junbesi wasn't far away, according to the guidebook, and I wasn't as fatigued as on other sections of the trek.

The lady brought me my cup and I played peek-a-boo with her grandchild behind the kitchen door as I drank. I'd miscalculated my thirst and needed a second cup but hadn't taken the small pot option. As I ordered my refill, the first trekker travelling in my direction stopped to take stock. He wore a contemporary turquoise running vest without sleeves, one-size-too-small vintage 1980s soccer shorts in a similar colour and black split-toe running shoes. His pack was compact, maybe half the size of mine, and he had dual walking poles. It wasn't his pseudo-Olympian outfit that drew my gaze, however, rather his most arresting feature, which was the port-wine birthmark on his forehead. It was a more perfect depiction of the hammer and sickle than the one on the Tashi Delek's door. I was staring at the

1950s summer camp version of Mikhail Gorbachev. A second later, my mind wandered back to Fez and I wondered if he'd been invited before my new comrade to explain how he was implementing the party leader's vision of glasnost.

"Namaste," he bid me, but there was no hint of Muscovy in his accent.

"Namaste. Where have you come from today?"

"Sete." I could tell from the intonation he was French.

"Wow, you walk really fast. Where are you headed?"

"Ringmo. If I go fast, I try for Trakshindu."

"That's hard core. I'm stopping at Junbesi. Trakshindu is another four hours, according to my guidebook, but I'm taking another 50 per cent on average above what it says, so maybe it's another six hours to Trakshindu. You could be getting there around when it gets dark. Are you sure you want to risk it?"

"Yes, zat is why I must hurry." And with a flick of his walking poles, he was off. He *was* fast and from the powder mist he lifted behind him, I thought I now knew the origin of the expression 'left for dust'. He was out of sight before I took another sip of tea and soon the clack-clack of his sticks was also out of earshot. The peek-a-boo kid was sent out to collect when I asked for the bill. I was happy to restart my plodding, thinking at his rate of knots Monsieur Gorbvitesse would be at Base Camp and back in Kathmandu before I reached Namche Bazaar, but at least I'd have seen something along the way.

The path widened onto a ruddy dirt road running high along the valley side and I consulted the guidebook again; it hadn't mentioned anything about this. Down below, I could see other paths and a more substantial rock or gravel trail on a riverbank. The map in the guidebook told me nothing of value to aid my navigation, so there was nothing for it but to plod on down the road and hope to meet someone to ask the way. The road now ascended to a corner cut into the cliff. No passers-by materialised to confirm my direction and it felt wrong the ancient packhorse route would follow this way. I hollered a "Junbesi" at a couple of farmers in the fields below; their response was to look up and walk on. At the corner, a yellow arrow had been painted on the cliff above. I fancied it wouldn't have looked out of place on the pilgrim route of the Camino de Santiago. But this was a long way from Galicia and, here, it could have meant anything.

I decided to risk where it directed, even though the path beneath the arrow looked hairy. The trail ran around the crag, the straight drop protected by a knee-high wall more broken than not. As I edged around the cliff, I was hugely relieved to see below me the path became a prolonged sandstone staircase. It baked in the midday sun. I was now sure this was the route and, better still, the drop was protected by an intact, waist-high drystone wall.

The staircase broke out to a path that coasted around the hillside halfway above the valley. It was now easy going and I reached a cobbled yard with well-tended evergreens providing shade, discovering it was the entrance to a monastery. I hoped it was the Tashi Thongmon Gompa as I wouldn't be far from my destination. I wasn't visiting so skirted around the sidewall to the front and, as I rounded a corner, my immediate reaction was: 'So this was where everybody has been hiding!'

A score of workmen were busy at renovations, with four men lifting a cross beam planned as the new lintel for the front gate. Other men were whitewashing the exterior walls and the chorten inside the grounds. I stopped and watched, fascinated by their way of working. Open pots of whiting were hoisted up by hemp ropes to the tops of bamboo scaffolding and daubed with an artist's precision onto the structures. There were no mechanical sounds; everything was done by hand. It looked like hard work. I moved on, content I was on holiday. Preoccupied as I was by their skill, a few steps later I nearly missed the mini yellow sign indicating the way to Junbesi was to take the steep stone steps down through the shrubbery on my right.

The steps were those which are neither one thing nor the other. Not a single flight, nor space for a full horizontal stride between them. Instead, it was one step down, a half-step shuffle, twist and down to the next step, the motion becoming increasingly hard on the knees.

As I descended into the shrubs, I could hear the chattering of children, although I could see nothing. I broke out of the bushes and the path ran down a stony ravine; ahead were groupings of four or five schoolchildren coming up the hill. Their regimented dress seemed out of place in the rustic setting. The girls sported blue-black tartan skirts and the boys grey shorts beneath their sky-blue jumpers. Hairstyles were shoulder-length bob for girls, buzz-cut for boys. The only concession to individuality was their backpacks; I spotted a Ben-

10, Dora the Explorer and Manchester United, judging the latter entirely inappropriate for *any* school. The number of namastes I issued that day multiplied by 100 as we crossed and, with my last greeting, the first lodges of Junbesi revealed themselves ahead.

The guidebook made a strong suggestion to stay at the 'Apple Orchard Guest House'. As I completed the staircase, I was thrilled to see I was in luck – it was one of the first buildings down to the left. It was only when I looked to my right, to see the 'Orchard Apple Guest House', and straight ahead for the 'New Apple Orchard Guest House', I realised the Nepali lodge owners were being canny again. The Apple Orchard wasn't going *carte blanche* to take all guidebook-guided custom. As I stepped down onto the town's main drag, it looked like every lodge in Junbesi was some flavour of Apple. I spied the 'Apple Orchard Lodge', 'Apple Lodge Hotel', 'Garden Apple Orchard Guest House' and 'Garden Apple Guest House'. Given the political tendencies in the district, I was half expecting a 'People's Revolutionary Republic Party of Junbesi Apple Orchard Guest House' and an alternate faction's 'People's Revolutionary Front of Junbesi Apple Orchard Guest House' but was left disappointed by their absence.

The choice was at once bewildering and straightforward. I chose something with an Apple in it. The guidebook had indicated Junbesi was around a four-and-a-half-hour trek from Goyem. Implausibly, I'd nearly kept pace with the author and, five hours after leaving the Tashi Delek, I'd arrived.

Junbesi to Nunthala

The Apple was built on a much grander scale than anything I'd encountered on the trek previously. The lodge was a recently whitewashed two-storey stone edifice in the traditional style, five olive-painted windows long by three wide. But, in my estimation, the timber bungalow extension, fitted with wrap-around PVC windows and forming a diner-kitchen, had failed in its endeavours to blend in.

A flagstone patio wrapped around the complex. Rectangular planters that bloomed with marigolds and precision sculpted shrubs were tastefully arranged around the perimeter. Entrance to the grounds was via a prayer wheelhouse that directed guests through the porch, an airlock to keep the cold out. As I opened the front door, I sensed the place was a cut above, by staying there I was going upmarket.

The vestibule was deserted. The aroma of dhal baat cooking drew me to the dining room and I called out a hopeful namaste, but it was met with no reply. Ten minutes later, a wee Sherpa lady came scuttling from the entrance's direction, carrying a plastic bucket in each hand, filled to the brim with potatoes. She took her new guest's patience nonchalantly, stopped momentarily, looked me up and down, sniffed and left through a door at the room's end. For some reason, I thought, was she thinking, 'Of all the Apple joints, in all the towns, in all the world, he walks into mine ...' when she clocked me?

Head poking back through the door, she opened formal trade negotiations with a price that would give a Russian oligarch cause to become a regular at the local pawnshop before joining me in guffawing at her ridiculous offer. My opening gambit in response was to point out her pricing strategy was unreflective of existing market conditions. She failed to concur, but as a special concession agreed to halve her original quote. Smelling blood, I pressed for a further discount of 30 per cent for being the day's first customer, but by her reaction, I'd pushed the game too far. Shaking her head, she led me into the kitchen.

The sight of four grandmothers chuckling while paring the spuds threw me for an instant; I couldn't fathom why they hadn't responded to my greeting earlier. It gave her time to retrieve the Guest House combined menu, pricing and terms and conditions booklet where the price she'd given was clearly stated. And so, with a wry grin of acceptance, the bargaining was concluded, both parties equally satisfied.

A cement staircase leading up from the lobby bisected the lodge, my room on the first floor along a mahogany panelled corridor. As I'd been shown to a first-floor room at each lodge, was it possible, I asked myself, that it was superstition or convention always to offer that location to the day's first guest?

A door of an ornateness belonging to a Victorian gentlemen's club secured the room. I was once again grateful the considerate owners had the forethought to cater for those unfortunates who'd broken their padlock. Inside, the two cots and half-height wooden cladding were made against a higher specification than anything else I'd seen along the route. I nodded my gratification, stowed my kit and returned to the diner to take lunch.

I was hungry so, after an unheeded succession of namastes, I walked over to the kitchen doorway, knocked on the doorframe and cleared my throat. The four ladies, almost done with their tattie-skinning, looked up at me in unison in bewilderment and started to giggle. Their amused stare said, 'Why had I knocked on the doorframe and cleared my throat, not called for their attention?' My shrug replied, 'I don't know, it was just something one did.' The owner took pity and manhandled me into the inner circle of cackling potato-peelers where she shoved the menu *et al.* under my nose.

I chose the life-giving Ra-Ra noodle soup for lunch, hoping for a repeat of Dagchu's ambrosia. The owner failed to acknowledge my order, so I stood there haplessly in the kitchen until a nudge in my back and push at my buttocks told me I needed to get out of the way. More laughter from the babushkas followed me back to my table; evidently my rear had met with approval.

The noodles were good, but not of Dagchu standard. I was disappointed but wasn't being fair; the noodles at Dagchu had been the perfect accompaniment for that place at that moment in time. There was no sign of anyone else arriving so, lonely for company, I returned to my room.

My quarters came with a power socket placed halfway up the sidewall above the bed, conveniently engineered in such a way that recharging of electronics was possible if the guest had had the prescience to bring along a two-metre cord. I wasn't carrying a firehose of cable, so had to jury-rig a rickety tower made from my guidebook, boots and first aid kit to support my phone. The power adaptor's pins protruded diagonally from the socket. But the proprietor wasn't going to sue for me for my disregard of the health and safety section of the terms and conditions of stay and my hands weren't wet, so it was all good.

As the phone charged, I busied myself with the repair of my sleeping bag zip. I felt yesterday's frustration even more keenly as, within five minutes of fiddling, I had the zipper back on its chain and the bottom stop bent to stop it coming off again. I made myself comfortable in the bag and tested the repairs. The zip held, so I decided not to try to find a tailor and settled in to read for the rest of the afternoon. As the sun dipped behind the hills, the room became chillier and I came to a break point in *Oryx and Crake*, so at 6.30 it was time for dinner.

The dining room was chock-a-block when I arrived, and I rued my lack of foresight in not booking a table. Guttural tones emanated from the first three tables; I reckoned there was a fair chance I'd caught up with the Germans Fez had told me about. They made up a group of around 15, a middle-aged crowd in a variety of mountain gear, nondescript apart from a couple of outliers. One was a short man who'd fashioned himself on a cross between the lead singer of an Eighties arena rock band and Albert Einstein, all grey poodle perm and bushy moustache. The other modelled himself on a leotarded Jean-Claude Van Damme in his heyday, his only concession to local conditions a pair of thick woollen socks tucked into his boots.

I hadn't passed them on the trail so was keen to ask them about where they'd detoured. I greeted them with a friendly namaste, but they seemed so engrossed in their conversation as not to have noticed, so it wasn't returned. The last table along the diner's length was occupied by two men around 60 in expensive fleeces. As I took my seat at the kitchen door, my namaste was again not reciprocated. I thought that strange; everyone else I'd met along the way had responded to the greeting and the people in the lodges had been friendly.

I contemplated the lack of response as I read the menu, which listed all manner of *haute cuisine* compared to that before Lamjura. Impressed by the choice, I decided to take the egg and chips. It was listed as one of the chef's international fusion specialities and, besides, I didn't want to see all those spuds go to waste. I hoped treating my insides to something familiar would help them glue themselves back together. So I was pleased to see the food wasn't served *à la nouvelle cuisine* when it came; there was at least one bucket full of spuds on the plate. I could tell my immediate neighbours were from France. I asked for the condiments in my version of French, hoping to break into some conversation, but they passed them over without even catching my eye.

The volume of the Germans' conversation increased when two porters brought in plates of bratwurst from the opposite end of the room to the kitchen. The sausages were served with hoots of appreciation and a couple of tankards of beer hoisted in salute. From my position, I could see all the way through the lodge, where outside the corridor the porters were cooking food amid a camp of tents. It impressed me they'd constructed the makings of a mini-Oktoberfest in the Apple's garden.

The Germans cleaned their plates of the first course, prompting the porters to cart in two tripods with mounted silver tureens on top. The group was joined by their guide who gave a cheery thumbs-up as the old plates and cutlery were refreshed with clean ones. I could see and smell that the cauldrons contained a main course of beef goulash and potatoes. It was greeted as enthusiastically as the first course, Albert Bon Jovi and the youngest of the group taking another beer to wash it down.

I was about halfway through my mountain of chips when the porters completed another trip to the campsite and replaced one of the now empty tureens with a kettle the size of a blast furnace crucible. What was next, I thought, black forest gateau? My guess wasn't far off – the porters brought a round pie dish and pot of custard on their next return trip. How they'd made all that food on a campfire, especially the pie, was beyond me. It could've been sourced from the village, but everything else looked piping hot when they brought it in. They'd made it themselves.

I'd finally won my battle with the fried potatoes and sat back to tea as the Germans got stuck into their dessert. I could tell by now they had no interest in anything outside their entirely self-contained group. That was fair enough, I thought; they didn't owe anyone else conviviality. The more I observed them, though, the less comfortable I was with their behaviour to their hosts. The guide and porters were smiling at every command, but they *were* commands. Drinks orders were dictated with a hurry-up rather than politely requested; food plates not gathered into a helpful pile or space made for ease of collection. I hoped I was reading it wrong but couldn't help but feel the subtext of behest and serve was something more than rudeness. To a certain extent, I understood the group had doubtless paid well and expected a certain level of service from their employees, but the way I saw it playing out in reality didn't sit well.

The French couple upped and left, not bidding the Germans goodnight either, and I thought, 'Well, at least it wasn't something I said'. I finished my tea and reasoned my time would be better spent with *Oryx* rather than observing more ignorance, so I headed up to my room. I opened the Kindle and read for a while, but I'd overdosed on literature that afternoon so wasn't in the mood. I switched to music, starting at track one of *Slinky* by the Milltown Brothers. Forty minutes later, it was time for sleep; it was 8.45pm.

The early night did me the world of good and I slept well, waking up refreshed. Yesterday's bloating and stomach cramps had abated, my single *Diary* entry for that day showing a marked improvement at a Type Five. Egg and chips and bed before nine would be my mantra from here on in. My only worry was my legs had stiffened considerably overnight; the steep descent must have stressed unused muscles and I hobbled down to the dining room.

The French couple had beaten me to it and were finishing their breakfast as I arrived; my good morning was ignored again. My appetite was back and, after wolfing down my porridge and milk tea, I paid the bill. The prices at the Apple were practically double those before pass but unmerited by the quality of the stay.

I passed by the German campsite on the hike downhill through the tidy village to cross the river in the valley below, reflecting it wasn't only their strange unfriendliness I found disagreeable, it was their mode of travel. They were camping in the grounds of lodges. Why not stay in the lodge? It would be warmer and there'd be less stuff to carry. If they were going for the full adventure experience, why not self-navigate, wilderness camp, carry their own gear and food and cook it themselves? It seemed that on the one hand they wanted to claim they'd camped all their way through the Himalayas, but on the other wanted to be supported by a team making everything relatively luxurious. It was one thing or the other for me, not their bizarre hybrid.

The short hike down via the chorten to the river did my legs the power of good and by the time the trail started its ascent, I was moving fluidly. I was glad to be on my way, to leave the aloofness of my co-guests at the Apple behind.

The track climbed through mixed oak and pine forest, taxing at first. I caught up with a porter who was carrying an octad of three-metre solid wooden beams lashed together with an ingenious set of tensed, knotted ropes. Three cross ties were held fast at equidistant positions by stick batons on the timber's topside. These were connected top to bottom. The rope tension to keep everything together and balanced was provided via a combination of the porter's head strap and his arms stuck out in front. The ropes acted as reigns, his hands steering the load. A rolled sleeping mat at the bottom of his spine provided the only cushioning.

Incredulous how he could support such a weight and gobsmacked at how he kept it pivoted on such uneven ground, I followed him for a while, not wanting to disturb his rhythm. He was the human fulcrum in a seesaw steadily making its way uphill. At a clearing in the forest, I was thankful to see his immediate labours were all but over, as the frame of a half-erected new cabin came into view.

The forest thinned out at a byre where a lady was watering her cow and the way became a slow gain through rolling meadow. Looking back, I could see Solukhumbu's Big Apple and more porters carrying monumental loads emerging from the trees. The track flattened out and I fell into an unlaboured, steady tempo. Its course lay on the opposing arm of the valley I'd trekked the day before and, as I travelled, I could make out the monastery glinting in the sun and the route all the way back up to Lamjura. Clouds smeared the pass's outline and seemed to contour in parallel with the head of the valley. If Austria had ever adopted terraced farming, it would look like this.

The porters bade me a friendly namaste as they levelled, motoring on past me. They were the folks who'd served the Germans, plus a couple of others. I caught up with them again taking their first tea break about 90 minutes out from Junbesi. The youngest-looking pointed to a mass of cloud overhanging the hills beyond the outline of a stupa in the distance.

"Look Everest!" There was a sense of ice and rock behind the grey swirls but nothing more.

"Everest, where?"

"Behind cloud, there. Wait, see." I did as commanded, but nothing emerged.

"I don't see anything?"

"Wait."

"Okay. I saw you gentlemen last night in the lodge, are you carrying all the tents for your group in your bags?" At my speed, I calculated, they could've broken camp and caught me up easily.

"Yes. Tent, sleeping bag, clothe, camp-gas stove. All for tour. Go slowly, ha-ha."

"You didn't look slow to me. How much are you carrying each?"

"Porter carry 35, 40 kilo."

"That's a lot. My pack is only 10 kilo."

"You trekker man, not Nepali man, ha-ha. Nepali man very stronger, ha-ha."

"I don't doubt it. Where are you heading?"

"We go Ringmo village next, eat dhal baat. Suman and Ved make."

"You're making lunch for the group, not eating at a lodge? How is that possible? How do you have time?"

"Yes. Tour all food make outside in camp. We go Ringmo, cook food. Tour come with guide, slowly slowly. Dhal baat good when people coming."

"Then you have to clean up, pack up and get to the next place before your tour group to make dinner?"

"Yes. Make tent camp. Make tea for guest arrive."

"I don't know how you manage it, that sounds like a tough job to me."

"Good job. Make many money." Everest was steadfastly refusing to show itself at its first opportunity, but I wasn't too disappointed as there would be plenty of other chances.

"Doesn't look like Everest is coming out."

"No, ha-ha, now big cloud all day. You no see, ha-ha."

"Well, if it's not coming out, I'm going to head off. See you later. Namaste."

"Namaste."

A dip into the course of a waterfall was the only deviation in the contour up to the chorten. Multi-coloured prayer flags were billowing in the wind from five poles that guarded the cliff edge. A trio of cows blocked my way around the stupa and, as I waited for them to move on, I idly wondered what number of cows constituted a herd. They eventually coalesced at the path edge and I was able to squeeze by.

It was good walking along the valley side. I drifted into a semi-trance-like state again, the porters not disturbing my reverie as they passed me again with a smile. The trail descended through broken pine. I spotted the porters crammed into the opening of a wooden shack nailed into a terrace above; it seemed they liked their tea as much as me. A boulder carved with Sanskrit messages painted over in blues, whites and yellows announced an increase in the downhill gradient. It also warned I approached the trek's first suspension bridge.

The bridge spanned the Dudhkunda Khola rushing below in a deep, wooded ravine. Two parallel metal cables ran from the cement blocks in which they were sunk at the top of opposite walls of the gorge. Iron fixings bolted into semi-circular concrete pilings provided their elevation, guidance and tension. These stood either side of the steps leading down to the bridge's floor, which was comprised of aluminium matting joined to the cross cables via thinner cords spaced at metre intervals. In theory, the chicken wire strung between them prevented a tumble into the abyss.

These contraptions could've only been invented by a sadist, the design maximising loss of balance at the span's nadir, as one reached the apex of one's fear of heights. I disliked these bridges immensely and so procrastinated about my crossing, deliberating to take a before and after selfie to show home. If I made it.

I heard the tea-refreshed porters stomping towards me, so I struck out. The footway was as unsteady beneath me as my feet were above it and I stumbled from side to side, my poor balance accentuating the bridge's side sway, throwing me further askance. I remembered from the Annapurna Circuit the trick was to dance across. The optimal technique was to take alternate firm and deliberate ballroom steps to counteract each swing. With my slow salsa, I reached the midpoint too tardily for the first porter not to disturb my crossing and another disruptive oscillation rippled underneath my feet. Now it was a matter of making it across.

The porters passed by again as I took that selfie on the far bank and I noticed, as they climbed through the forest above, that one of the men had an unusual gait. His left knee joint distended to the side and hinged at the front with every step. He must have been in some pain carrying his load; I only hoped it wasn't too much and he wasn't sacrificing future physical mobility for the money on offer.

The climb became difficult on a steep, stone switchback across the bridge and I struggled up through the trees, resting frequently. Once my breathing had calmed, I was struck by the bird call in the canopy; there was a riot going on of trills, cheeps, chirps, gurgles and warbles. I emerged at a sloth's pace from the cacophony to the mini ziggurat on which the first lodge of Ringmo was situated. The porters had set up their cooking gear and tables there, the smell from the great pots giving away something delicious was being prepared. My appetite was duly stimulated, and I headed inside to order a dhal baat. The owner stated it was going to be 30 minutes to satisfy my order and it was dark inside the lodge, so I went out to the terrace with my tea.

The Germans were now in sight, exiting the forest with varying degrees of strain etched into their faces. The unitarded muscle-man was the most relaxed, capering up from rock to rock, his poles folded in one fist. The lady accompanying Alfred BJ was suffering the most; he held her hand and guided her attentively, step by step. Bringing up the rear was the guide, who ushered them inside after they'd dropped their day packs in an untidy pile at the lodge's entrance.

I was trying to dispel my jealousy of the weight advantage the group enjoyed – they were carrying only day packs – when the chuff of helicopter rotors brought the porters scampering over from their field kitchen. A yellow chopper dropped from the mist and corkscrewed down in a buzz. Nose up, the pilot appeared to land in shrubbery uphill – he'd either executed a stunningly skilful landing or the quietest crash possible. Ved nodded when I asked if the copter must be evacuating an injured trekker.

Tea finished, I returned inside to realise I'd made the same mistake as I had at Junbesi, of not reserving my table. The tour group had occupied almost every seat in the restaurant, and I gestured to a sandy blonde-haired man if I could take the last remaining seat at the table. He failed to acknowledge my request, so I sat down and bid him a 'Guten morgen', his response being to stare straight through me with his dark blue eyes. Thinking he might not have heard, I made sure I was face to face to repeat my good morning. His eyes bored straight through me again for an uncomfortable few seconds before he turned around to chat with a friend. Despite my best efforts to let the slight wash by me and move on, I couldn't help myself from becoming annoyed, thinking it was one thing to feign indifference while at dinner, but such head-on-discourtesy was plain ignorant.

The porters brought in the steaming platters of food and I marvelled at how they'd managed to prepare wiener schnitzel and fries, not only because of the field-kitchen's locale. I'd seen plenty of cows and chickens in my roving but not a single pig *en route*. I wondered how they'd obtained the meat, my best guess being that, given the size of the porter's packs and their eagerness to please, it was just possible Suman had carried a wild boar up from Kathmandu.

The lavish fare and the repeat of the group's lack of manners or appreciation towards their hosts did nothing for my mood. I found the snapping of fingers calling for the emergency of the master's mobile phone needing charging particularly distasteful. As Alfred insisted on his second alcoholic accompaniment to his meal, my efforts at calming myself were failing. I needed to get out of there before I vented my frustration, so I shovelled down my dhal baat like Bart Simpson on speed. Ordinarily, I wouldn't have countenanced it, but I walked into the kitchen to pay my bill and speed my departure. The owner overcharged me by 100 per cent and so, severely irked, I made my way back out to the trail as plates of carrot cake were being butlered in the opposite direction.

I took my annoyance out on the trail and raced up 100 steps before breathlessness overtook my temper. I raged at the tour party's behaviour, not comprehending how they could treat their staff at best like servants, inconsiderately hog all the space in the dining areas and fail to have the common courtesy to return a greeting. I became irritated with myself; had I been more vexed at the dismissiveness of their staff or by their collective affront to me? I decided it a combination of both, but what the ratio was between them, I couldn't unpick.

I was disappointed with myself for not making a point of their poor conduct towards their employees but thought would that have done more harm than good? I could berate them, get some sort of reaction to satisfy my ego that I was better than that before moving on, content I'd done my bit. But I thought, what gave me any sort of right to press home my opinion? The young porter had said it was a good job. He, along with his colleagues rather than me, would have suffered any negative consequences of anything I could have said on their behalf. The entire episode confused me; the only thing of which I was sure was that I would give the group a wide berth if we crossed paths further on. If only to keep my temper.

My dash had stopped by the 'Himalayan Local Cheese Factory' which offered 'Butter, Cheese and Dry Cheese', according to its signage. Next up the hill was the 'Quitview Lodge and Restaurant'. There was nothing like the local advertising to help with my mood. Thoughts of quitters enjoying a last BYOWC (Bring Your Own Wet Cheese) before being whisked back to Kathmandu on the banana-coloured chopper cheered me. Feeling calmer, I made a short haul upwards to where the track was broken by a turmeric coloured road.

Beyond, the climb was harder, half-cemented angled rocks forming a punishing staircase ascending vertically within the walls of a wooded trough. My post-lunch burst of pace and the gradient started to take its toll and passing porters eyed me curiously as I lolled breathlessly against the walls. The trough broke into a winding path through the forest, but I couldn't yet see any sign of the monastery my guidebook had told me dominated the next summit.

Cloud rolled in and reduced visibility to 20 metres in all directions, so I resumed my head-down plodding technique employed in the ascent to Goyem and daydreamed. The path changed colour from gamboge to terracotta and I surfaced to consciousness; the trees had ended abruptly and I stood on a beaten earth terrace, the outline of a colossal chorten vague above. I'd reached Trakshindu La.

The stupa was the most ornate and best cared-for I'd seen outside Kathmandu. An aluminium fence surrounded it, presumably to keep inconsiderate selfie-seeking trekkers from clambering all over it. The throne of the Buddha was decorated by fire-maned lion-dragons and half-men, half-bird creatures underneath steps of golden Sanskrit. Corners were trellised blossoms. The vase was, indeed, filled with treasure, a seated gold statuette of Buddha a ruler's length in height. The 13 Steps to Heaven were alternated in gold and black hoops leading up to the fine filigree of the Umbrella of Protection and

Heart-Mind. Having finished photographing the chorten, I turned to see a lodge had uncloaked itself from the mist. I dropped my bag by its stone wall and ventured inside; it was time for tea.

The lodge was spacious, high-ceilinged and, astonishingly, heaving with customers. I wondered where they'd come from – I hadn't seen any other trekkers *en route* – but there was an intersection indicated above Ringmo on the map that met the 'Dudh Kunda Pikey Cultural Trail'. But the folks in the restaurant displayed no obvious outward signs of being art historians, lacking one cravat between them. I imagined the cultural trail was even less frequented than the trek to EBC and so couldn't see how it would account for the volume of trade. Yet I couldn't believe I'd caught anyone up, so it remained a mystery. There were no seats, so I changed my mind on the tea and filled the LifeStraw from a hose by the toilet shack outside. A thin man dropped his pack next to mine as I sipped.

"Namaste." He was already an improvement on the Germans, to my mind.

"Namaste."

"Where did you get your water from?"

"Hey! You're the first Brit I've met on the road, how are you doing?"

"Oh, I've had a tough day. That climb was awfully hard. My feet are battered, I think it's these boots," he replied.

"Yeah, I found it hard going as well, especially that stone staircase bit. Are you carrying your own stuff, too?" He nodded and followed with one of the standards of trekking small-talk.

"Where have you come from today?"

"Junbesi."

"Me too."

"You start in Shivalaya? Going to EBC?"

"Yeah, that's right. That bus ride was terrible, wasn't it? Oh, my back is still killing from that. Where did you stay in Junbesi?"

"People's Revolutionary Front of Junbesi Apple Orchard Guest House." I wasn't shocked the reference passed him by.

"Sorry?"

"Err ... nothing. What time did you set off? Have you just got here?"

"About eight. I've just arrived, yes," he answered. It was about the same time I'd departed.

"What's up with your feet?"

"Oh, it's these boots. I've had them for 10 years since my last trip to Nepal. I haven't worn them since, and I think my feet must have changed. I'm getting massive blisters."

"I have some Compeed in the bag, if you need?"

"Oh really, that would be nice of you." I undid the straps and proceeded to empty the contents, garage sale-style, across the top of the wall, making a mental note I hadn't taken notice of my mental note to pack the first aid at the top of the bag. He'd managed to get one of his boots off in the interim.

"Here you go."

"Thanks, but I don't see any blisters yet," he reported as he examined his foot.

"That's good, you should get the plaster on before it forms. Where's the heat from the rubbing?" There wasn't any sign of an ulcer.

"It's not really hot. It more feels sore from being bashed inside the boot."

"How about the other foot, is it the same?"

"Pretty much, yeah."

"I don't think the Compeed is going to do you any good, then. You just need to pad that area a bit more, maybe an inner layer of socks would help."

"Oh, really? Thanks for them, anyway."

"No bother," I said, repacking my bag.

"How much stuff have you got in your backpack? Mine is really heavy."

"It's about 10 or 11 kilos. I was in Nepal 10 years ago as well and I learned my lesson then. I had 15 kilos. It was too much. Plus, this is a new pack, it's a lot better than the one I'd back then."

"Yeah. Mine is 12 or 13 kilos but I have the same pack. It's really old. I don't think the straps are any good anymore, they're really cutting into my shoulders." Lacking tubular bandages or a splint to offer him, I offered what assistance I could.

"Maybe fiddling with the tension and putting more weight on your belt strap might help. I'm Lee, by the way."

"Thanks. I'm Aydin. Where are you headed for today? I'm going to Nunthala, I hope it isn't far."

"The guide says two-and-a-quarter hours but I'm not keeping pace with that. I think it's another three hours at my pace, but you'll be quicker. Where were you 10 years ago?"

"I did the Annapurna Circuit."

"No way! I walked that as well. Great, isn't it, so spectacular?" We chatted for a while about our relative experiences on the Annapurna Circuit, Aydin seeming to have had a rough time of it, and I could see that, while we'd been talking, the mist had palpably thickened.

"The weather looks like it's coming in now so I'm going to get going. I'll see you down in the valley somewhere, you're bound to overtake me. The water is over there, by the way."

"See you." He headed over to the lodge's rear and I repacked, ensuring the first aid kit and my poncho were easily accessible. I crossed a pair of weary-looking trekkers heading towards the lodge as I passed through the prayer gate marking the route. The cloud thickened and draped everything in a white shimmer.

There were going to be no spectacular vistas for a while, so I concentrated on my footing. Condensation had dampened the powdery surface, lubricating it to the point of slipperiness. I crossed a small wooden bridge surrounded by bulrushes. It led to a flat area where the trail's direction was unmarked. I consulted the guide as there was no-one around but, as it offered me no insight, I chose to bear left.

Twenty minutes downhill, I met a local gentleman who was obviously well up on the weather forecast travelling in the opposite direction. I thought he must have bought his coat and umbrella second hand from a city of London tax accountant circa 1959. His head shake and thrust upward arm answered my question as to whether I was on the trail to Nunthala.

I was disappointed to have taken a wrong turn, but at least it was only 20 minutes back to where I'd made the mistake. At the flat area, I took the right fork and a minute downhill, uncloaked from the murk, was a lodge where Suman and Ved were hastening the erection of tents in its grounds. Several of the Germans were milling around their encampment for the night. I hurried on, happy to pass them by.

The mist turned Scotch. A thin drizzle now bounced off the tree canopy and fell down to form rivulets in the track's centre. My balance and boots fared better in the slurry underneath than they had on the powder, suffering three near misses but no tumble. I crossed a steady stream of uphill traffic, mostly local people in their early 20s carrying small daypacks and brollies. The number of umbrellas and modern waterproof jackets seemed incongruous in the locale and I wondered whether folks were on their weekly pilgrimage to the local Gompa or were students returning home from a college in the valley.

They were in a rush to escape the dreich conditions so didn't stop to chat. The Scotch mist soon turned to a light rain as the footing became a different kind of difficult; the slurry had been replaced by a rock staircase covered in loose pebbles. The rocks were slick, and the pebbles were wont to turn an unbalanced boot into a twisted ankle.

I stopped to let a donkey train trundle up the staircase, propane canisters strapped to both flanks of each animal. Their drover stopped by for a chat as he ensured his stragglers kept up with the main body of the procession. As we were passing the usual pleasantries about where we were going, a Sherpa friend of his bowled around the corner. He'd constructed a novel way of keeping the rain off by lashing a wooden orange box horizontally to his chest, leather straps over each shoulder. Parallel rows of nails were tacked into the centre of the box's front edge, while inserted in between was an umbrella that had its handle sawn in half. Its canopy stretched over the box's front and over his head and back, so he remained bone dry. The language barrier prevented me from asking whether he'd filled the box with a pyramid of oranges that morning and sold out, or whether this allowed him to flog other dry goods around the hills.

The rain eased for a while. The cloud swirled away from the hillside and for the first time in a couple of hours the scenery became partially visible. The hills behind me were steep terracing spotted with dozens of farm buildings, in front of a broad valley. The misty conditions dulled the edges of the landscape, the overall effect leaving me feeling I could have been looking out over a glen somewhere in the Cairngorms.

The slippery rock gave way to a gravel path that widened away from vertiginous drops before passing under a spectacular waterfall to emerge onto a gravel road. The ancient pathway had been amended recently by the cut and the descent's end involved hanging on to uphill vegetation to avoid falling. I'd followed the road to a jumble of rocks that could've been the original trail's resumption when there was a downshift in temperature that heralds a downpour.

It was the kind of rain for which even spending a generation on the west coast of Scotland cannot prepare you. It fell in hawsers. I was thankful for my meeting with Aydin as my poncho was now at the pack's top. I took it out and prepared it for use, gladdened for the opportunity to give it an outing. I'd endured much ridicule at home for the poncho, not only because of its atomic tangerine colour, and soon I'd have some photos that demonstrated its usefulness in response.

The poncho is a wraparound that covers not only the wearer but also their pack, and is therefore highly effective in keeping the wearer dry but presents a challenge to put on unaided. The first arm is easy, but it becomes a wrestling match to find the cloak's tail behind the pack and wrap it around your body into position for the other arm. That isn't too difficult in itself but results more often than not in an impossible angle for the second arm to enter its sleeve, unless you're Harry Houdini. My record was 15 minutes of faffing before I found the sweet spot. That was less than ideal at the best of times but, in the cloudburst, meant I'd be thoroughly soaked before I'd donned more than a few square centimetres.

So I was grateful when a man in a green flowered topi folded and poked his umbrella into the dirt by my side, contorted my arm into the second sleeve and ensured the poncho was on. As his thanks, he wanted me to take a photograph of him resplendent in his green and red North Face jacket, modern hiking trousers and walking boots. He unfurled his brolly and posed, mean and moody, with one foot on the rock pile. He seemed incredibly pleased with the results when I showed him on the phone. Suitably encouraged, I asked him if he'd take a picture of me in the poncho with the valley in the background. He seemed to take umbrage at this and, with a cry in the negative, headed down a steep cut back on to the old trail. I thought it wasn't only the catwalks of Paris, then, that had their *prima donna* models.

The drencher rapidly turned the path to mud, so I appreciated it intersected with the road again, allowing me to choose that as a longer, but safer, option. I soon saw I'd made a mistake – beneath me on the footway was another suspension bridge. It crossed the stream I'd earlier forded and which was now a torrent. Boots wet through, I traipsed along the road as it meandered around the hillside while the deluge continued to pelt the poncho. I'd become a walking waterfall, front and back.

A short flight of steps served as a shortcut between switchbacks, and at the bottom a sign read 'Welcome to Nunthala Solududhkuna Municipality -1 Have a good safe journey' where I took that orange-clad selfie for the folks back home. I was glad to have made it to the municipality, but it took another monsoonal 10 minutes to reach the first lodge. The guidebook had indicated Nunthala was a four-and-three-quarter-hour trek from Junbesi. Five-and-a-half hours after leaving the Apple, I'd arrived.

Nunthala to Khari Khola

I had approached the 'Mountain Sherpa Lodge and Restaurant' from the structure's long side, rounding its tail to find the door. The lodge had been built into the hillside so that the under-storey was half the upper's width, its walls plaster trowel-smoothed in a Spanish grey concrete. A spirit level-flat courtyard had been recently laid in the same material, the T-square-precise change in the patio's hue – from light grey to gunmetal – marking safe passage from the downpour. It had the air of being a work in progress. I was unsure about spending a night in a potential building site but was more than tired enough to check it out. A friendly-looking lady, chuckling softly, greeted me at the open doorway.

"Namaste. Much rain." 'Yes, most of it falling on me,' I estimated.

"Namaste. Yes. A lot from Trakshindu La and all the way down."

"It always rain at Trakshindu. I like coat."

"Thank you. It keeps the rain off."

"You look like man in cartoon, grand-daughter like much."

"Mm ... cartoon?"

"France man cartoon."

"Ah ... French man?"

"Yes, France man."

"A *French* man in a cartoon? I can't think who that would be. Are you sure it's a *French* man?" The rain was still belting down, and I wasn't getting any drier.

"Yes, French France man."

"Mmm ... I can't think. Wait a minute, what about, what's his name ... Asterix?" She stared blankly.

"No, of course not, why would I be like Asterix, I must look more like his friend, the big fat guy. What's his name? Err ... Obelix, I think. He carries that big stone behind his back." I made a reverse flapping-cum-cupping motion.

"Obelix is bird?" She looked at me like I'd drunk a triple helping of one of Getafix's double Dutch-inducing magic potions.

"No, it's not Asterix or Obelix, then." The downpour kept trying to batter its way through the poncho.

"Obelix bird man, no. France French man sing lot of song. To pretty girl."

"Err ... Tintin? No, he's Belgian, isn't he? I don't think he sings. Is it Tintin?"

"I no know Tintin man. You no know France French man? Everyone know, even baby! Bad men chase with sword." My defences had been breached, the first cold percolation of water creeping down my shoulder.

"Ah ... one of the cartoon musketeers then? Is it Mickey Mouse?"

"Mickey Mouse is *USA* mouse. Not French France man!"

"Err ... yes. Even though, in character, he'd be playing a Frenchman." What was I saying?

"No Mickey Mouse."

"Can I phone a friend, then?"

"You have Nepal Telecom? Good signal in Nunthala."

"No, err ... I mean, never mind. A French man who sings a lot and gets chased by bad men with swords? Sorry, I really don't have a clue."

"He ring bell like monk. BONG ..."

"Like a monk, where would a monk ring a bell? In a monastery! Ah, you mean Quasimodo! Is it the Hunchback of Notre Dame?"

"Yes, France, French man. You look big orange Hunchback of Notre Dame French France man, ha-ha!" I rotated my shoulder cuff to divert the trickle away from skin.

"Do you have a room?" I asked, relieved the place not appearing to sport a campanile.

"Why you no ask? You stop much rain on head, ha-ha!" I was tired, bedraggled and my boots were sodden. I reckoned she'd done a marvellous job of softening me up for the pricing discussion, but I was mistaken – she quoted me a competitive rate and there was no need to haggle. But my experience in the hills meant I couldn't believe my luck. Looking at the freshly finished cement, I figured there must be something untoward going on, imagining a night snuggled up to a concrete mixer like an unwitting tour package holidaymaker in 1990s Benidorm. Conscious of falling into another trap, I asked to see the accommodations and squelched into the new block.

I had entered the corridor of a chalet of Val d'Isèrean luxury where wooden panelling ran top to bottom and had the perfume of forest pine. Half a dozen doors led off to a square dining room in the same oiled timber where the centrepiece was a wrought iron wood burner, rust weathered but unused. The padding on the perimeter benches had been undented by buttocks and the low-slung coffee tables were equally untouched.

The room was also very much more than a touch above; twin beds were topped by fat mattresses and thick duvets. Duvets! A power socket had been wired in below the windowsill so there would be no need to spend an hour jury-rigging, but the *pièce de résistance* was the viewing of the privy. The next entry in the *Diarrhoea Diaries* would record the expertly plumbed Western Style porcelain had received its maiden visitor.

"Dhanyabad. I'll take the room, thank you. Where's the light switch for the toilet for when it gets dark, please?"

"No light switch."

"Oh." As I was thinking that was only a minor fly in the ointment, that I'd have to keep the Powercap handy, she bundled me into the WC, shut the door behind me. The fluorescent tube stuttered into its first active use.

"Eco. Save light. Save planet," she extolled, beaming in her explanation as I popped my head back out. I didn't think it could get any better, could it?

"Do you have hot shower?"

"Yes. Two hundred rupee. Down stair." Bingo. I had a vision of a herring-bone, glaze-tiled wet room served *à la mode* by a recessed rain-shower head.

"Great. I'll take one later. Is there somewhere I can dry my poncho, please?"

"Yes, give me. I dry." She helped me disrobe and draped the poncho over the stair railing.

"You come see what you want eat now." We stepped back into the storm and I chose my evening meal of Ra-Ra noodles, arranging to eat at six. Delighted at my good luck, I slushed my way back to my room. The pleasure of removing my wet boots and damp socks was something to savour and I sat barefoot on the edge of my bed in a semi-dazed contentment. I was thankful for my good fortune and looked forward to the hour getting even better: it was time for my first shower since Bhandar.

The anticipation of the hot shower focussed my attention on how stale I smelled as I peeled off my fleece. The poncho hadn't only kept some rain out, it had also kept the heat in. The sweat from four days of heavy exertion meant I carried the odour of a cocker spaniel after an afternoon of splashing through muddy puddles. I selected what I speculated were my cleanest clothes – the ones at the pack's foot unused since the hike from Shivalaya to Bhandar – and headed downstairs.

The brief rest had played its trick of calcifying my thighs once more, so I took the stairs sideways, supporting most of my weight on the bannister. In the basement, a cubicle served as a combined bathroom and laundry, where the white cube of a brand-new washing machine sat next to a wooden bucket of soaking garments recently pulverised into cleanliness by a shillelagh. I was thrilled to see the shower was as state-of-the-art as the washer and, to top it all, there was a selection of shampoos and shower gels hooked around the hose.

I turned the knob and heard the faint whoosh of gas being ignited somewhere. As I stripped, waiting for the water to heat, I noticed a circular opening in the wall adjacent to the door frame and dropped my eye to waist level to squint through. There was nothing to see but darkness. As I stepped naked into the jet of hot water, the notion that all this opulence couldn't be provided at such a bargain price crossed my mind. There must be a surcharge, I must have to make payment in kind, I thought, hoping it wasn't going to take the form of servicing whatever poked its way through that glory hole.

I'd taken great pleasure in removing my boots and socks but that bore nothing compared to the shower. I lathered, rinsed, and lathered again; scrubbed away the grime under the steaming water; dolloped shampoo on my head and kneaded out my matted hair under the suds. Anyone spying through the glory hole could've been forgiven for thinking they were watching the euphoric bliss displayed in every brand of conditioner advert ever made.

With a fragrance of wild apple daffodils and scoured as pink as cherry blossom, I reluctantly stepped out of the water as it cooled. I towelled and dressed, slightly disgusted at having to fit my Wafer-Farm-clean body back into soiled garments, but it didn't last and, back upstairs, in the rapture of being washed and warm, the kitsch of the Warholian porpoise-motif duvet covers only added to my glee.

Six o'clock came around too soon; I'd spent a pleasant afternoon by the window idly reading and watching trekkers splosh their way down to the main body of the village. I finished *Oryx and Crake*; I'd enjoyed how the tale had told its message of not to mess with genetics, but was disappointed to find it was part of a trilogy and I hadn't bought the follow-up – I wanted more. I made my way to the dining room, unsurprised I was the only guest but wondering where my host was. Likely watching something on the Disney Channel, I thought. Six-thirty came, and a teenage girl peeked around the door frame.

"Not here, not here," she said and bid me follow her. I tiptoed in my socks around the courtyard's dry edge. She led me back through the doorway of the Quasimodo exchange before indicating I should take a seat at the table where my bowl of noodles lay cooling.

Strangely, I found myself in a shop where an L-shape of coffee tables opposed the counter. The store met all manner of consumer demands; stacked left to right in the glass-fronted cabinet opposite were stacked cigarette packets, plastic sachets of filter coffee, vertically balanced boxes of toothpaste, neatly rowed gold beer cans, half bottles of peach liqueur and bright orange single-size Fanta bottles. The shelves on the right catered for oils and sauces; one litre yellow square pouches of Swastik refined soybean oil dominated regimented bottles of red and green Druk chilli sauce. A full-length silver fridge sentinelled the doorway.

"Excuse me, I'm still hungry. Could I order something else, please?" I asked the teenager 10 minutes after sitting down. My Ra-Ra noodles, though good, hadn't sated my appetite.

"What you like?"

"Some chips, err ... French fry as on the menu, please."

"French fry." She spoke at a lithe man behind the counter, who brought to mind a recently retired Ethiopian middle-distance runner. His fleece matched mine but, underneath, he was a flat knot of muscles.

"French fry will be 30 minutes or more, sir," he apprised.

"No problem. Can I take a black tea while I wait, please? Small pot."

"No problem, sir." He put the kettle on and reached down into the counter's bowels to retrieve a quartet of potatoes. While the water heated on the stove, he peeled and sliced the spuds and pulled a Swastik from the shelf, emptying the oil into a steel pan he'd placed on the hob. The kettle whistled, he made up the small pot, switched the fryer onto the lit ring and gracefully placed my tea in front of me. It had been like watching some kind of domestic ballet.

"Where you from, sir?"

"Dhanyabad. I'm from the UK."

"UK nice people. You trek to Base Camp?"

"Yes, that's right."

"You trek alone?"

"Yes, I'm alone."

"Don't like guide? Don't take porter?" I wondered if Raj had phoned ahead, recognising this was all part of the set-up.

"Yes."

"No friend?" He delivered the line, but he didn't possess the teacher's comic timing.

"No, but I walk very slowly so I'd only hold up anyone I walked with. Alone, I can go at my own pace and stop when I want. It means I don't spoil it for myself or anyone who was with me. I want to try doing it carrying my own gear so no porter, but I'll see how I get on with that, maybe higher up I'll get one."

"No guide? How you know way to go?"

"I have a guidebook and looked at maps before I came. There are the signs and, if I'm not sure, I ask people along the trail. I haven't gone too badly wrong so far. So, I'm not sure a guide would be right for me."

"I am Sherpa guide for mountain."

"You mean for mountaineers rather than trekkers? If I was a mountaineer, I'd definitely need a guide." I wasn't sure if I'd offended him and was trying to soften my earlier comment.

"Yes. I have guided on many mountain."

"Everest?" He nodded.

"Mera peak, Lhotse. Many Khumbu mountain," he added.

"Wow. I think that's a lot more impressive than anything related to trekking. How did you get into that?"

"From boy, mountain guide is family business. Many Sherpa family from Nunthala mountain guide."

"I guess it isn't the season for expeditions to Everest now? What do you do when the mountaineers aren't climbing?"

"Yes, not season now, no expedition to mountain so prepare for next year. I guide in March, April, May. Now I work at lodge with wife. Sometime, if trekker want, I guide on trek?" There could be no mistake; it was an offer.

"Thanks, I think I'm fine without a guide. What do you think of trekkers without a guide or porter? Do you think that's wrong?"

"Better if trekker has porter and guide for safety but no problem if trekker trek alone, all trekker people are good. If trekker take Sherpa guide is more money for guide, he bring to village. Good for village like Nunthala. Problem for Sherpa people is guide from Kathmandu, they no know mountain and sometime have problem with altitude. Problem is no know local people, no take guest to best place. Only Sherpa people know secret place on trek."

"Are you talking about the organised tours from Kathmandu?"

"Yes. Big group, many trekker."

"They have guides who don't know the trek?"

"Depend. Some good, have Sherpa people, they know all place. If snow, know way. Some bad, only follow other guide and make problem in snow. Some good guide not Sherpa people. Depend. Trekker can have luck or no have luck."

"Yes, I guess so."

"More problem is porter. Kathmandu porter can have big problem."

"What do you mean?"

"Some Kathmandu porter never be in high mountain. First trek with group, too heavy pack, go too fast, get sick on mountain, need go down. Porter born in Khumbu best."

"So, if I wanted to get the best guide and porter, you're saying I should come to the Khumbu and hire one in, say, Shivalaya or Lukla?"

"Depend. Shivalaya better. Lukla same as Kathmandu. Can be good luck or bad luck."

"But that would be a risk, wouldn't it? You could get to Shivalaya and there would be no porters?"

"No problem. Always porter in Nepal."

"What did you say about the money? With a local guide or porter more money goes to the village? For solo trekkers like me, though, I'm not spending money on either."

"Trekker give money to Khumbu guide and porter better; money go to village. Big group, most money go Kathmandu, not village. Trek alone no problem, no money to guide, no money to porter but money go lodge in village. You pay my lodge in Nunthala, in village, not big trek company in Kathmandu. Porter bring Ra-Ra noodle to lodge, so porter get money."

"So, it's not a problem for Nepali people that I trek alone?"

"No, all trekker good, Nepali people like all. Better for you if have guide or porter for if have problem, but no problem for Nepali people, no problem for Sherpa people." He returned to the stove, where he determined the oil was hot enough for the potatoes; a satisfactory sizzle followed, and I broke the seal on the thermos.

The teenage girl pointed a remote at a TV elevated in the store-diner's corner and flicked through the channels to a music programme showing a mixture of pop music from the subcontinent and the West. The girl boogied unselfconsciously. The *Whenever, Wherever* video by Shakira finished and the show moved to what I expected to be the commercial break. But there were no commercials, instead more videos – this was the 'musical break'. In a music show.

A lady with an infant, bear-ears of their onesie poking up from the top of her papoose, entered the store. The lodge's matriarch, who'd been silently squatting behind the counter, rose like a chequerboard matryoshka on a scissor car jack. The lady with the child took a greaseproof package of sausages from the fridge and they greeted each other in a staccato wail. They both looked over in my direction and burst out laughing. I got the distinct impression I was being sized up, either as marriage material or the ingredients for the next batch of bangers.

"Namaste." I called to the lady the door. She giggled and returned the greeting.

"What type of sausages are they?" I was ever the Don Juan with my chat-up lines, and she giggled again.

"Meat." My host had put paid to any further flirtation with the pyre of chunky chips he laid before me and the disapproving side glance he made to the doorway. My date with the papoose lady was put on ice, her string of bangers disappearing out the door. I got stuck into the *pommes frites*, thinking at least I'd selected the optimal comfort food to combat my disappointment.

"Hot?" I questioned my host on the Druk chilli sauce's Scoville value; the chips were tasty but had reached the critical mass where they'd become samey and needed some livening up.

"Not for Sherpa."

"What's spiciest, red or green?"

"Same."

I tried the green, which was tangy rather than spicy and had a sour taste which complemented the chips well. Encouraged, I tried the red to see how it compared and a sear of pain worked its way up my tongue as the chilli sauce napalmed its way across my papillae.

"Feck me. That's hot!"

The slim man cast an amused glance that said serves you right for trying it on with my cousin. I slurped some tea, hazarding it would douse things down, but it wasn't much use. I reverted to plain chips, hoping there was no permanent damage to my taste buds. As the pain subsided, I realised I was going to pay for that chilli sauce in the morning.

No more meat-product shoppers arrived before I finished my tea, and everyone seemed content to let the evening conclude by watching the music show. I returned to my room and doubled up the dolphin duvets. It was going to be *so* good to sleep in a proper bed, under a proper duvet, my lullaby to be *A Walk Across The Rooftops* by The Blue Nile. I started on track two and, three quarters of an hour later, it was time for sleep; it was 9pm.

I awoke in the wee hours to scuffling, imagining Sherpa rats and slept-walked to the toilet, where the eco lighting wasn't working. Another power cut, I reasoned, but the flush didn't work either and I wondered if there had also been a water cut. I returned to bed, hoping to let the owners know before I needed to use the loo for the main event later in the morning.

The remainder of the night was restful, and I awoke refreshed to the sounds of slap-bass at 6am, the teenager playing the funkiest alarm call ever at teenager-level volume: 11 and a half. I was pleased to see the utility companies had completed emergency repairs overnight and light and water were restored in the WC. I recorded a Type Four in the *Diaries* and added a supplementary note to never take the red chilli sauce with one's evening meal.

The morning had that mark of freshness after a deluge where the air *smells* washed clean. My gear was mostly dried, the next few hours were an easy downhill and the sky was a cloudless cobalt as I stepped out into the courtyard. Everything had come together for the makings of a cracking day.

"Sorry, no apple." I'd ordered an apple porridge and milk tea in the shop-restaurant.

"No worries, that's okay," I said, thinking 'Oh my. What *would* they say in Junbesi?'

"Other fruit. You want banana?"

"Yes please." The porridge was so good it would've taken the gold star at the Dundonian Quakers Oats Society annual dinner. After no fuss with the bill or farewells, I stretched out onto the trail.

A mere 10 metres from my start, I was doubled over, my chest convulsed, dry retching. Concerned, I tried to reason why: Nunthala was only at 2,200 metres and I'd no headache; it couldn't be altitude sickness, so what could it be? I stopped dry heaving, took a swig of water and moved on again.

The gravel underfoot was saturated, and I could feel it sag with my weight as I strode along the broad track that wound its way through Nunthala proper. The high street was a silent parade of stolen-blueprint identical lodges, three storeys of whitewash and blue windows, proprietary gardens behind waist-high drystone walls. A battered tin shed announced itself as the Numbur snooker house, open 6am to 10pm. From the photos outside, it appeared Ronnie O'Sullivan and female anime characters were regulars. As I left the shed behind me, I dropped into thoughts about the poor porter who'd landed that gig, carrying the slate for the tables up to the village.

Beyond the stone stair that demarked the city limits, I stepped onto mudslide talus and my right boot slipped a metre, swiftly followed by my left as they gouged two walking-boot-tread grooves into the slope. My slide had been halted by the accumulation of mud from the grooves into wattle and daub fists wrapped around my boots. As I reached the flatter, more solid trail and scraped the gunk from my footwear with a handy stick and some broad leaves, I looked back with some glee at the 10-centimetre craters marking my path.

As I descended, the footing became at times a treacherous soft mud that sucked my boots down to lace level; open sewers of congregated donkey filth; smoothed rock stairs sparkling with films of wet; gravelly pebbles that collapsed and caved unpredictably; and fast-flowing runnels of slurry. I took each step carefully, the deliberateness amplifying the strain on my legs. Thirty minutes later, my knees were protesting each stair like a couple of pre-schoolers being dragged down to breakfast on a cold winter morning. There was little taxation on the lungs from the descent but all the reserves of strength in my lower body had been drained. I halted to rest, the optimism of breakfast having been dented.

It was a serendipitous place to stop. I looked back up a massive Y-shaped valley of broad, chartreuse cereal fields blending into pea-green terraces that erupted from the forests of deep green conifers cascading from the aretes at either fork. It was a moment to ignore my aches, creaks and clicks and let it seep in. I spent a quarter of an hour watching farmers move stealthily through waist-high crops, bending double to pull up a weed or thin their cultivars.

The path punished my joints for a while more before widening onto a horizontal where a stone tea garden had been constructed. As I procrastinated whether it was too early for the day's first tea break, two attractive women in their early 20s skipped down through the mud to join me. They had the glow of an inherent healthiness nurtured through years of balanced meals and a surfeit of dairy, only lightly tarnished by a temporary emaciation that betrayed at least six months on the circuit in Asia and a nutritional deficit possibly due to the effects of unfriendly bacteria.

The girls were pony-tailed, blonde and inked with a randomness of characters on their bare arms (the Gandhi spinning wheel, bursting lily and butterflies); they were further accessorised by a bird's nest of brass bangles and friendship bracelets. According to the Hindu Om Theorem, the Purple Haze would've been proud to call them customers. I was disappointed with the lack of local sensitivity in their choice of singlets and knee-length Lycra walking gear, but I thought at least they fitted it better than the guys in Spandex Ballet. They were from Denmark and were heading to Base Camp, on a tight schedule. My question about how they'd paid for their visa, combined with my other soporifically dull patter, meant after exchanging the usual pleasantries, they went on their way, me following in their wake.

A group of sixth form boys came racing up the hill, passed the Danish ladies and stopped, checking out the vision moving downhill, laughing loudly, needling each other. 'No chance, lads,' I thought as I passed them, but was gladdened they believed they had. I was also pleased their passing signified the trail's solidification into a stone staircase that ran through leafy forest glades. The cool rushing of a metre-high waterfall lulled me into a reverie once again. With each step, my knee pain seemed to lessen, allowing me almost to glide through a forest dissected by limpid streams tumbling steeply between mossed boulders.

As the trail flattened and the trees became twisted boles wrapped in the same hued moss, my meditation was interrupted by three athletic twentysomething men, competing in Lycra, who came storming towards me in an uphill slalom. They were the male equivalents of the Danish girls, but the musculature portrayed a picture that said they hadn't been backpacking as long. They'd completed a series of slippery mud switchbacks and, through the trees, I could see their route had taken them up the side of a narrow ravine. I could hear running water, something more than the streams that tumbled down to the trail, and I craned my neck to see if I could locate the source, the result being the mud giving way and my big toe cracking when my foot skidded into a rock. Recovering my balance and examining my boot, I hoped I hadn't broken a bone.

Toe throbbing, I reached a ramshackle farmhouse where a cock had been affixed to its wooden fence with electrical wire, pecking at imaginary specks on its topmost horizontal, and a minute later the source of the rushing revealed itself – the Dudh Kosi, the Milk River. I was glad to have my first sight of the river I'd follow on and off all the way to Namche Bazaar, but less pleased that, at 1,510 metres, this was also the lowest point on the trek. It *was* all uphill from here.

There was the small matter of the 109-metre suspension bridge to cross before I could start my ascent. I was spared any oncoming or tailgating traffic and, as I reached the far side, thought it strange I hadn't seen any porters that day. Barely discernible, etched into the rock and covered in lichen, was 'HMG Swiss Suspension Bridge Division' and some other characters lost to erosion.

Wondering whether 'HMG' stood for 'Hiker Murdering Gangway', I ascended gravelly switchbacks and the impressive, bubbling confluence of the Dudh Kosi and the Deku Khola, the river that drained the valley in which Nunthala sat, came into view. Thirty breathless minutes later, I discovered what I believed to be the first lodge at Jubling, the 'Hotel Riverside Juving'. Ignoring the minor spelling discrepancy, being taxed by the hike up from the bridge and wanting to take the opportunity to examine my toe, I ordered a small pot. Besides, I estimated, my early start had corresponded with a school assembly-time rather than mid-morning break, so I'd plenty of time to reach my destination for the day, which was Bupsa.

My order was taken at a small tea-cum-convenience store shanty in the hotel grounds. The gentleman who brought me my tea looked concerned as I removed my boot; from his face it was easy to read his thoughts, and they said I should've taken that shower in Nunthala with my socks on. My expert medical opinion was that the toe wasn't broken, just bruised. This assessment was based on the purplish colouring the digit had adopted and that I was able to wiggle it. Relieved, I took the other boot off, elevated my aching legs and aired my stockings on the plastic seat opposite.

The day *was* glorious. The morning chill had lifted and the heat of afternoon hadn't yet risen. I leant back on my chair, closed my eyes and sunbathed. Apart from the rushing of water, the only sounds came from bird call and an occasional flutter of leaves.

An hour later, the tea had been dispatched but so had my enthusiasm for the next stretch, and the basking had me considering this place as an overnight stay. I could relax in the tea garden, allow my knees and feet to recover, watch whoever was drying corn husks and be refreshed for the challenge of Bupsa the next day with a tan of which George Hamilton would be proud. Tempted as I was, I knew if I allowed myself to be seduced by each patch of paradise along the way, I'd take three months to get to Base Camp.

Stirred into action, I looked for the waiter and, instead, found a scythe three metres long. Either a team of men were required to heft it, or the Grim Reaper was significantly larger than he was depicted in the comic strips. I hoped Azrael wasn't having a quick brew before tapping the shoulder of that beardy geezer with the fatal metatarsal haemorrhaging. Not wanting to risk being asked to cash in my chips, I hobbled over to the shanty and paid my dues.

Juving was just one of the many alternative spellings of Jubling that littered the village as it threaded its way uphill in a narrow riband; others included Joving, Jubing and Jovling. It was a delightful village of whitewashed lodges and small shops festooned with hanging baskets of Mexican pink floral displays. I felt I was standing tall in the back of a limo in a ticker-tape parade by the manner the local ladies smiled and nodded at me as I hauled myself up the stone ladders and landings that constituted the high street.

At the village limit, a sign read 'Namaste Lodge and Resturent Cosmatic [sic], Fancy and Retail Shop Centre'. I wondered if the owners were trying for a new portmanteau with 'Cosmatic'. Among the usual opportunities to grab a Starbucks and McDonalds in the food hall, did the mall offer the chance to pick up some cosmic magic mushroom lip gloss and space-cake fake tan before leaving town?

Immediately out of the town, the trail drove on in thigh-pummelling increments. The archer's V-notch of the Dudh Kosi gorge lay always to my left, flowing into dark clouds that had swollen in the distance; it was raining further on. I trudged up into a hillside of shrubs similar to laurel bushes and strung across the view of the ravine was a cat's cradle of gossamer a metre across. A black spider with a bright orange Harry Potter lightning scar on its back sat among the carcasses of defeated usurper arachnids and half-eaten prey. To my mind, the spider was Shelob and the trail the hobbits' staircase to Mordor.

I was flagging badly as I reached a donkey-jam in the village of Churkha and only after the cops had issued tickets for flagrant disregard for lane discipline did the gas bottle-laden animals move on. Churkha hadn't been advertised in the guide and for good reason – it was little more than a level stretch of stone with a wooden house on one side and another elevated above a revetment on the other – but was authentically rustic enough for a man to be taking, in archaic parlance, rolls of photographs with an expensive-looking camera.

"Do you mind if I make picture?" he enquired in a heavily accented English.

"Fill your boots, mate."

"Fill ze boots?"

"Sorry. Yes, go ahead. Are you a photo-journalist?" He pressed a button and examined his viewfinder, checking the result. I missed the shutter's cluck; it at least gave an indication of the number of embarrassing portraits taken.

"No, I joost like make ze picture. I make ze picture of zis rajion of Nepal."

"I ask because your camera looks top of the range. Looks like you're serious."

"Yes, I am serious. I 'ave 25 kilo of camera equipment in my pack."

"What?! On top of your other gear? How much are you carrying altogether, in total?"

"I theenk 35 or more, maybe 37 kilo."

"Man, that's way too much, you're going to die carrying that. It's what the porters carry and they can only do that because they were born here and do it for a living."

"Yes. She is very 'eavy. I look for porteur maybe in next village." He was a social worker from Nice, the photography was a hobby, and he hoped to sell some pictures to local magazines. He'd taken his fill of shots in Churkha and stowed his gear into a front pack almost as big as his backpack. He was 30, shaven headed and looked in good shape, but even cleverly counterbalanced as it was, that weight was too much. I bid him *adieu* and he lurched forward, clearly struggling with the load. I figured it was possible he could be the only person I was going to overtake on the trek.

The Niçois had made a point of framing the lady in the alleyway, a potential National Geographic front cover. She was a lithesome 60-year-old whose most arresting feature was her golden nose piercings – an argonaut's shield had been speared through her left nostril and, dangling from her septum, was an inverted heart-mind. Her hoop earrings were made of the same precious metal. Her face was smooth, the crow's feet the only external betrayal of her advanced years. Her pink cotton blouse was warmed by a thick, crimson woollen cardigan, the sleeves of which were covered in tiny seed pods; her skirt bore a silver motif of dragon scales; and her feet were flip-flopped.

She'd been implored by the Frenchman for her picture, so I knew she had no English and I made the sign of spooning something into my mouth. She nodded in confirmation and nipped into the wooden house, returning with a printed menu in the green and black of a packet of mint humbugs. Keeping to my strict dietary regime, I ordered the cabbage noodle soup.

I was shocked when she disappeared and returned to the ginnel with a stack of long poles of firewood, not realising she'd have to make a fire to feed me. The wooden building I'd taken to be a roughcast hallway jutting into the passageway was, in fact, her kitchen. She thirded the poles with a hatchet, kindled some shavings and small twigs in a rectangular hole in the extension's rendered base and, within a minute, had a blaze going into which she fed the poles. A wave dismissed me inside while she chopped a white cabbage.

The eating area was a single table flanked by benches. The far wall was a cupboard of chicken wire cages that deterred thieves from making away with Ever-Ready batteries, Druk chilli sauce, Ra-Ra noodles, cases of San Miguel and hundreds of eggs, while the rest of the space was devoted to a store of 'computer sorted' sacks of rice. I couldn't spot a Cray anywhere in the background, although there were various tin bowls for measuring, and so wondered how that was achieved.

The lady knew her onions, or more accurately her onions and cabbage – the noodle soup was up there with one at the Dagchu, but I felt guilty I'd caused her to make a fire, so ordered a small pot to maximise the value from the flames and sat back out in the thoroughfare to enjoy the drink. A familiar face came tromping into the hamlet.

"Oh hello, fancy meeting you here," Aydin cheerfully greeted me as he dropped his bag.

"Fancy a cuppa? I've loads here."

"Okay, thanks, just a quick one, I've got to keep going."

"No bother." I hand-signalled another cup to the lady.

"Did you come from Nunthala today? I'm surprised you're behind me."

"Yeah. I started late today. That road to Nunthala, man, it took me 10 hours to get there in the end."

"Ten hours?! But you were only just behind me at Trakshindu La."

"Oh, I know, I got lost in all that mist. I walked for two hours and found out I'd gone the wrong direction. I had to go almost all the way back to where I'd met you to find the right track. My feet were really killing me by the end of the day. I woke up this morning so tired, my legs sore as can be and my shoulders aching from all that rubbing. It took me ages to get out of bed."

"How you feeling now? It's a knee-buster of a climb to here from the river, isn't it?"

"Oh yeah, my knees are killing me as well, I think all the ligaments are detached. You know, every step I hear clicking. I think you can hear me coming for miles around. Plus, my kneecaps are swollen, they must be twice the size they usually are. Honest, I can feel them rubbing against my trousers."

"You have pain-killers, right?"

"Oh yeah, but I'm not going to take them." He downed the dregs of his tea as a pair of young men dashed past with a friendly namaste. Aydin seemed to know them and hailed them to wait while he donned his gear before they set off up the hill together.

The climb from Churkha was harder than the ascent to it from the river. The noodle soup lacked the same fortifying kick that had made the first 20 minutes post-lunch easier on other days and it became a slog up stone flights interrupted by scrambles on all fours up minor landslides. The trail traversed a wooded hillside to reach firmer ground, a level flagstone staircase leading up to a red and blue painted ornate Tibetan gate. A further flight of stairs to the right led up to a chorten where sat the gentleman from Nice, enjoying a Gitane on the stone piazza of the lodge at the saddle's apex.

"Bonjour, monsieur. Can I invite you 'ave some tea?"

"That's nice of you, why not? Thank you," I replied, and detoured into the lodge to obtain a cup.

"How was the hike up?"

"She was very 'ard. I will take porteur if I 'ave enough monae."

"How much do you think it will cost?"

"I don't know but I theenk 15 'undred rupee for 25 kilo. It is a lot of monae, no?"

"Per day?"

"Oui."

"What's that come out at, err ... about €12, isn't it? That's not bad."

"But ze monae of social worker in Nice is not good. I 'ave to theenk very 'ard about theese." He stubbed out his cigarette as a plate heaped with noodles semi-submerged in black bean sauce was placed in front of him. I realised I hadn't only caught him up, but was going to overtake him! I finished my tea in a pettiness of celebration.

"Merci beaucoup for the tea. Enjoy your lunch! See you on the trail."

"Yes, see you. Au revoir and bon voyage."

I got back to my feet, but the rest had done no good and I lurched across the plaza. I was relieved the trail sloped gently downhill from the saddle and I traipsed unsteadily along its path to where a vista of a village strung along the wide valley unveiled itself. I reached it spent, disappointed to see it wasn't my target for the day – a sign welcomed me to Khari Khola. Deliberating my next step, literally, it was the sight of an unusual lodge which swung it for me. The guidebook had indicated Bupsa was a five to six-hour walk from Nunthala. Five hours after leaving, I was still at least an hour's climb away and, although I hadn't reached my planned destination, I decided I'd arrived.

Khari Khola to Paiya

What had drawn me towards the 'Tashi Delek Cottage Guest House' was the 'Cottage' part. Brightly painted in squares of Egyptian blue bordered in white, these were Brighton beachfront huts uprooted and transported far from any pier. Each white door was sentried by a pair of eye-height windows, the frames of which were in canary yellow. The image of an expertly completed game of Tetris came to mind. They surrounded a multi-level terrace set in a hollow carved from the hillside on three sides. An umbrellaed table and chairs topped the upper terrace, marigolds and marigold-strewn trees the bottom. A pair of orange smalls was drying on a washing line.

I tripped into the lodge, which itself was a fairly standard, two floors, whitewash, and blue-framed woodwork building. Before I could divest myself of my pack, a middle-aged lady was behind the check-in desk, arms splayed and palms flat on the glass counter. It was time to play *The Price is Right*.

"Namaste. Chiya? Tea?" A new gambit, perhaps, or maybe she'd miscalculated with her first move? After all, I was beyond early to need accommodation.

"No thank you, can I see a room, please? Hundred rupees?"

"Two hundred." Checkmate in one. She was a grandmaster in the art of blitz negotiation.

"I'd like to see the room first, please." She produced a butter-coloured fob from under the desk and bid me follow. We passed through a door curtain that led to the cottages, the way down comprising of a timber construction in the midst of a ladder-stair identity crisis. The ladder psyche had scorned the suggestion of a handrail, while the stair persona had conceded only a cosmetic width enhancement on the rungs. My unbalanced ballet of a descent was only made worse by the bottom of my pack hitting each level as I descended.

My host decided (I wondered if it was my socks again) to locate me in the chalet furthest away from the lodge. It was laid out in the same fashion as most lodges I'd experienced. Having been spoiled in Nunthala, I was faintly disappointed to learn I'd have to revert to the sleeping bag again, but nodded we had a deal. The lady showed me the outhouse, which was down a flight of stairs cut into the hill and painted in the same jolly tones as the other parts of the complex. I'd have to content myself with a Squat Style for the duration of my stay.

Dead beat, I stowed my gear, rolled out the sleeping bag and laid back to rest my eyes for a minute – and woke up three hours later. It was still too early for dinner, so I gathered the Kindle for a late afternoon of reading and sipping from a small pot under those damp tangerine pants. The ascent up the identity-fluid structure to the lodge was easier without my pack. After placing my order, I returned to the terrace and started *Cryptonomicon* by Neal Stephenson.

The first heavy drops of rain splattered in a loose change of tarnished silver, the thermos arriving on the cusp of the cloudburst. The lady completed her return journey to the door curtain as a thunderclap resounded around the hollow. The parasol above me was meant for shade, not shelter, and started to leak from its apex, so I decided to make a dash for it back to the hut.

My dash was more of an amble – I was, after all, no Usain Bloat. My shoulders took the brunt of the storm, soaked at the expense of everywhere else. I changed into a dry T-shirt and sat in the doorframe of my cabin, idly watching the downpour as it grew ever heavier. Sitting in the hut really was comparable to being on holiday in Brighton in June.

The tempest lasted an hour, after which the clouds lost their dark grey hue but remained squatting overhead. It was a surprise not to see any other trekkers dash in from the rain; for some reason, the cottages lacked appeal. On the plus side, dinner was now another welcome opportunity to hog conversation with the proprietors.

I made my way up the trans-grader staircase and was briefly greeted with an empty dining room before my host beetled out of the kitchen area next to the door curtain. She'd the same nose ring adornment as the lady in Churkha, and her attire was almost identical. The major difference in their appearances was their girth. If the Churkha lady was the flat tyre, the Khari Khola model was the fully inflated version.

She nodded at my request for food and came back with a menu booklet of eight pages. The restaurant served every combination of food imaginable based on half a dozen basic ingredients. The 'Spring Roll' section read:

Vegetable Spring Roll	Rs350
Cheese Spring Roll	Rs400
Sneaker Spring Roll	Rs400
Egg Spring Roll	Rs350
Mixed Spring Roll	Rs400

Tempted as I was by the third item, I worried the lodge's profit margin was going to take a big hit if they were using Yeezys as the chief ingredient. My mind wandered off to wonder whether the mixed spring roll came with an Air Max, Nike Predator, and a side order of shredded plimsoll? I moved on to the dessert section, pleased to see it, too, came with items of expensive footwear.

Apple Pie	Rs450
Banana Pie	Rs350
Mars or Sneaker Pie	Rs450
Banana Filter	Rs350
Apple Filter	Rs350
Rice Pudding	Rs400

The relative pricing got me thinking I'd seen plenty of apple trees but no banana fronds along the trek. Imported bananas should've made that pie more expensive than the apple. The apple pie's premium price seemed canny – every guidebook I'd read about Nepal waxed lyrical about that being the must-have dessert, so the lodge owners were simply being sharp in reading their market. With potential sharp-practice in mind, I moved on to the drinks menu, which read as follows:

Cock	Rs
Fanta	Rs
Sprite	Rs
Can Juice	Rs
Beer	Rs
Mineral Water	Rs
Local Raksi	Rs
Local Tungba	Rs

The lack of pricing was suspicious. If I ordered the cock, would I then have to order something else to take the taste away at London strip-joint prices? I wondered whether I'd been idiotically pronouncing *raksi* incorrectly as *rokha* in the other villages; that this was another entropic phonetic spelling; or this was how the word was pronounced in the dialect of this area.

I opted for the Yeezy-over egg and chips and a cup of tea. I was careful to request just tea, without the bag, on account of being keen to avoid any potential risk of confusion around tea-bagging, given the nature of the drinks menu. My host looked disappointed I hadn't selected one of the more adventurous items. I couldn't help but think somewhere behind the beach huts was a stash of never-worn Converse Fastbreaks she was anxious to get into the deep-fat fryer.

An hour later, I'd completed making as many puerile double-entendres from the menu as I could muster. I had bored of my phone's chess game and speculated the lady had gone to Churkha to purchase those eggs from her gracile cousin. An hour was long enough to wait for my meal so I called out. Receiving no response, I repeated the "Cooee" slightly louder. My call was again unheeded, so I walked over to the kitchenette, thinking something amiss. Behind the curtain door, there was no sign of potatoes deep frying or eggs sizzling in a pan, but my host and her daughter were both approaching their personal high scores on Candy Crush.

The owner looked up from her cramped, myopic posture with a look of shock and embarrassment that told me she was helpless in her addiction to 'Tasty' and 'Delicious' in-app purchases. Mortified, she apologised and escorted me back to my seat, turned around my tea in less than a minute and pulled the curtains shut again. I thought it a shame the mountains hadn't been left uninfected by the disease of social media and subtly monetised gaming, but it was clear from her behaviour it was here to stay.

My host had clearly felt guilty at her dalliance and attempted to make up for it 15 minutes later by piling on my plate a couple of ostrich-sized eggs and half the Khumbu region's annual potato crop. As quickly as she'd placed the food down, she was back into her kitchen area, indicating there was going to be no conversation tonight. I finished my food and headed back to my cottage, bidding the ladies an unreturned goodnight as I passed the galley. All I could see was a dull blue light peeking through the curtain.

The brief hop across the patio was enough to chill my bones and I was glad to warm up in my sleeping bag. I lit up the Nano and chose *Disintegration* by The Cure, hoping track six would get me off to the land of nod. Seventy minutes later, at 8.30pm, it was time for sleep. There was a finger drum on the corrugated roof as I closed my eyes; I would slumber to the soothing sound of more rain.

I woke early again and headed to perform my morning's hygiene. The WC was locked and, in my bleary-eyed state, I reasoned the door was jammed. I tried to force it and only realised I was in a tug of war when a stream of unknown words was spat through the jamb. The translation was something along the lines of 'A gentleman would know a lady requires time to complete her toilet in the morning.' A few minutes of shivering in my undergarments later, the lady had finished applying her make-up for the day.

"Namaste, sir. Nice morning." It was; the rain had abated and the clouds disappeared. I could see the snowy summit of a mountain behind the convenience's roof.

"Namaste, morning. Yes, it's beautiful. What's the name of that mountain over there?"

"I don't know, sir, ha-ha. I have lived in Khari Khola all my life but I don't know, ha-ha. I will ask husband today." She sprinted her way back to the lodge, keen to find out.

I was pleased the day's entry in the *Diaries* would be consistent at Type Four. Breakfast was another lonely affair of a tasty porridge and a milk tea, served with an almost Teutonic efficiency. After settling up without fuss, I set off, but had barely made it out of the doorframe when I started to dry heave, a repeat of the previous day. I managed to keep everything down and calmed my gullet with a swig of water before setting off again, worried about the root cause.

Khari Khola high street was frenetic, with a crowd gathered 100 metres ahead. I was caught in the wake of a swirling mass of blue-uniformed school children shouting and screaming along the strip as they rushed to join the throng. The cause of the melee was schoolchildren being thrown ballpoint pens and pencils by the Germans in the same way a SeaWorld trainer throws fish to an orca. I'd thought this kind of charity had had its day in Nepal a decade earlier but, from the delight on the children's faces, I was clearly mistaken.

As I marched through the scene, I couldn't prevent my dislike of the German group prompting a prejudicial conviction that they were only doing this for their own self-aggrandisement. The way they mistreated their porters was incongruous with this act of kindness and it felt disingenuous to me. I bustled through, guiltily ruminating I should think better of people, but knowing deep down that, in the case of the Germans, I wouldn't.

The path ran in shadow for a quarter of an hour down to a small suspension bridge where I met the porters from the German group adjusting their loads, our greeting similar to a first reunion of Korean relatives who'd been separated since the DMZ's establishment. They were, of course, rushing ahead to construct an outdoor kitchen that would serve their guests' indoor picnic at lunchtime and so our goodbyes came swiftly.

The river's far bank was enveloped in sunshine, a new road cutting across the base of the climb. A score of people were being marshalled for the ascent, their guide and porters straightening straps of day packs and maladjusted camera slings. I could see a duo of floppy-hatted half-centurions had made a start uphill.

"Coucou, Peggy," called a lady in the basal mass.

"Coucou, Sandra," responded one of the uphill ladies. The group were French, all well dressed in appropriate gear for the mountains and appreciative of the local culture, taking heed that on males past 50, Lycra is an even less becoming look than it was beforehand. The group had that air of polite disorganisation signifying the guide was going to spend some time fixing their clothes and backpacks, applying the same care and attention a mother would take for their child's first day of nursery.

I chose to pass them by and start the climb, the trail a tough introduction to the day. I heated up from the morning chill soon removing my Rab. A few hundred paces up the trail, the *coucou* lady was panting for air on the hillside. After a quick enquiry about her health – she indicated she was fine – I moved on. It was a new feeling for me – I found it hard to believe I'd overtaken someone who was carrying a daypack.

I reached Bupsa after an hour-and-a-half's strenuous climb. My new-found role as pacemaker deserved to be celebrated with a nice cup of something refreshing. The shaded table in the slot that was Bupsa's main thoroughfare was perfect for such an occasion and so I ordered a lemon tea. As I took my first sip, a heavily perspiring man heaved himself up the last steps to where I was sitting. His Johnny Cash of head-to-toe black had not been the best choice for the conditions.

"Good morning. Is this seat taken?" He spoke English with a syllable-by-syllable grammatical exactness.

"No, help yourself. Tough climb, eh? Did you come from Khari Khola this morning?"

"Ya. Extremely difficult. We bozth started in Khari Khola. I saw you pass by my lodge earlier."

"Oh, I didn't spot any tents by any of the lodges. Where was your group camped?"

"We have not camped, we have being staying in the Khari Khola Guest House." The abandonment of the pretence of camping seemed to provoke a new-found amicability.

"Why was that, did you find camping too cold?"

"No, we have not camped. To camp in the Himalaya? Who would do such a thing? Not me. I'm not crazy!"

"You didn't camp, are you not the German group? I saw you in Junbesi, right?"

"Ya, we are German but you did not see me in Junbesi. We started to trek in Ringmo."

"Ringmo? How did you *start* in Ringmo?"

"We came by helicopter. The weather was so bad that our plane to Phaplu could not land, so we had to return to Kathmandu. Our guide chartered a helicopter, we flew into Ringmo and started our trek there."

"Was it a yellow helicopter? I think I saw you fly in."

"Ya. Yellow."

"That must have been something. I saw the helipad, it's smaller than a merry-go-round."

"Ya. I don't know what this merry-go-round is, but our pilot was incredible. How he landed between the trees was wonderful." My new friend was Heinrich, on an exclusive organised trek of four. His four coffees arrived at the same time as Alfred BJ and what I'd reckoned was Heinrich's group materialised at the slot's base.

"This is the German group I thought you were with." He called out a good morning in German and Alfred BJ greeted him back, which left me wondering why Heinrich had been more successful than I had in that regard. They conversed for five minutes before Alfred BJ and his entourage recognised they'd blocked the street and needed to move away.

"They're so arrogant, so stuck up," he confided as the Muscle Man, the last of the band, departed.

"Yes, I didn't think they were friendly at Junbesi and they were downright rude at Ringmo."

"That is typical for Austrians!" He explained they were a group of doctors who were visiting a clinic in the hills their hospital supported. I thought, rather ungenerously, to remind myself never to get ill in Vienna; I'd have to run ahead and sterilise the instruments, balance the anaesthesia gases, perform my own open-heart surgery in a marquee outside the hospital and be thankful for the opportunity to do so.

Heinrich's colleagues arrived. Wolfgang was also around 60-ish, his shaggy beard and heavy metal hair matching his lupine name; Britta and Agathe were the two ladies, slightly younger. Britta was an Amazonian with short cropped grey hair, Agathe was darker and looking more like she spent most of her time browsing the cake section on Amazon. We chatted through their coffee until it was time to get going.

"Where is your porter?" Heinrich asked.

"I don't have one. I'm carrying my bag myself," I replied.

"Well, I admire your strength, you are stronger than me. Good luck." Ego ridiculously over-inflated, I set off.

Before I could warm up again, the trail became a turning circle where a digger was parked. A new road had been hewn out of the mountains to the right. It was either going to stop there or double back along the short cliff to Bupsa, so it was unclear which way to proceed. Two workmen were flicking the last of their ash onto the road as Ved and the young porter asked them something. I drew up and asked which way the path ran; the elder of the workmen pointed across the road to my right where a trail had been sculpted from the cliff. A wide-brimmed umpire hat came bowling around the corner in that direction, a grinning face beneath it.

"Lee! How are you, man?"

"Hi Aydin, how are you going? Did you stay in Khari Khola last night?"

"Yeah. That place was terrible, I'd a horrible stay in my lodge."

"How come? Mine was pretty good, they'd all sorts on the menu."

"Oh, well, did you see that rain yesterday? I got caught in it and was soaked through and the lodge had nowhere to dry my clothes. On top of that, the toilet roof leaked so I got all wet when I went for a pee."

"Doesn't sound like the end of the world."

"But that was a big problem because their food didn't agree with me and I spent most of the night in that leaky toilet. I hope I've not caught pneumonia."

"Did you take anything for the diarrhoea? I've got some Imodium in my bag if you need it?"

"Oh no, I wouldn't."

"Okay, are you heading towards Paiya today?"

"Yes, do you know which way the path goes?" I pointed up the cutting and he headed up, the porters hoisting their loads to follow. I would ascend in their slipstream. The new path led into a broken confusion of contorted trees narrowed to the width of a goat track which twisted and turned into distributaries and dead ends in the forest. My instincts told me this wasn't the right way. Aydin had disappeared, but I could hear the crunching of the porters' boots and the swish of branches being forced out of the way ahead of me. I broke onto a glade where Ved was marking the trail with an arrowhead made from sticks.

"Is this the right way, Ved?"

"I don' know."

The glade became a dell narrowing into a green funnel where I slipped and tumbled as I battled through a primary jungle of bushes and shrubs, my hands birched raw trying to arrest my fall. I tumbled to a stop on red earth at the Komatsu's side. A stone staircase that had been obscured by the digger's bulk led up the hill opposite.

"Bastards." I shrieked at the workmen bent over with laughter. I didn't think it was funny, not knowing whether Aydin had emerged or was lost somewhere above. I hoped he'd have had the good sense to retrace his steps and head downhill, and he was already ahead of me on the real trail.

The trail above the stairs was carved at a vicious angle into the hillside. My chest was heaving before I was a couple of hundred metres from the turning place, but it was a good place to stop, commanding a magnificent prospect over the Deku Khola valley. It was my last view of where I'd come from as the path now chiselled its way along the side of the Dudh Kosi gorge, the river sliding silently down the canyon 1,000 metres below.

The track climbed above the jungle line into terraces again, where the farms cultivated watermelons and also, with a certain peculiarity, grew pumpkins on their roofs. I approached a one-room narrow lodge nearing lunchtime and dumped my bag inside the curtain door, looking for something to eat. A man emerged from the lodge's rear.

I must have interrupted his Jane Fonda-style morning workout as he was attired in what could reasonably be described as an Olympic gymnast's outfit. Unreasonably, it could've been called a leotard, but what really caught my attention was the brilliant white matching towelling head and wrist bands colour-coordinated with his high-top basketball shoes. I wasn't about to tell him, though, that he looked like he was auditioning for the Bollywood remake of Flashdance, as he was built like the Colossus of Rhodes. He was head and shoulders above any Nepali I'd met previously and had iron-pumped his natural assets into the perfection of a Michelangelo's David.

"Namaste. Dhal baat. Chiya," he queried, his delivery inviting no dissent.

"Namaste. Dhal baat and chiya then, please. Just a cup. Dhanyabad." He returned, head bent, with my food a few minutes later. He was as taciturn as he was ripped, hunching off as soon as my lunch was on the table with a grunt that could've heralded successfully deadlifting one-twenty.

I ate alone, silently wondering how this giant had sculpted a six-pack in such a remote location and whether or not, when he worked out, the local police increased the avalanche risk in the valley below.

The food was passable, but he charged me at twice the going rate; I assumed he did it just because he could. I paid up in a hurry lest he changed his mind and calculated he'd undercharged me, or asked me to spot for him for the rest of the day.

The trail mainly seemed to serve as a bridleway for the next hour. The 1,000-metre plunge to death would've been merely terrifying if it hadn't been for the mule trains. It seemed as if 617 Squadron had breached a donkey dam upstream and the resultant wave of asses was funnelled directly towards me. Every five minutes or so, I found myself desperately flinging my body out of the stampede into any slight indentation in the crags on the inside of the way. The mules were armed with pairs of propane canisters doubling their width to almost that of the path; if they failed to knock you into the abyss, there was a good chance they'd get you with an IED: Improvised Eeyore Device.

I weaved upwards in petrified sprints and, after a few false summits, was brought to the prayer flags of Khari La. The good news was my guidebook had made no mention of the heart-stopping fear to be encountered on the section I'd completed, but it did advise to watch one's footing on the muddy, slippery, exposed and mule-clogged section immediately to come. Bloody hell, I thought, with worse to come, should I just swan dive over the edge now and get it over with?

I played a nip-and-tuck game of overtaking with a porter which took my mind off the conditions underfoot to some extent. He was tiny, all of 50 kilos, with a face more lined than the south face of Uluru. His load was suspended from a wicker basket lashed to a wooden vee with no consideration for max tare regulations. I asked myself if he could've been the progeny of one of those Sherpas who'd worked on the Hillary-Norgay expedition all those years ago. My thoughts progressed to what this section of the trail must have been like with 300 porters lumping their loads up the ravine together. I wondered what the local folks had made of the spectacle, as Nepal had only opened to Western visitors a few years earlier. The sight of the expedition might've been their first. From what I'd learned on the trek so far, I reckoned they'd have taken it all in their stride and, at the same time, made a killing on apple pie sales.

The pocket-battleship of a porter was taking things in his stride, too, even though the donkeys had churned the path into a sticky mud between a loose pebbling that served as the pavement. He was oblivious that the only thing between a misstep and certain death was, well, a misstep. As we raced across another chicane above the chasm, the weathered old man hit the nitrous oxide. With a wry grin, he sped off into the distance leaving me for dead either figuratively or, more likely, literally.

At my next rest stop, my fear was further ratcheted – I could see the bridleway now knotted severely back on itself around a promontory, where the turning was nothing more than a smoothed rock that stuck out over the void. I trudged up, my heart pummelling the chest strap of my pack, and scrambled over the boulder millimetre by millimetre. Around to the unseen side of the overhang, 50 metres away, was a wider section where the bluff was protected by another stone. I panted my way over and collapsed, fingers bloodied from where my clawing at the cliff rock had taken the skin off.

Britta gambolled around the scarp a minute later, unperturbed and without a sign of breaking sweat, her breathing so easy she could've given mouth to mouth. She reached me with a look of concern and asked if I needed a drink. 'Wow,' I thought, 'what a woman!' as I bobbed my head appreciatively. She undid her daypack to pull out a half-thermos of burnished silver so bright I could've sworn a mirror signal was returned from across the valley.

"Here, take the cup. There is only one," she offered.

"Thank you."

"Are you okay? Your face ... and look, your fingers are bleeding."

"Yes, thanks. It's just a graze." It was a vain attempt to try to restore some machismo after my brazen display of cravenness on the boulder. I knew she must have been watching my hopeless attempt at a side-pull and gaston.

"Wow, that's fantastic! Thanks. Where did you get that from?" The drink was a rich, hot lemon tea.

"Our guide fills the thermos each morning with whatever we ask for. There is black tea, milk tea, lemon, orange, and mint tea flavours. I like the lemon; I think it is refreshing. Do you want more? I have plenty."

"No, I couldn't possibly." I turned into an English fop at a garden tea party again, hiding my true desire. In reality, I'd have downed the entire canister.

"Go on. I can drink out of the can." I wondered if this were what a St Bernard would say about the brandy after rescuing someone in the Swiss cantons. 'Go on, have a sip. I'll join ya from the barrel, just to be sociable, like.' She took a gulp from the thermos to show me my pretence was acknowledged as nonsense and handed me a refill.

"Are the others far behind?"

"Yes, I think. Heinrich and Agathe are struggling to breathe on the climb. Wolfy has bad knees so is also going slow."

"They'll get there. How do you all know each other?"

"We don't. We met in the hotel in Kathmandu."

"Oh, I assumed you all knew each other. It's such a small group I thought you were couples or school friends or something?"

"Ha-ha, no. We are from a lot of different places in Germany."

"Where do you come from?"

"I was born in Munich, but I live in the Netherlands."

"Really? Whereabouts?"

"A place you won't have heard of probably, a town called Haarlem."

"I know it, it's not far from Amsterdam. How did you end up there?"

"I was married to a Dutchman, but am not anymore. It is funny that you know Haarlem, not many people know of this place, how do you know it?"

"I'd a girlfriend whose parents ran an underwear store there in the mall, called Livera. We used to go there to buy expensive lingerie from her mum. Needless to say, I don't need to go there anymore."

"Livera! I know it. I like it. I used to buy my knickers there, but since the divorce I don't need to go there anymore either!"

"Ha-ha. Well, I hope at least you bought some for *this* trip."

"No! I am from Bavaria, we always *'go commando'*, I think you say! Ha-ha. It helps a lot when you need to pee in the mountains, ha-ha."

I was liking Britta more and more. The tea was finished, and I felt revitalised enough to carry on, but Britta was going to wait for her team. I thanked her for the tea, said goodbye and headed off.

I continued to slither and slide my way down the muddy channel as it hung onto the cliff face. There were moss-coloured caves in which could be seen the charcoal remains of fires swept cold by feet. The guidebook told me these were old porter quarters, and I couldn't grasp how hard a life it was for them – as if it wasn't punishing enough to tightrope balance your own body weight up a mountain each day, at the end of it you had to kip in a hole in the ground.

There was some relief as the trail flattened out onto some sophisticated civil engineering, the path becoming a succession of brick ramparts connected by gentle stairs of long angular cobblestones. The route had turned away from the gorge back into jungle. The lessened peril, secure footing and downhill gradient meant I covered the ground at a speed unprecedented for me and I soon reached a tubular bridge spanning a small river. I gave way to a group of 10 or so who were crossing with heavy loads.

"Namaste," hailed the first gentleman to make it over. He looked their leader, a guide of around 30, wiry and garbed in serious-looking gear. He was all modern fibres, multi-utility pockets and adjustable strapping.

"Namaste."

"Are you going to Lukla? To Base Camp?"

"Yes, that's the idea. Have you done that already?"

"Yes, yes. We are going to Bupsa. To get the jeep to Salleri."

"I didn't know you could do that?"

"Yes, yes. A new road has been made."

"Yes, I think I met the guys finishing it this morning. I wouldn't trust a word they say if you need to know where to get the jeep. How was the trip, did everyone make it?" The rest of his group had made it across the bridge. They were equally well kitted out, matching paisley headscarves topping Ray-Ban and whisker combos only ZZ-Top could better.

"Yes. Everyone made it."

"How you doin', man?" I ascertained the first Billy Gibbons was from the Americas.

"Good, thanks. How was the trek?"

"Awesome, dude. Just like, awesome. Totally cool."

"Excellent. I'm looking forward to getting there."

"Enjoy it, man, enjoy." The suitably dusted Texan blues-rockers waddled off, leaving me with their guide.

"Where are you staying in Pangboche?" he enquired.

"I don't know, I'm just kind of turning up and seeing what's available."

"Here are the details of my friend, he has an exceptionally good lodge there. In fact, it is the best." A card was summoned from a pocket that had no right to be sewn in the place it was.

"Thanks."

"Where are you staying in Pheriche?"

"Same, I'm not sure." Another card arrived seamlessly from the same pocket with different details. I was impressed – he hadn't even looked.

"Thank you."

"I am a guide for Manaslu peak. In Annapurna. If you come back to Nepal in April, please come. I can guide you and you can stay in my sister's lodge. Please take my card." With another sleight of hand, I found another piece of embossed cardboard in my hand. If he'd pulled a bunny rabbit and bunch of flowers from his hat, I'd have had no right to have been surprised.

"Thank you. I'll look you up if I return."

"Thank you, sir, have a nice trek. Namaste."

I got the impression I was nearing Paiya, the track levelling off. I met a couple of post-coital ponies a few minutes after the bridge. Their coats were matted, more beaver pelt than horsehair, and their manes had been crimped in homage to Siouxsie and the Banshees.

A rusted iron pipe cut diagonally across the path provided some unwelcome hurdling practice. It must've been part of a sensitively considered hydro-electric scheme. One where an environmental impact assessment had inexplicably not made it to the local planning authorities. Telephone wires in the near distance betrayed the start of urbanisation and I crested a small rise to see before me a village. I forwent the first tea house in the settlement, the 'Apple Pie Lodge' due to a reluctance to encourage the proliferation of 'Apples' on the trek, so chose the next one along. The guidebook had indicated Paiya was a four-and-a-quarter-hour trek from Khari Khola. Six-and-three-quarter hours after leaving, I'd arrived.

Paiya to Thado Koshi

T he lodge's upper tier echoed a scaled-up marzipan house crafted by a master pastry chef, a smoothed magnolia plaster over drystone, windows merging softly into the walls. The basement had been left in its original state as if to emphasise the renovation's recency. Across the quadrangle of the patio was a secondary single-storey structure, bringing to mind the class of building typical in light-engineering industrial estates where independent garages and tile wholesalers ply their trade. I wouldn't have batted an eyelid if I'd walked up to find a rolled-up aluminium door exposing a jacked-up, wheels-off Suzuki minivan waiting forlornly for some attention.

The only issue with that image was there were no roads here. It brought into sharp focus that, apart from the two earthmovers, I hadn't seen a vehicle for over a week. It had been easy to get used to that as a new norm, taking for granted the air's purity and the absence of the rasp of internal combustion engines. My thoughts moved tangentially to the possibility that, as automotive traffic custom was absent, this facility offered the equivalent repair and maintenance capabilities for the mule trains that shuttled at breakneck speed along the way.

'Good afternoon, Mr Dhokha, I'd be grateful if you could have a look at Number Four, please, she isn't keeping up.'

'Not keepin' up is it, guv? Well ... that could be down to a lot of fings, mate. I can 'ave a look but cawn't promise nuffink,' would reply the lead-mechanic, scratching his chin.

'Yes, I'm quite worried about Number Four, and we need to get on down to Jiri. Will this take long?'

'Pfffff ... well, guv. I'd take a seat if I was you. We've got a bit of a backlog, you see; we're pretty busy right now with the Lukla donkey derby an' all.'

'I will, thank you.'

'Dawa, you comin' for a bite to eat? What d'ya fancy? Nice bit o' dhal baat for a change?'

'Err ... excuse me ... I thought you were going to take a look at my donkey?'

'Be right back, guv. Government regulations, you see, gotta give the mechanics an hour. Cawn't do nuffink about that.'

'Yes, I understand.'

'Roight guv, what was it, problem with the donkey, was it?'

'Yes, I know it's inconvenient and I'm most awfully sorry to press, but it's been two hours and I really need my mule seen to. Is that *raksi* I smell on your breath?'

'It was just a nip, squire, 'elps with the ol' digestion, so it does. Let's 'ave a butcher's then, up you come, Hee-Haw.'

'Did you manage to find the problem?'

'Well, it looks like the meniscus on the anterior posterior cruciate ligament rotator cuff side bearing could have a tear.'

'Is that serious?'

'Could be, guv, depends what we find when we get the hooves off. Do you want me to go ahead and get the pullers out?'

'Yes, please, I'd be most grateful if you could proceed.'

'Pfffff ... this looks a bit more serious than I first fought, squire. You see that white bit there behind the anterior posterior cruciate ligament rotator cuff?'

'Yes?'

'Well, that's yer lateral condyle patella tendon subacromial bursa. 'Olds it all together, see. Needs replacin', does that.'

'Will that take long?'

'Well, it's the parts, you see, guv. If we've got 'em in we can do it now, but I'll 'ave to check they're in stock. Dawa, can you check we've got a replacement LCPTSB for a 2014 Asinara?'

'Will this err ... what did you say, LBW replacement, be expensive?'

'Well, it's yer foreign model, isn't it, yer Asinara? Them Italian parts are 'ard to get, know what I mean? What's that, we got one in stock, Dawa? Yer in luck, squire. Should we get on with it now, I fink we 'ave a bit of an opening?'

'Yes please.'

'That's it all done, guv. Was a bit 'arder than I fought originally, we needed to get the coracoacromial ligament off before we could get to the LCPTSB. We 'ad to go to Nawang's place, see, to get the right tool for that.'

'Yes?'

'Well, yer Nawang see, 'e's a bit of wide-boy, innit, added a few rupees on, did that.'

'Oh dear, what's the final cost going to be, then?'

'Well, you've got yer labour for the initial diagnosis at a fousand rupees an hour, but we gave you a non-standard discount of not includin' lunch. Yer've got yer replacement LCPTSB part cost, yer CL tool hire from Nawang, did I tell yer 'e's a total villain that Nawang is, yer labour for the repairs, labour tax, value added tax and local government surcharge at 17 per cent. That'll be all-in nine fousand nine hundred and thirty-four rupees. Call it an even ten-k for you, guv.'

'My word, at that price it'd have been cheaper to put Hee-Haw down and buy a replacement.'

'Ahh ... why didn't you say, guv? We offer competitively priced abattoir services and I've got all sorts of used asses round the back, very reasonably priced if I do say so myself.'

A stocky gentleman interrupted my (mule) train of thought. He ushered me through a door into a small foyer and through another doorway protected by a green and yellow chequered curtain. I reckoned he wouldn't have looked out of place in the second row, his white head covering easily doubling as a scrum-cap. He seemed to be expecting me, so much so he asked me to register in a ledger he'd grabbed on the way in. We settled on the pricing without much fuss and it went on the first line on the new page dedicated to Mr Prescott's stay. The book's use to record the items consumed to inform the bill on check-out wasn't new to me; in the larger, more commercial places like the Apple it was standard and I found the write-as-you-go system generally worked well.

Beyond the curtain lay a shop-cum-dining area, similar to Nunthala, except here the shelves and glass-fronted counter were better stocked, and luxuries were on offer alongside the usual items. There were stacks of digestive biscuits in gaudy red sleeves, dark purple jars of jam and plastic squeezy bottles of home-made honey. The curiosity of an orange and blue painted plywood model of a lodge, complete with picket fence, lay mostly finished on the counter.

The wood panelling had been decorated top to bottom with a faux stone bricking-effect wallpaper covered in framed photographs of the owner's family and certificates of hotel management. The room's centre was dominated by the lodge's top attraction: a cast iron wood burner stove of such huge proportions it could have been salvaged from the *Lusitania's* boiler room. Its metal chimney ran vertically up through to the next floor. I hoped my host was going to select its next port of call as my room – I'd be happy to play off the risk of death by carbon monoxide poisoning against having central heating for the night.

My vision of slamming a brass handle around to full steam ahead and toasting my toes against the pipe wasn't to be. My host selected the room directly behind the shop space. I made it orderly and took my mid-afternoon tea on the patio. The cloud had closed in and the view was restricted to the tea houses immediately up the main street; the air became chillier and, after finishing my tea, I decided to spend the afternoon buried in *Cryptonomicon*.

The afternoon bled into early evening, the shop doing a brisk trade judging by the thumping and thudding that had emanated from the plywood partition's far side at regular intervals. It was time for dinner, so I headed to the facilities to wash. Dual toilets had been erected at the base of a stone staircase leading down from the courtyard; I chose the nearest cubicle, which had been recently modernised. Originally a Squat Style, the WC could now boast a Western Style loosely affixed above the long drop's midpoint. The inward camber and drainage slots had evidently proved something of an engineering challenge. The bowl allowed a degree of movement that was only checked by the boltheads that, in the loosest manner of speaking, sort of secured it. Using it would be as hazardous as trying to stay in a motorcycle sidecar driven in an Isle of Man TT race time-trial.

Back in the diner, I was thrilled to see the burner had been stoked; less so it seemed to be pressed into employment to dry the entire village's washing. Seeing the German group made up for that. They nursed their polished thermoses of tea, relaxing quietly with a contented look of well-earned fatigue.

"Ah ... hi Lee! Come and sit with us," Heinrich beckoned.

"Thanks. Nice to see you. I was expecting to be alone again this evening, I haven't met many people for the last few days. There was nobody in my lodge at Khari Khola."

"Ah, well, we are all here, we all made it, I am happy to say."

"How was your day?"

"Good, ya. Difficult. I was glad Wolfy and our guide Dote were there to help me. Having 65 years old, this climb is not easy for an old man like me."

"Ach, you're not old. You made it here okay, right? You just need to go slowly slowly, like they say here," I said, not believing my own words of encouragement around the age element. Heinrich didn't seem to notice.

"Slowly slowly, I have no problem with this, ha!"

"Me neither. Have you folks had your dinner yet?"

"No, not yet, Dote has just passed our order to the kitchen."

"Mind if I join you?"

"Of course, ya. No problem." My order was a vegetable and egg noodle dish that tasted exactly like the Chinese takeaway version in the UK. Somehow the chef had imported *bona fide* black bean sauce or had made up something from local ingredients as good as. I spoke with Heinrich, the conversation roaming across the usual topics and eliciting that he was a dentist from Hamburg. He'd been told by his wife to get his behind up into the Himalayas before he drove her insane with his gabbling about it. I was glad I'd met such a kindred spirit.

"So, tell me, Lee. Will Scotland become independent? There is a lot of curiosity about this in Germany."

"I don't know. The last vote on that was five years ago, and they said it was a once-in-a-generation event. At the moment, the UK government is dead set against another vote and the Scottish government dead set on having another one. It's a big topic in the news at the moment, there's a lot of hassle about it."

"I guess like in Germany, the UK government has the final say over the regional governments on such matters?"

"Yes, the UK government has the legal power to say yes or no to another vote, but the Scottish government, which is run by the Scottish National Party, is saying that because of Brexit there should be another one. They're saying leaving the EU has changed things so much that having another vote is justified."

"Changed what things?"

"Scotland voted overwhelmingly to stay in Europe, but we're leaving because the rest of the country voted differently. The SNP says the Scottish people are being forced to leave the EU against their will."

"The Scottish people don't like Brexit?"

"Yes, they voted something like 60 per cent to stay in the EU. What do people in Germany think about the whole Brexit thing?"

"We think Britain still thinks it has its empire and thinks it will be better off alone. Of course, in Germany, we think that is crazy! We don't understand how Britain thinks more trade barriers will make things better. We are sad the UK will leave but now it is like a divorce, ya, we want to see you out of our house."

"I can understand that, it has gone on for ages."

"And you, Lee, what do you think?"

"I agree with you, I think we're nuts to leave but it's a done deal and we just have to get on with it. Democracy is democracy, right, even if you don't agree with what it's decided. I think there are a lot of arguments from the Brexiteers that make sense, but I think we should've stayed in and tried to reform the EU from the inside, rather than leaving."

"Ya. We are not happy with all in the EU in Germany also. We pay a lot of taxes to support other nations, we would like reform from the inside also."

"The really sad thing is that I think the entire thing ended up as a protest vote against immigration. The irony of that was that the immigrants the backlash was against weren't coming in from the EU and, besides, the ones who do are the ones who pick all our crops, jobs that Brits don't fancy anyway. Regardless of all that, Heinrich, there's one overriding thing that I come back to about the EU that means more to me than all the other arguments."

"What is that?"

"Well, you're German and I'm British and we're sat here having a civil conversation, not shooting at each other. It was different for my grandfather 70 years ago. Your countrymen were dropping bombs on him. If nothing else, the fact that not a single person within the EU member states has been killed by conflict between them should be worth keeping."

"Ya, I agree. My father was in the Luftwaffe in the war, he never talked about it. I remember he told me when I was a boy it was good that the EU was set up so Europe didn't make the same mistakes."

The conversation moved on to other matters. Had he heard of a group called The Beatles and did Hamburg still have the Reeperbahn? Yes, and yes. Did the Hamburg supporters still think of Kevin

Keegan as a legend and what did he think of Jurgen Klopp? Heinrich couldn't stand football, but his professional opinion was Jurgen should be careful not to over-whiten his teeth. Were there still no speed limits on the autobahn? Yes, but he drove a Volkswagen Golf. Were the bagpipes really classified as a musical instrument? That was the topic of much debate. Was it true the British were the fattest people in the EU? Yes, but only for a while longer, soon they'd be the fattest people outside the EU.

It was a real pleasure speaking with Heinrich; under other circumstances we'd have reluctantly agreed to take a brandy before retiring but VSOP wasn't something the tea house stocked, so I bid everyone a goodnight. I brushed my teeth vigorously – Heinrich was a dentist, after all – and returned to my sleeping bag. I powered the Nano and started *Eye To The Telescope* by KT Tunstall at track two. Fifty minutes later, it was time for sleep; it was 10pm.

The night wasn't one of blissful, undisturbed slumber, sounding almost as if the Hatton Garden gang had targeted the safe deposit boxes hidden in the shop and had burst through the floor before midnight to ransack the place. They continued through the wee hours and I imagined bare shelves in the morning as I made my way down to relieve my bladder. The stair to the outside privy was coated in black ice and I almost suffered the ignominy of tumbling to my end from the smallest drop I'd encountered within four days' walk. Dote or one of the porters had started practising for the snoring category in the Namche Bazaar highland games when I returned, so the rest of the night was suffered awake.

Unrefreshed, at near first light I headed to complete my ablutions and make an early start to the day. I strapped myself into the capsule in cubicle one and managed to keep the buffeting down to that associated with only minor turbulence, but my bowels were keen to stay and experience it for as long as possible. The morning's *Diaries* entry would read a confusing Type One, followed by Type Five, Type Six and Type Five. Every time I stood to complete and slosh away, I needed to sit down again. I emerged a good 30 minutes after I'd entered to be greeted by Britta waiting patiently by the door. Shocked she wasn't doing jumping jacks in her underwear, if she'd chosen to wear any that day, and embarrassed she could've heard the previous half-hour's moaning, scraping, splashing and sploshing, I tried to deflect attention elsewhere.

"Morning, nice view." It was. Stunning. The sun had risen to illuminate snow-capped mountains along the valley that now seemed touchable. It was a moment and a place where it felt like I'd entered the Himalaya proper.

"Ya, I can't see it much, though." She pointed to her eyes. They had the swollen look of a habitual onion peeler allergic to steel knives and chopping boards. I knew I'd been in the cubicle for a while, but I didn't think the resultant emissions were *that* toxic.

"Your eyes look sore."

"Ya, it is the cold. I get it all the time in the winter in Holland." Britta had an Achilles heel, then, but she was still one hell of a woman in my book.

"Can you take anything for it? I have some anti-histamines in my first aid kit if that would help."

"No, thank you. It is very kind. I have already taken some."

"Okay, well, see you for breakfast." I left her to brave the Western Style-with-a-difference and brush her teeth. I found my breakfast of porridge was hard going, but it wasn't the porridge, it was me – I'd lost my appetite. I finished as best I could, washed it down with some milk tea, packed and made my way with my book to the foyer.

There was what could be described as a minor accounting error on behalf of my hosts, but it was rectified once I'd shown them how to use the addition rather than multiplication sign on the calculator, and we parted on good terms. I'd eaten alone, the German folks bar Britta not yet having risen. I chose to strike out, thinking I'd see them later in the day; Britta was bound to skip past me doing one-handed press-ups at some stage.

Thirty metres down the trail, I dry retched again, a more sustained attack than the previous day's singular dry heave. I stood bent over, waiting for some vomit to propel itself onto the path, but it failed to arrive. A train of dzhos whose load seemed mostly hawsers eyed me suspiciously as they tramped past. I was worried; I wasn't at 3,000 metres but I thought the retching may have been a sign of something altitude-related. There was nothing for it, though, but to carry on and see how the day went. If I became sicker, Lukla was only half a day ahead, according to the guide, and I could seek medical attention there.

I was thankful the trail was benign at first. That was soon established as a devious trick when the formidable sections soon made themselves present again. The footing ebbed between muddy troughs and dust bowl-dry promontories of such alarming exposure my pulse was hitting dartboard maximum every time I hair-pinned around one. I reached Chewabas, the day's first village, 10,000 heartbeats later. The settlement was perched on the canyon side, the lodges' width narrowed to the notch of flat land available. The 10-year-old in me surfaced, ready to meet a community of walking carpets. I imagined an aproned, hirsute restaurateur, subtly handling a delicate commercial situation with a golden customer:

'Sir, I must insist you've overcharged me for my dhal baat. My calculations indicate that I am owed Rs.50 in change.'

'Let him have it. It's not wise to upset a Wookiee.' A handsome rogue seeming busy arc welding the most decrepit-looking mule in the hamlet's saddle-strap clasp would interject.

'But sir, nobody worries about upsetting a trekker.'

'That's cause a trekker don't pull people's arms out of their sockets over loose change. Wookiees are known to do that.'

Surveying the village, my mind shifted to weighing up whether my appearance would warrant me classified as Mos Eisley scum and villainy or my burgeoning beard qualified me, in some sense, as a recently unretired Jedi. I espied the neighbourhood boasted a parking space lined with a circumference of whitewashed stones. They were centred with an H and I presumed that this was from where that mule would blast off to make the Kessel Run in less than 12 parsecs. It was at this point I knew I should drink more water.

Landing any craft there wouldn't be for the faint of heart; not only was there the flight up the gorge, with its buffeting winds and the dearth (I thought Darth – and once again, committed to taking on more fluid) of landing space, a pilot also needed to remember to instruct their passengers to exit using the craft's wall-side doors, lest they have an exceedingly short trekking experience. My Jedi senses detected I wasn't alone in taking in the scene.

"Hi Aydin. How are you doing?"

"Oh, hi Lee. Not too bad. My feet and shoulders are still painful, especially my feet, but my tummy has calmed down," he reported while busy with his camera.

"Cool. Where you headed for today?"

"Oh, I don't know, maybe Phakding. How about you?"

"I'll see how far I get; it depends on how I feel. Maybe Cheplung. I'd like to make the hike up to Namche as short a day as possible."

"Where's Cheplung? I might stay there as well."

"It's a little bit past where this trail joins the one from Lukla."

"Oh, I might go farther than that, then."

"Are you walking now? Want to hike together for a bit?"

"Okay, I'll be going slow, though, because my boots are still rubbing."

"Don't worry, I doubt I'll keep up with you." We set off in tandem, our pace evenly matched, if only because Aydin fancied himself as a budding Ansel Adams and stopped to take a double exposure of every second bush. The trail reverted to its hair-raising best a few minutes later and I saw that, given his injuries, Aydin seemed to cope with the threat of imminent cessation far better than I did. A vista opened where our future path could be spied, hiding in the canyon side shadows. In my mind's eye, the path was little more than a hopscotch across triangular, apex-balanced rocks that coiled around a rim of a 1,000-metre vertical drop. I stopped; my shoulders slumped.

"Will you have a look at that, Aydin? I thought yesterday's path was bad, but that looks 10 times worse."

"It probably looks worse from here than it will when you get there."

It wasn't. I repeated my nail-abrading technique around the cliffside switchbacks, and we finally reached a section that had the reassurance of three metres of twisted tree trunks between the path and crag side.

"You really don't like the exposed stuff, do you, Lee?"

"No, I'm not good with heights. I don't get vertigo, just an unashamed terror of falling off. I know it's irrational, Newton's laws and all that, but however hard I try, the fear always comes back. You seem to cope alright."

"Oh, the heights, they don't bother me, but I think the local council could do a better job of maintaining the trails, though, just look at all this mud! My feet are sliding all over inside my boots."

"The local council? I'm not sure the local councils work in the same way as back home, mate, I'm not sure Solukhumbu district council has much of a budget for pothole maintenance and street furniture."

"Yeah, but someone should do something. If this was London, it wouldn't be as bad as this."

"Where in London is your local council, Aydin?"

"In the north, a place called Barnet."

"And how, may I ask, are the roads in Barnet?"

"Just awful."

Aydin was as unperturbed by the track's extremities as I was terrified, but his chirping on about the deficiencies of life in the capital took my mind off things. He was a computer programmer who'd taken seven weeks' leave from his job to walk the Three Passes Trek. Aggrieved he'd been overlooked for a promotion, he had used his position as the single point of failure in his company's information technology department to insist he could have the time off.

"I work in IT as well. I used to do coding work, must be getting on for 20 years ago now."

"What sort of languages?"

"Object oriented and some database stuff. I'm on the delivery side now."

"What sort of delivery? Database stuff or coding?"

"I specialise in delivering the nasty integration jobs, you know, the big complex programmes that have failed or need turning around, the ones that are usually a nightmare to get over the line. There's always a mix of datacentre, hardware, database, code, networking, security et cetera involved. Plus cloud now, of course. So, why are you so pissed off about missing out on promotion?"

"Well, they brought in a junior consultant, who I trained up, and then she applied for the same role as me. The bosses said she got it because she was more qualified! I think it was more because they think I'm too disruptive, because when I see something wrong, I tell it like it is! She just told them what they wanted to hear."

"That's fairly common, I'm afraid. In my experience, organisations bring in ex-management consultants who know diddly squat apart from how to schmooze and do PowerPoint presentations, and then promote them to their level of incompetence. They cock things up and then it's usually up to the likes of me to come in and clear up their mess. I shouldn't complain, though, I've made a decent living from wiping their bum for them."

Like a montane Statler and Waldorf, we moaned our way up to the next rise in the trail. The festoon of prayer flags marked it as Paiya

La, the last pass before we reached the junction at Cheplung. I wondered if Aydin, had he been the local council leader, would've made it someone's job to keep the prayer flags at a certain standard and subsequently employ an inspector to check up on compliance.

The trail now eddied down a series of slurry chutes through an increasingly bird-rich forest. We came across a solitary tea house on the shoulder of a ridge. Aydin decided it was time for elevenses, so we bid our *adieus* and I descended for a while before an overpowering smell alerted me to a visitor heading the other way.

The fragrance belonged to a young man of perhaps 20, his quiff reaching me far in advance of the rest of him. He was attired in blue jeans, Converse and a Letterman jacket, his aroma that of a Parisian *parfumerie*. I wasn't sure whether my own pungency was acting as a contrast to highlight his bouquet, or he'd emptied an entire bottle down his shirt that morning. He swished passed me with feline grace and with what could've been 'than'youverymuch' mumbled under his breath.

I could see, from where we crossed, the welcome sight of the village of Surkhe in the crook of a side valley below. The rest of the hike down to my lunch stop was easier, across a path firmed by placed rocks. The Everest View Lodge took my fancy as the place to eat.

"Ça va, monsieur?"

"Hey, 25-kilo man! How are you doing?" He was sitting in a nook that hosted a single-room shanty that was a porters' tea stop. Unsigned, trekkers would miss it.

"Is good, no? I 'ave found a porteur. 'E 'elp a lot. 'E is very reasonable, boout 'e doesn't speak Eengleesh."

"That's excellent. I thought you were going to have a tough time with all that weight. How are you speaking to each other?"

"We do ze signs, you know, for make eat, sleep, sheet."

"So, what are your plans, now you have some help?"

"We go Phakding today, zen Three Pass. If I 'ave enough monae for pay Dawa, zen we go Gokyo and ze ozher place."

"Well, I'm glad you got that sorted, I thought you were going to die with all that weight. Have you had lunch yet?"

"Yes, we 'ave finish. After zis cigarette, we go."

"Bon voyage, then, I'm off to get something to eat, maybe see you on the trail." I left him to enjoy his smoke and headed over to the Everest View. For a lodge cradled in a subsidiary river valley hanging above a canyon, it was an optimistic boast; unless the View had a 1,000-metre periscope hidden in its bowels, guests were never going to catch sight of the mountain from there. I went wild in my choice of lunch: vegetable noodle soup and, inspired by Britta's kindness, ordered the decadence of a hot orange 'juice'. The 'juice' was an advertising gimmick – the powder used to make the drink may have once been in a box transported with some satsumas, but that was the closest it was ever going to get to real citrus. Still, it was more than passably refreshing.

The lodge was a fine, cavernous place in dark teaks. I was joined by an early middle-aged Russian couple who took a distant table. I could make out they were Russian mostly because of their matching outfits of white, red and blue striped spandex and the badge portraying the double-headed eagle on the man's fleece. They had the chiselled features of folks who worked at their physique for the majority of the day. I imagined that, in a Bond movie, they'd be the evil hench-people entrusted by the arch-villain to try, fruitlessly, to kill James. I bid them a few of my words in Russian but a wan response was all I received in return; there would be no lunchtime conversation today. Next time I saw her, I'd have a word with my partner's mum, Olga, who insists 'Red dog baby is crying. Vodka, cheers!' covers all eventualities in any Muscovite conversation.

I finished my noodles and was swept by a wave of lethargy, causing me to deliberate on taking a room at the Everest and having a long nap. I decided this was possibly not the best course of action, given the pair of FSB assassins were slurping through their noodle soup at the far table. The subsequent inquiry into my sudden death would reasonably conclude I'd chosen an unfortunate dish for my lunch, Surkhe being well-known locally as a radioactive hotspot, and somehow my plate must have been left in its nuclear nucleus. It would be confirmed the two Russian trekkers spotted in the vicinity were only passing by, there only to see the famous temple.

Wearily, I crossed the makeshift wooden bridges spanning the river and started the ascent on the far side of the main village, where the same cobbled pathway I'd descended to reach the hamlet continued steeply. I could tell the strike at the ass-cloning factory in Lukla had ended as the number of mule trains that came bolting down the path seemed to double on this section. After half-an-hour of breathless ascent, I reached a decision point: the pathway up to my right led to Lukla, so should I head that way and see a doctor; or carry on and double back at Cheplung if I felt ill?

As I weighed up the pros and cons, a porter I recognised from Heinrich's tour joined me. He dropped his load next to me and we exchanged the customary greetings. He took a bunch of green flyers from his pocket before risking life and limb by dashing through the traffic, a human version of Frogger, to place one in the hands of every muleteer. The flyers were cursorily examined and stashed in back pockets with a look that said they'd be used as toilet paper later.

"Are you a Christian, sir?" he asked as he handed me a green square.

"I was christened, yes."

"I am a Christian too, praise Jesus Christ, he is my Lord and Saviour. What Christian church do you belong to, sir?"

"I was christened, but don't really go to church, just weddings and funerals mostly."

"But sir, I do not understand, why have you renounced the way to salvation? You must know the message of love, that Jesus Christ died for your sins on the cross and only by following his teachings can you reach heaven?"

"That's how the story goes, yes. I'm not sure you have to belong to a church to follow his teachings, though, I think you can be a moral person by following some of his teachings and live a good life that way."

"No, sir, that's not what my Lord and Saviour Jesus tells us. The only way to his heart is to follow his message of love as it is written in the Bible."

"I wouldn't be so sure of that; I studied the Bible and the way it was written came from a tradition that wasn't meant to be literal. The parables are meant to convey a message, not be the message itself."

"Sir, I can assure you that is not true. The word as written in the Bible is God's word and God's word is the truth of all truths. All praise him, the heart of my heart, Jesus Christ almighty!"

"I'm not sure I agree the Bible scholars wrote down the word of God verbatim. The Bible was translated from Hebrew to Aramaic to Greek to Latin. What language is your Bible in, English?"

"Yes, sir."

"Well that's another translation on top of those, then. It wasn't God who did the translating, was it?"

"No, sir, it was a human person, but a human person who God's light shone through."

"And that makes it the word of God?"

"Yes, sir, and following its teachings will save your soul. Will you come to my Bible study group in Namche?" It was the last thing I'd have hoped to add to my itinerary.

"What church do you belong to?"

"Pentecostal, sir."

"And do you think with one session you'll be able to convert me?"

"If you are willing to let Jesus into your heart, yes sir. I am sure with the guidance of the Gospels a good man like you can begin to see the true path."

"Hallelujah!" I cried sarcastically, beginning to get fed up with his proselytising.

"Hallelujah! Praise the Lord my God and all his angels in heaven." He hadn't detected my tone.

"Can I ask you something, please? You're the first Christian Nepali person I've met. That's unusual, isn't it? Most Nepalis are Hindus or Buddhist, aren't they? Did you grow up a Christian?"

"No, sir, I was a Hindu. Missionary came to my village and showed me the true way is to be a Christian. Hindu religion has many gods, but this is not true, there is only one God and his son is Jesus Christ my Saviour."

"Yes, I think you mentioned that already. How many Christians do you have in the village, just you?"

"No, sir, many people have converted, since four years ago we have a church in the village."

"So, Christianity is growing. Did the missionary make you carry those flyers and tell you to hand them out?"

"No, sir. Now I am a missionary for the Lord and I make my own flyers. I try to bring the light to the people in the mountains."

"Well, I wish you good luck with that. I guess I'll see you on the trail to Namche?"

"Yes, sir, please keep my flyer. I hope you will come to our study group when you reach Namche, the address is at the bottom. I am sure my Lord and Saviour Jesus Christ will welcome you back into his loving arms. Hallelujah."

"Okay, thanks." There was a gap in the constant stream of donkeys and I made a break for it. I hadn't been nauseous since the morning, so chose to carry on up to Cheplung and reassess the situation there. The climb was another trudge up the relentless stone that hung above the canyon. I was spared the morning's terror because the trail was firmer underfoot and wider so my nails were left unbloodied.

I crossed a small suspension bridge framing a spectacular side valley waterfall where Aydin was calculating the correct aperture setting for the hazy light and we resumed our complaining trudge up the gorge together. We came across a rusted wrought iron bridge crossing a small stream. I needed to rest, so Aydin tramped off solo.

"Namaste kaki!" I could tell the greeting from the mule driver wasn't a compliment. I knew I could do with a bit of a scrub-up, but he wasn't too Suavecito himself. The iron bridge led into a village that broke into a trident of streets. I chose the one that ran by the snooker shed, pleased to see Ronnie O'Sullivan and the anime girl cued off here as well. The anime girl had also invested in a boob job since her last frame in Nunthala, by the looks of it, her cleavage augmented to spill over the green baize.

The source of the kind of wealth that could attract major stars of the international billiards circuit was obvious beyond the village; situated at the top of an escarpment, it was surrounded by broad fields of cabbages. The market garden led down to the tree line, where the views into the canyon were obscured. Never had I been more grateful not to see the view.

The gradient became almost flat with a stone pavement underfoot and I strolled along, blissfully comparing it to the earlier toils along the canyon side. I passed through a district gate where a discrete sign confirmed I was on the way to Namche. Beyond was a linear chorten complex with a wall of prayer flags and more flat terrain interrupted on occasion by small flights of stairs. With the easy going, I found myself in the rhythm of reverie for the first time in days, a farmer porting a haystack on his back only registering subconsciously. I weaved through a dzho train with the effortless grace of something born in a yak pen before finding I'd glided through the beautiful village of Chaurikharka with what I imagined as the poise of Nonagenarian Neo.

I reached the T-junction at Cheplung and was awoken from my daydream with a shock; the last week's sleepiness had been replaced by something more akin to the scene in *The Fifth Element* where

Korben Dallas opens his window in the morning. A score of Japanese trekkers came up the valley from my left, moving their walking poles in synchronisation behind their leader. To the right was another group of perhaps a dozen, their origin obscured by floppy hats, sunglasses and monikered face scarves. Aydin stood, mouth agape, across the road. It was at this moment Britta and, surprisingly, the rest of her group, including the missionary, caught us up.

"Hey, did you bring any of that hot lemon?! I could do with it now."

"Ha-ha, sorry, no, I drank the last of it as soon as I saw you in the distance!"

"Ha-ha. This is a bit different, isn't it? I think I saw more trekkers in the last 10 seconds than in the whole of last week."

"Ya. I hope they're not all going to Phakding," she said.

"Is that where you're heading? It still looks a long way from here on the map."

"Ya, Dote, how long is it from here to Phakding?" queried Heinrich.

"Around two-and-a-half hours. It's easy, all downhill from here!"

"I think too much for me today. How about you, Aydin?" I asked.

"It's coming up 4.30 so I think I'll try for Ghat. That looks like a nice place on the map."

"Want to get going, if we can find a gap in the traffic?" We set off, another group joining the throng *en masse*. There was a strange sense of confinement in this. The Himalaya's majesty spread all around us and yet I could only focus on having to dodge trains of oncoming trekkers. This sparked an increase in my pace and soon I'd left Aydin and the rest far behind.

The trail was broad and, as Dote had said, mostly downhill, so I made quick progress. I crossed a small bridge in the basin formed by a tumbling stream that was almost a waterfall and pushed myself up the ramp on the far side. That was when the fuel feeding my afterburners ran out. I was at a tea house standing proud above an extensive paved terrace ringed with paint cans filled with marigolds. The guidebook had indicated Thado Koshi would be a five-hour trek from Paiya; eight-and-a-half hours after leaving, I'd arrived.

Thado Koshi to Namche Bazaar

T he lodge was two storeys, appearing to have been clad partly in redbrick wallpaper. It gave the impression it was going through an identity crisis, with its Dr Jekyll the Saino lodge and its Hyde the Hilton, or vice versa, depending upon your point of view. What drew me to the place, apart from my tiredness, was the notion that if the proprietors were house-proud enough to hang paper on the outside, what would the inside be like?

The lady in charge got up from peeling vegetables and greeted me at the counter, behind which was a partitioned kitchen so well provisioned it would take even the most indolent of teenage male cooks a month to get to pot-washing. The dining area was fitted with a wood burner similar to the one in Paiya, but much bigger. It only served to emphasise the transition from the little-visited road from Shivalaya to mass commercial tourism. I knew from speaking to the lodge owner in Kenja this wouldn't be a place that figured in most visitors' itinerary; Thado Koshi was too near Lukla. The guidebook also recommended folks stay in Phakding for their first night in the mountains. How much more commercial would it be there?

We made short work of the haggling – I think the lady was grateful for the custom – and she showed me up a pine stair-ladder to the upper floor where the smell of fresh sawdust pervaded. The lodge was undergoing renovation and extension, the landing floor unpainted plywood boards. My room was equally unfinished, but I was pleased to see the cots had plump, as yet unused mattresses, complete with polythene protectors.

The bathroom had been plumbed in that day and I'd be the first to use the shower should I choose to do so at, of course, the usual premium. The state-of-the-art, firmly seated Western Style was also brand new, its price sticker not yet unpeeled from the cistern. It was already a comely place, but when the final finishing touches had been completed it was going to be a pure belter.

My last top-to-tail cleanse had been at Nunthala. I reckoned a proper wash would help to revitalise me, so crossed the hall in my undies and made to deflower the shower unit, only to be left frustrated. The promise of a hot lather failed to materialise and at full power, fully opened the shower head produced the sort of discharge with which even a dehydrated 50-something with an enlarged prostate would've been disappointed. I craned my semi-nakedness down the stair-ladder and asked if there would be any hot water.

The lady responded that the workmen had gone home, and it would be tomorrow before they could fix the problem. I did the best I could to wipe away some grime using the hand basin by the toilet and retired to my sleeping bag. It had grown cold and I took note to try not to parade around in my shorts in unheated hallways at 2,500 metres in future. I heard another guest being shown to their room. While they were receiving the spiel about the washing facilities, I drifted into a comfortable, exhausted slumber.

An hour later, I awoke with a start normally associated with being late for work after hitting the snooze button twice and forgetting to wake up. I hoped I hadn't missed the evening dinner slot, so flung on my clothes and slid down the stair-ladder with firefighter urgency. Aydin was chatting to a couple of young trekkers at the nearest table. Somehow, I knew the discussion focussed on the latest trends in podiatry.

"Hi Aydin, I didn't expect to see you here, I thought you were heading to Ghat tonight?"

"Hi Lee, yeah, I was going to go to Ghat but that last walk up from the bridge was too much for my shoulders. I've got a massive rash where the straps have been rubbing. This is Marcus and Jenny, by the way."

"Hi Marcus, hi Jenny, good to meet you. Have you just flown into Lukla or come on the Jiri trek like us?"

"Neither, we follow't t'trail up from Joonbesi to 'ere as part oft' Pikey Peak trek. Fust off we got a jeep to a place called Dhap and then walked over t'tops at Pikey Peak. Trail then joins t' Jiri trail at Joonbesi."

"How was that?"

"T'views were amazing," Marcus replied. "They reckon Pikey Peak has one oft' best views int' Himalaya, or certainly of Theverest range. They're only just openin' oop t' trail, trying to promote it ont' basis of t'views an' as an alternative to Lukla. Facilities are pretty basic, thew, there aren't many lodges. Whin we got ta Kenja we thought, 'Wow! They've got windows 'ere!'"

"I take it you didn't mean the operating system, ha-ha?"

"Ha, no, nowt much o' anything roond there."

"It sounds pretty hardcore."

"Aye, but twas fantastic, best trek ever I think! Most oft' time we'd t'whole mountain to us selves. We didn't see any other trekkers fort' first three days. Th'only negative I can think of was it was freezing at night because there were no glass int' windows. Oh, and the were nowhere t' wash in t' bhattis. When we got t' Joonbesi everything was smelling so bad I'd a shower in me pants and socks and washed everything with soap." Jenny joined in.

"That's a good idea, my socks are pongy too, I wish I'd thought of that."

"It also means you've less chance of getting a verruca."

"There's not much chance of getting a verruca, is there? My feet are bad enough as they are," Aydin piped up, looking genuinely worried. Marcus and Jenny were a couple, both in their late 20s, both from Yorkshire, apparently nowhere near a Taco Bell. Marcus was an electrical engineer, Jenny a vet, and back home they spent their weekends in the great outdoors. They reeled off an itinerary of off-the-beaten-track treks for their three months in Nepal that told anyone they were hardcore outdoorspeople. I imagined them at the door of their cottage in the Dales as a force nine blizzard that would flay the skin off a fully armoured knight raged outside.

'D'ya think I need t'put t'hat on or not today, Jenny, luv?'

We chatted over their shared pastry that was advertised as apple pie but more resembled a pastie; they told me it was scrumptious and I ordered the mixed pizza on their recommendation. My vision of thin crust topped with tuna and red onion sweating with oil was dispelled when it arrived. The pizza was more vertical than horizontal, its overall shape approaching a cylinder. The doughy base was mounted by such a thick layer of cheese I figured I'd missed the 'Night in Savoy' promotion, the chef using my order to dispose craftily of a surplus raclette wheel. Above that was the tuna surmounted by a coral reef of crispy, caramelized onions. When I tucked in, I realised what it lacked in presentation, it more than made up for in flavour – the recommendation had been well made.

The young couple finished their meal, politely made their excuses and headed up to bed. Aydin looked disconsolately over the remains of his dhal baat and followed them, muttering something about always ordering the wrong thing from the menu. Sated, I returned to my sleeping bag not long afterwards and listened to *Strange Kind Of Love* by Love and Money from its start. Fifty minutes later, it was time for sleep; it was 9.40pm.

I awoke late. I'd enjoyed my best night's sleep of the trip. After recording a brace of Type Threes of a flaxen gold colour in the *Diaries,* I made my way to the dining area, asking myself what I could've eaten to cause such colouration. I didn't recall having the Rapunzel-flakes for breakfast in Paiya. Aydin was finishing off an omelette and I ordered the rice pudding and milk tea, hoping for a repeat of the delights of Goyem.

"Morning Aydin, been up long?"

"Yes, since the crack of dawn, I'd a terrible night's sleep, to be honest."

"How come?" I guessed he must have been kept up fretting about the dzho parking bylaws or what was the correct council tax band into which the Cheplung cabbage magnates should fall.

"My back and shoulders were aching all night. I think I'm carrying too much weight, Lee. I reckon that's why my shoulders hurt so much."

"Mm, yes. Could be."

"I'm going to ask the lodge if I can leave some stuff here that I don't need and pick it up on the way back."

"Sounds like a good idea."

"Yeah, I've brought some things I thought I'd need but really don't. I have my nail clippers here. I keep asking myself, what *did* I bring them along for?"

"Exactly."

"I'm going to leave them here if I can, and my flip-flops."

"Should make all the difference to the weight of your pack."

My rice pudding arrived. It more than rivalled the Goyem version, its texture and sweetness were post-Sunday-roast-granny-made perfect. Aydin had agreed terms and stashed his unnecessary items in a cubby-hole by the stair, so bid me a good day and was on his way. I took my time over breakfast; today was going to be a hard climb and I wanted to make sure I was properly nourished before I set off.

And the view wasn't bad, either – the valley's wooded crag sides cupping in supplication the trident of snowy peaks that was Kusum Kangguru.

It was a place of easy distractions; I watched children tramping uphill in school uniforms my own children could have worn on their way to their classes. Unlike the kids I'd seen at Junbesi, they didn't seem to have any backpacks or books with them. I wondered if my friend from Deurali was giving one of his electronic tutorials in the region today. The passing of the last of their giggling gangs was the signal to get going, so I finished my tea and made ready for the off.

I'd timed my departure well, as there was none of the previous day's traffic. Anxious to avoid a repeat of the last few day's dry heaving, I started with a few slow strides which seemed to help; the dry retch was only a single episode. I'd made a couple of hundred metres of progress along the flat, cobbled street when my first encounter caused me to double-take. A young man walking in the direction of Lukla had a mono-board peeking above the top of his backpack.

"Hi, have you come down from Base Camp?"

"Sure have, man."

"Were you able to snow board up there?"

"Nah, there wasn't enough snow to catch a slide, man," he replied in an American accent. I tried to relate to the man, how he could even contemplate being able to snowboard down the side of Everest, but could do nothing more than be inspired he'd even consider such a thing. Warmed by the idea, I marched on.

The good night's rest, the carbohydrates, the sugar and the flat terrain, or downhill as Dote would've called it, combined to turbo-charge my morning. I caught up with my first gaggle of people assembled in line at the trailside. They mulled around with the slightly perplexed and disconnected look of a primary three school trip who'd been told to wait on the museum steps while the teacher counted them up. They were universally resplendent in their shop-new outfits, wicked hiking tees under Gore-Tex blousons. Multi-pocket trousers were clearly essential preconditions for this tour. The faintest dusting of beige despoiled the pristine appearance of rubber-soled boots. Their heads moved in Wimbledon centre court unison as I passed. I imagined they must've thought I'd deliberately rolled around in barbed wire and emptied the ashes of a fire over my head to look so worn a single day into the trek.

The trail had become a boulevard, a snow-park U of crazy-paving bordered drystone walls where the flagstones had a visible inward camber, the compression of a million eager, scuttering footsteps. The way was directed across a plateau of grasses ready for scything, refreshments offered at 500-metre intervals by tea houses that would've been the crowning glory of any lower village. A backdrop of peaks redolent of the Yosemite Valley and, in particular, Half Dome framed the scene

I stopped at a pair of metre-high prayer wheels mounted on rusted iron, factory-purpose shelving straddling a courtyard wall. The luxury of their gold curtaining and Sanskrit lettering only served to emphasise the weather-beaten condition of their support. A wooden plaque implored 'Please turn this mane to purify your sole [sic]'. As I did as requested, I fancied that's what a lot of Premier League defenders would be despairingly hoping for when playing against Sadio this season – but also it was not likely what Lama Dorjee had in mind when he'd placed the wheels in position.

The Dudh Kosi had now become an impassable ford, scouring its way through the valley. I wondered where it had joined the canyon I'd trekked after Surkhe. There must be a huge waterfall or set of rapids somewhere that catered for the drop.

Thinking Russ Abbot must have run out of tartan paint before he could add the 'Jimmy' at the 'See You' lodge, I entered Phakding. In some ways, the village could have been paying homage to an Austrian ski resort, the window of the 'Sherpa Hermann Bakery' shamelessly flaunting brownies, flapjacks and other delectable confectionery. It also offered Illy americanos, cappuccinos, lattes, and mochas.

A lodge had pinned a lawn of fake grass onto its terrace and situated faux leather cushioned recliners underneath an iron pergola, its cross beams cast in infinity swirls. This achieved more of an Ibiza chill vibe, but equally could've been at home as the last on-piste stop for a Glühwein before après-ski proper. I was unsure what to make of all of this; it was such a different experience to my first week. Should I be aghast at the blatant commercialism of it all or be happy I could gorge myself on lemon drizzle cake?

Pondering over the authenticity of such a place (did its very presence make it authentically Nepalese because that's what Nepalis do here; or was this some form of occidental corruption which made it inauthentic?), I crossed over the suspension bridge to upper Phakding. A slight incline brought me to the bright yellow sign of 'Hermann Helmers' bakery. Their selection put the poor Sherpa bakery to shame: 'Beans coffee, pie and *strudel*, pizza and sandwich, bread and rolls, muffins and doughnut, cakes and cinnamon rolls, cookies and more'. I wondered what 'more' there could be. I'd have enquired whether they had a gingerbread man with smarties for eyes, but the place was closed, presumably for baking.

It was coming around to the time for the day's first tea break. Atop a half-flight of stairs, I came across a sunny courtyard that seemed a honeytrap to trekking parties. I realised why none of those resplendent lodges down valley had had any customers – they were all here.

"Namaste Dote, namaste Britta. Hi Heinrich, Agathe, Wolfy."

"Hi Lee, come and join us. We are taking coffee," called Britta.

"Thank you. This place is popular, isn't it? It's mobbed, what's going on here, Dote?"

"It's a good place for first break. All trek from Lukla stop here."

"Seems strange everyone should stop at the same place and, yet, here I am as well." Dote's group had made it to Phakding the previous night at eight in the evening. It had proven a chore for Agathe and she was finding the morning heavy going. Further discussion was difficult because an overweight, bellowing Englishman continually interrupted our conversation. Sporting curtains of greyed hair and eyes like overripe blackcurrants, he waved around a *stein* of beer straight from a Bavarian Tourist Board poster.

"And the Treaty of Utrecht, 1715 dear sir, was when Spain ceded Gibraltar to the British, signalling the end of the War of the Spanish Succession." He was lecturing to a man in his early middle years who contrasted his evident athleticism with an understated hippy chic, beads and bangles over a Lycra sports vest, his look replete with a grey topknot.

"This cemented Britain's hegemony in sea power in the Mediterranean and was also, arguably, a watershed in that it validated the British policy of maintaining the balance of power. This allowed us to establish our colonies in north America, while the French were fighting everyone else, and this is where *you* come in, dear sir, your hometown of Boston of course being part of British America before

1783. Now, the Seven Years' War ..." Topknot slid on his wrap-arounds and sighed as he leant back in his chair, his irritation obvious to everyone apart from the overbearing Brit. I imagined he'd paid a lot of money to come for a workout in some of the most awesome scenery on earth, with possibly some zen meditation thrown in, not to be lectured to by an amateur Niall Ferguson on amphetamines.

"So, Verity wants to go on the helicopter to Namche, who else wants to go on the helicopter?" The Historian had been interrupted and forced to switch topics.

"I'm going to go on one of the horses. What about you, Monty? Are you going in the helicopter with Verity or coming with me on one of the horses?" Topknot was becoming increasingly testy at being organised by the Historian, grimacing into his chia seed infusion.

"So that's it settled, then, Verity and Monty will go with Jeremy and one of the guides in the helicopter, Richard and I will go on two of the horses and everyone else is walking. We just need to finish our drinks first and then we will be ready for the off. Where was I, yes, 1763, that attested to the rise of Prussia ..." By the crimson hue of his face and the trembling of his limbs, that topknot was going sub-orbital when its owner's frustration with the Historian erupted. I'd finished my tea and considered it prudent to get away from the potential stooshie; besides, I could see the throng was mustering to leave. I wanted to get ahead of the crowd, so I said another goodbye to my friends and made off.

The promenade had given itself over to a more standard beaten-earth track, the four lanes constraining to one where a stall which straddled its width sold plastic souvenir Dorniers and fridge magnets of 'Lukla Nepal', manufactured in China. An uphill train of dzhos passed through when the traffic lights changed. I descended to a temporary plank footbridge with another train heading my way. The bridge had been erected over a gushing brook while repairs were being made to the concrete one further downstream, the ancient skills of bamboo scaffolding lashed together with hemp contrasting with the cement mixer at its base. The opposite bank necessitated a steep ascent back onto cobbles.

"Mister, mister. Here must pay local trekking permit fee." A voice emanated from a sliding window secreted into a concrete pillbox above a pair of smooth cement revetments.

"Ah, okay, namaste, I already got mine in Kathmandu. I'll come up and show you." I hauled myself up to the smooth ledge by the window and extracted my permit.

"This is no good, mister. Here you need *local* trekking permit. All trekkers pass Tok Tok have to pay local permit to trek this area."

"The guidebook didn't mention that, how much is the permit then, please?"

"Two thousand rupees." I now had a potential problem. I had Rs.6,000 left in cash, which I'd estimated ample, even allowing for inflation, as the guide had indicated the national park entry fee up ahead was Rs.3,000. An extra Rs.2,000 was going to cut it fine afterwards if prices had gone up significantly, but it appeared I'd no choice but to pay the fee. I left with a hint of dread I'd have to hike back to the bank at Lukla from the park entrance if I were short of funds at the gate.

The path undulated under pleasant shade provided by riverine magnolia forest. I passed a pretty, recessed waterfall before heading up a stone staircase. At its summit, the trail was funnelled towards the Sagarmatha national park gate, the entrance squeezed between a lodge repurposed as a government office and the rocky cliff wall opposite. Men in fatigues manned a painted green checkpoint. Imagining this the Gates of Mordor, Nepalese style, I thought that, although my pack was feeling heavier, I'd forgotten to pack the one true ring and so couldn't sneak through using its powers of invisibility. I hoped Aydin hadn't stashed his elven cloak in Thado Koshi with the rest of his weighty items. I might hear about it later if he had.

The park entry area reminded me of Ratna Park, only less organised. Porters and guides were massed aggressively, gesticulating and shouting, while tour group members stood and watched, hoping for something to progress, but not sure when that would be or what shape it would take. Trekkers sporting rite-of-passage 'Everest Base Camp' T-shirts clicked their walking poles in the opposite direction back through the gate. The soldiers shuttled back and forth to the office, chits of a variety of colours grasped in their hands.

It was clear there was a menu of things to do to get past the hubbub and through the gate, but I hadn't been provided with any of the ingredients. So I patiently jostled and shunted my way through the mosh pit until I reached the permit counter. All pretence of respecting personal space had gone at this point; a few of the guides couldn't have been more intimate without performing a colonoscopy. I handed over my TIMS card and Tok Tok permit to a relaxed official. She was unfazed by the tumult and I was more than happy when she seemed satisfied with my credentials.

"Three thousand rupees." 'Yippee!' I thought, ecstatic I was going to get in and also that I'd enough money for lunch. With a freshly stamped coupon, I squashed my way back through the multitude over to the military where the dread from earlier intensified as a buzz-cut examined my prayer-flag colouring of permits. 'What is it about skinheads in pyjamas that induces such a feeling?' I mused. 'It's probably the machine gun,' I thought. 'Yes, definitely the machine gun.' He nodded sagely and indicated I should move on. 'Marvellous! I'm in!' I realised happily.

Beyond the gate, the path descended a steep, cobbled staircase banked by massive granite blocks painted in white mantras. Buoyed by my success I skipped along the trail's next part in short order entering a village where a painted mural welcomed me to Jorsale. It was time to eat before what I'd been warned was the most taxing part of the day, if not the entire trek – the ascent to Namche Bazaar.

I stepped down to a restaurant towards the river side of the dorp. The owner showed me through to a sunny terrace overlooking the river, its tables decorated with tins of marigolds and shaded by yellow and blue parasols. I'd been fortunate with my choice again. I ordered the tomato vegetable noodle soup, variety being the spice of life. My first blue sheep was a mother and its young ballet dancing across the rocks at the water's edge. I watched a moving haystack crawl along the bank amid the woods above them. The restaurant's service was as relaxed as the setting, my complex order not yet delivered when Dote and the German gang stepped through to join me.

"Are you stalking me, Britta? Ha-ha."

"Ya, I heard you carry a lot of money and, from the way you walk, I want to be there to collect when your heart gives way." She sat down at the table opposite, Dote fussing around to get everyone settled. Once he was convinced everyone was comfortable, he took their orders, making me jealous as he mentally acknowledged a variety of three-course meals. My noodles arrived and we spent lunch talking about how this stretch of the trek felt so different to the ones before yesterday.

"Hi guys. I saw Lee's hat through the doorway and thought I'd come and say hello."

"Hi Aydin." By now, I'd learned asking how he was mightn't be the best way to start the conversation.

"Oh, I've got to say that I'm a bit pissed off. Did *you* have to pay that extra 2,000 at Tok Tok? My guidebook doesn't say anything about that."

"Dote handles all that for the group. We have already paid, no problem," Heinrich replied.

"Yes, I paid it, mate, I think it's some new swizz to get more money off the trekkers. I don't think you can do much to get out of it. Are you stopping for lunch?"

"No, I think I'm going to get something in Namche."

"Are you sure? I think Namche's a few hours away and it's supposed to be a hard climb. Might be best if you loaded up on carbs beforehand."

"No, thanks but I couldn't at the moment, I had a ginormous chocolate chip muffin at Helmut's bakery so I think that'll keep me going." He waved us goodbye and, finishing my tea as Dote's group were being served their main courses of spaghetti, omelettes and chips, I was soon packing up to follow him.

"Namaste. Praise our Lord Jesus Christ, the one true saviour." The hallelujah man dropped his load as I was leaving the restaurant.

"Hallelujah."

"Hallelujah, sir. Please do not forget the study group in Namche."

"Don't worry, I haven't forgotten about it. Your group is through there, are you joining them for lunch?"

"Thank you, sir, yes I am."

"I hope they have loaves and fishes on the menu." Before we got into the literality or symbology of the miracle, I'd made my escape. The trail crossed the river onto the east bank and descended onto a level gravel of blinding whiteness. The sun was high overhead and a wise porter stopped to tell me to cover my scalp; as I located my hat, dread ahead, I could see the dual spans of the Hillary Bridge.

I wasn't in favour of suspension bridges in general, but this was the one I looked forward to the least. The first bridge constructed across the gorge had been deemed not frightening enough by the local authorities and so they'd upped the ante and built one on top of it. At 100-plus metres, it also wasn't short enough that gritted teeth and closed eyes would be enough to get across the chasm, which was a death-defying 300 or more metres deep. The trail up to the span became an ascent of broad, smooth cement terraces, almost as if the local civil engineers had gained some malicious glee in placing the most solid underfoot part of the trek directly adjacent to its most unstable. The steps were deceptively steep, so I reached the bridge's stanchions with the sound from my lungs resembling the inward compress of a set of punctured bellows. I sat down to recuperate and admire the metal pathway swaying gently in the breeze before me.

I could hear a tour group gaining on me while I sat there. There was no opposing traffic, so there was nothing to do but go for it before I was caught and had to deal with the increased resonance of other boots on the footway. I clenched my teeth and set off, my gaze fixed on the concrete pillar in the distance. The bridge increased its sway and, at approximately halfway across, my feet became more unsteady. I knew someone else had entered the bridge behind me. The span's sideways oscillations became more pronounced, the metal slats beneath my feet seeming to move in chaotic angles to an irregular beat. Before long I fancied I knew what it felt like to be an unfettered barrel being tossed around in the hold of a sinking Spanish galleon. I reached the far side and collapsed into a concrete bench as my pursuer, a fully laden porter, passed me serenely with a look of complete bewilderment. I didn't move until I could no longer feel the blood stretching the veins at the base of my throat.

"I'm glad that's over. I diden' enjoy that, Dai! 'Ow 'bout you, then?" The tour group's vanguard had followed the porter across.

"Bloody 'ell, that *was* 'orrible. I bet I've got some good fillum of that on my Go Pro, mind."

"Look at Sian com-an' across, she's bricken' it, isent it?"

"What you laughin' at, yar couple a bastards?" Sian wasn't amused.

"You were shitten it, Sian, go on, admit it." The rest of their group made it over with cheery, encouraging words of well done for the more serious members and unabashed taunting for those who they knew could take it, ignoring the crumpled figure bunched over on the seat to their right. My heart had calmed and I moved on, leaving the bench for those who were in equal need of it for recovery purposes.

The bridge was at the confluence of the Bhote Kosi and Dudh Kosi rivers. At first, the trail climbed in a series of dusty, forested switchbacks overhanging the former river, some hairpin apexes so badly eroded the only way to progress was by scrambling on all fours. Other places required hauling oneself up by exposed tree roots and so I was coated in a tawny dust, sweating and out of breath, in short time.

The muleteers had finished their lunch and a postprandial cascade of donkeys surged down the trail, barging a pensionable lady below with a propane canister as she was being helped up a head-height crumbling step. She fell on her behind and the rest of the herd's hooves stampeded by, only centimetres from her body. Her face was covered in churned muck and tears when her partner helped her, shocked and unsteady, back to her feet.

"Fuck off, FUCK OFF THE LOT OF YOU!" she screamed at the last of the hindquarters disappearing below.

"There, there, come on, love. Not hurt, are you?" asked her husband tenderly.

"I don't think too bad, I just landed hard on my bum."

"Good job there's *plenty* of padding there, then."

"You're a total bastard, so you are, Brian James Conway."

"Ah, but that's why you love me and agreed to marry me all those years ago, my beloved Margaret. Come on, now, let me see you. Looks like you're alright, let me get a wipe and clean that dirt off your face."

"Is it going to be like this all the way, Brian? If I'm going to be run over by bloody donkeys every five minutes, then I don't know if I'll make it." The tears welled up in Margaret's eyes.

"I hope not, love," Brian replied quietly. I regained my feet and left Brian some privacy to attend to Margaret. The trail continued to wind its way up through the pines flattening out into a broad shaded area, where the group from the bridge trudged up as I rested.

There were 15 to 20 of them, at a guess, their ages ranging from mid-20s to mid-50s. None of them looked like they'd completed any sort of training programme for the trek, even though they'd dressed for it. Spare tyres bulged from base layers of the youngest and beer bellies stretched the fabric of the oldest. They were all puffing from every exertion with short gasps I knew only too well. By their darkened underarm patches I could see the wicking of their vests was being road-tested to the utmost. The first couple decided to take a break and plonked down beside me.

"Go on, give us another one of your sweets then, Sian." She reached into a utility pocket and pulled out a nugget of translucent green in a clear plastic wrapper.

"Fox's Glacier Mints!" I couldn't help blurting out. "I haven't seen one of those for years. I didn't know they still made them."

"Yar, best in the world, they are. Do you want one, love?"

"Ooo ... I wouldn't say no. Where are you guys from in Wales?"

"I'm from Cardiff and my wife Sian 'ere, she 'as the serious misfortune to 'ail from Swansea. What about you?"

"I'm originally from Liverpool but live in Glasgow. I'm Lee, by the way."

"Gareth."

"Edwards?"

"I wish, it's Davies."

"With a name like that you must like rugby?"

"Yar, with a belly like this you can probably tell I used to be in the pack. I used to be a lot fitter when I played, mind."

"Ga', stop ya lyin', you've always 'ad that same belly for the 20 years since I've known you, love." The rest of their tour had now caught up and perched on rocks strung out downhill of us. I sucked lustily on the candy, savouring its sugary-minty taste bliss.

"That's a lot of people for one group."

"Yar, we make up six of 'em, though, so we're not *all* strangers. That's Dai and Ruth, they're friends from Cardiff, and those two are Johnny and Mike. Mike's English, but we 'ave to put up with 'im because 'e's married to Sian's big sister."

"How's everyone doing? Must be hard with a big group going at different paces?"

"Yesterday from Lukla was fine, wasent it, Ga'? It was all down 'ill! This morning was alright, but this is hard goin' since we stopped for dinner. What about you, Lee, 'ow are you findin' it?"

"Pretty tough. This is supposed to be the hardest part, though. Seven hundred metres straight up, so the guidebook reckons. I've been going eight or nine days now and climbed similar. It was supposed to have acclimatised me and made me fitter for this but doesn't seem to be working so far. It's definitely made me wish I'd done more training for it than walking to the local pub."

"Come on, ya can't go wrong going to the pub, now then can you! Nine days, mind, where 'ave you been for all that time?"

"I came in from Shivalaya, down in the valleys. The idea was to follow the route of the Hillary-Norgay expedition to see a bit of what it was like back in the day."

"I'm glad we didn't do that, aren't you, Ga'? This is 'ard enough for me, isent it? I'll be glad to get to Namche and 'ave a nice 'ot shower this evenen'." I hoped Sian wasn't going to be too disappointed with what she found in that department in Namche.

"At the next rest stop, hopefully, we should be able to get our first glimpse of Everest. Well, I'll see you there." I moved off and fell in tandem step with an oriental man in floppy hat and face mask and, although his steps felt pained to me, it wasn't long before we reached the Everest viewpoint.

In all its wisdom, Namche municipal council had decided the stunning view of one of the natural wonders of the world would be best observed at the side of a latrine. This was the only public lavatory for the three hours between Jorsale and Namche, so the queue to the WC was longer than for the ladies' at midnight in a basement nightclub. Seeing the need to crowbar myself through the crowd to get a view was enough to put me off. I decided, as I'd been waiting practically 30 years to see Everest in person, another couple of days wasn't going to make much difference. I continued my traipse, thinking to myself Aydin would be up there, busying himself taking notes for the stern letter he was going to send to the local assembly about the state of affairs.

The oriental man had been joined by a younger couple. The ascent had flattened out and the young man dashed to a tree at the trailside. I guessed he was catching up on a missed opportunity at the viewpoint and so tramped on with the old man and his younger companion. The man came racing up the hill and pulled up beside us, his hands cupping a handful of berries. He offered them around and, as the others popped them into their mouths, he made a signal to say I should try them. They had a lemony tang that cut through the earthen taste in my mouth. Seeing my reaction, the man gave me a smile and thumbs-up but the berries failed to have the same revitalising effect on the old man. He grimaced, held out his hand to pre-empt any offer of help and parked himself on the path's upper bank.

"How much have you got in your pack, mate? Sian says you've been carting it for a week." It was the eldest of a trio of the Welsh tour's youngest members, who'd caught us up.

"About 10 or 11 kilos."

"That sound's mad, mate. Don't fancy that myself."

"You get used to it.. It's only when you take it off and then have to put it back on again that you feel it. Ten isn't bad, I met a French guy who was trying to cart 30-odd kilos of camera stuff up and down the hills."

"Are you kiddin'? Is he still alive?"

"Ha-ha, yes. He ended up getting a porter."

"They're great, the porters, I'm glad ours are carrying all our stuff. Water and snacks are plenty to be carting up this slope."

"Vere is your het from?" asked the other man who, for some reason, reminded me of the character on the 'Welcome to Skegness' logo.

"Scotland. It's a Tunnock's tea cake. It's a national delicacy."

"Looks like Poland fleg. Ve are from Poland. Ve hoop you Poleesh."

"Sorry, no. I only know two words in Polish, 'Grupa dupa'."

"Ha-ha, thees is not good Poleesh vord to know. Vant to know ozzer?" As my new friend gleefully taught me some other coarse Polish language, the Historian plodded by on his horse, riding bolt upright like an Arc'teryx Don Quixote. Richard reclined in his saddle behind, the Patagonia of his Sancho Panza a less expensive second. The horses attracted the attention of two men who were bowling downhill.

"Good morning. Are you people of Spain? We are Mexican! Viva Me-hi-co!" They were speaking Spanish but I could tell they weren't native speakers.

"Good morning. How are you?" I replied, also in Spanish, this time passably well.

"Very well. How old are you?" I wondered if they'd only reached the first lesson on one of those language courses Matthieu had said were a necessity for guide work.

"Fifty-three." They looked flummoxed; I hoped they were staggered by my evidently youthful appearance, but considered it more likely the Nepali-Mexicans hadn't yet reached that number in their lessons. They continued to hurtle down the trail, laughing and proclaiming their allegiance to Pancho Villa.

Our next stop was for the inspection of our paperwork at a coffin-shaped shack, set at an unnecessary dip at the trailside serving as a police checkpoint. This was another bottleneck where trekking parties mulled around in confusion, but I was prepared for that and pirouetted my way through the mob to the open window to present my ticker tape of permits. The guard was clockwork efficient in stamping everything and he dismissed me within seconds. My new companions needed to wait for their guide so I said I'd see them again in Namche.

I set off with a sudden onset of fatigue, my energy dramatically drained like engine oil into a sump, and my trudge deteriorated into a stagger. I reached a fork in the trail where a flight of stairs rose abruptly ahead, while a longer, sweeping trail to the left promised another precipitous flight in the distance. I chose straight ahead and crested the stairs to find a town, a proper town, not a village, semi-circled beneath me.

The lodges were bigger here and there were more of them than anywhere I'd seen since Kathmandu; they were an audience that sat in an amphitheatre, the stage set at the edge of a scarp. My lungs thanked me as I descended into what was now, to my eyes, an urban sprawl. The entry to lodgings was a cobbled alleyway running between hotels on the uphill side and shop fronts on the downhill. I chose a hotel, expecting to see a reception desk once I'd entered the doorway, but I'd made a mistake; access was three flights further up. Legs aching, I crashed gratefully into the reception area. My guidebook had indicated Namche Bazaar would be a six-hour trek from Thado Koshi; seven-and-a-half hours after leaving, I'd arrived.

Namche Bazaar to Tengboche

The Hotel Kamal's reception-cum-dining area followed the same blueprint as I'd found in the lodges, only scaled up threefold. A trio of ladies were busy behind a dogleg counter in the corner opposite, the older lady, garbed in the matriarch's uniform, sitting intent at her books. The flourish of her pen could've been marking secondary school jotters. The two younger ladies, dressed in jeans, down jackets and flip-flops, pottered at their tasks with the half-heartedness of underemployment; that completed homework didn't need restacking again and again.

I asked for a room and prepared to do fiscal battle but, instead, was presented with a laminated booklet with a price list that said take it or leave it. I realised I'd gotten lucky in Thado Koshi; the rates there were only marginally more expensive than in the lower valleys but in the Kamal the price hike was steeper than the trail up. I knew there wasn't much to be had from looking for cheaper lodgings elsewhere in town; there was the smell of price-fixing, cartel-based economics around.

The room was passable, featuring emaciated mattresses in polka dots over dual cots. It sat nearest the bathroom. The tiny window's glass seemed to have curdled – it didn't offer any sort of view – but thankfully some light was making it through. I was too tired to go anywhere else, so I took it. The young lady's laminated booklet served as an informational along with details of what the restaurant offered. It made it clear orders for dinner needed to be made by 5pm. I needed to hurry or go hungry.

The restaurant was one of the contemporary, ground-breaking, Italian-American-Indian-Chinese fusion movement trending across the globe, the menu offering everything I could think of except for 'Sneakers Pie'. I guessed Sneakers were possibly not in season this time of year or were difficult to import all the way from Khari Khola, which could've explained why my young host had to suffer cold feet in her flip-flops. I'd also have to get my 'Cock' elsewhere, by the looks of it. My inner carnivore couldn't resist the lure of the exotic and I chose to try the yak burger and chips at a wallet-emptying Rs.850, a Royale with Cheese on the Champs-Élysées a bargain by comparison.

I returned to the reception counter at 4.55pm to comply with the regulations. The Schoolmistress was still busy correcting what could have been an obscure branch of trigonometric algebra, from the scribbles she ticked off in the books as she went, and she didn't look up. Inexplicably, I regressed 40 years: 'No miss, it wasn't me who defaced my jotter, it was that nasty Mike Rees'; but I stood there awaiting my corporal punishment, nevertheless.

Eventually, Teach raised her head and sniffed a reluctant acknowledgement of my existence. I hesitated before my ego kicked back in. Damn it, I was the customer here! I placed my order and, playing the Schoolmistress at her own game, made it equally clear I'd like my murdered furry beast served promptly on the dot at 6pm, and retired to my room content I'd made my presence felt.

Nausea struck on resting my head on my pillow, a shudder of weakness writhing its way up from my aching calves to my shoulders. Namche was at 3,400 metres, well within the zone for altitude sickness, and I hoped it wasn't that, rather the ascent taking its toll. If it was exhaustion, the food should help and so six o'clock couldn't come around quickly enough. The minutes dragged until it was time to raise myself from my bed with the fluidity of Lazarus. I limped my way to the dining room to find it busier than a Saturday evening Nando's with a two-for-one special on. I found a free table and contemplated what the etiquette was: should I wait at the table to be served or announce my punctual arrival at the counter? Ever the Limey, I waited demurely, anticipating some sign my food was on its way.

There was a serving hatch behind the counter I hadn't noticed when I'd checked in and I could see into the kitchen from my table. In contrast to the charm of the home cooking in the lodges, this was a regimented factory with a rigorously enforced hierarchy. Minions hastened around chopping boards and saucepans while being harangued by the sous-chef. All that was missing was the harridan head chef mussing over his hair transplant while expletively berating the apprentice not to overboil the effing dhal.

Completed orders were slapped on the hatch with breakneck regularity, accompanied by a chef's cry. The two younger ladies had now been catapulted from indolent underutilisation to harassed waitressing in the space of an hour. They whizzed past my table bearing balanced plates of world cuisine, but by 6.15 my food hadn't arrived.

It gave me time to observe my fellow diners. I was, from their assemblage, the only solo trekker in the hotel. There were several couples but mostly it was larger groups, seven or eight in each party the average size, all accompanied by guides. A group of four in their 20s caught my attention, not by the brash loudness of their American accents, but by their guide. He was shuttling back and forth to the counter and giving the Schoolmistress a hard time about the food he'd sent back. Cowed, the Schoolmistress would nod acceptance of his complaints prior to barking a reproach through to the kitchen.

The guide was equally unsatisfied by the waitress service, making his feelings plain about that. When the food was returned, having been improved to his satisfaction, he chose to steward it over to his charges himself – with his one arm! He repeated the waiting duties for the Americans' coffees and teas and, as his errands became more onerous, I felt increasingly uneasy. It was the group's non-recognition of his actions that struck me as unfair. Not only did he have to guide them, look after their daily needs, and perform waiting duties but he was doing it with only one arm. The least they could have offered in return would've been the odd thank you.

I accosted a passing waitress and, after a couple of instances of being passed off, my dinner arrived. The burger was somewhere between McDonalds and hipster gourmet, the yak chewy, more akin to a skirt steak than burger. To my amazement, it came with real sliced beefsteak tomato and lettuce. The chips were perfectly fried chunky wedges and I finished disappointed by the portion size only because it was so good.

The five-metre trip back to my room worried me. I arrived at my cot shattered. I lay on my bed hoping, as my dinner digested, the fatigue would abate and glad that, as the next day was dedicated to acclimatisation, I wouldn't be travelling too far. I listened to the precisely titled *Greatest Hits, Vol. 2. The ABC-Dunhill/MCA Recordings* by Bobby Bland, starting at track four to prepare me for bed, and an hour later it was time for sleep; it was 8pm.

I dozed for a while before Ed Sheeran plugged in his shrunken guitar and warmed up his crowd with *Galway Girl*, starting around

9.30. A highlight of my itinerary was going to be a well-earned visit to The World's Highest Irish Pub to sink a couple of pints o' der black stuff and hopefully sing along to some Thin Lizzy tracks on the jukebox. A recent DNA test had shown my genetics to approximate those of a Dublin bar stool, so I felt I owed it to the place. It was a measure of how knackered I was I couldn't stir myself to make it the 50 metres down the street to the boozer. The Rip Van Winkle-awakeningly loud show went on until around one when the pub turfed out the drunks, the majority of whom seemed to be staying next door.

Through the particle board partition, a gridiron team were debating the premier state from which one could originate in the good old US of A. Rather remarkably, they settled on Idaho. I'd nothing against Idaho, but couldn't think of one thing or person associated with the locale, the state not possessing an attraction such as the Grand Canyon or Golden Gate Bridge that would've drawn me to visit. It struck me as the kind of place similar to Lincolnshire in the UK – it is probably passably nice but not somewhere you'd ever bother to visit, unless you desperately needed to sell a pony and trap.

After a spiral down into an extended mutual congratulation on their compatibility as friends, they turned in, enabling me to make a scientific breakthrough that will no doubt bring me a Nobel Prize in physics if my work in backpacker bar-dynamics remains unrecognised: the discovery that the only thing in the universe louder than a pair of Americans conversing through plywood, is a pair of Americans snoring through plywood. I was almost sad I'd parted company with the Austrians, as I'm sure Alfred BJ would've been able to verify my findings. Ultimately, exhaustion won over the snorting sibilants and I managed to doze off again for a few hours.

The scuffling of porters making ready for their day in the corridor woke me pre-dawn. My call from slumber corresponded with a realisation that the richness of the food had stimulated a powerful reaction. I recorded a double of Type Fives in the *Diaries* before daybreak. Making the five metres from my bed to the toilet had also not been without trouble; I had the beginnings of a cough and had brought up a thimbleful of greenish phlegm, fortunately at the Western Style's door. It wasn't a promising start to the day but, through the door, I'd heard the kitchen opening while I'd been busy, so decided to be one of the first in for breakfast.

I was far from the earliest customer – the full complement of porters had packed their kit and were taking tea before their guests awoke. I ordered the 'Full English' breakfast, hoping some stodge would replace some lost solids and help me feel a bit livelier for the day ahead. The menu listed its ingredients as toast, eggs, bacon, and roast potatoes with a milk coffee thrown in for good measure. There's nothing like roast tatties on toast to get you going in the morning. As I waited to be served, I mulled over what the day's itinerary might be. In my planning for the trip, I'd outlined two possibilities for the acclimatisation day based on the night passed:

Option 1: Having behaved sensibly in The World's Highest Irish Pub
1. Wake up with a clear head around eight.
2. Gorge myself on a Full English Breakfast.
3. Change money at the bank.
4. Head off on a day walk towards Thame, take in some mountain scenery, and return before dark.
5. Dinner in the hotel and an early night.
6. Awake refreshed and ready for the trek to Tengboche.

Option 2: Having behaved not as sensibly in The World's Highest Irish Pub
1. Wake up with a raging hangover around noon, hopefully in my hotel room.
   a. If in my hotel room, proceed to step 2.
   b. If not in my hotel room, establish if I'm in police custody
      i. If in police custody, pay fine(s) due or mentally prepare for *Midnight Express*-type experience.
      ii. If not in police custody, establish who my new friend is and ask directions on how to get back to my hotel.
2. Change money at the bank, if still in possession of wallet.

3. Go back to Irish pub for Full Irish Breakfast (same as Full English Breakfast but substitute potato scones for toast) and the hair of the dog.
4. Establish if barred from The World's Highest Irish Pub.
    a. If unbarred, proceed to step 5.
    b. If barred, retire to the aptly named Liquid Bar for breakfast and hair of the dog, go to step 7.
5. Discuss from a bar stool what else could be more Irish than roast tatties on tattie scone washed down with a Guinness with a barman who goes by the name of Mick O'Sherpa.
6. Spend rest of the afternoon unsuccessfully looking for darts for a game of five-o-one with Ed Sheeran.
7. Liquid dinner over a game or two of pool with Ed and back to the hotel for an early night.
8. Awake sort of refreshed and not so ready for the trek to Tengboche.

No doubt fortunately, things had turned out closer to being Option 1. I'd have another chance on the way back to visit The World's Highest Irish Pub, so I wasn't too disappointed.

I expected the porters to sit among plates of pewter skid-marked with the muddy browns of lentil residue or their spoons galloping to and from heaps of dhal baat, fortifying themselves for the day's haulage but, instead, most contented themselves quietly with only hot drinks. For the few who'd chosen to eat, their dishware was occupied with miniature Tibetan bread rolls in various states of crumbly demolishment. Replace the tea with espresso and the place could've been a Duomo-side café, barring all the hand-waving drama.

Porters and guides arrived in the dining room at regular intervals and to a set pattern. The first action after entering was to head to the white plastic tower block of about a bedside lamp's height at the counter's end. Its windows were power charging points. A mobile phone would be slipped from a pocket. On reaching the 'Tower of Power', a head movement approximating a snooker player calculating their angles would follow, after which a charging cable would be inserted into a socket and the phone laid on the counter. The owner would order their drink and possibly bread before taking a seat with their colleagues.

This procedure worked well at the start of the morning, but as the diner became busier some inherent flaws were revealed. The etiquette around which socket to select and where one's phone should sit hadn't yet matured into any sort of regularity. My inner 'form an orderly queue of one' Britishness expected the tower's early users utilise the lower sockets and extend their charging cables along the counter to their furthest extent. All subsequent users would work their way up the tower's floors and place their phones inward, thereby allowing easiest access to the next socket and avoiding double-deckers of phones dangling from snarled cables.

Needless to say, the locals did it differently. As the rat's nest of wires became more entangled and the stacks of mobiles rose, each additional power-starved mendicant would position themselves in front of the tower with the caution of a Buckaroo player with only the bucket piece left to hang. If there were no sockets available, an unwritten rule seemed to be to examine the percentage level on each phone and replace the one with the maximum charge with one's own. For less scrupulous users, an alternative was to select the one easiest to yank out and replace it. I was astounded that this didn't seem to cause any irritation or conflict, but then again six in the morning was kind of early to start an Old West saloon-type bar brawl.

I reminded myself my phone would need charging later in the day. Unlike in the sophisticated lodges of the valleys below the room lacked a power socket included in the room rate. The Kamal was going to charge me for the pleasure, a concept I'd first come across in Paiya, but the charging arrangement there made the 'Tower of Power' look almost formic in its level of organisation. Its use was only advisable in rubber-soled boots. At checkout, the lodge owners hadn't charged me for it, presumably because the costs incurred were offset entirely by the danger money they owed me for its use. I made a mental note to contact the marketing department at Salomon when I got home; what my boots lacked in their slip prevention performance, they could more than make up for in electrocution suppression.

At the Kamal, there were various tariffs associated with the charge level at which the phone was extracted from the tower. A 'full charge' cost Rs.150, a 'half charge' 100 and an hourly charge was priced at 50. I tried to work out how these costs could be calculated; did the 'full charge' mean the phone needed to be presented with a flat battery for the full 150 to apply? If I had six per cent left and opted for that pricing, would I pay 94 hundredths of the cost? Did the half charge only apply from zero to 50 per cent or from 50 to 100, or both; or could I also choose to charge from 25 to 75? If I had 46 per cent left, would I have to make sure I was at the counter to withdraw at 96 to avoid a nasty surcharge?

I appreciated the hourly option was easier to administer from a business angle but, from a customer perspective, what did that translate to in terms of power uplift? Would I get more than 25 per cent in my 60 minutes and therefore be pro-rata better off if I selected that option? The entire set-up was less decipherable than a dual-fuel white meter bill. I wondered how the ladies behind the counter could hope to police such an operation. Not only would they require codebreaking abilities in excess of those possessed by Alan Turing to assess the tariff, they'd also need the memory skills of an idiot savant to keep track of who plugged in which phone, where, when and at what rate, combined with the mathematical ability of Hypatia to reckon the final bill. Maybe that was what Teach was working on when I'd arrived the previous day?

The arrival of my breakfast corresponded with the first trekking group's appearance. They were a quartet of Nipponese senior citizens who deferentially congregated in the nowhere space between the counter and crockery cabinet at the room's midpoint, appearing baffled by what to do next and uncomfortable at not having anyone to ask. Their leader was an older man who, from my angle appeared to have been looking after himself. From the back, he could've been a teenage track athlete but when he turned around his countenance was more of someone run over by a race of track athletes. He'd attempted to mask his pocks and pustules with a coating of grey fur that fell to beneath his chin but had been only partially successful. But he'd salvaged his look with a fantastic hat that must have been a souvenir from a Seven Dwarfs ride in a Tokyo theme park.

The other three were ladies, significantly shorter in stature and wider in the hips, wearing the kitsch of a uniform that – to my European eyes – was slightly off kilter in the way only a Japanese interpretation of Western fashions can be. There was something amiss about the floppy headgear, fleeces, waterproof trousers, and modern footwear I couldn't place; it could have been the white bandanas that led down from under their cherry blossom patterned hats to knot under the ladies' chins, but I couldn't be sure. They busied themselves examining the flags pinned to the ceiling but found naught to comfort them. As my eyes followed, I couldn't spot a red circle on white background either. They resorted to examining the state of their boots for a while as more confident guests arrived, swerved around them, ordered, and took station at their tables. Their guide arrived to a wan smile of relief from the man, followed by some bowing and a gentle conveyance of words before he showed them to their table.

The Full English was Rs.800's worth of excellence, or 400's worth downwind of Phakding. The banks weren't scheduled to open until after 10 and I'd nothing better to do, so I settled back for a second milk coffee and to watch how the morning unfolded in the diner.

By 7.30, the place had returned to the thrum of six the preceding evening. I was joined at one of the last available chairs by a young lady who confidently told me she knew she was going to be the first Icelander I'd met trekking. I couldn't resist a response that said it was funny she'd said that because I'd passed Gregor Clegane carrying Björk downhill yesterday. She'd completed the Three Passes Trek and was on her way down, accompanied by her cost-conscious combination of guide and porter in one, who chose not to sit with us. I was shocked by how skeletal he was, but the girl from a village not too far outside Reykjavik asserted it wasn't due to illness, he was naturally emaciated. We chatted through the usual pleasantries and moved on to talk about Skyr, whether Lazytown was still going and the rules around how surnames worked in Iceland. It was something that had fascinated me since watching a stop motion animation adaptation of the *Eyrbyggja Saga* while coming into land at Boston.

"You see Gregor, the World's Strongest Man, he's named after his father Bjorn, so he's a Bjornsson. If he'd been a girl, then he would be Bjorndottir."

"If he'd been a girl, then you'd have to be pretty brave to ask her on a date. So, it's add '-son' or '-dottir'?"

"Yes."

"So, if your father's name was, for example, Magnus Magnusson, what would your name be?"

"My first name is Elisabet, so I would be Elisabet Magnusdottir."

"So, say you got married to a man called, what would be a common Icelandic name for a man?"

"Jon."

"For a woman?"

"Viktoria."

"Okay, so if you got married to Jon and you called your daughter together Viktoria, she'd be Viktoria Jonsdottir?"

"Correct."

"So how can you tell in Iceland, with different surnames, you're Mr Magnusson's daughter and he's Viktoria's grandfather? Is it not possible to tell that you're related?"

"This question doesn't make sense. In Iceland everyone is related!"

"Ha-ha. So, what about same sex-couples, do you have same-sex marriages in Iceland?"

"Why? I don't think Hafþor would go on a date with you! Of course, we have same-sex marriages, for a long time now, just because we're all related doesn't mean we still live in the 19th century. You know we have the world's oldest parliament, don't you?"

"I do think I remember that, yes, founded by the Vikings. So how does it work for kids where there's no man?"

"Don't they teach biology in Scotland?! There's always a man, even if he only plays his part by a syringe."

"Ah, yes, let me rephrase the question. So, where you have a lesbian couple, which woman's name would the child take?"

"It would be the name on the syringe and the woman who made the baby. So, if the baby was called Viktoria, the father's name was Magnus and the mother's name Elisabet then the name would be Viktoria Elisabetdottir Magnusdottir."

"Wow, I'd hate to be that kid on their first day of school. The teacher would be pissed off having to write all that in their assembly book. I'm not even going to ask what happens for a gay couple who're having a baby with a surrogate mother!"

"Ha-ha, yes, it gets complicated, but the good news is there isn't much happening in the winter in Iceland, so we have plenty of time to figure out what the right name is for someone and then spend until spring arguing about it."

"I've read one Icelandic novel, I think. It was called *World Light*, by Halldor Laxness. I don't remember it too well, but nothing seemed to happen in winter in that either, or summer for that matter."

"No, you've remembered that book perfectly, that is the summary of the story." Elisabet had finished her breakfast and prepared to leave, the skeleton falling into lockstep behind her as she paid her bill. She gave me a friendly wave as she left, her scraggy shadow following in a strangely menacing wraithlike silence.

The banks were about to open, so I returned to my room to dress for a stroll around Namche. As I donned my gear, I was thankful the food showed no signs of making a sharp reappearance and the last few day's dry heaving seemed to have abated.

I'd been drawn by the idea of Namche Bazaar ever since I'd first heard its name. The Bazaar part of the name was evocative of a montane souk occupied at every corner with turbaned cobra charmers. I imagined residual descendants of the Nazi baddies from the inn fight in *Raiders of the Lost Ark,* bullets fired from their Lugers ricocheting off piles of kitchenware hanging from open-fronted stalls as they pursued the grandchild of Indie's untold dalliance with a Nepali lady. Belloq's great-nephew would be casually examining an arcane artefact in a hookah bar while the combatants steadily destroyed the village brick by brick as the battle raged up and down its twisted alleys and wynds. It was with a scintilla of that expectation I made my way down the stairs into the alleyway that ran between shops below.

The settlement's principal thoroughfare was a passageway of a mule's width at its widest. The five-storey stone terraces on either side brokered no sun to warm its broken flagstones, but the chill atmosphere was suitably evocative of foreboding. Splintered, overhanging balconies painted white and blue five storeys up would provide blackshirt henchmen with ideal sniping positions. Dark recesses of shadow could offer areas of respite for the hero to dash between the sprays of bullets before clambering up the stone face of a hotel to dispatch the fascists with his bare fists.

The pieces of the cinematic jigsaw I imagined fell away as I made my way up the alley; the vegetable stalls from which Dr Jones Junior Junior would start his climb were instead dedicated to hawking ubiquitous wares. Daypacks and larger were slung down from awnings, padded jackets displayed from plastic hangers and lower trekking poles arrayed on wooden frames. T-shirts boasted slogans of macho achievement and dhal baat power and there were buffs, knitted muffs and headscarves. At ground level, shelves stacked with boxes of water bottles, ponchos and lockable diaries dominated. At a push, I could see Dr J-cubed using a trekking pole to skewer a Hitlerite, but in truth my illusion was broken.

I came to a T-junction at the top of a stair, at the Lord Buddha pharmacy, and contemplated whether or not he'd have approved. The drugstore's signage seemed to suggest the only way to nirvana is a life of monastic inner reflection, but if that doesn't work take a couple of Diamox with water after food. Even though I wouldn't appreciate it yet, a pyramid of toilet paper that would've served the needs of even the keenest of Covid-19 hoarders had been stacked on the table outside. I thought the pharmacist was nothing if not canny, playing both ends of the market. 'Enjoy the savings of the triple pack of Imodium and six-roll price combo deal', the arrangement screamed.

I turned left in the bank's direction, finding the town more of the same, interspersed with the odd bakery, cyber cafe and bar. Disappointingly, the Rastriya Bhanijya bank, when I reached it, was closed and showed no sign of operating soon. It was a Saturday, but it was supposed to open from 10 until noon. I'd have to exchange my cash at a reduced rate with a local Shylock.

He was a jolly, rotund fellow who became even jollier when he saw the fold of dollar bills I wanted to convert into rupees. When he let out one of his frequent bellowing laughs, the jowls of his face moved towards each other in a kind of pincer movement. His day-to-day business model didn't cater for the appearance of a scrubby-bearded Rockefeller with more petty cash on him than Pablo Escobar on a visit to the most pliable of his local politicians, and so he told me he had to leave his office to cover my needs.

As I sat at his desk, I wondered why it thrilled me to see his empty safe left open at my behest, but also so worrisome he'd disappeared cradling all my money and passport in his hands. I'd only just met him, after all, and was that a helicopter I heard revving up? He returned, beaming, with a roll of rupees Pringle-canister thick and criss-crossed by elastic bands in his chubby mitts. I wouldn't have been at all surprised if he'd nipped around the corner and they'd opened the bank especially for him.

He stretched a thimble across a single digit and, with a Scrooge-like glee, counted out the trade, his mood only sullied when he came across a slightly torn $20 note. Despite my protestations, he wouldn't accept it. I wasn't sure what his issue was; it was not likely I'd flown halfway across the world and tramped for eight days to palm off a counterfeit 20. No matter, I reckoned, I'd more than enough lucre to keep me in yak burgers for the next couple of weeks.

I set off for Thame. After the bank, the centre's tourist tawdriness rapidly dissipated into dwellings for the locals, an urban version of the villages I'd seen on the lower trek with the additional trappings of municipal pollution. There had been enough shit in the Central Business District's alleyways to put the 16th arrondissement's trophy dog-fouled pavements to shame, but here it was a flyblown carpet mixed with forgotten Dasani bottles, weathered corn snack packets and discarded cigarette packs.

I reasoned such squalor couldn't be apportioned to lack of pride in one's surroundings or negligence; rather, it must be that the day-to-day fight against poverty took precedence. I was sad to think I could happily munch away at a fillet in the Steak House 100 metres away and here there was such privation. As I headed onto the trail, the growing magnificence of Kwangde as the backdrop for this district only acted, if anything, to magnify my feelings.

I'd walked little further than these unofficial city limits when I needed to add to the filth on the ground. My dry retch had eventually succeeded in promoting itself to full-blown vomiting and I threw up at the trailside, immediately faint afterwards. It was obvious Thame was out of the question and so, an hour after cheerfully leaving the Kamal, I was despondently back in my room. The walk back hadn't been easy, a navel-deep dry heave repeating itself every few steps. I reached the hotel toilet just in time for my body to try another expulsion of something that wasn't there to expel. I lay on my bed breathing hard and hoping the spasms would stop. Eventually, my chest calmed, and I closed my eyes to rest; three hours later, I awoke to the drone of vacuuming.

I was the only visitor for a belated hotel lunch, ordering a small pot of lemon tea to try to replenish lost fluids, the Café Florian pricing of no consequence given my new-found opulence. I recovered with a couple of cups and decided to extend my munificence to a bowl of noodle soup with egg, placing my order with an uninterested Teach.

Teach shouting my order through the hatch was the opportunity for her son to make his escape from under her skirts, the shaven-headed pre-schooler gleefully snatching a smartphone from the lap of his sister. The toddler jumped from her seat and hopelessly chased her one-shoed brother around the diner, screaming with an intensifying despair that was met by an increasingly mocking taunt. She gave up and went to mum for sympathy, but none was given; she was too busy on her own iPad with a game that pinged with the music of a one-armed bandit. The boy seated himself at the far end of the room. With the fickleness only small children or the Twitter account of a recent American president can exhibit, his sister jumped up to sit at his side.

"Mission Accomplished. Level 1." The squeal of delight was the only sound from the pair in response to the electronic announcement.

"Mission Accomplished. Level 2." Another squeal.

"Game Over." Another squeal, but of a different nature.

"Mami ..." The mother looked up without interest and squawked something to her boy before the phone was passed back with a look of contempt that said he'd make her pay for this.

The noodles were good and, reckoning there wasn't much chance for conversation with the electronically addicted mum, I decided to go back to my room. I spent the rest of the afternoon at *Cryptonomicon*, attempted to crack the first challenge in my Codeword Puzzlepad and, at five, ordered my dinner.

I figured a hot shower would help me feel better so enquired at the counter, where one of the younger ladies told me the key was out. I wondered what that meant, the key was out of what? I waited patiently for the key to come back in and, 20 minutes later, an unabashed young lady presented herself at the counter, clad only in a damp travel towel and tangle of wet hair. She dangled a rusted key from her hand and I was slightly disappointed to learn it wasn't part of the latest Mammut chastity belt trekking gear. My instructions were to use it to unlock the shower a flight below.

The key was for a padlock out of proportion for any kind of threat a potential shower thief could pose, securing the shower room's equally overengineered sheet metal door. Inside, the chamber resounded with the memory of quivering steel. Its walls and ceiling were painted light mustard. I imagined that this is what it must feel like stuck inside one of the ship's boilers on the Yellow Submarine of Beatles fame. I was disappointed at the lack of complimentary soaps and shampoos, thinking that with all that hair, Miss Exhibitionist upstairs could've used them all up in a frenzy of Pantene lathering. The water started at a skin-blistering temperature, turning five minutes later to slightly above freezing. The controls failed to respond to any sort of encouragement. I couldn't phone the lady in Bhandar for advice on thermal equalisation techniques, so reluctantly I towelled off, my skin a mixture of red welts and blue frostbite. I was clean but dissatisfied; the shower was nowhere near Nunthala standard and three times the price.

At six, I took up my table ready for dinner. I'd remembered my phone and managed to secure a mid-tower, mid-counter spot for charging, after working through four pages of quadratic equations to choose the hourly tariff. The matriarch was on her evening off or had been removed by social services for neglect, her place taken by the children's father who sat with his daughter, both busy accomplishing electronic missions in his lap. Mysteriously, he was wearing sunglasses.

The dinner clientele was mostly the same as the previous evening, together with some fresh faces and some familiar from breakfast. The four Japanese folks had merged with another group, tripling their size. A Nepali man who looked more like Ken Jeong from *The Hangover* than the actor himself orbited around them. He was something of a raconteur, judging by the regular laughter coming from the dozen. I was hugely impressed, thinking it was one thing to master a different language but to be funny in it, too, must be incredibly difficult.

There were a couple of Sherpa guides drinking long glasses of beer. That came as a shock; for some reason, I'd expected all those golden cans of lager were reserved for the trekkers. But I realised I hadn't thought about that at all, it was another subconscious prejudice. I wondered whether, because I hadn't seen a Nepali take anything other than the local spirit, I'd pigeon-holed that as their only choice and filed beer drinking as something I'd never expect to see.

Now a regular, I was served promptly and my dinner of chicken and vegetables with chips passed quietly. At the expiration of the full hour, I went to retrieve my phone to find some enterprising wag had replaced my phone with their own. I was irked enough to unplug everything and arrange the cables to look like the interloper's phone was still on charge. I knew it wasn't what the Man with No Name would do in the same situation, but it made me feel better.

Back in my room, I'd learned from my mistake of trying for an early night and worked my way through more puzzles. I read some more but reached that saturation point where it becomes a chore rather than a pleasure and so I fired up the Nano in expectation of the long, interrupted night to come. I started *Infected* by The The on track six and, an hour later, it was time to try for sleep; it was 11pm.

Saturday night was quiet at The World's Highest Irish Pub compared to Friday and I thought perhaps it had been full of rowdy bankers over-enjoying their night, safe in the knowledge they had the next morning off. The Pride of Idaho Sibilating Society had also moved on, so I managed a good night's rest.

The next morning I made it to the diner in time for rush-hour. I sneaked my phone cable into a slot around the back of the tower before ordering porridge, hoping its weight in my stomach would help keep everything down for the day. The Japanese groups now seemed to have formally signed an alliance and were in the process of moving off together as I waited for my breakfast. I was dispirited to see the one-armed man flitting around his guests again. Lukewarm porridge came as I was joined by a young lady who told me she'd completed the Gokyo trek and was spending a few days in Namche to experience the benefits of high-altitude yoga before heading back home. Breakfast had only been saved by her company and the milk coffee we shared.

I made a trip to the Western Style. I entered a Type Four in the *Diaries*, appending a technical footnote to ensure the plastic seat was firmly affixed to the porcelain before use. My cough hadn't worsened, and I was thankful not to feel sick, so after deduping my bill and querying the correctness of the derivative used in calculating the phone charge, I was ready to trek again. I left via the upper entrance past a Scandinavian lady who was organising via phone what sounded like a climbing companion to come to meet her. Either that, or she'd swiped right on Namche Tinder.

The morning was a silver of grey clouds, my breath visible in the chill. I'd been forewarned about the staircase out of Namche and found it steep, but nowhere near as bad as the descriptions I'd read. My ascent coincided with peak hour and so my experience was more like the jostle up the left-hand side of a London Underground escalator than a trek in the Himalaya. The cool temperature and the incentive of competition meant I reached the huge mani stone at Chhorkung in good time.

As I took a breather, my deep inhalations turned into a dry retch with globules of phlegm brought up via a hacking cough in the interstices between spasms. I gave a weak smile and thumbs-up to each concerned trekker who passed me for the next 10 minutes before drowning out the dry heave with water from my LifeStraw and moving off along the path. It was mercifully flat, a broad, dusty sand crushed and crenulated with the imprints of hundreds of rubber soles.

Dwellings backed on to this part of the trail and the local means of refuse disposal seemed to be to slow burn everything in a wok in the pathway's centre. I thought if I was mistaken, then I pitied the poor traveller who was going to be served for breakfast this morning the least appetising plate of fried noodles on the entire subcontinent, but the acrid smell of melting plastic told me otherwise.

I wasn't sure if dzhos, rather than mules, were the pack animal of choice above Namche, but there was a perceptible increase in their numbers on the first part of the track. They came at me in a rolling slow motion, bells tinkling. I thought of them as animals of contradiction. Their huge horns gathered inwards to points that would be terrifying if in pursuit at Pamplona, but here were rendered as unthreatening ornamentation by the animal's placid demeanour. Their legs seemed too short in relation to their bulk, as if transplanted from a Shetland pony. They had short hair mottled in blacks and browns while at the same time sprouting tufts of shaggy red. Here, they were carrying small yellow sacks incommensurate with their load-bearing capacity and I wondered if their downhill trip largely consisted of bringing back discarded trekking gear.

I climbed an uneven set of steps and rounded a switchback nearing the completion of its apprenticeship for a job at Paiya La. It was the first time on the trek my breath was truly taken away by anything other than the climbing. The green downward arrow of the valley's craggy slopes framed a parabola of reclining rocky alps; from its vertex rose a hazy sierra cloaked in white, two aiguilles dominating. To the right were the twin shards of Lhotse, to the left the twisted trapezoid of Everest. The panorama was stunning and it took a moment to take it in, followed by another to be shocked into realising that it was real.

I now knew the real meaning of having to pinch yourself. I was humbled by a vista both awesome in the true sense of the word and painted by a master artist in the hues of a perfect ratio. Small wonder, then, that grin tickled my earlobes. Practically 30 years on from my first attempt, a decade after my second and a week on from Phurteng, the weather had finally been kind. I'd realised my lifelong ambition to cast eyes on Mount Everest. It was only 'Mission Accomplished. Level 1' but I didn't think it inappropriate to let out a squeal of delight the kids from the Kamala would've been proud of.

If there had been a chautara at which to sit, I'd have stayed for hours but, as it was, the gathering crowd of photographers spurred me on. A corniche ran along the valley's left-hand slope, leading to a chorten announcing another switchback. The aspect from the far side of the stupa broadened to include Ama Dablam to the right and more aiguilles to the left. The spectacle of five minutes past was surpassed. As I took some photographs, the Historian trotted up behind me, this time on his own feet, and I was glad that even he was dumbstruck for a few minutes.

"Oh, hi Lee."

"Aydin! How are you doing?" I enquired, instantly thinking 'Oh, shit, I know I shouldn't have asked that.' But the detail of his latest ailments washed by me, I was too mesmerised by the view, and then I noticed something was amiss – he'd stopped moaning.

"Did you see Everest back there? It was unbelievable, wasn't it? I've been waiting decades to see that. I can't believe I've finally seen it," I blurted out in a staccato response to the silence.

"Yeah, I've got some great photos. It's a shame about the cloud though, I could've done with some blue for contrast. The local council could do with putting one of those seat things there, I could've stayed around and waited a bit more for the clouds to go away."

"I'm sure there are going to be plenty of opportunities throughout the day. Look, the clouds are even being burned off by the sun just now. How did you sneak up behind me like that, by the way? I thought you'd be miles ahead by now?"

"Yeah, I wasn't planning to, but I got stuck in Namche for a day. I had a headache and felt dizzy. I thought I might have got AMS."

"Oh dear, that's not good. How are you feeling now?"

"My headache's gone but I'm still a bit dizzy now and again."

"Are you taking anything for it, the Diamox?"

"No, I couldn't possibly take any tablets for it, they'll do you more harm than good. I've heard they paralyse your hands and feet."

"I don't think I've read that but fair enough. So, where are you headed for today, Tengboche?"

"In that direction. I don't want to stay in Tengboche, though. I think it will be too expensive. How did you find the prices in Namche? I couldn't believe it when I first went into a hotel and asked how much for a room! I thought she was a *right* rip-off merchant. I tried five places in the end, but they all wanted to charge me the same. Eventually, I found somewhere where someone would bargain a bit. It cost me Rs.750 for dinner, mind!"

"Sounds like you got a deal. I paid more than 800. It's still cheap, though, isn't it? I mean, it's only like six quid for an evening meal, you wouldn't get that anywhere at home for a sit-down except crap fast-food places. They have to cart up the food and all that stuff to cook it with as well, so I can understand why it's more expensive. Plus, they've got a limited season – imagine what the same grub would cost if you ordered it in a French ski resort, you'd have taken out a second mortgage by now."

"Yeah, but it still feels like a bit of a rip-off."

"I know what you mean but there's not much we can do about it. So, what's the plan, try the lodges in the smaller villages and hope they're cheaper?"

"Yes, I think that'll be better."

"Well, I think we've got a fair way to go. I think that settlement on the ridge on the left could be Tengboche. I suppose if you're knackered when you get there, then you always have the option of staying. Even if it costs you another Rs.100 a night, it's not exactly going to break the bank, is it?"

"It might do for me. I only changed £200 in Kathmandu and that's nearly all gone. I tried to change some American Express travellers' cheques in Namche but they wouldn't accept them."

"Two hundred quid! Is that all? You're doing well, I spent 300 to get to Namche and changed some more yesterday. I didn't know they still did travellers' cheques? I thought everyone got cash out with their cards nowadays."

"I'd them left over from my last trip to Nepal."

"Ten years ago?"

"Yes, Amex say they're still valid."

"And they're still accepted, 10 years later?"

"Not in Namche. So, I have to watch my budget. I only have £600 for the whole seven weeks."

"Jeez, that's cutting it. I hope you've got enough." He wasn't taking any pictures from this viewpoint, so set off. I feared for Aydin – things weren't going to get cheaper with altitude. I was unsure what he'd do if he ran out of cash at 4,000 metres; it wasn't as if, in an emergency, he'd be able to sell his nail clippers for cash any more.

The corniche swept into the piazza of the Ama Dablam View Lodge Restaurant at Kyangjuma. The lodge was tastefully built into the mountainside, the plaza forming the roof for the rooms below. The restaurant was a semi-enclosed belvedere, the top of its half-stable door had been flung open and the shop to its left was open to the breeze. The view from the interior wasn't preferential: every table in the handsome courtyard had been occupied by trekking groups, pride of place at the wall. From this angle, to my mind, Ama Dablam was Gandalf reposed with knees up to his chin, cloaked in a mottled blanket of whites and greys, the wispy clouds the shapes he blew from his long clay pipe.

Beyond the tea house, the woods through which the path hacked could also have been penned by Tolkien. They were cresting waves of ancient, spindly trunks that broke downhill into ashen thickets, a tunnel to an elven lair. The woods thinned and led to a crooked signpost in a banana yellow that pointed the way unequivocally to Tengboche, while another fork signed for the Gokyo trail. The sub-lettering for the Tengboche route read 'UNDP-GEF-SGP/KSCCS/KBZUC'. I made a note in case it was the Wi-fi password for the lodges further up the valley.

The woods changed nature and became stronger, more individual, with mature, deciduous specimens of waxy leaves sheening in the bright sunshine. A blackened log chautara, forming a cliffside corner above the Dudh Kosi sweeping through the valley hundreds of metres below, announced the approach to the village of Sanasa. The trail was funnelled into an alleyway where all manner of miniature Tibetan prayer wheels, decorative beaten bowls, etched slate plates and carved Hindu Oms were on offer in an open market that fronted the stacked counters of the trailside lodges. I opted not to load my pack any further and moved through the hamlet; souvenirs were for on the way down.

Afterwards, the route broadened to bring Ama Dablam into domineering focus above shoulders of dark green pine, my course dead ahead towards it. The exceptional vista took my mind away from worrying too much about the cliffside exposure of this section. It cut inwards to descend once more through the mature forest of birches and rhododendrons. I reached the tiny settlement of Lawichasa. It buildings could've been glued, crag side up, into a niche in the cliff. I decided to take tea and some sun on the bright terrace recessed a handful of steps down from the path.

There was no way without unkindness to describe the appearance of the lady who attended. Any aspiring make-up artist struggling for ideas for Macbeth greasepaint could do no better than a visit to Lawichasa for inspiration. Along with her steepled namaste, she greeted me with a smile that Heinrich would've considered a career-changing opportunity. What she lacked in beauty and youth she compensated for with vigour, however, as her movements were the salsa of a long-player set to 45.

I soon discovered the patio was prime real estate for people-watching. Everyone and everything emerged from the trees and took a single step of reassurance that asked, 'What does this next bit look like?' The scene was evocative of a parade of ham actors momentarily milking the applause on their first stage entrance of the matinee performance. Whoever was coming through would adjust a strap and nod to a companion to confirm readiness for continuing, speed up and understeer through the turn where I was sitting and oversteer out the other end. I now knew why, in the Latin part of Europe, this activity was so popular.

I was enjoying myself watching the world go by, sitting in the startling sunlight, supping my second cup of the crone's excellent black tea when the Historian's party edged past in dribs and drabs. Another porter with a builder's merchant's worth of timber pivoted on his head stopped to rest and the crone's grandson joined me. He had the insistence of a four-year-old who was convinced by his argument that it was more effective to hop on one foot between the kitchen and the water butt, rather than concede to put on his other shoe. The extended Japanese group walked on by and, as the procession seemed to draw to a close, I finished my tea; this was the signal to settle the bill and move on.

The trail descended steeply afterwards on eroded, beaten earth where hazes of dust were hoofed up by the trains of ascending dzhos. My knees buckled as I sidestepped down the awkward steps interspersed between exposed tree roots. I'd soon caught the Historian who'd stopped mid-trail, tenderly helping his wife down a difficult stair of thigh-height conglomerated rocks. I waited for him to guide her gently down.

"Wait there please, darling, let this young man go. He's an expert."

'Young? Expert?' He couldn't be referring to me.

"Take your time, don't worry, I'm in no rush. I'm no expert, either."

"Thank you. Come on, darling, please be careful on this next step."

"Is it going to be like this all the way, darling? I don't think I can do it. My knees aren't going to take it."

"You're doing wonderfully, darling," he encouraged.

"But it's so hard. I didn't know it was going to be this painful. You never said," she croaked, in a dry voice somewhere between a broken rasp and a tear.

"Yes, but it will get better. Come on, now."

"I don't think it's too far to the river now, you should be able to get a bit of a rest there," I offered.

"Oh really? Thank you, young man. You see, darling, we're not far away now. I can ask the guide to sort you out on one of the horses and you can go up on that to Tengboche." I was warmed that, out of public gaze, the Historian was a much different man.

The couple graciously let me overtake and I completed the patella-pounding descent through the forest to the Dudh Kosi. The trail to the first suspension bridge curled around on itself and up onto a patio. Those in the know would deem this an even better people-watching spot than my perch at Lawichasa – the rushing river beneath complemented the magnificent panorama. It also boasted the added comedy factor of unbalanced trekkers wobbling their way to the other bank.

The second bridge led shortly afterwards to a tea house that warned it was the last food and drink outlet before Tengboche. Its sunny quadrant opposite couldn't have been located in a prettier spot.

Even if I hadn't learned my lessons on missing lunch, the location was enough to persuade me to stop and so I looked for a menu.

"Hey, man, are you on your own? Come and join us."

"Yeah, I am. Thanks for the offer. Can I sit here? Where are you folks from?"

"I'm Jim, and this is Josh, we're from the US."

"I'm Xavi. From Chile."

"Xavi? Like Xabi Alonso?"

"Yes, my name is Gabriela, but everyone calls me Xavi from when I was small."

"I'm Lee, from the UK. Are you from Santiago?"

"No, a lot more south."

"By the Torres del Paine national park?"

"No, a lot more north."

"Puerto Montt?"

"No, I am from Concepción. But how do you know this place? No-one knows it outside Chile."

"I was looking at the Torres del Paine trek earlier this year and it looks like you have to get a boat from there to go to the national park. I couldn't work out how to get there but thought it's probably easier from the Argentinian side. It didn't look like you could get a bus from Santiago, can you do it that way?"

"Yes, you can go, but you need to know how to do it." Xavi didn't elaborate so I changed tack.

"So, where in the US are you guys from? You're not from Idaho, by any chance?"

"Idaho, why do you think we're from Idaho?" Jim asked.

"Oh, no reason, I just heard that it's very nice, that's all."

"I wouldn't know, never been."

"I guess you're not in the horse trade. So where *are* you from?"

"Ohio."

"Let me see if I can get my guess for your town completely wrong as well, then. Is it Pittsburgh that's in Ohio, no it's Pennsylvania, isn't it? Err ... is it Cincinnati, is that in Ohio?"

"Yeah, but unlucky, man, we aren't from there. Have another guess."

"Err ... now I'm stuck. Sorry, I'm not too good on the Midwest. I think the only other place could be Columbus? Is that in Ohio?"

"Great guess, man. You heading to Tengboche today?"

"Hopefully, that's the plan. Have you folks been travelling together for long?"

"Nah, we just met in Namche this morning." We chatted through a delicious lunch, vegetable noodle soup for me, plates of heaped dhal baat for them. The boys were recent graduates, a few days into their two-week vacation. They were making the most of it by cramming in the Three Passes Trek.

The guys were everything for which the Founding Fathers would've wished in their vision of an ideal American citizen – bright-eyed, confident, smart, engaging and challenging without any of the cynicism of old Europe. Their guide was a smiling, lithe boy in his 20s, wearing powdered jeans and going by the name of Taha. Xavi was of similar age. She was travelling solo across the world, a more seasoned traveller undimmed in her enthusiasm for the excitement of new places. She bore my attempts to communicate in my halting Spanish with more good humour than they deserved. I liked them a lot.

After lunch, we set off together for the climb up to the monastery, but a minute after repacking our bags we were unpacking them again for the army checkpoint. It was set back in a glade and could have been an early timber prototype for a British Telecom telephone box. The guard who took my paperwork was far more laid-back than those at the Sagarmatha park entrance, examining my permits with the chilled tempo of a Jamaican in the second week of a beach holiday.

"You start in Gaurishankar park, Shivalaya? Ha-ha, you are terrible slow, man!" I could've been mistaken but was sure I detected a Marleyesque lilt in his accent as he handed me back my tickets.

"Thanks, mon, I and I've heard dat before, see you on de way down."

The trail now ascended through rhododendron and pine that grew with a deep green lushness on the valley side. The river's rush was soon lost below, and the trail broke into stands of trees interspersed between long, dusty ruts exposed to the midday sun. The gradient had become ferocious, and I was soon labouring under the effort and with the heat. The footing in places was obstructed by angular rocks cemented into the path with the deviousness of Fortress Europe tank traps. Screes of pebbles made the footing treacherous. A young trekker who I'd crossed slipped 10 metres below me, crashing onto her behind to set off an avalanche of 100 stones that sprung down the hillside. Fortunately, she was dusted and grazed but no more.

An hour in, the needle on my noodle power gauge flickered between a quarter and flat. I'd kept pace with Josh, Jim, Taha and Xavi but now it was time to urge them on ahead and I took advantage of a shaded stone chautara to sit down. I breathed in the view of Kantega, directly ahead in a notch above the pines. Clouds swirled around with the flourish of a matador's cape, revealing a different snowy aspect minute by minute. I rested for half-an-hour, enjoying the theatre of it.

The porters who joined me were as indifferent as they were taciturn but became animated when our dawdling was rewarded.

"National bir' of Nepal, feasan'!"

A family of Himalayan monal burst from a thicket and dashed across our path into hiding.

As I climbed, my pace slowed to that of a delivery man shouldering a 1950s refrigerator up the final twist to an attic apartment. The train of the combined Japanese party rolled by as I sat on a rock, chest heaving, taking the last of my water. The switchbacks flattened into a long haul upwards, then returned, and I was grateful for the shade they afforded. I came across a black hose at the base of a massive boulder, thoughtfully engineered to capture the spring water, and I filled my bottle and took a deep draught that made me feel better. A porter passed and shouted some words of encouragement; around the bend to Tengboche, he told me.

I hoped he was right and pushed on to find a tourist information board where three laminated signs had been pinned. The one in Roman script pronounced 'Keep Silence in Monastery Area'. I was conflicted, happy to be near enough that volume control was considered a potential issue, but dejected there was no sign of a monastery when I looked up, just more brush and blue sky. I wondered if the monks had a kind of motorway exit distance marker system in place, three warning signs to keep silent or else, and this was the first one. Head down and a little disheartened I still had a long way to go, I trudged upwards and felt something grip my arm. The trail's final crest deserved a helping hand to yank a trekker up and over and that was best provided by a beatific, smiling monk.

He was garbed in the talapoin's traditional dress, the only concessions to modernity the addition of a puffer jacket colour coordinated with the crimson of his robes, a pair of square spectacles and, of course, the mobile phone he was talking into. The 'Keep silent' instruction was clearly for visitors only. I span the prayer wheels as I passed through the ornately painted kani and stopped dead at the belvedere, the scene ahead surpassing all those from earlier in the day.

"Get moving, Englishman! You are blocking the way. As usual!"

"Ah ... Britta, ha-ha. Will you have a look at that?"

"I would like to, but I can't see anything through your backpack."

"Oh, sorry." I moved out of her way. Down valley to the right was Ama Dablam, a shoulder of mist rolling in above the hills that bowed to it; ahead were Everest and Lhotse; and to the left the exotic splendour of the monastery.

"Ya, it's something else, I think is the way you say it?"

"Yes, indeed. Most definitely worth coming for." We stood reverently for a few minutes.

"Are you staying here tonight?"

"No, Dote has arranged a place for us tonight further on. It will be the most luxurious of the trip. I don't have to share with Agathe, and it has hot showers. My first one of the trek!"

"Sounds great. Are you waiting here for the others to catch up?"

"Ya, they will be a long time, I think."

"I'm going to stay in that lodge there, I think. If you want to come in, I owe you a cup of tea or two?"

"No, thank you, I will go to see the monastery, I think. Also, I have some magic tea in my thermos to drink."

"Okay then, say 'Hi' to everyone for me when they catch up and enjoy that shower!"

We parted and I headed to the imposing fortress of a lodge that loomed to my right. The guidebook had indicated from Namche Bazaar it would be a four-and-a-half-hour trek to Tengboche; seven hours after leaving, I'd arrived.

Tengboche to Shomare

T he citadel was approached by an outer gate and stone corridor, presumably designed to allow archers to rain down fire on an army of heretics, those who'd rebelled against the monastic code of silence, laying siege to the place. The fortress was three storeys of grey-mortared blocks and Tudor-painted windows. A feasting hall was to the inner portcullis's left which had been made to the same scale as the Kamal. On entry, I was glad to see the other guests who were a-feasting weren't overtly Viking berserker in their appearance and the chamber wasn't about to descend into a Valhalla justified axe fight. Rather, the place was empty bar a couple who resembled medieval peasantry in their smeared tunics and the chief steward at the counter.

The steward looked up from the parchment unfolded across the counter with, initially, a wearisome slowness that betrayed he perceived my arrival as a chore. He collapsed the paper and strode to meet me with an urgency which said I may be an unwelcome distraction but was potentially a profitable one. He couldn't hide his displeasure at having to see to me, though, scowling with the pursed lips of King Richard III. My half-formed greeting of 'Good morrow, sir innkeeper. Hath ye quarters for a weary knight a-questing?' somehow translated into the usual "Do you have a room?" The man harrumphed and led me back out to the passageway.

The chamber was a floor up. Its standard dual cots offered a distinctly ill-suited view of a mobile phone mast that trebled up as a hitching post for woolly ponies and upright support for a washing line. Beyond that was a vertical wall of rock and ice illuminated in the mid-afternoon sun. We agreed on the ransom for my quarters. As he stomped off back to his reading I heard the American boys' upbeat chatter from the room opposite, their door ajar.

"Hey fellas, looks like we're going to be neighbours tonight."

"Hey Lee."

"Have you just got here? I thought you were miles ahead of me?"

"Yeah, we were, but we slowed up towards the end. I guess you didn't do too bad for an old guy. We're going to get some tea, wanna join us?"

"Ha-ha. Sure, see you downstairs in five." I didn't let them know, but the offhand comment was an ego boost. Having struggled on the way up, it was good to know I wasn't entirely decrepit in the eyes of youth. Just mostly decrepit, but I'd take that.

I made my way back to the feasting hall, where the walls were pinned with the jousting vestments of the knights of Brazil and Argentina, the names of their vanquished foes embossed in blood afore. I sat down on a wooden bench where Sir Josh and Sir Jim had secured a kingly flagon of mulled spiced tea to refresh the assembled knights-errant.

"Are Taha and Xavi not coming down to join us?"

"Xavi, she's feeling the altitude, man. She had a major league headache on the last bit before we got here. She's taken some Diamox and is going to stay in her room to see if it gets better. Taha is arranging some stuff for tomorrow."

"I hope she's okay. How are you guys feeling?"

"Pretty bushed, that was a hard climb. I think I brought too much stuff. How much are you carrying in your bag?" asked Jim.

"About 10 kilos."

"Man, I knew I'd too much stuff, mine is about 13. I gotta lose some of my crap."

"You could ask the lodge to keep it for you," I suggested, hoping they'd enough storage to cater for three kilos of nail files.

"We aren't gonna come by this way on the way down, so I might need to ditch some stuff." We chatted for a while about life in Ohio and trekking in different parts of the world. Inevitably, the subject came around to the incumbent in the White House. Josh wasn't a fan.

"Man, he makes the US look like a bunch of assholes."

"Yeah. I think he's done real damage to America's reputation internationally."

"Yeah, we know, everywhere we go everyone asks how can we have elected this guy."

"It's strange how quickly things can change. I remember I went to a Leonard Cohen gig on the night Obama was elected ..."

"Leonard Cohen?" queried Josh.

"Yes, you know, Leonard Cohen."

"Never heard of him."

"Really?"

"Nope."

"Honestly, I think you millennials are a lost cause sometimes. No, actually, all the time. He was a poet, a writer and a singer. He started off way before even my time, in the 1950s as a poet and then later became famous as a singer."

"What's his stuff like, then? If he's from the 1950s, is he like Elvis or something?"

"No, pretty different, definitely not rock 'n' roll. The best I can say is he had the voice of an idling chain-saw."

"I'm not sure I'd look him up, then."

"Sorry, you should, he's really good. His lyrics, especially, are brilliant. I guess that's down to all that poeting, if that's even a word."

"Okay, I'll check him out on Spotify when I get a signal. What would he be under if not rock 'n' roll? Country? Americana?"

"I don't know, maybe folk, but he wasn't American, he was from Canada. You know, like a lot of really talented people who people assume are Americans but are actually Canadian, like Mike Myers, Dan Aykroyd and ... err ... Justin Bieber." I couldn't resist the opportunity to tease.

"Man, who're all these people you keep talking about? Mike Myers, who's *that?*"

"Yeah, you know, like Shrek."

"Shrek? No way ... Shrek is *Canadian*?!" roared Josh.

"Yeah, well kind of ... I think the accent was based on Mike Myer's time in Scotland. So, I think Shrek is Scottish, which kind of makes sense if you walk around Glasgow city centre on a Saturday afternoon. Most of the men look like that, except I think Shrek has much better skin tone. Sorry, what on earth were we talking about again?"

"Leonard Cohen and Obama."

"Oh, yes. Let me just check you've heard of President Obama before I move on?"

"Ha-ha, very funny," mock-chuckled Josh.

"Just in case you were wondering, he isn't Canadian, by the way. Even though he's a really talented guy, he's actually an American."

"Let's not get into that."

"Okay, so what I was about to say was on that night, it was such a surprise that a black man had been elected as president of America. Outside the US, we didn't think that was possible with all of the history. I remember thinking when Leonard played *Democracy,* which is one of his more famous songs, that it was a bit of a watershed moment. It probably sounds corny, but I thought that the American people had shown the world what they could do, you know, back to being the leader of the West, democracy and all that."

"I was too young to vote, but I remember Obama's time as president, so I think I know what you mean. Things are a bit different now."

"Yeah, now look what you've got, a useless, narcissistic Wotsit in the Oval Office."

"Wotsit?"

"Fake Cheetos."

"Ha-ha."

"Sorry, I'm doing a disservice to the usefulness of Wotsits there, at least they serve some purpose – they taste good."

"Oh, right, well, you know, we know, man, we *know,* but it's not just the US, you've the same kinda asshole in charge of the UK now, right?"

"Yeah, only I think our candy floss-haired narcissist is a bit smarter. He's fooled everyone to think he's as much of a numbskull as The Donald by spouting random stuff no-one understands in Latin, but he's got the same kind of ideas."

"Latin?"

"Yes, ergo pissum on me amicum Orangius obesiutus morbidium, prostitutae Russianium?" Or, at least, a similar collection of English words, suffixed by -um, tumbled uncontrollably from my mouth.

"Ha-ha. So, you live in Scotland right, what's the deal with it? Is it going to be independent of England?"

"Well, Scotland isn't part of England, even though the English think it is sometimes, it's part of the UK. I really couldn't tell you if it will become independent."

"So, what's the UK? It's not just England, it's England, Scotland and Ireland, right?" Jim joined in.

"No, but are you sure you want me to *try to* explain all that?"

"Sure, we got time. As long as you do a better job than you did of explaining where Leonard Cohen was from," retorted Jim.

"What do you mean?"

"You said he wasn't American."

"Yes, he was Canadian."

"Well, Canada is on the continent of North America, so technically he was an American."

"Touché. Do you still want me to give it a go, given my evident geographic incompetence?"

"Yeah, go for it."

"Well, okay, you did ask ... I'm not sure I'll get this right, even though I should know it, geography degree and all, but as you've rightly pointed out, that may not be worth much."

"Come on, man. I was just teasing."

"Okay. So to start with, you have England, Wales, Scotland and Northern Ireland. They're all separate countries but bear with me on that for the moment."

"Okay, we got it."

"England and Scotland are kingdoms. Wales is a ... err ... principality. England and Wales were politically united hundreds of years ago and then Scotland joined in the 1700s. Together, these three make up Great Britain."

"Got it."

"Add Ireland and together that became the United Kingdom of Great Britain and Ireland."

"When was that?"

"I'm not sure, I think around 1800, but there's loads of history between England and Ireland before that. I'm sorry I don't know much about that, I'm afraid."

"I'm disappointed in this already," Jim joked, determined to enjoy himself as much as possible at my expense.

"I'll try to get my act together. In the 1920s, the southern bit of the island of Ireland became a separate country, the Republic of Ireland, Eire, and the northern bit remained part of the UK as Northern Ireland."

"Okay."

"So, now, you've the island of Ireland which is Northern Ireland and the Republic of Ireland. They're separate countries, except for when it comes to rugby, when they play as Ireland."

"Jeez, that makes a lotta sense."

"Yeah, well I did say ... but it gets even better. The UK has a government and also Scotland, Wales and Northern Ireland have their own governments, for their own countries. While they're separate countries, they're politically part of the UK."

"So, they're separate countries, with their own governments, but they aren't separate countries?" asked Josh, reasonably.

"Correct. Except for England, of course, which is a separate country that *doesn't* have its own government. I told you I'd struggle to explain it, but it's your own fault for asking. Do you want me to carry on?"

"Yeah. So, who runs England's government?" replied Jim.

"The UK."

"The UK government is England's government as well as the UK's?"

"Yeah, there was talk of the English having regional governments a while ago, but in typical English fashion, they couldn't be arsed with it in the end."

"So, I guess the Scottish could be *arsed*. What's Scotland's government?"

"The Scottish government."

"So, man, what's the point of all these governments?" queried Josh. "It sounds a bit like state and federal in the US."

"Kind of, yes, the Scottish government can do things like hike income tax rates and waste the money raised, but only within Scotland."

"Sounds like the way the state government works in Ohio ..."

"Why does that not surprise me? The UK government concerns itself with squandering tax money at the national level, the nation in this case being the UK, not the nations of England, Scotland, Northern Ireland and Wales."

"Sounds like how the federal government works ..."

"Again, I'm not surprised. Anyway, that's how it's put together, the only exception to this, of course, being when Team Great Britain means the nation at the Olympics."

"Err ... okay, I think I get some of that. Does Team GB include Northern Ireland?" asked Jim.

"Yes, it does."

"Isn't rugby sevens going to be in the Tokyo Olympics? Who'd the guys from Northern Ireland play for then?"

"Team GB, I think."

"But I thought you said that all the rugby guys played for Ireland?"

"Except when they play for Team GB."

"Jeez, how do you keep track of all this, man?"

"I don't, I'm just making it up."

"Sounds like it. Keep going," goaded Jim.

"So, Scotland has its own government, England doesn't have one and Wales and Northern Ireland have Assemblies, which are their governments."

"Okay."

"Except the Northern Ireland Assembly hasn't sat for a couple of years, so they effectively have no government."

"Oh man ..."

"At the moment, nothing can be approved because they've no parliament, so at least they aren't blowing all their tax money. Some would argue this is the most efficient the Stormont government has ever been."

"Ohio state government again ..."

"So, getting back to your question, Scotland had a referendum in 2014 on whether to stay or leave the UK and the vote was 55 per cent to stay against 45 to leave."

"So, that's it done, then. Scotland will stay in the UK?"

"Not quite. So, the UK is in the European Union. So the UK is subject to European laws, mostly about the degree of bends allowed in bananas and how much Merlot should be poured into the wine lake each autumn. This has caused a lot of fuss for years, so in 2016 the UK had a referendum where it voted to leave the EU." Even as I tried to explain, I found myself wishing the Nepali gentleman *en route* to Trakshindu La would bowl in through the door; in my mind's eye his orange box an ideal platform to launch my impassioned declaration of where I stood on all this under the haughty gaze of the Union's medieval nemesis.

'Yes, I do agree, Sir Lordsnooty of the Duchy of Procreation, Albion has issues with immigration. I find it particularly harrowing that qualified Florentine surgeons dare to come to the UK and save lots of lives in the National Health Service, not to mention have the impertinence to pay their taxes on time. I'm sure we can *quite* do without the droves of artisans from Krakow burdening villages like Little Xenophobing in Surrey with their highly competitively priced home extensions. It's such a nuisance hordes of Wallachians land in Lincolnshire each summer to steal all our highly desirable fruit and veg picking jobs. I can see your point regarding these country-sinking disadvantages ...'

Before I could drift too deeply into my dark-age fantasy, which in my head was developing into a scene where my recusant peroration had been ill-received by the authorities, resulting in a pair of far-age henchmen clad in camel-skin, covert-style tunics wrestling me from the hall with orders to take me to the dungeons of Whetherspew's prison for waterboarding by competitively-priced keg beers and torturing by Silk Cut branding irons, Jim interrupted to haul me back to reality.

"So, everywhere leaves, right? All the countries, nations, whatever are part of the UK?"

"Yes, but in the 2016 referendum, Scotland overwhelmingly voted to stay in the EU. So, the Scottish National Party, which is in power in Scotland, is saying that it wants another referendum for Scottish independence because the Scottish people are being taken out of the EU against their will."

"So, what's going to happen?"

"I don't know, but the UK government is saying they can't have it. They're stuck with Brexit at the moment, anyway, so it depends on what happens next with that."

"So, if they allow it, then Scotland would be independent and then they'd go back into the EU?"

"That's the idea. You've the SNP wanting to break away from the Union because they want more local control to then join a larger union, so they can have less control; and the UK government wanting more local control by breaking away from the EU, except this doesn't apply for its constituent countries, of course, where there's more than enough local control already. To be honest, I've lost the will to live with it all."

"You're not the only one." I was spared any further explanation of the Irish backstop and what the UK would be called if Scotland left the Union, Nova Borisium possibly, by the arrival of Xavi and Taha. She was improved and keen to take in the ceremony at the monastery. I declined to tag along as I had a rest day in Tengboche the next day. I would go to the morning version. I retired to my room to read some more *Cryptonomicon* and bask in the phone tower's irradiative glow.

As the day drew to a close, a shadow moved down the massive rockface with the stealth of a stalking snow leopard. It became so cold in the room I could see my breath. I layered on my thermal gear and snuggled into my sleeping bag, covered with the blankets the lodge had provided, but the drop in temperature brought on a phlegmy coughing fit that lasted until the early evening. At 7pm, I headed to the banqueting hall to see if I could halt the cough with some mead and fortify myself with a roast quail or two. The place was humming in a modern-day Chaucerian kind of way. The others were there but there was nowhere to sit next to them, not even a chair to pull over, so I asked an old man if the seat on the bench opposite was free.

"Aye, tekkit," he answered. From his bruising, the man appeared to have been beaten on the left side of his face, which did nothing to complement his folded, lined features and scraggy beard.

"You okay, mate? Looks like you've been in the wars a bit?"

"Aye, took a wee tumble, tha's all. No' as bad as me mate."

"What happened to him?"

"We were comin' doon fae Gokyo and he slipped on a pebble, took me oot and we both ended oop on wor arses. He's go' a cracked rib, mind."

"If he's worse than you, he must be in some state, is he okay?"

"Nae, no' really. He's oop in wor room, drooged tae the eyeballs wi' painkillers. There's nae meer doctors till Namche, so it's the best I can do. Its tekkin' fookin ages tae git him doon coz he cannae walk wi' the pain."

"That sounds terrible. Can you not get a helivac or rent a donkey to take him down?"

"Nae insurance fae tha' laddie. Tae much money."

"Oh, okay. What about you, are you on painkillers as well? Your face looks bloody sore."

"Aye, an' antibiotics. The doc at Gokyo said I'd AMS an' a respiratory infection, so he gave me some tablets for tha' an' all."

"Sounds like a bit of a nightmare trip?"

"Nae, just the last bit, up tae then it was fab. Mind, I'll be glad tae git back tae Aberdeen to heal up." We chatted for a while and my food arrived. I'd ordered the macaroni cheese, imagining an *al dente* pasta oozing with semi-melted, slightly burned cheddar. The congealed lump of rubber held together with gelatinous snot fell way short, my first meal in Nepal that was genuinely disgusting.

The Aberdonian's respiratory problem had taken a turn for the worse, turning into a sneezing and coughing fit. I was fearful of catching whatever he had, so wished him well, made my apologies and bade goodnight to the gang. Back in my room, the 10th track of *The Heat* by Dan Reed Network was where I started the music and, an hour later, it was time to for sleep; it was 9.30pm.

I awoke to ice inside my window at 5am, needed the lavatory and was surprised to have to join a queue. A group of three Americans were fully clad and in the process of the last of their ablutions before heading out on the trail. I failed to see the point of trekking in the dark, so left them to their own devices. I returned to bed before heading for a 6.30 breakfast of porridge, eggs, toast and milk tea, hopeful of making the ceremony at seven. Taha came to join me while his charges were strapping on their packs upstairs. He told me he was 20 and hailed from a lowland village in the Dolpo. Over our drinks, he showed me a Nepalese card trick that would earn him a fortune if he ever made it to Vegas.

"How long have you been a guide, Taha?"

"One year, this is my second season."

"Do many people from your village work as guides?"

"Yes, it is good money."

"What about the women? I've never seen a female guide, do many women guide?"

"Some, not many. Mostly for girl trekker, alone."

"Speaking of women, the other thing I don't think I've seen here is a pregnant one. I've seen loads of kids and babies, but don't remember seeing one pregnant lady. Do they stay indoors all the time when they're pregnant?"

"No, all the women are in Kathmandu. Too dangerous to have a baby in mountains."

"What, all the pregnant women from the mountains, *all* of them are in Kathmandu?"

"Yes." I found it hard to believe and reckoned he must be pulling my leg; it wasn't like having babies was a recent development and could only take place in hospital.

Fully laden Jim, Josh and Xavi entered the diner, keen to get moving, so we said our goodbyes. Breakfast finished, I made my way over to the imposing edifice that was the Tengboche monastery. The entrance to the monastery was an ornate open gate that reminded me of the similar structure in Chinatown in London. A pair of squat dragons in an Italian tricolour of reds and greens on their white bodies guarded each pillar, those Anfield red, affixed with a quartet of multicoloured plaster medallions depicting demons and gods. The cross-beam spread outwards as it gained to a roof of burnished gold summited by a pair of resting animals, possibly deer or cows, focussed on an ace of spades-shaped jewelled spear. An angry elephantine dragon showed its trunk in warning at each corner.

The gate led to a flight of stairs up several terraces to the monastery itself, a pink-beige box three flights high, its wedding-cake tier of roofs disappearing above. The rectangular shape of its brown windows was fooled into trapezoids by black painted mural surrounds.

I climbed the steps and passed through into the inner courtyard where, ahead, was a wall of vermillion brick. Centred was a white curtain, featuring motifs of what I guessed were vases with crowns of flowers. They were pulled back to offer a triangular entrance to the interior. The crazy-paved courtyard was cloistered at one storey high, balconies affording hooks to hang the yellow and green drapes that fringed all around. A monk in robes and crimson bomber jacket and beanie pottered around.

Inside the curtains, a yellow plaque explained the monastery rules. Beneath was a worn stone that was an elegy to the dedication of a previous monk, his soles having eroded deep gouges. I took off my boots, pulled back an inner curtain and entered the interior, dimly lit and incense scented by candles.

Three sides of the temple were lined by be-socked, cross-legged trekkers of all descriptions; the last occupied by what I took to be the head monk, recumbent in front of a golden altar depicting gods slaying demons. To his left was a monk with a brass instrument something akin to a French horn without all the intestinal brass. To his right a line of monks sat perpendicular, overseeing a cushioned structure that ran up the interior's middle. I wasn't sure if the monks had dispensed with their orange under-robes or this was a higher rank in the order, but all were clad exclusively in crimson.

The same hushed awkwardness and stifled coughs of the wait for the start of a Christian service pervaded the chamber before the entrance curtain was closed and the ceremony began. The head monk incanted. The line followed in a susurrating hum, before the next in seniority took the lead and incanted with a thrice of finger cymbals to emphasise his chant. The other monks followed and, mid-murmur, there was occasionally an arrhythmic tuba-like reverberation of the horn. It was fascinating but beyond strange. I tried to figure out the pattern, but it failed to align with anything I could call on as a musical frame of reference.

After 15 minutes, some trekkers had seen enough and made their way out. I persevered for another 15 and was rewarded with more emphasis on the finger cymbal and horn. I anticipated something was building for a climax, but the murmurs settled back into the quiet cadence of the ceremony's earlier parts and silence indicated it was over. I was baffled by the entire thing, but thought it was wonderful still to have been able to see something so cryptic, so undeniably foreign.

The ceremony was over in the nick of time; even as I reached the barbican, I was bent over with stomach cramps. I made it to the toilet and spent the next hour locked in an uncomfortable embrace with the Western Style. The *Diaries* that day would record exploding Type Sixes and Sevens that ran well into double digits by morning's end; clearly I'd made the mistake of seasoning my eggs with gunpowder rather than pink Himalayan salt at breakfast.

I staggered back to my room feeling drained, the diarrhoea having been kept good company by the hacking of phlegm. My plan of a short acclimatisation walk followed by coffee and cake at the renowned bakery 100 metres down the slope was forfeit. So I spent an uneventful day reading, cracking codeword puzzles and visiting the water closet. I ate a lonely lunch. The afternoon was a drift in and out of sleep to awake in an icy darkness; the sun having been blocked by the massif behind my window. The descent to the diner was breathless and I ordered dhal baat, hoping the chef couldn't possibly get that wrong. It was as good as the macaroni cheese had been poor. Spirits raised, I tempted fate with a double helping of boiled rice while trying to rehydrate and calm my innards with some mint tea.

The diner was the polar opposite to the night before, devoid of life, which was as well because I was feeling sorry for myself and disinclined to chat. I made it up to my room overwhelmed by nausea and reclined in my sleeping bag, unreasonably miserable. I read some more before choosing track six of *Echoes, Silence, Patience & Grace* by Foo Fighters as the start point for my evening music. An hour later, it was time for rest; it was 8.30pm.

The night was a difficult one – my cough had become much worse and I used the last of my handkerchiefs to catch the sputum. There were a few visits to the garderobe around midnight. It entertained in my mind a debate about which day a particular entry in the *Diaries* should be classified; should the day be aligned to start or finish of business, so to speak? Talk about First World problems.

Breakfast did nothing to lift my spirits. The lodge must alternate chefs, I surmised, as it could only be the same person who could so ruinously concoct the macaroni cheese who'd be able to burn cold porridge. I chose the start as the determining factor for the entry-to-be in that day's *Diary*. So the morning's tally was a more tolerable trio of Type Sixes by the time I crossed the moat and left the fortress behind to start my crunch across the hoar frost down the valley.

The novices were unperturbed by the cold, persisting with bare arms as they whitewashed the chortens. They were doing better than myself – by the time I'd reached the bakery, I'd a quintet of dry retches under my belt and half a lung of phlegm expelled. My infirmity contrasted with the rude health of the morning: the sky was powder, Everest, Lhotse and Ama Dablam shone with a brilliance painful to look at directly, the rhododendrons were clasped in rime and the air was brisk. The undiscernible downhill gradient, the retches and the fresh air seemed to combine to reinvigorate me. I gained a rhythm, my sloth's stagger gradually becoming an end-of-day trudge that evolved into a stroll.

I made my way down through another Tolkienesque forest, a feature of the landscape which hadn't been lost on the owners of the aptly named 'Rivendell Lodge' at Debuche. I resolved to stop there on the way back, if only to check the proprietors lacked pointy ears.

The trail flattened off through the village. I passed a huge mani wall that pointed the way to a nunnery where the track was blocked by an untethered bull, from his implored baying desperate for love. I wondered if he'd mistaken the French horn-type instrument at the monastery for the call of an equally desperate lady cow. As it happened, there *was* a lady cow, or persuadable short-horned bull, in the forest across the trail to Mr Horned Horny. Unfortunately, the route of my passage was directly between the two lovers.

I figured it prudent not to get caught in the middle of the two or, even more perilously, be mistaken for a rival, so cravenly hid behind a tree trunk waiting for the bull to cross. For a male desperate with lust, the bull made a remarkably snail-like crossing; he was either a master of anticipatory foreplay or all baying and no trousers. Eventually, with more sexual posturing than your average Nate Dogg video, he made it across the pathway to his new girlfriend. I took the opportunity to remove myself from behind the tree and tiptoed past the start of their passionate liaison.

I was above the Imja Khola which flowed beneath me on my left. Ahead a group of stonemasons were busy with hammers and picks, breaking grey rocks and affixing them to the top of the embankment they were constructing. I was almost upon them before I realised there was no way past and I'd have to take a dirt track cut into the friable riverbank. It was made of a pebbly conglomerate glued together with gritty sand. The local folks nonchalantly skipped across this landslip in the making. I'd no choice but to do the same, although my interpretation of their skip was to take single, studied strides causing a tailback of porters to Debuche.

I saw the reason for the earthworks as I completed my traverse. A suspension bridge swayed above a massive landslide. It had caused the original metal-strutted bridge to fail. It lay on the valley side, crumpled into a deformed shiny heap like the discarded tin foil from a Sunday roast dinner.

The crew had completed a fantastic new, level path and were busy finishing the final section as I crossed the Imja Khola suspension bridge. The new trail was ideal footing, a series of stone steps interspersed with long stretches of beaten earth pavement which allowed a trekker to catch their breath, their course seeming to lead directly towards Ama Dablam glowing in the distance. Regrettably, this superb workmanship didn't last, and I was soon back on an ancient dusty track to continue my ascent.

I passed through another smaller kani which replicated the one at Tengboche. It led to a hanging valley patchworked with stony fields. The fields were marked out with low-slung walls, the overall effect that of a well-curated Roman archaeological exhibit, the stones the foundations of villas.

The settlement's stone lodges became evident as I tramped up the shallow incline. A few minutes beyond a yellow billboard informing me I'd reached Pangboche, elevation 3,985 metres, I entered the village's main street. It was dhal baat time, but I wasn't hungry. I fancied a cup of tea and almost immediately found a pretty lodge with an expansive terrace and also, luckily, that I was ahead of the crowds.

I sat out on the terrace but found the sun too strong for sunbathing so retired inside. I ordered a black tea and a Snickers bar, which the enthusiastic owner offered to bake in a pie for me. As I was savouring the chocolate, I was joined by a quintet of sweating, dusty trekkers.

"Ger us a couple of Mars bars while yer up eh, Roberto."

"Fer fooksake man, how many Mars bars have ya had tudday, like?"

"Away, gaan ger us 'em, will ya?" Their guide stepped in to keep the peace and presented the petitioner with his confectionery; he'd made short work of both bars by the time I'd paid my bill.

I intended to keep ahead of the rush so headed out of the village past waterwheels and ladies pummelling their washing in the open-air laundry built at the side of a stream. Dzhos stood idly downstream, gargling up the suds.

The village outskirts also constituted the tree line and the path now became a long, dusty up-and-down along the valley side above the river. In the distance I could clearly see the next village, dwarfed by Everest and Lhotse as its backdrop. It was hot work beneath the overhead sun, and I was soon down to my T-shirt. The trail split above a group of prayer wheels. I traipsed along silently with a couple for a while until we came upon a group of 15 or so trekkers queuing by a public convenience, the door swinging open as we passed.

"Holy shit, man, I can't go in there. I'm gonna throw up." The speaker was a man fat in the way only Americans seem able to achieve.

"If not go, go behind rock." The dubious advice coming from their guide.

"Man, I can't go over there. Everyone will see my ass."

"Not more option. We not look. Believe, no-one want to see ass."

"No, man, I can't do it." He was genuinely disturbed by the idea, welling up. Another of his group, a young lady in Spandex leggings, had no such qualms and, taking one look at the earth closet, decided to take his spot behind the rock. I hurried on.

The next village was preceded by a slippery flight of steps over which a rubber hose seemed to be draining the unused water from the first few lodges across the path. At the top were two restaurant sun terraces where trekkers basked like semi-leotarded iguanas. Hungry – and alarmed at the various states of undress outside – I ordered a noodle soup in the interior of the first place.

The noodles were excellent and, after an hour relaxing, I crept through the prone bodies of the nudists reddening in the sun outside to head uphill. The first post-lunch task was to haul myself up a near-vertical stone staircase funnelled between two lodge walls. It was only 10 or 20 metres in length. Reaching the top was too much.

My target in the morning had been to trek to Dingboche. I hadn't made it but thought it unwise to push on any further. I had another rest day scheduled there so I'd make tomorrow a short walk rather than a complete rest. The guidebook had indicated from Tengboche, it would be a three-and-a-half-hour trek to Dingboche. Three-and-a-half hours after leaving, I was at Shomare, still an hour short of my destination – but I'd arrived.

Shomare to Dingboche

I t was clear the tea house had originally been just that before the owner had ingeniously managed to wedge a low-slung extension between the diner and uphill terrace wall. This amounted to four rooms plus a lavatory strung out under a tin roof. Compared to the lodge at Tengboche, this was more Carwash than Carcassonne, but at the same time it was quite charming, with its recently painted doors matching the chalcopyrite colouring of its roof.

A fortysomething man was raking the gravel courtyard. He looked up from his labours, raised an eyebrow modelled on a more expansive moment in Roger Moore's career and tilted his head to beckon me over. He placed his rake at the lodge entrance and disappeared for a moment to emerge with a key hanging from a perfect imitation of a yuletide log. He showed me to the third room along from Room One. Room Two.

The room, cool inside, was dual bunk and I nodded my acceptance sagely before my host went back to his combing. I was loath to break the code of silence I'd established with Roger, preferring to lie back in the room's shade and recuperate, so the haggling could wait. I dropped my gear and lay back on the cot not a moment too soon as a fresh wave of nausea swept over me.

Two hours of discomfort followed. I wanted to be ill but every time I rose to go the toilet my stomach seemed to calm, then I sat for a while becoming nauseous again, and so on. Reasoning some mint tea, sun and fresh air might help I took a seat at the circular plastic table at the raked quad's edge. My host was now busy pruning purple flowers with an exactness of attention worthy of a Victorian watchmaker. The blooms had been planted into recesses on the uphill wall and were evidently something of a passion.

"Would you like some tea, sir?" Roger enquired. He was about 40 and carried a burliness that wasn't in keeping with the delicateness of his horticultural endeavours.

"Yes please, mint if you have it."

"We do." He headed to the door and popped his head back out again a moment later.

"Small pot or big?"

"Small, please." As I waited, I admired Ama Dablam shining in the sun; from this angle its shape was more evocative of the statue at the Lincoln Memorial rather than of Gandalf. My host returned with a silver platter and thermos and we agreed the pricing, which was far more favourable than at Namche or Tengboche. It seemed staying at a place not listed in the guidebook as a standard stop meant the owners had to try harder for less money.

I got the impression Roger's easy-going charm was effortless. We shared a cup of mint tea while chatting about the usual things: where home was, family and how business was this year. The conversation amicably tailed off and we sat in silence watching the trekkers funnel up the stairs, enjoying a comfortable familiarity that would befit a pair of old school chums.

The hikers stumbled up, lungs labouring with each ligament-stretching step. It amazed me how the guides kept their groups coherent, every tour seeming no more spread out than 20 metres. The trekkers came in as many heterogeneous shapes, sizes and ages as could be imagined. It was a real art the way the guide made allowance for the dainty grandmothers to keep pace with the New York marathon finishers. The technique appeared to be to halt at the top of major climbs to allow everyone to catch their breath and the weaker members to catch up, but I suspected there was something more to it.

The trekkers supported each other, egged each other on in something more than mere camaraderie. There was something, too, in the shape of the train always being the same, the stronger members upfront, ranked behind the guide, followed by middling abilities, grouped side by side in twos and threes, and finally the weaker colleagues, arms searching ahead for support, head down, puffing into their neckerchiefs.

I never heard a group member shout a 'Come on!', 'You can make it!' or even whisper something similar; it was as if the encouragement came from an unspoken collectiveness, that somewhere along the trail, each party had somehow self-organised and achieved some kind of hive-mindedness. Everyone knew their place in the hierarchy, what their role was and how to carry it out. I wondered whether this was a natural phenomenon the guides had learned to harness or something they'd cultivated over the decades.

My host jumped up, his focus shifted uphill. A second later, a pair of stubby-legged horses flew past and down the stair, their riders swerving between the narrow stone walls, guiding their steeds with reins gathered in one hand. The men were dressed in brown skins and the fur-flapped hats that in my mind are associated with the hordes of Genghis Khan. The cord of their dislodged hats stretched taut behind them. I half expected to see a chasing posse of Tangut Imperial Guard streak past in pursuit. As the clopping dissipated, my host, who had followed them downhill, returned with a look of disgust. It told me this type of boy-racer behaviour was frowned upon. He gathered his rake again and took out his frustration on the gravel with some unneeded re-combing until a call from his wife drew him inside.

I sat and watched more groups lurching uphill. These later-in-the-day parties seemed to struggle more than the earlier ones. With their heads dropped, backs bowed, imploring hands and floundering missteps, they resembled a forlorn *tableau vivant* of a party of lost Antarctic explorers. But as they trudged past, they seemed to garner some energy and pushed on, anxious not to let their plight be observed by the man on the terrace.

A snaking train was interrupted by some downhill traffic. Two gentlemen appeared atop the stair, one of them helping the other as he hobbled down the steps with a grimace. Even with my poor Spanish, I could tell the man lending assistance asked his friend if he wanted to rest and take some tea, and they came to join me.

The men had the mutual familiarity of those who have decades of shared history. The hobbler was larger, heavyset and wore the privations of his trek with discomfort; the low savannah of his grey stubble transitioned into asymmetrical clumps of beard proper on his cheeks and chin. He threw his sunglasses on the table in frustration to reveal dark, rheumy eyes; bragging rights dictated he had to keep up with his smaller lifelong friend or suffer the consequences for evermore. The helper, for his part, was wearing his trip much better. He stood a head lower in stature than his friend but lacked his girth, avoiding the trap of running to fat that can befall shorter middle-aged men. His tan and litheness told of a lifetime of outdoor sports. His shaved head dovetailed in a manicured perfection with his imperial goatee. Were it not for his wrap-arounds and modern attire, I thought I could've been looking at a 17th century colonial ambassador fresh from his posting in Hispaniola.

"Hello, how are you?" It appeared I'd at least mastered that expression.

"Good, you speak Spanish?" the more elegant man replied, Don Cervantes now in my mind.

"A little." A wild boast indeed.

"Some tea?" I suggested.

"Yes, please. Thank you very much. Are you heading up or down?"

"I go ascend. And you?"

"We are going to Pangboche. This morning we were on the peak of Kala Pattar, to see the sunrise over Everest. I think Pangboche is another hour, uh? To go there will be enough for today."

"Incredible! This morning, what hour can be you leaving?"

"At 5am."

"Already, you is here! Very good. Much quick. The sign of Pangboche to me says 20 kilometres and 15 hours is to walking to Base Camp."

"Yes, but that is going up, now we go down. It is much quicker. Kala Pattar is only 200 metres but it takes two hours to climb and 30 minutes to descend."

"Yes, but already again you much quick. You walks much in Spain?

"Sometimes, but my friend Carlos and I live in Madrid. It is a long way to the Pyrenees or Picos de Europa, so we go when we can. I am Alvaro."

"My name is Lee."

"Lay? Nice to meet you, Lay." At least I wasn't the only one with linguistic issues.

"Pain, Carlos foot?"

"Yes."

"Carlos, yours feets are pain? Stop must feet pains?" Carlos looked understandably perplexed.

"I conduct my day-to-day business with people in the USA, so we can continue in English? Carlos doesn't speak it," said Alvaro.

"I try make to do best my Spanish."

"Very well, I can continue in English and you can continue in Spanish, I will translate your Spanish to Carlos for you." The cheek.

"What is you problem with feets ills?" Carlos pulled his nearest leg off the chair and took off his boot and sock to reveal a bandage wrapped tightly around his ankle. He unwrapped it to reveal a display of purple and green bruises that mottled a swelling. I could understand why he was hobbling.

"My god! How are able you to walking? Is a big problem, no? Fall down?"

"Yes. Carlos twisted his ankle on a loose rock at Kala Pattar."

"I have ... errrr ... pain ... to make die." I imitated the swallowing of tablets.

"Thank you, but Carlos is taking Ibuprofen already. We will get more help in Namche."

"I am hope Carlos is more best."

"He will be fine, he's a strong man. Also, I give him no choice, or he has to stay in Nepal. Thank you for the tea but now we must go. We are leaving from Kathmandu to go home in five days. It is a problem, eh, to have only two-and-a-half weeks' vacation?"

"Yes."

"Good luck with your trekking. Goodbye." Alvaro gave Carlos the thumbs-up and he returned it more through obligation than enthusiasm. He rebandaged his foot, gingerly inserted it into his boot and headed down the stairs, holding onto the wall and leaning in with shoulder arched as he took each step.

I sat idly until the sun started to set, the encounter having encouraged me. If they'd been on Kala Pattar in the morning, I wasn't far away. In spite of my deteriorating physical condition, I'd hope of making it.

The sun had set rapidly and the temperature had dropped to below freezing even quicker, so I headed for the dining room for warmth and sustenance. It was cosy, only five tables arranged around the three walls opposite the reception counter. They were all occupied except one, which I took and ordered a plate of egg fried noodles. A young man with a topknot and Lycra under hiking shorts pushed his empty plate away from him and departed; the first dinner sitting must have been done, I thought. My remaining dinner companions were a blond, bearded man directly to my left, a man of pensionable age directly opposite and an Asian man at right angles to me.

"Hi, good evening."

"Hi," replied the blond man. He was mid-20s and clearly annoyed I'd disturbed whatever was engrossing him on his iPad so returned to his hunch and finger-poked his device in an almost contemptuous dismissal. Fair enough, I thought, but his loss – he was going to be sorry when he realised he was missing out on the badinage that would be bouncing across the diner between myself and the older raconteur.

"Hi. How are you?"

"Hi." The older man looked up from his phone.

"Are you heading up or down?"

"Down."

"Were you able to make it to Base Camp, then?"

"No."

"Oh dear, did you have a problem?"

"No."

"Oh, are you doing a different trek, then?"

"Yes. I stop here." The banter was really getting going now. See what you're missing, Beardy Blond? Encouraged, I decided I'd ratchet things up by pursuing a different topic.

"So, where are you from?"

"Switzerland," he responded, dropping his gaze back to his phone before momentarily raising an eye towards me. His face told me that, for a second, he was conflicted between an old-school politeness and the blue glow's lure. His device won out. Having covered all the usual topics earlier with my host, I now had one remaining option for an evening of sparkling repartee.

"Hi." The Asian man looked up from his dual screens, so I went all in, gambling on another failed language.

"Nihon-jin desu ka?"

"Hai."

"Irigisu-go?" The Japanese shook his head. He looked at me, hoping for an advance on that, but I'd exhausted my Nipponese apart from the phrase to ask him the way to a taxi-stand in Tokyo, which for some reason I'd retained for 30 years, so I nodded, smiled wanly and allowed him to return to his dual screening.

The three men seemed content in the company of their electronics and paid me no heed. The room, nevertheless, felt horribly awkward and I cogitated on why that should be. They were all perfectly comfortable to ignore each other, digits swiping left and right. Was it because I was offended by the wanton violation of the unwritten law that says trekkers should be gregarious? Was it because of my quaint 20th century conditioning that it was rude to ignore a fellow human in favour of a computer? Or was it because my pride was hurt that my fellow diners were more interested in what their apps were saying to them than in what I might possibly contribute? Regardless, I sat there twiddling my thumbs waiting for my food, wishing I'd brought my phone.

The noodles arrived and so did a bowl of steaming broth for the Japanese man, and I stole a peek at what Beardy Blond was doing on his device. He was playing one of those God games where you start off with a settler and have to chop down swathes of forest so you can arm your expanding population with clubs to go and bash some other poor sod who hasn't finished chopping yet and steal all their food. Bloody hell, I thought, didn't he get enough deforestation by looking down the valley each day?

I wondered whether he was playing with the Swiss and Japanese by Bluetooth and who was winning. If they were, it wasn't an exciting contest – the room was as animated as an open analysis of the Ruy Lopez opening at a librarian's chess club – so I was grateful when the Japanese started his meal. He was a black belt seventh dan in slurping and was performing an advanced kata by the irregular rhythm of his sucking. I knew it was wrong, but I took a perverse satisfaction in every interrupted glance from the Swiss and Beardy Blond with each clamorous slurp.

I finished my dinner, resigned to an evening of reading. I spent a couple of hours at my Kindle, thinking take that you three, you may have your phones but I bet you don't have one of these fancy things with you, do you?! My musical choice to round off the day was *Woodface,* by Crowded House. Track eight was where I started and an hour later, I was relaxed enough for sleep; it was 9pm.

The night had been another rough one – my cough had grown worse and sleep came in only broken snatches. The *Diaries* would see a Type Six recorded which, together with my sore throat and the start of a runny nose, meant I was in poor spirits as I entered the breakfast room. Beardy Blond was leaving as I arrived and passed me without a word. The Swiss was being attended to by a guide who'd been absent the previous evening and there was no sign of the Japanese boy. I wished them a good morning and ordered toast with eggs and a black tea.

"Did you sleep well?" The Swiss was a morning person, or his phone was elsewhere on charge.

"I didn't sleep much, actually, maybe it's the altitude."

"It can be a problem. I saw many people on the trail to Gokyo with this problem."

"So, you've been to Gokyo?"

"Yes, Tashi my guide took me there."

"I didn't realise you had a guide. Where was he last night at dinner?"

"He was in our room." I was surprised at that – it was the first I'd heard of a room-share arrangement, the norm being to pay for separate board for porters and guides.

"You're sharing a room?"

"Yes. We didn't at first but Tashi is my friend now, he is more than a guide. He took me to his village in the valley of Gokyo. His house was one room and I stayed with his family. He wouldn't take any money for this."

"That sounds like a great experience." I was beginning to put my initial impression of the Swiss to bed; he must have been having a rough time the previous night and I could relate to that.

"Yes. It was very different to how we live in Switzerland."

"I can imagine. Where in Switzerland do you come from?"

"Zurich. The German-speaking part."

"I've been there once, many years ago. I remember it as being genuinely nice but ridiculously expensive."

"Yes, it is still expensive, but not so nice anymore. Now we have too many immigrants. They have come to Zurich and are spoiling our way of living." With that, my impression of him changed again.

"What do you mean?"

"Do you believe the Swiss government allows 60,000 people to come to Switzerland each year?! It is too many, they take the jobs of Swiss people, this is not fair."

"Okay, but just so I'm clear, do you know what the level of unemployment in Switzerland is at the moment?"

"Yes, I think three per cent."

"That's pretty much full employment, I'd say, so these immigrants aren't taking your jobs. If the UK is anything to go by, they're probably doing all the shit jobs that Swiss people don't want to do."

"No, I don't think this is the case. You in the UK have the same problems with this type of people and are making Brexit to stop this happening."

"That's not completely correct, in theory we're leaving because of self-determination. But you have it right it's the same hate-fuelled misunderstanding of immigration that has in part caused Brexit."

"I am not misunderstanding these immigrants, they take the jobs and do not become part of our Swiss culture. It is the same in the UK, I have seen the mosques and the men with the long beards."

"So, what exactly is Swiss culture, mate? Cuckoo clocks and dodgy bank accounts? I don't get it, mate, on the one hand you've just said spending a night in a Nepali home was an amazing experience, so you seem open to different cultures, but on the other, it sounds like you're not open to that at home?"

I'd expressed my point in more of a rant than I'd intended and he looked at me with a chagrined grimace that said the conversation was well and truly over. We were both glad when Tashi came to collect him and we could part company. I sat there in an irritated silence and, with no appetite, pushed the eggs around my plate. It took me an hour to finish them, pay my bill and set off.

It was another stunning morning – a clear blue sky above the hazy whites of the Himalaya in the distance. Shortly after the village, the valley widened out. Ahead, the trail's gypsum-like dust broadened and split into multiple paths trodden by feet into different levels. I was grateful the upward camber was indiscernible, thinking if Paiya had been a double diamond black run, this was an easy blue.

Except it wasn't. I lasted 50 metres before collapsing on a grassy bank and, with each lungful of air, I became queasier. This time my retch wasn't dry – the liquid brown of my tea immediately followed by everything I'd eaten that morning. Worse still, I failed to avoid my trousers.

This was now serious – although I lacked a headache, the vomiting was a good sign I had mountain sickness. I cleaned up as best I could and decided to give myself an hour to rest; if I was still being sick at that point, I'd call time, descend and possibly try again tomorrow or the next day if my condition had improved.

"Waiting for a bus, mate?" joked a young trekker, who poled past me as if he was on his way to the local shop to buy the Sunday papers. I'd no energy to think of a riposte, all I could manage was a weak smile. Feeling sorry for myself, I dreamed that if Usain Bloat had pulled up in his Supper Deluxe and offered me a ride to Base Camp, I'd have snatched his arm off. One hour and more than a score of curious looks later, I'd recovered sufficiently to heave on my pack and take my first strides without any reaction from my innards. It was the green light to continue.

The terrain I trudged through was now devoid of trees, a canvas of sand-coloured grasses upon which had been scattered brown dwarf shrubs as the trail undulated among mossy grey boulders. It was as if the liver-spotted skin of a jaundiced centenarian had been draped across the landscape like a hurriedly made bed. Above the vista of the alpine zone ahead were the slopes of the valley sides, where I could see the same shrubs had spread in a pattern redolent of bacilli under a microscope. Towards the summit, they thinned out and disappeared first into a brownness and into a gunmetal grey rock which formed, above everything, the jagged massif.

A short while from my unfortunate stop, in the middle of the valley, was a solitary lodge that seemed utterly desolate. It was strange to see a place so clearly purpose-built for the trekking industry, and not part of an ancient village, that was evidently so unused.

I was soon mixed into the morning rush-hour of dzhos heading downhill and trekkers up, and imagined I saw the porter from Lawichasa again. He was carrying the same burden, with the addition of two cardboard boxes roped to the planks above his head. Although the climb was gentle to the eye, it wasn't to the lungs. I was breathing hard when I finally reached a summit which revealed the path tumbling down to a wooden plank bridge over the river below.

I crawled up the opposite bank – hard going but mercifully short for the steep, exposed section. The path led to the shoulder of the hill, where a rudimentary chorten had been constructed. As I rounded it, I could see ahead the outline of a settlement in the valley, behind a porter coming the other way. I was elated to be so close. The trail headed down, back up and undulated again. Dingboche had seemed so very near at the chorten but I didn't seem to be making much headway towards it.

"You want help?" asked an Asian man, possibly 30, pallid from a lifetime of indoor pursuits and garbed in top-of-the-range gear doing nothing to hide his pudginess. Behind him followed a similar specimen, only more bulbous. Their patent lack of athleticism made it harder to bear they'd caught and passed me with ease.

"I'm fine, thank you, I'm only going to Dingboche." I pointed at what I was now convinced was a mirage.

"I see you make *big* mistake, mister, you carry bag. I have 25-kilo bag, much bigger, but I have porter carry for me."

"Lucky you."

"Yes, I bring lot of good thing. He bring my bag to lodge and I send him to you, I make him carry bag for you."

"No thanks, I'm fine. It's not far."

"I help you, you go faster. Look at us, we go fast like Mao Zedong on Long March. Chinese people are too smart, don't carry bag by self."

"No, thank you. I'm sure Chairman Mao didn't have someone to carry his bags on the Long March."

"My friend. You don't understand Communism, Chairman always have bag carry for him. All comrades equal, beneath party leaders."

"I can believe that. Thanks for the offer, but no thanks all the same."

"No problem, no problem. We see you in lodge, if you still alive, har-har." With that, he strode on with his companion. There was no sight of their porters, who were presumably labouring up the slope behind. Spurred on after my brief Sino-political exchange, I finally seemed to gain some ground on the village spread out over the hillside below. The track flattened out and I could see a painted blue tin roof proclaiming 'Peaceful Lodge'. The guidebook had indicated that, from Shomare, it would be a two-hour trek to Dingboche; four hours after leaving, I'd arrived.

Dingboche to Dughla

I approached the teahouse through a stone-walled chute that suggested panicked sheep, flanks dodgem-crashing as they mindlessly careened to be shorn. The lodge seemed to take its advertising seriously; the only sign of life was a lone plastic chair, casually pulled up against nothing, waiting for its first sunbather to baste on the well-tended lawn.

The arrangement of the place brought to mind how the desks at a corporate presentation would be fashioned, with the gate to the chute positioned where the projector screen would be set. The main building of two long and slim storeys sat under a cobalt corrugation of iron, its upper floor a three-one-two of uPVc panes set within a cladding of Brahmin-blue painted panels. Underneath, a lower arcade of glass sheltered beneath the jut of a tin roof. The right arm was a single storey, traditional in its native stone and economic with its black painted windows; the limb to the left was a budding greenhouse, the incongruous terracotta of its roof keeping the sun at bay.

As I entered the main building, I imagined the complex could've started as a field hospital that had ossified in the cold. Inside was still. I waited, thinking service would be provided with equal tranquillity, but after a while I realised I'd mistaken desertion for serenity. This wasn't the reception area, it seemed, despite the usual set-up of counter and tables, and so I decided to try the hothouse-like area.

A girl on the cusp of leaving the trauma of her teenage years behind was basking under the glass in the midday sun. She was dressed in traditional attire; her tan line would be abrupt where the tightness of her headscarf was wrapped. She had her plastic chair leaning back on two legs, her own planted firmly astride for balance aside in an unseemly, manspreading pose. Her eyes flicked open in an embarrassed stare; guests were clearly not expected yet. It took an instant for the lady salamander to extract the buds from her ears and I recognised something tinny yet familiar.

"Five Five Five?"

"Yes!" she replied, seeming nonplussed by my expansive knowledge of the local *oeuvre*.

"*Budi?*" Now she was plain flabbergasted.

"You know *Budi*, Nepali music?" she asked, her face cut by a broad grin.

"Yes, of course."

"He's very cool man." She seemed impressed. I wasn't about to contradict her impression of the ancient Western fogey being *so* down with the kids, but I thought it was a good job she didn't ask me to name another one of his songs. Once she'd gathered herself, the girl was all professional bustle, the conversion seamless from slovenly teenager to accomplished receptionist. I made a note to ask her dad, if I could find him, how he'd achieved this in her upbringing; it was something I could take home with me.

We returned to where I'd waited in vain. She popped her head through the curtain behind the counter where an argument with someone with a man's voice followed. Now confident to fix the price, she took me down to the end of a long corridor and showed me to the room. The price was more than reasonable for the standard of the accommodation – I'd been offered a corner room where light streamed through half-length windows on two sides and the cots had double-thickness mattresses. A fitted sheet and duvet in washing-powder-advert white were wholly unexpected and welcome bonuses. The bathroom was a couple of doors up, replete with Western Style, fitted vanity unit and a power shower, of sorts.

Outside my window I had a pair of sierra views to select from. At ground level, I was astounded to see there was an ambition to grow vegetables. A half-dozen polytunnels hugged the ground, their ripped edges flapping gently in the breeze. I was grateful I'd been so lucky to find a premier place to stay and recuperate without having to exert myself in the slightest.

I cleaned myself up as best I could in the bathroom; with no washcloth, it was a delicate balance between trying to clean the dried stain of illness from my trousers and not soaking them so much I'd have to take lunch in my smalls. I wasn't yet ready to brazen it out and parade into the glasshouse in just my underpants, pretending I was looking for an almost-all-over tan. Besides, I'd been rotating the same four pairs of briefs for the last couple of weeks.

An hour of hand sponging later, I was ready to try the local brand of noodle soup, hoping the quality matched that of the lodgings. The sunroom had filled up while I'd been at my laundry. The same group who'd stripped the store bare of Mars bars in Pangboche had arranged themselves each at their own individual tables.

"Namaste, hi."

"Alreet, mate," murmured the group's largest member, a beefy giant who was snap-flipping cards into a game of patience. Roberto, I remembered, was what his friend had called him.

"Are you guys heading upwards?"

"Aye. Beys Comp, like." He grinned as he drew some royalty, which meant he could move a pile of cards over to an empty slot and release a line.

"I saw you guys down in Pangboche, day before last I think it was. I think you cleared the lodge out of chocolate bars."

"Wil, that's that fat bustard Joao fur ya, man! He's a reyvin chocaholic, that lad, canny keep 'im off it, like." A gentleman in the corner flicked the bird.

"I hope you've left some for my dessert after lunch?"

"Wil, I dunno, but I'd git in quick now, Joao's lookin' hungree, same as usual, mind." The gentleman repeated his middle finger gesture, so I decided to move things on to less emotive subjects.

"Have you guys just got here today, the same as me?"

"Nah, man, we gaan heyar lust neet, this avvy is oor furst rest, like. We've gut the afternoun off coz oor guide, Gorpal, took us oop an acclimatisation wauk this monin."

"Where did you go? How was that?"

"Oop the valley at the top of the village, Chhukhung I think it was called. It was alreet waukin, like, though Joao found eet a bit huard at the top, didn't ya, Joao?"

"Aye, I was puffin' n' pantin' a bit but it was worth it, mind, the views whin youse get around the corner up theyar are spectacular, like. Whit about you, where have youse come from?"

"Shomare, just down the valley. I'd planned to come to Dingboche yesterday and do the same as you, but I was so knackered when I got there I decided to stay and make the walk up this morning my sort of rest day." I finished my recap as the girl came to take my order.

"Aye, it's tough in places, like," pronounced Joao, a compact, pocket Enrique Iglesias.

"How are you dealing with the altitude?"

"No real problems so far, like, but I'd a bit of a leet head yesterday."

"That's no change frum any uther daiy, then, is it, Joao?"

It seemed the card player couldn't help himself, but this time Joao just smiled. I made light work of my noodles. We chatted through tea and the men agreed to head off to the village bakery to see if Joao could empty the shelves of any chocolate-covered doughnuts they may have.

I retired to my room thinking it was a good job Joao hadn't been on the 1953 expedition. Norgay would never have had a chance to leave his offerings at the summit. I was better for the food and tried to read but, half an hour into my book, I developed a pain at the front of my skull. This was the moment I'd been dreading. Up until then, I'd been able to convince myself I'd avoided altitude sickness because I hadn't had any headaches but this, combined with the nausea, meant in all likelihood I did. I wasn't going to descend that afternoon but decided, if the pain hadn't gone away by the morning, I'd reached the point where I'd have to turn back. To carry on would be folly – high-altitude pulmonary oedema or, even worse, high-altitude cerebral oedema were life-threatening conditions.

Until this point, I hadn't seriously considered failing in my desire to make it to Base Camp. In my mind, although I was ill, I was still able to overcome that inconvenience and soldier on stoically – a bit of a cough, the odd bit of vomiting and some phlegm weren't going to stop me – but now I was potentially risking my life. The words of counsel I'd airily dismissed in Goyem came back to mind: 'Anything can happen to you and no-one would know'. Altitude sickness could be a silent killer; if my body gave up, how long would it be before anyone found me deceased in the corner room?

I found the idea of not making it curious, at first, and hard to process in my own personal context, as if it could only possibly apply to someone else, someone less robust and less determined than myself. But it dawned on me the person I was thinking of wasn't me anymore, it was the me of a decade earlier. It was with a certain degree of irony and sadness the notion I could be over the hill seeped into my mind. I tried to dispel those thoughts which bothered me far more than the concept of 'failure'. That I could deal with – I'd be disappointed to have made it so far without reaching my target, but it would only be *this time*, I could go again. But the idea I could *not* go again I found distressing, and wondered how Hillary had dealt with something similar.

Despite being one of the first two men to the summit of Everest, never mind Base Camp, he'd suffered a debilitating bout of altitude sickness in later years. I wasn't sure, but thought he could climb no higher than Tengboche. It wasn't a bad place to be able to reach but no Everest; how had he dealt with that? With these thoughts echoing in my head, I spent the rest of the afternoon in bed, in and out of sleep. At six, I awoke with headache and nausea gone and my anguish morphed into a cautious optimism. Maybe I could still make it, after all.

Dinner could only help my situation. I made my way to the sunroom, only to find it closed and be told that food was being taken in the reception area.

"Comon join us, man," invited Roberto. He had his deck with him, and he and his three companions were busy at a game.

"Thanks, how was your afternoon?"

"It was a greet, mon, Joao gut himself a jam downut from the bekery an' I gut a brownie, it was deee-ad tasty."

"So, I guess they didn't have stottie cake, then?"

"Ha-ha."

"I forgot to ask something earlier but can I ask it before we talk anymore?"

"Sure, as long as it's not if you can 'ave the other jam downut Joao is savin' for hees midneet snack, like, he'll no be 'appy wi' that." Roberto was met with the middle finger again.

"Ha-ha, it's not that, it's can I ask where you guys are from? I don't want to say the wrong thing and get myself in trouble as I've done that before, so are you guys Geordies or Mackems?"

"John and Gus are from Scotland but me and Joao are Geordies, man. We thought *youse* might be from Sunderland, with that hat on."

"No, it gets a lot of attention this, hat, but it's a Scottish Tunnock's tea cake. But I'm not from there. I'm from Liverpool."

"Aye, wil, that's good for youse, then, dependin' on wither youse a Red or Blue?"

"Red."

"Yav gut a good team a' tha moment, think youse 'ave a good chance o' winnin' it."

"What about Newcastle, how d'you reckon they're getting on?"

"Nycasl are shite this season, the only blessin' this year, mind, is that a Tunnock's tea cake has more chance o' winnin' anythin' than Sunderland."

"Ha-ha. So, how do you guys know each other?"

"Wil, John has the misfortune to be married ta me sista, Gus an' I work thegither on the rigs and Joao is like a hanger-on. Canny get rid o' the fukka, like."

"Do you have Portuguese heritage, Joao? It's not a name you usually associate with Tyneside."

"I'm from Brazil originally, I came to the UK with my parents when I was 10 and never went back."

"Oh. So, you're like Geordinho?"

"Nah, he's so shite at fitba he's more like Geord-in-ya-oon-goal-o, man." Joao had no retort this time to Roberto's considered opinion.

"So, how come you're doing this trek together?"

"John is a keen walker, like, a Munro bagger, an' Gus is deen it for personal reasons, for 'is sista. I've always wanted ta come since I read Ranulph Fiennes' book an' Joao thought we were gaan on a shaggas holidy ta Magaluf."

"Ha-ha."

"Whit aboot youse man, youse trekkin' alone?"

"Yes, I was inspired to come by reading the biography of Hillary. I've come along the route the 1953 expedition took, through the lower hills to Base Camp. I was at a talk by Ranulph Fiennes a few years ago, by the way, he's some boy. He's got brilliant stories and he tells them superbly, he's really funny."

"Who's Ranulph Fiennes?"

"Ya never heard of Ranulph Fiennes, Joao? Ya moopet." Roberto couldn't resist.

"No, who's he?"

"Greetest living explora. Been oop Everest, crossed Antarctica hoppin' on his left bollock, like."

"First I've heard of him."

"Tha's nooo hoop for youse, man."

"Aye, shoot oop, man, will yazh?"

"As yazh Billy-No-Mates, do ya want to pley some cards? We can deal youse in an' you'll not have ta listen ta any meer shite from Joao," gently offered Roberto.

"Sure, what game are you playing?"

"Shithead."

"That's a bit rude, I was only asking."

"Ha-ha. The game's called shithead, yazh shithead." The game was one where you needed to get rid of your cards, and the person left holding onto their own at the end became the 'shithead'. We played for an hour and I found I was even more of a shithead than any of my close friends had repeatedly reminded me.

My pizza, when it came, was fantastic. I washed it down with a small pot of peppermint tea. Several hours of fun at cards, the convivial chat, great food and refreshing drink had done me the world of good and I was revived when we broke to get some rest. Back in my room, it was time for music so I started the *Hurt & the Merciless* by The Heavy at track 10 and, an hour later, I was ready for sleep; it was 10pm.

The night was a strange mixture. I needed to visit the lavatory three times and the *Diaries* would report a grand total of four Type Sevens by the time I'd paid my bill, but in between excursions I'd fallen back asleep almost immediately and slept soundly. My headache had abated so I was in good spirits when I took my seat at the table for breakfast.

"Mornin' shithead." I'd lost the final game before we retired.

"Morning all, sleep alright?"

"Sound, like." They were in fine fettle. Gorpal attended to their every need as they munched their way through pancakes with syrup. I plumped for porridge and black tea, a match for the previous night's pizza.

"Where are you heading for today?"

"We are going to Lobouche," replied Gorpal.

"I'm going to just head to Dughla. The guide says don't ascend more than 200 metres a day, so that's about right for me, I think."

"No, no. Lobouche is best, with acclimatisation yesterday Lobouche is no problem. Nothing at Dughla, no good lodge."

"Okay, thanks, but I'm taking it easy and I've plenty of time."

"Aye man, good job youse not with us, yad have hud the yak bell evury day," interjected Roberto.

"Yak bell?"

"Aye, if ya come in last pleys to a toon, tha' nixt dey youse have to carry the yak bell with ya an' ringit whenever ya pass another groop."

"Yeah? In that case, as I'm so slow, I'd be deaf by the end of the trek with all the ringing I'd have to do." Inexplicably, visions of Nunthala popped into my head.

"Yazh canny be slowa than Joao, man. He's slowa than Sunderland's back line." We chatted until they'd finished their breakfast, Gorpal gave them the signal they needed to ship out and I left to pack.

As I walked back to my room, I was struck by a bout of dry heaving that surpassed any previous episode. I made it to the WC, vomited my breakfast back up and immediately felt better. I waited for an hour and the nausea didn't return; I hadn't had a headache since the previous day and so concluded it was safe to carry on. I donned my gear, paid my bill and headed out into the cold.

The steep ascent out of Dingboche up to a ridge of chortens was in shadow. It was a difficult climb for first thing in the morning, causing me to stop frequently to catch my breath. The trail was multi-threaded up to the shrines. It coalesced to one point on the ridge on which they sat, the footing a scree of small pebbles that slid back down the slope with each misstep.

"Hi, Lee!" This was by now a familiar voice; the call coming from over my shoulder where Aydin appeared from the side of a chorten like a Midwest cop pulling out to chase a speeding car.

"Aydin, where were you hiding? How are you?"

"I was looking at this chorten and I saw that hat of yours. It seems like I've been following it for two weeks."

"This hat is beginning to get a bit of a reputation. Did you stay in Dingboche last night?"

"Yeah, it's really cold, isn't it? I was freezing this morning, so expensive as well."

"How are you doing for money?"

"I haven't run out yet, I'm not eating lunch and watching how much I spend on tea."

"I can see what you mean with the tea but not eating lunch sounds a bit Spartan. Are you sure you're alright with that?"

"Yes, but the belt on my walking trousers could do with pinning now, I wish I hadn't left my sewing kit in Thado."

"Where are you headed for today?"

"Lobouche. I did a walk to acclimatise yesterday so I hope I'm going to be okay with the altitude, although I have a bit of a headache this morning."

"I'd one yesterday, it's gone now, though. I'm sure you'll be fine if you keep hydrated. You did that acclimatisation walk so I guess you've been higher than Lobouche already?"

"Yeah, it was miles in the end, though, you know, the village never seemed to get any nearer. It was hard on my feet, I really should get new boots." I knew better than to ask him if he needed blister plasters or Ibuprofen, or suggest that he was going to struggle to find a cobbler in Lobouche.

"Well, good luck. I'll see you on the trail, no doubt." And with that, he was off. I was now walking on a shoulder of land high above the Khumbu Khola river braiding its way through the valley. I made it to the shadow line, beyond which frozen puddles were beginning to thaw and the day had become warm enough to strip to my fleece.

The terrain was now flat and there were magnificent views of the range that arced around from my left to ahead, all gunmetal grey rock summitted by a powdering of snow. I could see that, although there was still some dwarf plant growth at my level, it wouldn't be much further before I was above the shrub line.

I only realised my speed when a train of 20 trekkers passed me, neckerchiefs pulled high beneath their bucket hats as they scratched along with their poles. They hardly seemed to move but still left me for dead. A little disconsolate, I sat down on a rock to rest and a shudder of fatigue worked its way down from my shoulders to my boots. I'd been going for less than an hour.

"Do you have a problem, sir?"

"Just taking a breather." The look on the guide's face told me he wasn't fooled.

"Are you sure? Do you have a headache?"

"No headache, I'm just feeling tired, thanks."

"If you have a headache, you must be careful and go down. Here is 4,500 metres, it is dangerous for altitude sickness."

"I think I'm okay, thanks. I've ascended very slowly; I think I'm only tired because of stomach problems."

"Ah yes, the Delhi belly!" A pair of 20-something ladies had now joined us.

"What is that you are saying about *this* Delhi belly?"

"Are you ladies from India?"

"Yes, from Delhi, but we are not in possession of these Delhi bellies you are speaking of."

"Ha-ha, I think you're the first trekkers I've ever met from India."

"Yes, I am not surprised, for us it is a new thing; it is becoming more popular now." I reckoned that true; I hadn't encountered any Indian or Chinese trekkers a decade earlier but had met both on this adventure.

"If you don't have a problem, sir, we will carry on. We will wait for you at Dughla and if you have a problem, I will help you with whatever you need. Maybe a porter to carry your bag."

"Thank you." I followed the trio for a while but couldn't keep pace, struggling to make ground. I could now see the village of Pheriche behind me in the valley below. Ahead was an enviable young powerhouse who'd clambered up a boulder by a yak herder's hut for a picture. The track was generally level, the terrain a tawny beaten earth of overgrazed grass, but then a slight incline meant the need for another sit down.

"Do you suffer?"

"Excuse me?"

"Do you suffer?" My interrogator reminded me of *Spy vs Spy*, the black of his face scarf matched by the felt of his fedora and knee-length jacket. His trousers and boots were the colour of coal. They matched the hue of his backpack.

"I'm finding it difficult, yes."

"I suffer." His voice had a slightly eastern twist with the intonation of a 45 played at 33.

"With the altitude?"

"I suffer with everything."

"Yes, it's tough. Where's that accent from?" I enquired, intrigued.

"Romania."

"Whereabouts? I only know two places in Romania, Bucharest and Transylvania."

"Yes." He didn't offer confirmation or otherwise but, with his lack of exposed skin and sonorously hypnotic voice, I assumed he hailed from the Carpathians.

"Are you heading for Lobouche?"

"I suffer, I will go to Dughla, take drink." My jugular pulsed.

"Okay, do you want to walk together for a bit?"

"Yes, but I suffer, I cannot breathe." That was a surprise, I thought his kind had no need of breathing. We walked together for 100 metres before he needed to rest, I supposed because the sun was directly overhead.

"Are you okay, mate?"

"I suffer."

"Do you want me to stay with you for a while?" Not meaning for the next five centuries.

"No, I suffer. I suffer alone, you cannot help me."

"Okay, I'll see you at Dughla, then?" The fedora bobbed in agreement and I headed down the track now gently descending to a broad white scar in the hillside ahead. It could've been that a flood had swept down the valley and scoured away the banks, depositing a field of table-sized boulders in the valley.

The river was crossed by a plank bridge that seemed no more than a boot's height above the milky torrent roaring below. The path wound its way through and over the boulders, the scramble becoming awkward. Where there was no easy route, the trekking parties concertinaed into a bottleneck of packs and poles and it became a wait for the traffic to clear. One last steep scrabble was required to reach the balcony of trekkers sunning themselves on the terrace that served a couple of lodges. The guidebook had indicated that, from Dingboche, it would be a two-hour trek to Dughla; two-and-three-quarter hours after leaving, I'd arrived.

Dughla to Lobouche

The teahouse was called the Yak Lodge and I approached hoping they allowed humans to stay as well. It was a two-storey grey block approached across the sun terrace, nothing remarkable about the place other than the mortar between the bricks. It was strangely pronounced in the way the first squeeze of toothpaste from a fresh tube lands on the bristles.

I'd caught up with the many trekking parties which had passed me in the morning, and whose members all now seemed intent on basking in the sun while they took their late-morning refreshments. I fancied joining them after I'd sorted out my lodgings. I weaved through the thickets of sun worshippers arrayed on their plastic deckchairs and searched, without luck, in the grey building for the reception.

I had more success in the restaurant which stood at a right angle. It contained a receptionist, a man in his early 30s who was either sensitive to airborne particles or moonlighting from his position as bagman for the Dughla Dzho Rustler Gang. When he rolled down his black Paisley neckerchief, which he did in a way more suited to the maître d' of the Dorchester demonstrating to a junior waiter the correct procedure to fold a napkin, what was striking was his uncanny resemblance to the actor John Leguizamo.

My host showed me to my quarters, Room 101. My first impression of the interior was that The Ministry of Love would've been satisfied with the arrangements for anyone scheduled a visit whose worst fear happened to be mattress stains of an indeterminate origin. The dual cots which lay silently putrefying beneath the peeling paintwork were well suited to O'Brien's dark arts. The room was a wooden box and I knew from one look my sleeping bag would have to be enough to keep me warm. The grubby window revealed a gravel circle acting as a helicopter landing pad. I'd seen no arrivals so we settled on the price without fuss. Overall, I adjudged Room 101 functional, but down-at-heel compared to the Peaceful; my only real gripe was the pair of squatting stalls that served as the khazi were at the far end of the corridor. A black hose, fed from a blue plastic barrel above a porcelain trough, comprised the washing mechanism. I made a note to check whether water would need to be taken into the stall to conclude one's business; it would be unseemly if one had to return to the sink.

The terrace had become even busier while Leggy had been giving me the tour of the facilities. I wasn't going to find a seat outside, so returned to the saloon to take some tea. A different member of the Dzho Rustlers came to take my order of a small pot of mint tea; he was more casual in hiding his identity, with his red bandana slouched across his neck. Unfortunately, his serving skills failed to match his yak abduction abilities and he brought me a pot sullied with milk. He must have recognised me as the Man with No Name and didn't want to risk being gunned down in the courtyard, so his apology was to replace it with a big pot painted in orange tulips, with a cricket ball of tin foil acting as the stopper. Satisfied by his grovelling, I re-holstered my six-shooter.

The tea was timely as the cough that hadn't troubled me on the walk to Dughla now chose to reassert itself. I was struck by a fit that took the pot's first half to suppress. I signalled to Leggy I'd like something more and he moseyed on over, pulled down his neckerchief and glared at me expectantly.

"Well ... ?"

"What's in the club sandwich, please?" Not what Blondie would've ordered or with the same coolness and force, but I was hungry so it would suffice.

"Dunno, mister." Leggy's reply was delivered with a curled-lip snarl of which his doppelganger would've been proud.

"Okay, I'll have that, then." Well, I thought, you've got to have some adventure in your life.

I could see that Leggy, when he brought the plate to me, was being more accurate than awkward with his description; the club was three slices of toasted bread with a layer of orange chips stuffed between the first two and an unidentifiable mulch in the other. I think it might have been rustled dzho, although, alternatively, it could've been something shovelled out of the moraine uphill. I ate it more out of a sense of duty than enjoyment and struggled to keep it down.

Trekkers bustled in and out of the restaurant in groups of threes and fours, but the place seemed more of a quick in-and-out stop than somewhere where a conversation would be struck. Aydin was nowhere to be seen so I guessed he must have carried on, one of his cost-cutting measures to skip lunch. I found myself missing his company – there was plenty to complain about in the restaurant and I was sure he'd have made a fine job of doing so.

I finished the rest of the tulip pot and went to my room to read, thinking I'd take a mid-afternoon drink on the patio when the crowds had departed. I finished *Cryptonomicon*. I'd enjoyed it overall but felt the ending unbefitting of what had gone before. My cough had grown steadily worse as I read, possibly due to my posture. I'd run out of tissues so made my way to the bin at the end of the corridor, salvaged a plastic water bottle and cut it into thirds with my penknife, discarding the top two.

My next read was another science fiction book, *Gnomon* by Nick Harkaway. I soon found myself appreciative of the Kindle's inbuilt dictionary. I passed a couple of hours reading and filling the bottom third of my bottle with a greenish phlegm before taking some sun and a ginger tea in the late afternoon on the plaza. The rest helped immensely with my recuperation; my nausea had disappeared and my cough cleared, so at six it was time to empty the spittoon and head to dinner.

In contrast to earlier, the saloon was almost empty. This gave me the opportunity to charge my phone and Kindle fully for the dzho ransoming sum of Rs.600. There was a dual-lead charger plugged into a socket, so I attached both devices. I'd argue on check-out 600 was the price for the socket, not per device, and fill any varmint who disagreed with a belly full of lead.

Leggy took my order of tomato noodle soup with his customary disdain and I settled back to see if there was going to be any engaging company that evening. My only companions were a trio of Frenchmen – two young, orange-bearded men and a clean-shaven older man who I discounted as being their father on the basis he was recounting a story about his recent visit to India. It failed to strike me a father-to-son conversation and, besides, they were so different genetically. The older man was of such short stature he'd have needed a stepladder to have a *tête-à-tête* with Toulouse-Lautrec, whereas the others could have played in Toulouse's back row.

What he lacked in physicality, the wee man made up for with force of argument as he held court. The group's ambience reminded me of the mid-afternoon political debating shows I'd seen on TF1. The older man was earnest, looking for approval and respect from the younger men for his experience. The younger two were looking for credibility in his eyes via counter-point. He was into the fine detail of border control, the chaos of the trains and tuk-tuks and how bribing the police worked. I wondered if I was as boring when telling my kids about my travels. I rapidly put that idea out of my head, already knowing the answer too well.

The noodle soup was passable but not filling and so I summoned Leggy over and troubled him with a request for spaghetti and, to fill the wait while it was prepared, a ginger tea. One of the younger Frenchmen reached over to my table and helped himself to my tray of chilli sauce and salt and pepper without a by-your-leave. The raid was swiftly followed by the other swiping my napkin holder, again without any recourse to proper manners. I imagined this was a deliberate provocation of the Man with No Name; Leggy had called in some hired guns to help him be rid of me and this was the first move by Shorty Escargot and the Gingembre Twins Gang.

It was fortunate my spaghetti arrived just before I could turn the situation into a fully-fledged Sergio Leone Western lead-fest. The spaghetti amounted to no more than a sludge of wet pasta that had been washed in a congealed malaise of ketchup. After forcing it down, I took a mint tea and waited, Smith and Wesson cocked under the table, ready for another slight from the outlaws. Shorty's gang, however, was now engrossed in a discussion on Indian cuisine, no good cheese apparently, and I was able to sashay out of the cantina without recourse to gunslinging.

I retired to my cell and read for an hour, frustrated my Kindle was only 30 per cent charged. The evening's musical choice was *Version 2.0* by Garbage, played from track eight, and an hour later my coughing had abated enough to allow for sleep; it was 9pm.

My stomach woke me shortly after midnight so I slipped on my boots and somnambulantly headed down the corridor in my pants and thermal top. I pushed open the left-hand trap's door to be greeted by one of the Gingembre Twins, or more precisely his penis. My first thought was, 'Why is this guy standing in the hallway with his knob out?' My second, 'Ah, he's French, that explains it.' And my third that I had the hired guns' names wrong – this guy wasn't one of the Gingembre Twins, he was possibly Billy Le Demi-Frite or, by the looks of it, Billy Le Champignon Bouton.

"Pardon." I wasn't sure what to make of that. It wasn't like a Gaul to excuse himself for swinging his wanger about in public; I understood in some *départements* it was a popular competitor sport. It was only when his eyes directed me to the floor I understood what he was apologising for. His trousers lay crumpled around his boots, soiled in no way I'd seen before. It was if they'd been through an entire 60-degree cycle where diarrhoea had been used as the fabric conditioner. I was mesmerised, not because I'd never seen a Frenchman with such a small willy, but because I'd no idea so much waste matter could've been expelled by a single person, and I'm a father-of-two.

"Pardon." I saw Billy was close to tears and I wasn't sure what to do: explain it was all in the technique, not the size? Or did he want something else?

"Mon ami, Loic? Il m'aidera."

"Yes ... err ... I go. What door in you sleeping?" The improvement in my French was immeasurable in a crisis.

"Twenty-four."

"I agree." I drowsily headed back along the corridor and down the stairs but couldn't find room 24. I guessed I'd made a mistake in the translation and returned to the site of the toxic spill.

"Excuse me, there is none 24."

"One hundred and four. Please." He showed me with his fingers.

"I agree." This time I found the room and tapped on the door. There was no sound, so I poked my head around and the second Gingembre Twin, or whoever he was, awoke with a start, looking ready for a fight.

"Excuse me. Your friend. Toilette. He ... lots of shit. Big problem. Help you. Over there." It seemed to get the message across, and he pushed past me to go and help his compadre. I still had my own business to attend to and followed him. Thankfully, he'd pulled the door shut to allow for some modesty in the clean-up operation, but I could still hear the sad, low wail and snuffling tears of Billy as I closed the door of my room.

It was difficult to get back to sleep after the episode, but I managed after I heard the reassuring clump of boots returning to room 104. I awoke without any need to visit the Squat Style. The *Diaries* would record an entry of one Type Five (as my deposit had been completed post-midnight) but I'd also add a footnote to remind me to write to the Bristol Royal Infirmary (Department of Stools) to propose a new Type, the suggestion being a Type Eight would be the equivalent of Type Seven but on the scale of the Great Flood.

Shorty Escargot was enjoying a breakfast of eggs when I returned to the saloon but there was no sign of the Gingembre Twins. I imagined they were already on their way upwards, leaving a visibly miasmic trail of *ordure colon* in their wake. I couldn't blame them for making an early departure; I wouldn't have wanted to share my embarrassment at breakfast, either.

My porridge was a thin gruel that left me disappointed. I washed it down with a black tea before arguing my case successfully on the charging arrangements. I think Leggy felt guilty about the extortion of Rs.600. Bill paid, I packed my gear but, before I could finish, I dry retched. I took this as an improvement on the last couple of days – at least I hadn't brought everything up. More worrying were the additions I'd made to the spittoon as they were now a thick green. I finished coughing, cleaned up and left for the trail.

The sun was up and the sky cloudless as I started on the morning's brutal first climb; the series of dusty switchbacks, cut through a terminal moraine, soon had me struggling for air and I couldn't help thinking the Twins must have been suffering badly on this stretch. The trail was braided, cutting through vegetation little more than a dry scrub of gnawed grasses interrupted by the odd stunted shrub, with cairns of stones keeping me on the right path.

The scenery above and around was as dramatic as anything I'd seen but I'd no eyes for it; I was head down, focussed on my laces and making sure I took the next step. Soon I'd worked my way into a rhythm and imperceptibly entered the trance of my approach to Goyem, my thoughts amounting to no more than the crush of gravel under my boot.

"Not too far now, mate. Once you get to the ridge there, it's only twice as steep as this." My persecutor was the younger of two men heading downslope, his accent faintly West Country.

"Oh, shit. You're kidding me, right?" The interruption to my reverie had broken the unconscious blotting out of the difficulty in breathing.

"Yes. Sorry to be mean, once you get to the top here it's pretty level to Lobouche." A helicopter passed overhead.

"I wonder if that's that French guy, dad?" The younger man was looking skywards.

"French guy? There were a couple of French guys in my lodge last night, one was in pretty bad shape. Do you know what happened?" I hoped Billy hadn't collapsed on this tough stretch.

"I heard a French guy died at the lodge in Lobouche last night," said the older man. "He was put in a body bag this morning. They were going to helicopter him out so other trekkers wouldn't see him. I reckon that's him in the helicopter that's just flown over."

"Are you serious? This isn't a wind-up, is it?"

"No, I wouldn't joke about a thing like that, mate."

"Jeez, what did he die of, do you know?"

"Nobody knows, mate, he went to bed and didn't wake up."

"Oh, okay, thanks for letting me in on that. I hope I don't get his bed in whatever lodge he stayed in, I don't want to make it two from two."

"Ah, you'll be alright, mate." The father and son headed downhill and, 10 minutes of worrying later, I was on the ridge at the top of the ascent. I knew to expect the memorial ground, but I found it had crept up on me all the same when I stepped down from underneath a string of prayer flags onto a gravelly area. To my left was a parade of monuments which stood in line and brought to mind the Easter Island heads.

Ahead of me were modest shrines, some rock built, almost mini-chortens, others simply plaques bolted into boulders, each commemorating a loss on Everest. A few had etched images of the dead climbers on brass affixed into cement, while an orthodox cross marked the place of fallen Russians. I stopped at the tribute dedicated to Bulgarian climbers. The alpinist club of a place called Sliven had been hit with three tragedies and a person called Ivan Tomov had been lost only six months earlier; he was only 35.

Deep within, it felt wrong to be rubber-necking at these remembrances. I was drawn in, like everyone else who passed, by a morbid fascination to see who was commemorated there in stone. But they weren't my loved ones, not even anyone I knew. I considered a dedicated place further away from the trail would be more fitting, allowing dignity for the fallen and privacy for those who came to visit them. The memorial statues on a ridge in the distance were, in my opinion, in the right place.

Uncomfortable, I didn't tarry and headed off down the track, which was as level as the young joker had promised. I was on the right bank of a stream that seemed more composed of boulders than water. To my right, all was scree, rock and boulder that spread down to the water level, another moraine I guessed; the left bank was greener, with the same cropped grass as on the trail up. The massif that had seemed so imposing and unreachable a couple of days earlier now seemed climbable, a day trek – but the memorial downhill told me otherwise.

Pumori was an equilateral of snow to my left and the trail ahead a brilliant white of dust that cut along the ablation valley's side. My cough had eased again as I'd climbed, I reasoned because of the infection working its way out. I wandered into my trance again on this much easier section, plodding along in a rock-scape that had been scoured, ground and churned into something starkly beautiful.

"Lee!" I'd have passed her without noticing, were it not for the salutation.

"Xavi! How are you doing?" I replied in English; it was easier for all involved. She greeted me with a kiss and a hug that belonged more to the visit of a beloved uncle rather than someone she'd lunch with once, but I didn't complain.

"I am great, thank you."

"I guess you're on your way down? Did you manage okay in the end with the altitude? Did the Diamox make a difference? Did you make it?" I babbled.

"I made it to Base Camp, but not Kala Pattar. The altitude was too much, but I am so happy to make it to Base Camp, I can't believe that I did it!" I was delighted for her.

"Congratulations! What about the boys, did they make it too? Are they still with you?"

"They went to Kala Pattar this morning, they will be coming down soon, I think." We chatted for a while and parted company with another hug. I left her encouraged and hoping to see the American guys and congratulate them, too. I crossed over to the stream's far side and filled my LifeStraw.

"Bonjour, monsieur."

"Ah, hello." It was the older lady from the trio I'd met at Bhandar. Her porter gave me the thumbs-up. She told me that her group had split, the younger girls regrettably suffering from mountain sickness and having to descend, so there were now only the two of them. She seemed, if anything, stronger at 5,000 metres and strode off into the distance at a faster pace than her downhill chicaning to Kenja. As I bid her goodbye, a young, curly-haired man came to sit down next to me.

"Hi, I see you have a LifeStraw."

"Yes, it's a brilliant piece of kit."

"I have one, too. I got it in Thamel, Kathmandu."

"Is it real, or do you think it's a fake one?"

"It's real, it cost $30. I have the guarantee."

"I got mine back in the UK. It cost more than that, so you got a good deal, I think."

"I bargained hard."

"I guess so, $30 is a really good deal."

"Do you want a coconut cookie? I got these in Thamel, too, they're good."

"That would be great. Where are you from, Israel?"

"Yes, how do you know? Because I drive the best bargain? Ha-ha."

"Ha-ha. No, I walked with some Israeli guys 10 years ago, the last time I was in Nepal, so I got to know the accent a bit."

"Ah."

"Have you just finished the, what is it, two years in the army?"

"A bit more, but yes."

"Going around the world?"

"Yes. I feel like a cliché now."

"Good for you. How long have you got?"

"One year."

"Well, I'm sure you'll have a whale of a time, if you aren't already. Are you doing it solo?"

"No, with a friend from the army, here he is now." His buddy caught up and the rest of the coconut cookies were dispatched without hesitation. We chatted for a while and agreed it was time to push on to Lobouche. We'd stopped short of the first vista of the village and 10 minutes of steady walking later, I was there. I fancied staying somewhere away from the main trail through the settlement so headed towards the upper part of town where a lady was fussing around outside a lodge.

"Do you have a room, please?" She looked up at me enquiringly for a second, eyebrow raised.

"Why not?!" she replied, bidding me follow. The guidebook had indicated that, from Dughla, it would be a two-and-a-half-hour trek to Lobouche. I was delighted to see I'd kept pace for the first time because, two-and-a-half hours after leaving, I'd arrived.

Lobouche to Gorak Shep

I followed the lady through a door curtain into the lodge's welcoming reception-diner which I estimated to cater for around 30. The space was illuminated by a wall-length bay window, the late-morning sun reflecting through the polished glass. Wooden tables and plastic chairs gathered around a black iron burner. They sat under the green frills of an interior bunting. Flat yet plump cushions and woven tablecloths in gold and black gave the place a homely, well-kept feel more like the family-run businesses of the lower trek than the pseudo-industrial lodges of Namche onwards.

"You are my first customer of the day. You must share a pot of tea with me!" I thought this must be a new stratagem – drug me with some sweet nectar and lure me, half-sedated, into agreeing to an exorbitant price – but the offer had caught me unawares and I hesitated.

"Caamm on ... don't be shy! What type of tea do you want with Sangmu?"

"Err ... I'll go for a lemon tea if you have it, please."

"Coming right up!" Sangmu disappeared behind another curtain door and yelled something in Nepali, giving me the opportunity to survey the interior in more detail. A cornucopia of manufactures were stashed behind, under and atop the counter, upon which a throwback calculator, larger than a modern laptop, sat waiting for input. I could see the place was once a popular hangout for Korean visitors: a calendar announced something was happening between 26th March and 11th April 2015. The discreetly taped notice advertising in italics to the discerning clientele that they could purchase a heli-rescue flight and oxygen service only served to bring home the dangers at this altitude and my associated condition at Dingboche.

As I sat pondering how the mechanics of the heli-rescue service worked, Sangmu returned. She was mid-40s and moved with an energy that said it constantly needed shedding lest she explode. Her hair was bundled under a pink scarf worn Little Steven style, the rest of her outfit a charcoal puffer jacket, black leggings and sandals. Her constant smile and bustling movements gave her an air of jolliness. She made me feel as though she was genuinely pleased not only to see me but also to have me as her guest. She put the tea tray down on the table in the sun under the bay and patted the seat next to her.

"Come here, sit next to me in the warm." The delivery was jovial, almost laughing, but the message was clear: this was to be considered an order, not as advice.

"Err ... okay." I sidled over to the table, for some strange reason feeling like a fly which has found its legs are suddenly all sticky.

"Don't worry, you are my first customer, there is no charge for the tea. Do you want sugar, sugar? Ha-ha."

"No thank you."

"If you don't want sugar, I have honey, honey? Ha-ha."

"No, thank you, I'm sweet enough as it is, ha-ha."

"I am sure you are, but you will need all your energy here."

"I'm fine, thank you." She handed me over a steaming cup and I took a sip; it was as refreshing as Britta's magic tea and it struck me I hadn't seen her for a few days. I wondered where she was. One thing for certain was she wasn't shopping for underwear.

"Wow, that's good."

"Yes, thank you, you know Sangmu is good at a lot of things. Let me know if you change your mind about that honey."

"It's fine as it is, thanks, more than fine, in fact, it's great."

"You look cold, why don't you come warm up next to me." I obeyed, shuffling closer.

"Caamm on ... move closer now, it is warmer here." If I'd gotten any nearer, I'd have been sitting in her lap. I moved shoulder to shoulder, which seemed satisfactory.

"Where are you from?"

"The UK. I live in Scotland."

"Do you have wife?"

"Yes."

"Is she here on the trek with you, or in Scotland?"

"Scotland."

"That is a shame for her." She increased the gap between us; now at least one existed.

"What about you, is your husband here? Is he a guide, perhaps?"

"No, he is in Kathmandu. He runs our other businesses." She shuffled a buttock a centimetre away.

"So, you run this place all alone?"

"I have a boy who helps me, he is in the kitchen." The other buttock now followed, she shouted a name and a boyish face appeared at the door curtain.

"That must be hard work, being here alone for the season?"

"Yes, but this is my business, I am used to it. I come here for the trekking season in September. I have one more month and then will close in December, it's too cold for trekkers then. I will open again in spring, for the trekkers and mountaineers. When I am here, my husband takes care of our trekking businesses in Kathmandu."

"Do you have any other family? Aren't they able to help out?"

"I have two sons, here, look at these pictures." Both buttocks jumped back towards me. We were shoulder to shoulder again as she placed her mobile in front of us and scrolled through her gallery, beaming.

"This is my older son; he is studying in Portland Oregon. A postgraduate degree in ICT. And here is my other son, he is also studying in the USA."

"What's he studying?"

"Business. Here is another picture of my first son, on his graduation." She flicked to a family portrait and Sangmu was transformed, regaled in finery and jewellery.

"Wow, you look fantastic in this picture. What's that jewellery?"

"It is called a Sherpa Star, made from gold and coral. It costs $20,000." The tea house business was clearly more lucrative than I thought, then – two children in American colleges and 20k of bling wasn't what I expected for the proprietor's lifestyle when I walked in.

"Hello, do you have a room for a good price?" asked one the Israelis. Sangmu nodded and unglued her hips from mine.

"I show you. Scotland-man, you come too."

"Hey, Scotland-man, how did you get here before us? We were ahead of you."

"Old age and treachery will always beat youth and exuberance, my friend." He was as nonplussed by my epigram as much as I was after I'd said it. Sangmu led us upstairs to our quarters, showing me to the mirrored corner suite with heart-shaped vibrating bed, decorated in red velvet cushions. The Israeli guys were to share the adjoining box.

The room followed her template, the freshly laundered duvets on the cots in keeping with the little details that made the lodge feel more homely. The cost was reasonable and there was a petty satisfaction to see the rate I'd agreed wasn't discounted any further for the arch-negotiator from Israel. Luggage deposited and room secured, we headed downstairs, Sangmu looking disappointed when I took up station at the table with the young men. We ordered a small pot of black tea, which came before we'd fully settled into our seats.

"So, what are you guys called, where are you from?"

"I'm Amos. I'm from Jerusalem and this is Noach, from the north. Do you want a coconut cookie to go with your tea?"

"I thought you'd finished them off? Yes, that would be nice."

"Amos always has coconut cookies, he's addicted."

"Where in the north are you from, Noach, by the sea of Galilee?"

"Not far, yes, I'm from Nazareth, you may have heard of it. Do you want some dates?"

"Wow, you guys are a walking larder. Where did you get dates?"

"We got them in Kathmandu, they're Iranian."

"Are you sure you're allowed to eat them, then?"

"No, we know we made a mistake and that's why we are feeding them to the gentile, ha-ha." The texture and sweetness of the dates reactivated my tastebuds after the trekking diet's sameness.

"These are exceptionally good."

"I hate to say it, but I agree. Here, take the bag."

"No, come on, I couldn't do that."

"No, really, I'll give you a special discount, ha-ha." He split the bag open and we munched our way through the fruit as we finished the small pot.

"We're going to walk over the glacier this afternoon, towards Chhukhung. We will see if we can get to Kongma La. Do you want to come with us?"

"Thanks for the offer, I'd love to go but wouldn't be able to keep up."

"What do you mean?! You beat us here and, besides, you don't look *that* old."

"Believe me, I feel it at the moment. I don't think I could keep up with a couple of guys who'd just graduated from professional couch potato school, never mind two who've been running around Negev obstacle courses in their budgie-smugglers for the last three years. I'm pretty done, to be honest, so thanks for offering, but I'm going to have some lunch and spend the afternoon in bed, I think." Sangmu looked up from her phone and cocked her head.

"We're going to head off now."

"What, before lunch?"

"Yes, I'm from Nazareth and we have some bread and a tin of tuna, so we won't go hungry. Ha-ha."

"Okay, good luck." Through the glazing I could see the boys head back down the trail and I ordered a vegetable noodle soup. It came without the vegetables and the boy in the kitchen was subject to the full vent of Sangmu's wrath. I was told to finish my bowl and it was soon replenished by another more in line with the original order.

"Boy made a mistake, there is no charge for this, for you."

"Don't worry, anyone can make a mistake."

"You will have some tea with Sangmu to make up."

"Okay." I finished the vegetable noodles – the boy had made up for his error, they were approaching Deurali standard – and Sangmu beckoned me over to take my tea.

"Here, for your face." She handed me a hot towel.

"Solar-powered facecloth, very good uh?" she explained.

"Yes, this is great." And wiping off the morning's grime was. Sangmu flicked through more family portraits and, as she explained who the aunts and uncles were, it became clear she was missing her family terribly. I got the impression she was bored with lodge life at 5,000 metres.

"When you close down in December, it must be difficult to know you still have a three-day walk to Lukla. I guess you fly to Kathmandu from there?"

"Three days! No, Lukla is two days. I am a real Sherpa lady!"

"Two days! You must walk quickly."

"It's all downhill, very easy for Sherpa people. Sometimes I go in helicopter, even quicker."

"That must be expensive?"

"When they have space for Sherpa lady, they charge same as for box of noodles, so it's not expensive. It is better coming back after the winter – I get helicopter to Dughla and walk two hours."

"I can see how that would be better. I've felt more than once that it would be nice to be in one of the helicopters I've seen flying up and down the valley."

"But I see you are a trekker! You show you are a strong man."

"I don't feel too strong at the moment. If you'll excuse me, I'm going to go to my room to rest for a while, I'll be back down in a couple of hours for some more tea." She nodded gently. Back in the room, I threw the covers off the velvet bedspread, fed a purse of coins into the slot for the love machine and got ready for action.

I increased my vocabulary fourfold with an hour of *Gnomon*, my cough gradually returning, and after an hour I was ready for a nap. I awoke, confused, and slightly panicked I'd missed dinner time as it was dark outside and cold in. I was relieved when I found it was only six o'clock and went down for Sangmu to greet me in the restaurant.

"Scotland-man, I thought you were coming back to see Sangmu? I was going to come and get you, I thought you must have a problem."

"Sorry, yes, I was feeling exhausted and fell asleep."

"You feel better now? Ready for dinner?"

"Yes, thanks." The tea house had filled up as I slumbered, with Amos and Noach sitting in the circle of a larger group. Two hirsute young men who'd passed me in knee-length Spandex on the trail up to Namche were settled into a corner. The Japanese super-slurper from Shomare was sucking up some soup through a straw at a table on his own.

I was invited over to the circle, the group all Israelis who'd recently completed their service in the Defence Force. Shimon had left the army still wearing his fatigues, by the looks of it. With his compact frame, half-peaked beanie hat and glasses, he was Radar from *M*A*S*H*, only more aquiline. I asked Yisrael if his name caused confusion when people asked.

"Yah, Yisrael from Israel, very funny."

As he seemed to bear that with good humour, I asked whether his parents had got fed up naming their kids and whether his siblings were called Xisrael and Zisreal; and then pushed it further to see if he had a brother whose name began with J. Yisrael was taller than Shimon and held himself in an unnecessary stoop in his yellow padded jacket.

Chava sat cross-legged in a beige fleece, her hair scraped back to emphasise a dream-catcher of earrings dangling from her lobes. Her friend Esther was quietly focussed on her hot drink and Lior robotically busied himself with a packet of Pringles, his focus to keep the crumbs from his dark curly beard. Amos was about to turn another bag of coconut cookies into crumbs.

"It is dark now and he's still not here." Noach said to Shimon.

"Yes, but we should give him time, until we've finished dinner."

"What's going on?" I asked.

"We met a Chinese guy on our way up to Kongma La. We said that we'd meet him here for dinner," Noach answered.

"And he hasn't showed up yet?"

"No."

"How long ago was that?"

"At around 3.30."

"How long did it take you to get back here, then, from where you met him?"

"An hour and a half, maybe a bit more, maybe a couple of hours."

"So he should've been here by now?" I queried, trying to work out the cause for their alarm.

"Yes, I think so but the guy was going really slowly, though."

"So, he may arrive at any moment?"

"Yes, but I'm worried because he had no food and not much water left when we met him. Amos fed him some coconut cookies to keep him going. Even though he was going slow, we think he should be here around now. We were thinking he may have got stuck, the way across the glacier isn't easy to find, even in the day."

"It's only just after six, he could've made it down. Are you sure he isn't here, in any of the other lodges in Lobouche? He sounds like he'd be exhausted; maybe by the time he got here he chose another lodge instead."

"No, we haven't checked," replied Shimon.

"Maybe an idea would be to order some dinner and, in the meantime go around town and check whether he's arrived anywhere," I suggested. "Your dinner will be waiting when you get back and, if he's in one of the other places, then it's all good."

"Yes, I agree, let's go guys." The Israeli men stood, grabbed their gloves and affixed their headtorches, Shimon the ranking officer and the rest following his orders. The light of their Petzls was soon lost behind the silhouette of the nearest lodge and I was left with the girls, Slurpy and the two other men.

"Damn, it's cold out there." It had taken 20 minutes to complete their door-to-door.

"Was he there?"

"No, no-one had seen him," reported Shimon. "I think we need to go and search for him on the glacier. We've come back to eat dinner quickly first."

"You're not thinking of going onto the glacier on your own, in the dark, are you?"

"Yes, we should go soon, it's so cold out there. If he's stuck on the glacier, he will freeze to death."

"Hang on a minute, Shimon, you don't know the glacier. You can't get lost out there as well, stuck on the glacier somewhere. You need some local guys who can guide you in the dark. If all you lot end up wandering around in the night not knowing where you are, God knows what could happen. Sangmu, do you think you could ask some of the villagers who know the trail across the glacier to Kongma La to help out?"

"Do you know this man is not in Lobouche?" she replied, with some dubiety.

"They have checked, Sangmu, he's not in the lodges. Could he be anywhere else? Maybe he came off the glacier and went the wrong way, down to Dughla instead, or went back to Chhukhung or Dingboche?"

"Not Chhukhung or Dingboche, it is too far from where the Israel-men saw him."

"Can you call the lodges in Dughla, to see if he's made it there?" She picked up her phone and 10 minutes later we'd ascertained the Chinese man hadn't made it to the Yak Lodge. There was a momentary hiatus while the Israelis bolted down their food.

"Can you organise some help from the local guys, Sangmu?"

"He is not in another place in Lobouche? I will make sure before I ask, the local people will be very angry with me if this man is in another lodge." She rang around but there was no sign of the man.

"Sherpas are coming now." Another 10 minutes passed before a trio, clothed for an Arctic night, bowled in.

"Okay, let's go," Shimon ordered. The Israelis stood to attention while the two other young men donned their outer layers, gloves and headtorches and Amos gave me a nod. He knew I wasn't joining the search party and I found myself disappointed to learn it had also been expected and accepted, unspoken between the group.

"Good luck." It was the best I could do, rationalising I wasn't well enough to go and help, that I'd be a burden to the younger and fitter men. That was true enough but also an excuse to hide my fear; I was afraid of being so slow as to risk being left behind on the glacier. If I hadn't had the excuse of my rasping cough and exhaustion, I wondered whether I'd still have ventured out into the dark to look for someone I'd never met, hoping I'd have gone but not sure I possessed the courage. As it was, I was left with the women and the Japanese man. He sat perplexed at his empty bowl watching the line of headlamps fade.

I didn't enjoy being left behind one bit, in the category of women and children. It hurt my pride, my machismo. Such shame would normally have been enough to send me out into the dark, macho peer pressure winning the day rather than any act of selfless nobility like the others had displayed. I was also hurt there was no offer or brokerage to involve me in the rescue attempt; the young men had considered me too old, too sick, a liability. I sat there telling myself to get over my pride, to accept the facts and hope the young men would be successful in the search.

Two hours passed from the expedition's start eating dhal baat with the girls, discussing life in Israel and where they were going to go next, but the small talk felt awkward and I went outside to scan the darkness for moving lights. I stomped my feet outside the door on the ice and wandered down to the corner of the next lodge, but there was nothing bar the barking of a dog. Back inside, we'd reached an uneasy silence when the door was flung open and one of the Sherpas said something to Sangmu.

"They found him."

Sangmu barked an order into the kitchen and the boy came into the diner with a Swastika box of dried dung. Sangmu fed some discs into the burner and, evidently frustrated, lifted the lid and tipped the whole box in, instructing me to fan the flames.

The door burst open again. The other two local men brought in a lithe-looking oriental man, dead-legged, supported between their shoulders. No more than a teenager, as he was placed by the fire, a Cheshire cat smile spread across his face. Sangmu forced a bottle of Coca-Cola into his hands and with a single glance told him to drink it all down. The rest of the search party was soon safely back in the room and gathered around the fire.

"It was the Canadian boys who found him," reported Amos.

"Where was he?"

"He was on the glacier, in his sleeping bag," explained the longer-haired Canadian. "He was almost in a crevasse or something, whatever you call it, and I saw his head light flashing."

"Yeah, and then I saw Jack heading up," said the other Canadian. "He looked like he was cutting across the trail, up away, so I just followed him. The local guys were off to the right, but I shouted them over. It was down to them that they got us back safely."

Sangmu brought out a large pot and made sure everyone received a cup before a snickers bar was forced down the Chinese man, followed by some tea with honey. The search party members were justifiably ecstatic, their excitement building more and more as they recounted the rescue. Noach and the Canadian men circling around, high fiving everyone, laughing as they went.

"Well done, guys. You are real heroes." I congratulated them, delighted they'd made the rescue but conflicted that I hadn't really been part of it. My involvement had consisted of advising the Israelis not go out without guidance, but no more than that. In my mind that had been nowhere near enough. I was sure Norgay would have been first out of the door regardless of his own condition.

Still, I reckoned they were something, those folks who'd gone out and risked their necks on the glacier. I was convinced the Chinese man, who'd now regained some colour in his cheeks, had had a close scrape. I was glad that he was grateful; when he'd recovered enough, he thanked everyone again and again.

Sangmu treated the locals to a tot of whiskey before insisting the rescued man finished off a plate of dhal baat as more rescue details emerged. The man had left Chhukhung at 9.30 rather than the 7am recommended, not realising there was going to be nowhere to eat, and little or no water, along the way. He was tired by the time he'd crossed Kongma La and, because he hadn't eaten, got into difficulties on the descent. He had reached the glacier at nightfall and had reasoned it was the lesser of two evils to tuck himself up for the night in his sleeping bag and start again in the morning, rather than risk falling into a crevasse in the dark.

Despite Sangmu's protestations many a person had spent a night on the bare mountain, I believed the search party had as likely as not saved the young man's life. He was lucky to have had the bravery of the combined Israeli Defence Force and Canadian Hippy Trekking League to count on. An hour of congratulations later, I thought to take my leave and let the heroes enjoy their moment. I returned to my room and looked for something to calm me down, my choice falling on the title track of *Hotel California* by Eagles. An hour later, I was ready for sleep; it was 11pm.

The night was a poor one, although not as poor as the Chinese man's could've worked out, my improvised spittoon brimming in the morning. What sleep I had was in fits and starts and I was awake long before dawn, so I sat in my sleeping bag, waiting for daybreak and the chance to try to work the infection from my lungs on the day's hike. It became evident Noach was suffering a milder version of the same thing – as I joined the queue for the bathroom, he let an unheroic gob of phlegm fly from the landing window.

I had to break the ice on the outside Western Style and the water butt used for flushing, but was more than pleasantly surprised to record in the *Diaries* my first Type Three for a while, less pleased to cut my finger on the water butt's rusted rim. I ate a breakfast of soupy rice pudding with a bandaged hand.

After a milk coffee, hugs and shakes of everyone's hands, I was ready for the off. There was no sign of the hapless Chinese man; Sangmu told me he was still sleeping, and she wouldn't let him out of his bedroom that day. Wondering *exactly* what she meant by that, I set off with the relief of a clear head and, even more reassuringly, no sign of the dry heaving that had plagued me for so many days.

I descended through the village and crossed over the stream under a blue sky. A washing area had been constructed among the rocks and black hoses sprouted off to all quarters of the village, the remnants of a film of ice clinging to its sides. On the other bank, I started my ascent and was soon at the sign for the turn-off to the Italian Pyramid. The Italian Pyramid: I thought it sounded like a team sport from one of Berlusconi's *bunga bunga* parties and was thankful the sign didn't sport a picture of Silvio mid-game.

"Hey ... alreet man."

"Hey, it's the shitheads! How are you doing? Have you done it, made it to Base Camp?"

"Wae'aye man. Beys Comp yesterdiy and Kala Pattar this monin."

"Congratulations. What's it feel like to have made it?"

"Marvellous, like, we anly went hulf-wey oop Kala, smashin' view from theyar, mind."

"I'll make it there tomorrow, hopefully."

"Aye, youse'll be reet, mon. Wearin' that Mackem hat guarantees last pleys, but at least youse'll finish, like."

"Ha-ha. See you for a game of cards in Namche or Lukla, maybe?"

"That'd be alreet, but I think we're gaan a different way home, man. Portsee or some other pleys," interjected Joao.

"Yazh fookin' spanner, Joao. That's on the wey. Hoo ya gaan to get hame if we divnae go via Lukla? Fookin' start flappin' ya wings an' hoop ye land in Kathmandu, like?"

"Well, congratulations again, lads, see you downslope." I plodded on into a boulder field, the trail holding level as it wound its way through it. Ahead rose the icy shark's tooth of Pumori, beneath its peak the path rising sharply on the muddy brown of a moraine. I thought I could make out the half-silhouettes of people on the top; it seemed a long way off and much steeper than I'd hoped for. Lobouche sat at over 4,900 metres, Gorak Shep a tad below 5,200, so I'd expected a slow, steady climb up the valley; but it wasn't going to be, this amounted to another straight up 100 metres of pain.

As I neared the obstacle, I became increasingly downcast, dwelling on my lack of participation in the previous night's rescue, the same doubts surfacing about my suitability to be here as those which had bothered me at the Peaceful. I genuinely wondered if age wasn't just a number and I was too old to be doing this kind of thing; the search party had returned from hours of scrabbling around in the dark bounding with energy, and I'd struggled to make it up the stairs back to my room.

It felt like a watershed moment as I neared the base of the climb – I was among some of the most dramatic scenery the world could serve up and yet I wasn't able to enjoy it. My mind was focussed on the slog the walking had become, the pain in breathing, and now I was about to put myself through yet another rocky scramble. 'Why the hell am I doing this again?' I kept asking myself against a constant background murmur of, 'I could die of AMS here'. These thoughts followed a natural path to, 'If I called it quits now, then it was a good effort,' and I stood, head down, hand on a boulder for support at the bottom of the moraine and considered turning back. The urge to quit battled with, 'Come on, get a grip, you're almost there, fancy going home and saying you nearly made it, you were only a few hours away. Join the ranks of yet another famous (in your own lunchtime) English failure.'

"Hello you. 'Ow are ya doin', love?" While I'd been wrangling internally, a long train of trekkers had descended the dusty eroded into the slope and mulled around where I stood. I raised my eyes and my spirits were lifted by the sight of the same spare tyres and beer bellies that had offered me encouragement at the Hillary Bridge.

"I'm not feeling so great, but I'll tell you what, one of those Fox's Glacier Mints would help a lot, if you've got any?"

"Good to see yar still a cheeky buggar, love. 'Ere you go, take an 'andful, I've got loads left," Sian graciously offered.

"Thanks, you're a lifesaver." I popped a sweet into my mouth.

"Have you been to the top, then?" I asked, struggling to get the mint to rotate in the dryness of my mouth.

"Yer, everyone made it to Base Camp yesterday and three of us went up Kala Pattar this mornin'," Gareth answered.

"Congratulations, you must be chuffed?"

"Yer. It was great to do it, like, but I'm glad we're goin' back now. We're pretty knackered. I don't know if you remember Charlie, the young boy? He made it to Base Camp with us yesterday but was taken ill when he got back to Gorak. They had to helivac him back to Kathmandu in the afternoon."

"Oh shit, have you heard from him? Is he okay?"

"Yer, he's fine. They put 'im on oxygen and he was right as rain in a few 'ours, they reckon. I bet he'll be in the pub this evenin', braggin' about his exploits to any girl who'll hear 'im. I wish I was with 'im, like. Anyway, there's our guide tellin' us to get goin'. Good luck, Daft Hat, keep goin', you're nearly there now."

As they hooped the wristbands of their poles, I started the climb, my doubt from five minutes ago replaced by a nothingness of determination. I'd show the kindly Welsh people I was going to make it, if for nothing more than not to let them down. No internalised Rocky Balboa hurrah of 'I'm going to do it' accompanied my ascent, my mood more akin to a small boy showing his dad he could climb the ladder to the treehouse all by himself. I made it to the top, ribcage pounding and gasping for air, the Welsh group now lost in the distance. I popped another mint into my mouth and took a moment to admire Pumori and thought 'What was I thinking about calling it a day? Have a look at that, for feck's sake, you feckin' pillock!'

Stunted grasses were all that grew here now, and then only sporadically. Over a steep precipice to my right was the glacier grinding its way down the valley. It was mostly grey rock, the texture of a child who has rolled in the sand after swimming in the sea. Where the ice had stressed and smashed itself, rock cones angled up into hummocks, revealing an underbelly of white, while floes melted away from the edges of frozen ponds.

The canal of ice cut through the terrain in a trench that couldn't be far from collapsing in on itself. I was soon walking on a single-lane path through an area of the same, the Changri Shar glacier's terminal moraine. The trail snaked its way through boulders and rocks marked by cairns, the landscape seemingly alive. Pebbles bounced at me from above, the ground groaned and creaked and I could hear scree avalanches tipping themselves onto the ice not far below. I sensed the way crossed something unstable, the uncertainty of the glacier itself, and wondered if terminal moraines were named in honour of trekkers who'd dallied too long on their shifting forms.

The going was a dangerous undulation – fresh carvings of avalanches left sections offering an uninterrupted cliffside view of the fall below. I tried to put that out of my mind as I descended into a cleft in the moraine. Steeling myself for a climb around an exposed shoulder of rock, Paiya La came to mind once more. I made way for a train of dzhos and took my chance, falling into their slipstream with the reasoning that if their bulk could pass through safely on the narrow track, so could I. After the turn, the path was on a ridge less treacherous. I could see lodges at the bottom of a long, steep slope, down which I trudged. Unhesitatingly, I selected the first lodge. The guidebook had indicated that, from Lobouche, it would be a two-and-a-half-hour trek to Gorak Shep; three-and-a-quarter hours after leaving, I'd arrived.

Gorak Shep to Gorak Shep

The lodge was an untidy agglomeration of buildings that appeared to have been sown organically into the dust, nothing new about their blue tin roofs or grey stone walls. Entry was a zigzag through a courtyard into a corridor that served both a wing of rooms from a right angle at one end and the door to the reception-diner at the other. I dropped my pack and headed to enquire about a room.

The man at the corner counter was busy totting up his takings and cross-checking them against what had been written in each room's order book. It took him a while to acknowledge me, his way of doing so to sniff at a young man who was syphoning salt from part-used shakers into full cellars and refilling the empty ones. Why didn't he unscrew them all and fill them up from halfway?

The salt man beckoned me back through the doorway and down the corridor to a blue door without uttering a word. He stood, waiting for my nod, an offer of take it or leave it. He knew I was too exhausted to leave it, which was unfortunate as what lay behind the door was, without a doubt, the least inviting room to which I'd been shown on the trek. Built into the hillside, the cell's only light came from a paperback-sized porthole built into the stone above the single bed. The three other wooden walls were in various states of decay but had in common the fact that the feet of their planks were rotted by damp. The cot was covered by a bedsheet in an over-washed, Y-front grey that had been stretched to ripping point, while the only light, a neon tube, cackled above.

It was midday, but the chamber was cold, so cold the miniature portal still held fast a frame of ice for its watercolour of condensation. It was as if the blueprint for an oubliette had been turned on its side and built by a bunch of cowboys. It did nothing for my mood, but I reckoned I could tolerate it for one night.

My plan was to eat lunch and make my way to Base Camp before trying for Kala Pattar the next morning, thus minimising my stay in the lodge. So I returned to the restaurant to take a seat, waiting to be served. The diner was set out in a similar way to many others but was more function over form, booths aligned against each wall ice cream parlour style. A replica of Lobouche's burner sat unlit in its centre. A split-door serving hatch was set into the wall next to the counter and a table for condiments and cutlery stood next again.

The youth who'd shown me to my room eventually finished with the salt, picked up a laminated menu and placed it on the table. I ordered a small pot of lemon tea as my cough returned at double amplitude. Half an hour later, there was no sign of it and the trekkers who'd entered the room in dribs and drabs after me were lunching. If being made to wait for the salt cellar work to finish before I could place my order hadn't left me in good humour, I was now more than cheesed off. I swivelled on my bench and asked the boy where my tea was, the question posed more towards the aggressive rather than assertive end of the scale. He looked embarrassed and my tea was with me within a minute.

The act of drinking seemed to take an unreasonable amount of effort, only calming my coughing marginally. I realised I was approaching exhaustion. I hoped a double helping of noodle soup would be my salvation. I so strode up to the counter and made myself clear to the boss I wanted two bowls of noodle soup, one garlic and one vegetable, as soon as. He remained mute and signalled to the youth again.

The striding had been a mistake; I almost collapsed back onto my bench. The boy took my order and I sat back with my tea prepared for a long wait, in which he didn't disappoint. I twice had to pull him up to remind him I'd ordered and a good 30 minutes later my food arrived. The vegetable noodle soup was devoid of anything remotely organic. The garlic noodle soup was equally lacking in its top-of-the-bill ingredient, instead flavoured by a full grinder of peppercorns. I sent both back and the youth returned with my vegetable noodle soup, to which had now been added a floating piece of cabbage. The garlic noodle soup followed soon afterwards beneath a similar arrangement of a couple of unpeeled cloves of garlic. I hadn't realised how easy it was to get boiling water, instant noodles, chopped veggies and some seasoning so wrong but understood I was now being taught an expert lesson by someone with a doctoral thesis in ineptitude.

I forced myself to finish, something I'd never contemplated I'd need to do with noodle soup. I got up, thinking at least it would fuel my attempt at Base Camp that afternoon, but by the time I was twisting the key in my padlock, that thought had been dispelled. The walk along the corridor had been an ordeal and I needed to rest, so I squeezed into my sleeping bag, deciding I'd give it an hour before trying for Base Camp, there being enough light left in the day. Three hours later, I awoke, shivering.

I'd missed my chance, but I wasn't too downhearted – I'd make Base Camp in the morning and try for halfway up Kala Pattar as the Geordie guys had done. Although I was cold, the sleep had done me some good. It satisfied me that putting on my boots hadn't left me exhausted. It was only five, but I figured by the time I'd placed my order for dinner and been served, it would be bedtime, so I returned to the restaurant and took a space in the one remaining booth.

The evening crowd resembled a cross between a disaster relief reportage and the finish line at a marathon. Those guests not shuffling about in the confused slow-mo of a newly resurrected zombie moved around as if fast-forwarded from table to table. The head-bowed walking dead stared, obsidian-eyed, into their steamy drinks; the finishers sloshed theirs as they gesticulated in an exaggerated semaphore.

A pair of old age pensioners signalled they'd like to take the place opposite me. The lady resembled a non-airbrushed Nana Mouskouri. Her husband was harder to assess due to the black wraparounds he sported between his salt-and-pepper goatee and slouch cap. It was clear to see he'd been educated as a gentleman, though, and after showing her the bench, he attempted to help his wife into her seat.

She was unsteady – whether from her advanced years, the demands of the trek or both – and her first buttock hadn't made the cushion before she slipped and lost her grip on their combined walking poles. They scattered and skittered across the floor, spearing the boot of a 26-miler. He was explaining to an uninterested automaton opposite how his stride pattern had allowed him to achieve a personal best.

The accident quietened the room in an Old West-saloon-piano-player-stops-playing sort of silence, the collective attention directed towards Nana. I expected her to well up in embarrassment, but she was made of sterner stuff. If I'd envisaged a melodious, light jazz tone to her voice, I couldn't have been further from the mark. She directed a guttural bark toward her husband. He gathered the poles, sat down beside her and took off his sunglasses to reveal a second pair. I wondered whether that served some practical purpose or if he was just beyond Beatnik cool. He rubbed the under-glasses, which took the form of *Django Unchained* circles, and slid them back up his nose. I thought there was no doubt about it – despite the pole episode, Nana and Django Senior were the epitome of hip.

Unfortunately, the UN Emergency Hospitality Commission hadn't been able to helicopter in its crack relief waitering squad between lunch and dinner and the service remained dire. Django had recited Allen Ginsberg's entire repertoire and was gearing up for a creole rendition of Kerouac, accompanied by Nana on damyin, before any of the hapless staff had paid us any attention.

I ordered a tomato pizza, my logic being that if the chef could make a mess of noodle soup everything else would be equally inedible but at least I'd be able to pick at the base if he burned the cheese. Nana was completing the post-production for her latest double album, a Cambodian throat-singing of *Naked Lunch* set to Galician gaitas, when the waiter returned bearing a cone of charcoal. I was wrong about the base being edible. I picked my way through what I could and ruminated over ordering a dhal baat, aware it was possibly a life-or-death decision: would I have died of AMS by the time my order was completed?

The conversation had been stunted with Nana and Django. Between adding to their oeuvre, they only had the odd word of English, while German wasn't a language in which I'd yet managed to acquire my customary abjectness. They finished their dinner of feta cheese and beetroot salad, downed their last glasses of retsina, tossed their crumpled empty packets of Gitanes into the wastepaper bin and sauntered off.

As I waited for my replacement dinner of dhal baat, I was joined by the French lady I'd met in Bhandar. She looked worn. She had no English, so she was going to have to suffer my attempts at a language in which I'd a master's degree (distinction) in failure.

"How are you?" I nailed that one, thinking so far, so good.

"Tired."

"Today, go you to Everest Base Camp?" She must have considered that was close enough to merit a response.

"Yes."

"Go, Kala Pattar?"

"Yes."

"Very good! Tired very? The mountain is big." I exuded nursery dialogue, but I'd settle for that.

"Yes." Were my attempts at the language of love so execrable that all she could summon were single-word answers, or was she as tired as I was? I decided to change the subject to something with which she'd have to engage.

"Your daughters. Sickness. What is happening?" I queried, convinced I'd nailed it in perfect Parisian.

"My daughters?" She looked perplexed and I worried maybe I hadn't nailed it after all.

"Yes."

"I don't have any children." That was harsh, I thought: just because she'd made it to EBC and they hadn't didn't mean she had to disown her kids.

"The two girls, at Bhandar. Your daughters?"

"Ah, you misunderstand, sir, they aren't my daughters. They're friends who are trekking together. They're from Marseilles but I'm from Besançon, we met on the first day of the trek."

"Oh, sorry. I thinked you are their mothers."

"No."

"Therefore, what is happening? Sickness of mountain?"

"Yes, the doctor said they must descend and they went down with Matthieu. He phoned my porter to tell us they're well." Well, I reasoned, at least that was something.

The UN Emergency Hospitality Commission Sikorsky must have been using the latest stealth technology and the Special Ops team completed their silent mission in the kitchen as two orders of dhal baat arrived in less than an hour; it was impossible otherwise.

I was grateful for the food's arrival – it was passable and it was proving a real strain to try to keep the Gallic going. We managed to place an order for a small pot when a culinary Ethan Hunt disguised as a clueless waiter came to clear our plates. As we shared the small pot, the conversation faded out and the lady from Besançon opened her puzzle book and got to work with her pencil. As I supped my tea, I couldn't help but think any new arrivals to the restaurant would think we were a couple in the comfort of a dull marriage of 30 years.

After what I considered was a reasonable time not to be thought rude and jealous of the excitement of her word finder, I retired to the icebox. I started on my own Puzzle Pad, only to find my brain couldn't cope with the effort and I put down my first attempt within five minutes. I hoped music wouldn't be too much and chose to play *The Original Movie Soundtrack Saturday Night Fever* by Various Artists from the start. If this were to be my last night on Earth, I'd go out dancing on a bellyful of dhal baat. An hour later, I was ready to sleep; it was 9pm.

My cough kept me awake through the night. After paying a visit to the latrines, what sleep I could grab was haunted by the Dantesque scene I'd encountered there. I knew it was difficult to hit the bullseye on a Squat Style at the best of times, but thought it was easy enough to aim at least somewhere in the vicinity. I could see how the black verglas would be worrisome – I wouldn't have liked to slip inside the cubicle either – but how fellow trekkers could think it acceptable to leave an unnavigable maze of stinking mounds leading up to and inside the stalls was beyond me. I'd gone for a number one and ended up gagging up my dhal baat. The only positive side-effect was I'd nothing left to digest and didn't need to return before breakfast.

I was early into the diner and took a seat next to the condiments, thinking I couldn't fail to attract a waiter's attention in such a prime location. But I hadn't counted on a successful overnight counter-insurgency against the UN Emergency Hospitality Commission by the Gorak Shep People's Revolutionary Garçons. It took 40 minutes to place my order for jam on toast and a milk tea.

The Nepali standard for jam on toast was two slices of dry toast accompanied by a pair of silver cups, one of butter, one of jam. My toast came, but without the accompaniments, and I pointed this out to a GSPRG. He looked at me with an exasperated expression that said 'What kind of Western neo-colonialist dogma is this? How dare this imperialist dog demand *actual* coverings for his bread?' He was even less impressed when he returned with the jam and I asked him for a knife to spread it with.

I sat and nursed my milk tea, munching desultorily on my toast, until the majority of my breakfast companions had left. I wasn't in the right frame of mind for the trek to Base Camp; the tiredness, sickness and cold had got to me. I ventured back down the corridor to gather my things with more of a resigned 'Let's finish this effing thing' rather than 'I'm going to Everest Base Camp today; it's going to be awesome', but failed to even reach the door of my room.

I'd be forever grateful to the poor sod who'd hosed down the lavatories down before I arrived. With the turd obstacle path's removal, the correct trajectory of my vomit was therefore easy to calculate. The expulsion was immediately followed by stomach cramps, but I was grateful to record a Type Four in the *Diaries*. I spent the next hour in my room before I had the motivation and energy to don my gear.

The lodge's insistence water needed purchasing did little to improve my humour, nor did its price. If the old lady at Sagbanda was the ultimate hill-shark, the owner of this lodge had to be a mountain-orca. So I set off down past the dried lakebed in a mood that more befitted a journey to meet with Her Majesty's Revenue and Customs to discuss the finer points in one's accrual accounting than it did an ascent to the top of the world.

The snows summiting the bowl of mountains were glossy under the greys of the sky. I trudged up through white dust to cross the lakebed and around the shoulder of Kala Pattar. I found the rhythm of a grumpy reverie as I traipsed up a long ridge of scree. Apart from a mottling of moss and a solitary clump of grass or two, all here was battleship grey rock and enamel white. The well-trodden, undulating path was marked by cairns. The place didn't feel hostile, or at least not as hostile as it should, given my experiences downhill and what the West Country men had told me about the French trekker.

"Hey, Lee, you look like you need a coconut cookie?" I gratefully accepted Amos' offer. It appeared the entire Israeli Defence force was going to complete this exercise together.

"Where did you guys get to yesterday? Any more rescues?"

"Ha-ha. No, we climbed Kala Pattar."

"Congratulations. I hope the views were worth it?"

"Yes, it's amazing! But it is also very hard. We got to the lodge near dark and Esther was dead at the end." The group swivelled in sympathy in her direction and she nodded sheepishly.

"I'm going to see how I feel after Base Camp and then maybe try later or head back down."

"Okay. Well, see you at Base Camp, then." And with that, the formation moved out. I was envious of their vitality, even poor Esther, who was their weakest and yet was wearing seven league boots compared to the pace I was setting.

The scree's undulations continued, and I passed a rusted oil drum topped with a coolie hat painted to decree it was proudly part of the Namche recycling effort. I didn't envy the local bin man this pickup.

A cairn directed me downslope to the right and I could make out colours among the grey. I was now on the glacier proper where pockets and puddles of ice were scattered amongst the ground grey of dust and rock. I picked my way across pebbling and the colours became more distinct: prayer flags. Nearer, I could see they were strung from two boulders that drew my eyes to a rock in their centre. The rock was an inverted Chinese spoon, its bowl supported by a melting block of ice and cairn pillars. Spray painted in blood red on its side was:

'EVEREST BASE CAMP 5364m'

The morning's angst and grumpiness dissolved as it dawned on me I'd made it; in its place came a warming sense of peace and, as if to celebrate with me, the sun broke through the clouds and a clear blue soon surrounded the bowl. I hadn't known what to expect to feel if I reached Base Camp; something akin to a fist-pumping high-five moment or a cursory, numb acknowledgement before turning back perhaps? I was aware the former would be out of character – subconsciously, I'd deem it not befitting of the place – and so reasoned the latter more probable; but in reality it was neither, more a sensation of deep tranquillity.

I had Base Camp to myself, which I considered was in keeping with my trek – the journey had been alone and it seemed fitting I should arrive solo. I sat down on a rock and breathed in the serenity, my mind turning to what it meant to be sitting here and what had inspired me, the Hillary-Norgay expedition. I imagined the contrast with how the glacier must have appeared on their arrival 66 years earlier – the commotion of 100 Sherpas cooking dhal baat, making tea, setting up tents and affixing the paraphernalia that goes with a military operation. For their expedition, Base Camp was the start, not the destination. So I thought their emotions must have been the polar opposite of mine: excitement and trepidation rather than quietude.

The mountaineers had almost three-and-a-half kilometres more to climb from where I was sitting on my rock. Although my trek up from the Swiss Bridge at the Dudh Kosi equated to roughly the same ascent, the two weren't comparable. It was only then the nature of their accomplishment became real to me, what the phrase 'superhuman feat' meant: to make it to the top of all that ice and rock was something far beyond my comprehension. I was humbled to have been able to follow in their footsteps to reach this point, to have followed them along the old way to Everest Base Camp. I was happy with that – it was more than enough.

I wasn't sure if it was the air's thinness or the ataraxia, but my vision seemed enhanced and I found myself seeing in a kind of hyper-lucidity; everything was more vivid. The legendary Khumbu Ice Fall's seracs spilled down, whites whiter than white, from a high place on to the glacier ahead. Encircling me were the peaks of some of the highest places on earth, universally magnificent; underfoot, the glacier quietly creaked and groaned like an old schooner straining at its moorings.

The post-rescue doubt and despondency of Lobouche had evaporated with my repose, the inner challenge of my right to be on the mountain met. I'd almost convinced myself I was too old and too sick to belong here, but I was here regardless, and I wondered what that meant, if anything. I knew the rescue was by far the finer achievement, a story more worthy of telling than my trek, but at the same time knew without doubt reaching Base Camp was something with which I could be satisfied. I'd seen the EBC trek described as nothing more than a strenuous walk but my experience had been far more difficult, the journey something far richer for it. So while I rested there, on my stone, I couldn't help but feel quietly exultant.

The guidebook had warned me to expect to be disappointed by Base Camp – nothing there, it said – but as I sat there in the warming sun, I couldn't agree. The scenery around was astounding in all its brilliance and the sense of peacefulness worthy of any destination. In my estimation, it was the perfect spot and I reckoned even the lower-case notation for the 'm' on the EVEREST BASE CAMP graffiti was spot on.

Footsteps behind me broke my reverie; I'd dallied long enough and so there was only one thing left to do before I returned. I opened my day pack to take out the Rabbid so we could take the picture for my daughter but found he hadn't deigned to make the trip, presumably remaining cosy in my backpack at the lodge. I was disappointed but it didn't spoil my mood; my daughter would understand and, if not, there was always Photoshop.

To my left, I heard the unmistakable throat-clearing vowels of Dutch being spoken. This was another one of my failed languages, although in the past I'd learned how to order a liquorice pancake while bicycling, so at least I'd mastered the basics. Failing that, I knew if I interjected *lekker* at every other word in my sentences, the average Dutch person would be so amazed to hear anyone speak their language they'd ignore my other mumblings.

The ladies who were speaking were the epitome of the non-politically correct poster image of milkmaids of the Netherlands tourist board of yesteryear. So, I figured I was on solid ground that they came from the low countries. Either that, or they were a couple of linguistic perverts who were conjugating obscure verbs in one of the more grammatically obtuse languages on the planet.

"Could I ask you to take a photograph, please?" I asked in my best Nederlands. At least, I thought that is what I asked, in what I thought was their language. They both looked at me with an unblinking, unbelieving stare.

"A photograph, please?" This was met again with wide eyes. I didn't think my pronunciation could've been any better and so concluded that they were probably shocked I'd said please.

"A photograph?"

"Ah, are you schhpeakink Dutch wisch us?!" The taller milkmaid asked, in English of course, but I wasn't to be defeated so easily and continued in Dutch.

"Yes." They seemed to recognise the validity of my pronunciation.

"No problem. Hop up on dat rock. Wit de schijn. I'll take it der."

"Hop up that rock? I can hardly even stand up! Thank you, though, could you take it here, please?" I asked, back in my native tongue.

"Der you go."

"Thank you."

"Zo, you schhpeak some Nederlands?"

"A little bit." I was being modest; in reality I could order any kind of pancake.

"Datsch unuschual. Not many people can schpeak our beautiful language."

"I spent a bit of time in Holland."

"Den why aren't you fluentsch in it, den?" she joked.

"I think it's quite a difficult language."

"Ja. We haaf 40 per schent de English words and we schay dem in a foony English acshent, den we haaf 40 per schent de German words and schay dem in a foony German acshent and den de udder 20 per schent are de French words, we schay dem in a micschture of foony English and German acschents. Ha-ha."

"Ha-ha, yes, that's what I mean, and that's before you get to the grammar."

"Ah, dat's easy, we joosht make dat up asch we go along."

"I could never get my head around those split verbs like 'Opbellen'. I never knew where to put the bell and the op."

"It goes where you feel like, like I sched, we make it up asch we go along."

"Thanks again for the photo." Their guide had returned from a trip to the moraine at the glacier's far side and they were heading back. I sat back down and couldn't resist quietly enjoying the sun for another half an hour, wondering why the Israelis hadn't passed me by. They were likely at the top of the icefall, Amos having confirmed his ration of coconut cookies sufficient for an expedition to recover all the abandoned gear on the Western Cwm before lunchtime.

It was time to head back myself; my elation had masked how hard it was to breathe while sitting there. The ascent back up to the ridge pulled me back to reality, as I had to complete it in sets of three steps at a time. The two Canadian rescuers passed me in the opposite direction, having scaled Kala Pattar that morning. They told me that, after Base Camp, they were going straight back down as far as they could make it.

I fared no better with my walking when back on the ridge and the Canadians had soon passed me again in the same direction. By the time I rounded Kala Pattar's shoulder, I was having to rest after every step for twice the length of time it had taken me to make it. By the dry lakebed's end I was shot. I shuffled up the small incline to the lodge in half-steps, but wouldn't suffer the shame of inching along the courtyard and so reached the door gulping for air. The guidebook had indicated that, from Gorak Shep, it would be a six-hour round trip to Base Camp; somewhat incredulous, four hours after leaving, with my return, I'd arrived.

Gorak Shep to Pheriche

The manager was waiting in the lobby, not seeming at all pleased to see me. I'd checked out that morning, agreeing I'd check back in if I were going to try Kala Pattar in the afternoon or next morning. It shouldn't have been an unwelcome or wholly unexpected surprise when I creaked back into view. I surmised that he was the Gorak Shep Linguistic Perverts Society's chairperson and the Dutch milkmaids had ratted me out on one of my mis-conjugations of one of the myriad of verbs used to describe eating Gouda. He vented his fury.

"I have let your room go, now I have to find you another one." But my cheeriness at having made Base Camp couldn't be broken, his chagrin the first thing in a couple of hours I took effortlessly in my stride. There wasn't much scope for my room to be downgraded but I'd marvelled at Nepali ingenuity before, so I crossed my fingers as he took me back towards the oubliette. My upgraded suite was upstairs. It was a wooden box that must have seen work as a double for the cooler in *The Great Escape*. I dumped my stuff, grabbed my catcher's mitt and got to work on the baseball.

Two hours later, I emerged more like Steve McQueen after his stint in solitary in *Papillon*. Drained again, the hacking cough had returned as I rested. The ascent to Kala Pattar was out of the question that afternoon. The cough was enough to convince me that, unless I was remarkably improved in the morning, I wouldn't risk it the following day, either. I shuffled back to the restaurant, hoping a serving of fast food would sort me out.

The diner was empty save a couple of hesitant Asian folks who looked like they'd opted out of whatever challenge had been set for them by their guide. They looked numbed. They doubtless thought the same of me, with the addition of dirty, smelly and looking way too pleased with himself.

I'd undergone something life-changing that morning. Like a shy teenager who'd finally 'done it', I'd lost my Base Camp virginity and could now sit smugly, full in the knowledge of her ways. I could tell they hadn't 'done it' yet by their lack of confidence in their surroundings. I hoped they hadn't got this far to find they couldn't make it any further; that would be agony. I made to give them a thumbs-up but thought better of it. I didn't want to patronise them, even though they couldn't have known where I'd been.

The GSPRG must have declared the afternoon a national holiday, perhaps to celebrate a victory in the march against preserves, as there were no serving staff to be found. I placed my order of garlic noodle soup, careful to emphasise with the chairperson it should contain at least one clove of garlic, throwing in a split infinitive while doing so just to annoy him. It appeared I'd got my message across because the soup, when it came, tasted vaguely of something, possibly even garlic. But by 3pm, the restaurant had gained no customers and, in the absence of anyone to listen to my boasts of becoming a man, I returned to my cupboard to read. My brain couldn't manage it and I closed my eyes, hoping 40 winks would help with revitalisation.

I don't know why I was shocked it was dark outside when I awoke, it was becoming a habit. It was dinner time, another opportunity to strut my stuff among those unsullied by the carnal knowledge of EBC. Someone had rewound to the place in the restaurant scene from the previous day, only this time I saw the theatre for what it was – the zombies were those hoping to get lucky and the finishers those who had.

I figured the Israelis must have decided to make an igloo for the night somewhere around Camp IV as there was no sign of them, and so I took up a place in the only booth with a bench free. My companions were an older man and younger lady who, from their appearance, were either father and daughter or monozygotic twins who'd experienced vastly different exposure to sunlight.

"Have you done it yet?" I titillated.

"Yeah, mhate, we wir at Base Camp dis avvy," answered the more crinkled of the two.

"You're Scousers?!" I exclaimed.

"Yeh. I'm Brian and dis is me doorther, Angela."

"Me too, I'm Lee."

"Yer dewn't sound it, mhate."

"No, I haven't lived in Liverpool for nearly 50 years. Bloody hell, did I just say that? I hadn't realised it until then."

"Dewn't knoew if yer still qualify, den. Are yer a red or a blew?"

"Red."

"Well den, yer definitely dewn't qualify, la!"

"Bloody hell, I've trekked all this way and got to 5,000 metres and I have to meet a bloody Toffee!" I laughed in mock disgust.

"Evertoneyan to yews nonbelievers, please, mhate. Sew, where dew you live now den, like?"

"Glasgow."

"Dat's a bit like Liverpewl but widtout de weather, isen i'?"

"Yeah, pretty much, plus at the moment, the second-best team in the city plays in blue as well, but they don't moan about it as much as you lot. Mind you, they've got Stevie G in charge now and he seems to be doing a good job, maybe Everton should try the same thing, get Jamie Carragher to come and manage you."

"Ha-ha. Neow way, I'd rader av Marco Silva than Carra an' dat's seyin somethin'."

It seemed the GSPRG Day of National Unity Against Conserves had ended but, by the paucity of staff around, had been replaced by wildcat strike action. They amounted to a skeleton of picket-breakers on duty and I managed to collar a non-union man as he ignored past.

"Could I have a hot orange and plate of chips for myself and two portions of the finest seasoned stew of beef, potatoes, carrots and onions for the proper Scousers over there, please." The manager temporarily fulfilling a union job was, unsurprisingly, non-plussed by my request.

"Dewn't listen to the plazzy Scouser over der, mhate, tew vegetable newdels and black tees fher us, please." The manager nodded his comprehension. I reckoned that some achievement as 'TOO YOUNG' still struggled with the Liverpudlian accent after 17 years.

"So, how did you find the trek?"

"We're glad we came, ahren't we Ange, luv?"

"Yeh." She nodded.

"Bu' never again, like. It's tew cold an' derhty. Ange's noews can't stop runnin' and I cahn't breathe arfada time. Tew be 'onest, we're a bi' fhed up and we'll be glad to get backh tew Kathmandu for a shower an' den 'ohme."

"Me too. I was knackered at Base Camp and even more when I got back here. I wish I'd done a lot more training – somehow carrying

10 kilos of books in my backpack seven miles along the West Highland Way to the pub didn't prepare me for this."

"Yeh, bu' at least yew've go' some mountains to practiss on wir youse live, all we've go' is Billinge Hill an' dat only takes an hour."

"Yeah, I know it well. The crazy thing is that I've been taking around one-and-a-half times what the guidebook says I should to get places, but today I did the round trip in four hours and the guidebook says it should take six."

"I think dey might 'ave mooved de camp a bi' nearer dis year."

"Oh, so I might've had to walk a bit further before this year?"

"Yeh, but oo kerrs, la'? Its wir dey go from neow to climb Everest, dis Base Camp. Yews cahn't go any fuerdher trekkin' now, like. I think de camp spreads out across de glaseeyer anyways, so oo knoews wir de centre of de camp is, like?"

"Suppose not." I'd been more than grateful for the two fewer hours. It was more likely three or four in my case, so I was untroubled that I mightn't have been sitting at the exact spot from which Norgay and Hillary had set off for their summit attempt. I'd travelled the same route the expedition had taken and was sure their camp had spread to where I'd sat on my boulder; I was only missing out the easy bit – the three-and-a-half kilometres still to climb – so wasn't in the least disheartened.

Brian and Angela, it transpired, were part of a larger group with whom they'd got on passably well but without having met any real kindred spirits. The most important thing they'd wanted from the trek was a reaffirmation of their father-daughter relationship. The pace of the tour party had left them frustrated. They wanted more time to soak up the atmosphere together in the monastery at Tengboche but were hurried on. The majority of their group wanted to cram in as many photo opportunities per day from as many different viewpoints as they could manage.

But they were philosophical about it: "Rewl of da dice, la'. Rewl of da dice."

Their noodles, tea and my hot orange arrived but the blackleg looked baffled when I asked how my chips were coming along. I chatted with Brian and Angela until they'd finished their meal and were on their tea, by which time there was still no sign of my fries. I assumed arbitration had been successful as there was a sudden influx of waiting staff, ready to get stuck right into a shift of work-to-rule.

The first one I accosted agreed to check on the status of my chips, of which he'd no knowledge, of course, as the order had been taken by scab labour on a notepad unapproved by the union. He returned, reporting the kitchen knew nothing about chips, a statement I found difficult to contest, but he agreed to take my order on an officially sanctioned jotter.

I chatted with my fellow Scousers until their bedtime. My fries were still an abstract concept, but I was determined to get them even though I'd long since gone past hungry. Trekkers retired for the evening in quick succession until I was left alone. An hour and 40 minutes later, my burnt raw-centred spuds arrived. I emptied a bottle of ketchup over them in a vain attempt at salvage, but left the diner at 10 in a desultory mood.

My departure seemed to correspond with an influx of porters. I thought they were perhaps waiting for the last Westerner to leave before they hoisted the glitter ball and got their boogie on. Back in my room, I chose to join them in their disco dancing to *Let's Groove: The Best of Earth Wind and Fire*, starting the funk at track four. An hour-and-a-half later, I was ready to sleep; it was 11.30pm.

It was as just as well I was expecting to get no kip that night – after all, I needed to get up within an hour to place my order for breakfast so it would arrive around lunchtime – but that wasn't the cause of my sleeplessness. I soon realised that, for all its lack of charm, at least the oubliette's stone walls retained some heat, whereas my upgrade lost heat faster than a Glasgow council tower block. The freeze irritated my chest again. By 3am, the spittoon needed an empty, unfortunately necessitating another trip to the cavern of stalacshites where the conical scatological architecture equalled that of my previous visit.

On my return, my nose decided to come out in support of Ange's and a pounding headache developed, too. I was feeling so miserable I hardly noticed I couldn't breathe and I met the dawn not having slept.

I'd been last out and was now first into the reception-diner and thought how the staff were going to admire my staying power. Unopposed, I secured the place by the condiments and collared the solitary server for my toast with jam and tea. He must have been the new apprentice because the full order arrived, intact and piping hot.

In my mind I could see the shop steward reprimanding him when he arrived for the morning shift that afternoon.

I finished breakfast but my stomach, now unused to properly prepared and cooked food, revolted. The *Diaries* would record a triplicate of Type Sixes but only after my breakfast had been expelled, and that before I could complete my hosing down of the floor of the nuraghe turd exposition. It took me an exhausting 20 minutes of disgusting toil to repair the cubicle and I vowed never to see the place again.

As I pulled on my pack, I decided it would be folly to attempt Kala Pattar, reckoning I could likely make it up and back, but be so exhausted on my return it would mean another night in Gorak Shep. That wouldn't only be unappealing, given the sheer volume of turd cleaning likely to be involved, but also dangerous. It was better to live to fight another day. I contented myself with the knowledge that the proceeds from my exhilarating book on my adventure would undoubtedly cover the hire of a luxury helicopter to whisk me up there next time.

I trudged out of the lodge and faced the climb back up to the path over the Changri Shar glacier's moraine. I was already exhausted, and I hadn't started the day. I recalled the section as the most arduous and the idea had now wormed its way into my head that crossing in the other direction was going to be twice the pain. I stood at the bottom of the slope back up, which in reality was a short incline, and contemplated the traverse across the glacier. It was, in fact, less than an hour of scrambling but in my mind's eye it had magnified into something else – I was a Wildling about to attempt The Wall.

I took my first step and realised I'd underestimated my task. Make my challenge that of a paraplegic Wildling, the Night King's hands clasped around his throat choking the air out of him and Samwell Tarly strapped to his back. The best I could muster was the pace of my return from Base Camp. Bemused dzho drivers and trekkers passed by every few minutes, querying my existence. Head down, I managed uncomfortable step after uncomfortable step to reach the groaning moraine.

The cairns seemed less obvious from this direction and I stopped not from breathlessness but from being unable to read the trail. I was fortunate: a guide bounded ahead of me and vaulted around a boulder. I don't know if he was rubbing in his obvious superiority on the mountain, but I thought the full twist at the end of his handspring was a bit much in the circumstances.

I was heading down into the bight in the moraine that had creaked and avalanched so worryingly on the way up. Luckily, this afforded a view of his head bobbing between the rocks and I was able to replicate his path. I reached the moraine's edge at approximately the same time as he was enjoying his tea in Lobouche, but I was enormously glad to be over it. I was blessed again with where I'd stopped – I could hardly believe the view of the derailed grey train that was the Khumbu glacier scouring its way down the valley was so improved in this direction.

I plodded on, the gradient now in my favour, and reached the steep slope that had seemed so daunting on the way up, only to find its descent looked even worse from the top. It left me rueing the chances of being egged on by peer pressure or the bribery of a Fox's Glacier Mint were nil. As I procrastinated, pretending to plot my way down, or more accurately my downfall, I heard the trampling of hooves behind me.

I stood, a transfixed trekker in the headlights of a dzho train coming at me at full throttle-stampede speed. The animals split around me and flung themselves over the lip of the descent in threes and fours. They dusted a terrified group of oriental people who'd frozen in the middle of their ascent. A boy of 15 skipped past me with a long, reed-like branch, whistling sharp tones of encouragement to his herd who were now at a dead stop, looking for some stunted grass to chomp. I thought it best to get on down before the next express freight came hurtling through.

I blamed my boots again for the loss of footing which caused me to slide five metres down into the first oriental gentleman, who kindly halted my tumble with his legs. The second oriental gentleman also proffered his assistance by stopping the first, with his legs, and so on. An apology and thank you in English and Japanese were all I could muster. I was grateful it seemed to suffice as the fallen dominoes righted themselves and let me on my way.

I fared only marginally better with my footing on the rocky descent to Lobouche. By the time I was at the *bunga bunga* pyramid, I was debating whether to stop in Lobouche and spend the night at Sangmu's, so to speak. At this hour, I was bound to be her first customer, so at least guaranteed a free cup of tea along with everything else bound to be on offer.

As I crossed the stream back into Lobouche thinking losing as much altitude as possible was my best hope of improving my condition. I'd continue down, but only after taking full advantage of the confectionery on offer at the World's Highest Bakery. After all, I'd made it to Base Camp and deserved to celebrate.

The bakery had the sort of American backwater advertising that made it unmissable. According to the garish plastering of laminates on its exterior, I could expect a barista-made café latte crafted into the Bat-Signal and a black forest gateau so rich it would keep a week-long post-birthday-party sugar rush going for a coach trip of primary fours from Baden-Württemberg.

To my mind, the interior was more Florida Keys tiki bar than French boulangerie; at five kilometres up, the designers of the place settling on a false ceiling of rattan matting as the most practical finish. Its wall of faux blackboards stencilled with educational 'Know your coffee' cups wouldn't have looked out of place gracing the most hipster of Soho brasseries. But it appeared it was too early for the 40-inch flat screen to be tuned to Vampire Weekend MTV. The floral bench cushions were complemented by the single pink flowers protruding from the simple porcelain vases that sat on each table.

There were some upmarket concessions to the bakery's location in Nepal – the freshly pressed prayer flags were explained in the fashion of the periodic table. A sign declared 'Fixed Price'. I fancied this must have been another subcontinent signage accident; surely in this place it should've read 'Price Fixing'. I knew to expect to have to pay a pretty penny for my cake and wasn't too worried as I had a stash of cash left after my exchange in Namche. But I had a vision of poor Aydin stopped at the door, counting out his last few rupees, looking forlornly at an unattainable slice of carrot cake. I'd missed not seeing him for a while.

The price fixing included an element of self-service at the counter. I sidled up to see a mini chalkboard that listed the baked goods and their prices in a font so small it was almost as if the proprietors were ashamed to display them. Conditioned by the experience of larger coffee chains in the West, I placed my order at the counter's left, expecting to be asked my name so my cardboard pail of freshly ground milk slops could be identified at the other end. Instead, the barista lady asked me to take a seat after enquiring what pattern I'd like in my coffee. My café latte and chocolate chip muffin would be served to me at my table. My expectations were exceeded when they both came in short time; not only was the quality excellent, I thought the barista had outdone herself with the foam version of *Guernica*.

"Hi!" My lissom photographer from Base Camp greeted me as she came through the door. The Dutch ladies had changed into their lower-altitude gear. They were now garbed in black boots, black trousers, black thermal top, black buff, black shades and black headbands, as if they'd cleaned out the last summer ninja collection at Vroom and Dressman. They both looked delighted on surveying the interior and I decided I'd give it another go at impressing them with my command of Nederlands. It was as close to a brown café as Nepal was going to get, and I was sure I'd seen a liquorice pancake on the menu.

"Hoi." The smaller milkmaid chose to ignore my mastery of the greeting in what I understood as the subtlest of north Randstad accents.

"Dis is a nische plasche."

"Yes, it is gezellig." I self-congratulated myself with that, scoring a point with the ultimate in a Dutch description of anything nice or, in fact, anything at all. They both autonomously nodded their agreement and we moved on to other matters.

"How isch de coffee?"

"Lekker." I was on a roll now. *Gezellig* and *lekker* in two sentences.

"And de chocolate chip cookiesh?"

"Lekker. The cute cookies are lekker." I couldn't have played that any better, I thought – I'd added a '-je' to the end of the word for cookies. This made them cute in the Dutch language, the linguistic equivalent of an Instagram kitten picture. It was top marks for me.

"What is this 'likker'?" their guide questioned; he clearly wanted to get to know his charges better. They both broke into wide grins.

"What is funny?"

"Lekker meansch 'nische'. *Likker* is someding elsche, even nisesher, but you don't need to know dat for now, maybe in Kathmandu." They were both laughing now, the guide at a loss.

"An esphpresso and muffin please," the smaller milkmaid asked.

"Lik ... no, lekker."

Buoyed by caffeine and sugar, it was time to move on. I handed over the brick of bills to which the reckoning for the refreshments amounted, arranged to meet the ninja milkmaids for lunch at Dughla and headed out.

I was back on the level, riverine stroll to Dughla, soon drifting into a meditative state. My cough had disappeared, my breathing had become even and I'd found one of those gaps in the traffic that implied I was alone on the mountain. Before I knew it, a train of trekkers was upon me. I missed the chance to pull up the crazy soul who was heading uphill in a kilt to ask him if he was a true Scotsman and whether his travel insurance covered frostbite in the regions usually described as nether.

Back in my reverie, I was soon at the monument to the fallen and realised I hadn't appreciated its extent on the way up. I spent a little time examining more of the tributes, bittersweet feelings evoked by the number of people who'd died fulfilling their passion. My dusty descent to Dughla was choked with parties of stumbling, breathless trekkers struggling to ascend. I knew exactly what they were going through with 'This is horrible,' and 'How much more of this?' doubts battering at their self-confidence.

"Not too far now, don't worry, it's flat at the top and then you're at Lobouche. Keep going." I was unsure if it encouraged or patronised, but I hoped, as it had done for me, that it helped.

I reached the stone ramparts of Dughla and chose the alternative lodge for lunch, reckoning I needed to take the Dutch girls somewhere that would impress. The Swiss chalet style bar, specials menu and checkerboard tablecloths all spoke of a quality that far exceeded its neighbour. The restaurant was packed, the food smelled wonderful and the ambience suitably *gezellig*; I'd chosen well.

The only challenge was finding somewhere to sit among the groups. The lady in charge, who looked nothing remotely like John Leguizamo, which I'm sure she'd have been pleased about if she ever got to consider it, insisted on pushing tables together so each party was as cosy as could be. This left me the choice of squeezing into the seat that nobody wanted where the tables joined within a group, or waiting. Squeezing in between sweaty trekkers was far too *gezellig* for me, so I took up a seat at the bar, ordered a straight-up hot mango juice and waited.

My luck was in almost immediately – one party left, another smaller one of four Spanish gentlemen arrived and I was ushered to a corner seat to join them. I was unsure if they were suffering from the climb or were miserable by nature. They didn't respond to my conversation starters with more than one-word answers, so I sipped my mango and waited for my lunch date until what I believed was the appointed hour. They were 20 minutes late before I realised I'd been stood up. It wasn't my first time, so I took it in my stride. I joined the guys from Barcelona in their wailing and gnashing of teeth and consoled myself in the best way possible by ordering a slap-up chicken noodle soup. It turned out to be top-notch and the service couldn't have been more in contrast to Gorak Shep.

The Catalan folks had munched their way through a full four courses by the time I'd finished drowning my sorrows with another hot mango juice. Bill paid, I was heading out when I spotted an Asian lady who'd sat down in the corner I'd vacated. She was weeping tears of despair; I was sure she was telling her husband this was her end of the road.

"Don't worry, after the next climb it's all flat to Lobouche, you'll get there." My comments seemed to register and there was a momentary break in her sobbing before it intensified. She seemed inconsolable and I worried that, somehow, I'd done more harm than good. Her husband gave me a look that said 'Thanks, but I'll deal with this' and so I headed out onto the terrace.

The boulder-field crossing to the torrent at the bottom of the village was more difficult from this direction. I was thankful to make it across without spilling into the water. I was even happier to be taking the low road to Pheriche, rather than repeating the higher trail back to Dingboche. The path arrowed straight down after the bridge putting me back on a green carpet of gnawed grasses. The trail was badly eroded and its braids darted between clumps of dwarf shrubs. Below, the river plaited itself within a tray of white boulders; ahead, the Ama Dablam massif presented its reverse view.

I achieved a steady rhythm with the descent and fell into the trekking torpor, happy to let my mind empty and to drift along, listening to the rushing water that grew ever nearer. My thought-free consciousness was only interrupted by an involuntary look up at the helicopters that called this part of the valley their flightpath. As the afternoon wore on, they seemed to descend more frequently. Each time I craned my neck, I hoped they weren't dealing with an accident or that the passenger wasn't the Asian lady, that she hadn't thrown in the towel; but who was to know?

I'd completed the descent and was now on a gentle gradient down to the village that nestled in the crook of a river bend ahead. A tributary cut across the trail repeatedly, making the going boggy in places, and I was pleased my boots coped well with the challenge.

As I reached the solitary farm building that lay between me and the village, I caught up with a trio of trekkers, an older hippy and his acolytes. He was complaining about needing to be sick again and why that was making him so slow today. It was in contrast with my own experience – once I was past my morning sickness and walking, the nausea had abated. He acknowledged he was fine when I passed by and he seemed well cared for, so I moved on into an area of drystone walling straight from the North York Moors. It was only the quartet of dzhos that raced past me as I marched down the narrow alleyways that reminded me I was nowhere near Yorkshire.

The alleyways soon widened into a biscuit-coloured, beaten earth track and the lodges were upon me. The guidebook had indicated that, from Gorak Shep, it would be a five-hour trek to Pheriche; seven hours after leaving, I'd arrived.

Pheriche to Debuche

T he Snow Land Lodge took pride of place on the Pheriche strip. It was a complex of interconnected bungalows whose appearance was in keeping with a village where the town council had acknowledged the voice of tight planning regulations. Its grey stone walling had been altered to accommodate an octet of windows framed in pea green, with its signage – a handsomely gothic yellow on black background – pinned above. Everything appeared freshly made and, to my eyes, the place had been attended to with care, thoughtfulness and taste.

I entered the reception-diner where the care and attention were equally impressive. The mahogany brown of the hardwood shone and smelled of polish. The dining tables similarly glinted in the sunlight. Each was topped with dedicated condiments, an extensive 'coffee alternatives' menu and a twin-set of sauce bottles meticulously scraped clean of any residue. Curtains were clasped at their waist in a figure-of-eight inward twist. The centrepiece burner had been buffed back to its foundry-made burnish. 'This'll do,' I thought.

There was no-one to greet me, but I could hear an interference of babble that was a TV show emanating from somewhere behind the reception desk. I spotted an old-fashioned brass bell on the counter and waited what seemed a polite length of time before I flapped the plunger down. There was no change in the show's audibility and so I tried again. There was still no response and so I increased the frequency until I was soon pinging the bell with the frequency of a dystonic Basil Fawlty.

With still no sign I'd ever be attended to, I dropped my bag, flipped the counter back on its hinges and strode boldly into the kitchen. Two young men crouched around an iPad, staring intently at the screen.

"Sorry, sorry, sir. We didn't hear you arrive."

"No worries, what are you watching? Nepal's Got Talent?"

"The X-Factor India." I imagined what the subcontinent's version of Simon Cowell would look like but rapidly dispelled the notion, thinking not even the best Mumbai tailoring could cope with the demands of a nipple-high waistline.

"Ah, we have the same in the UK. Not the Indian version, I mean, the UK version. Do you have a room, please?"

"Of course." He paused the show and directed me to my room. I was in Room 101 again but, in keeping with the rest of the lodge, its interior was not remotely Orwellian. The walls were smoothly plastered and thick foam mattresses sat atop wooden beds where freshly laundered sheets and pillows were arranged. There was a throw rug on the floor in a kaleidoscopic Sixties' acid trip motif and the stout wooden door even had its own key lock and a handle!

After thanking my host and agreeing the rate, I started unpacking. As I spread out my things, I was shamed into a realisation that my fetid dishevelment wouldn't do in a place such as this. The date of my last shower was hazy I but smelled I could do with one now. I returned to the restaurant and was only mildly shocked to see the two hosts in full synchronisation to an enthusiastic, yet tuneless version of *YMCA* coming from the iPad. I think they were at the 'Y' when I entered the room.

"Young man, I'd like to get myself clean, I'd like to have a good meal, I'd like to do whatever I feel." I couldn't resist joining in for the 'MCA' bit, but then again, can anyone?

"Excuse me, sir?"

"Err ... when you have a sec, I'd like to use the shower, please."

"The s'ower is no problem, sir, 10 minutes please. I will join you there." I thought he might have been taking the whole YMCA thing too literally.

"Okay." It was only when I was naked, in the shower cubicle, I realised why he'd wanted to join me, and it wasn't to help look for the soap. The lodge's Achilles' heel was the arrangement of the shower; while the watery bits were inside the cubicle, the propane tank and dials that made the watery bits go hot and cold were outside. This design meant at least two people were needed to operate it unless you happened to have arms with the elasticity of Mister Fantastic or the inhibitions of a Swedish naturalist.

I asked my controller to turn the water on and was met with a gelid blast straight from the top of Ama Dablam.

"Could you maybe make that a little warmer, please."

"Yes, sir." Thirty seconds later, my skin had been blowtorched raw by a geothermal jet.

"A little bit cooler, please."

"Yes, sir." Ama Dablam again.

"A little warmer, please." It was at the point where my eyeballs had melted I deduced it was better to come out at least freshly scrubbed and warm, rather than waterboarded and frozen, so I ceased further instruction. It turned out to be a good move as either my shower-mate had mastered the controls or the alternating hot and cold temperatures had equalised karmically. I was able to soap up and scrub down before one final polar blast encouraged me to get out.

I emerged from the banya expecting my assistant to have left me to dry off alone, but he was still there, twiddling the controls. It appeared the shower had a more complex shutdown procedure than an RBMK nuclear reactor, so I could understand his exactitude. I gave the signal he'd successfully avoided a core meltdown for the day and we were done.

He didn't leave, though, presumably following an unwritten code that said, although I'd indicated I was done, the reality was I wasn't. I'd now give a knowing wink and ask for my naked back to be unknotted Turkish hammam style or go all-in for the leaf-birching flagellation. I declined the undeclared offer of any extras and my controller went back to the dance hall. I hadn't realised what a difference being clean would make and I returned to my room wet-haired, feeling marvellous.

Dried off enough to comply with everyone's granny's 'Don't go outside, you'll catch your death of cold with that wet hair' edict, I followed the controller's advice and took a cup of hot sea-buckthorn juice outside to see what was going on. Helicopters were flying along the valley and spiralling downwards to land on the river's nearside gravel bank. Groups of two or three people would rush forward in the head-down crouch everyone knows they need to do when they're getting into a helicopter, and the machine would spin back into the air to head back towards Lobouche. There never seemed to be anybody getting off, so the place was evidently a pickup point, but I was unsure for what or where. The juice was like sucking hot orange rind. Refreshed after draining my cup, I headed back into the lodge.

The 1,000-metre descent had done me the world of good and I spent the hour before dinner time with a clear head stuck into the Kindle.

I was disappointed my hosts weren't slapping the floor to *Oops Upside Your Head* when I pitched up for dinner as I reckoned I knew all the moves to that one, if not necessarily in the right order. But I understood why the guys had needed to make their own entertainment; I was the only guest. The lack of patronage was a pity for such a top-end establishment and I felt that, somehow, I owed them some proper business. As I was in celebratory mood I splurged on a garlic soup starter with egg and chips for a main, giving warning I might take the lodge up on their apple pie as a dessert and follow up with one of their coffee alternatives. In other lodges, I'd be wary of a menu item listed as an alternative.

'What we actually mean by alternative, sir, is the cappuccino is made using the yak dung technique.'

'Oh wonderful, you mean like Kopi Luwak, where the beans would be filtered by a yak rather than a cat?'

'Beans, sir?'

Not in the Snow Land, though – I knew whatever they presented would be pukka. The food *was* pukka; plentiful, delicious and leaving no room for the apple pie. My hosts had kept themselves to themselves *Walking the Dinosaur* in the kitchen. There had been nobody to share my evening with, so I gave a second thought to phoning Sangmu and asking her to come down valley to par-tay. But, in the end, I anticipated she was probably involved in hosting another rescue celebration for the Israeli Defence Force, so instead went back to my room to read. Afterwards, still in disco dancing mood *White Women* by Chromeo was my choice of bedtime music, starting at track two. An hour later, I was ready for sleep; it was 9.30pm.

I'd stopped in Pheriche for a specific reason and it wasn't because of its world-famous hot showers. A doctor friend from home had worked as a volunteer at the Himalayan Rescue Association aid post in town, way back in the 1980s. A couple of weeks before I set off for Nepal she'd invited the family around to her place for a 'slide show'. This was not a Glaswegian euphemism to eat some marvellous paella and drink all the wine in the house (actually it is but, then again, anything is a euphemism for this type of behaviour in Glasgow). Rather, it was an invitation to view a ring of high-quality photographs displayed by a mechanical projector onto a pull-down screen. Talk about retro!

I hadn't seen photographs displayed in that way for at least 20 years and had forgotten how good they could be compared to digital. I know nothing about photography except to point the phone vaguely in the direction of the thing you want to shoot, or press the selfie button and adopt a pout like a pursed duck's arse in front of said thing; but the old-fashioned pictures seemed to have a depth and warmth missed by modern cameras. Our friend had asked me to 'pop in' and take a few pictures of the HRA. The idea was I'd show them to her when I returned home or leave them to her in my will if I didn't make it back.

I awoke after my first full night's sleep for what seemed like weeks with the photographic mission in mind. By any measure I'd overslept – it was 8.30 – but by Nepali standards this was practically halfway through the day. The night had been freezing– I'd doubled up on the duvets over my sleeping bag – but after a short period of coughing, it had been blissfully uninterrupted. I opened the curtains to a bright morning filtered through a layer of rime a pound coin in thickness on the window's inside.

The water butt serving the sink by the shower controls required a vigorous shake before I heard the ice crack inside and it allowed me a dribble of water to brush my teeth. I was doubly vigorous with the butt inside the toilet, wanting to make sure I could flush and rinse the Type Four that would be recorded in the *Diaries*. The memories of Dughla and Gorak were still all too vivid It was too cold for the ballroom to be graced by the Pheriche disco dancing champs of 2019 and so I went searching for some assistance in the kitchen again.

It turned out my controller was pleased to have something to do; the iPad was out of battery and was charging, precariously balanced on a ledge like a Liverpudlian trekker traversing Paiya La. I watched the helicopters fly in and out as I enjoyed my tea, toast and jam, which were all as good as the rest of the food at the Snow Land. Refreshed and fuelled up, it was time to fulfil my mission, so I paid my bill and bid farewell to my hosts.

Outside was chillier than brass monkeys and I was in full layering as I headed around the corner to the aid post. There was no sign of a retch or even dry heave, which I considered was just as well as I was going to see the doctor. I knew if he asked me whether there was anything wrong with me, I'd start with upper-body ejections but somehow the consultation would end at the very least with an endoscopy.

The aid post was approached via a side alley off the main drag; at its end was an aluminium cone, mounted with its point thrusting skywards. The cone and its position at the passageway's end brought to mind the cinematic portrayal of medieval workshops where an iron sign indicating the artisan's wares was displayed outside. A black iron plough for the blacksmith and coins for the moneyer. So I could only draw the conclusion this was an odd place for a craftsman to have set up to cater for Madonna's needs in the brassiere department. As I drew up to the sculpture, I could see the cone had been cleaved in half and so added to my assessment that the atelier also offered a service for more flat-chested clientele.

I dropped my pack at the door and, oddly self-conscious, took some photographs of the building, yard and HRA signage. The aid post is effectively the highest hospital in the world and I knew it was funded by donation, the doctors who manned it volunteers. If I hadn't been aware it had been successfully operating since before my friend had worked there in the late Eighties, I'd have been able to glean something from the sign pinned to the door their model had a good chance to work anywhere in the world where health services are provided as a luxury commodity. I learned the surgery was open from nine till five each day, emergencies seen anytime. Consultation fees were within the range of most trekkers. For US citizens, a flight to Kathmandu and charter helicopter to Pheriche on top of the going rate to get your ingrowing toenails fixed would be cheaper than having them done at home.

It was also clear the money raised helped to subsidise local medical care. The cost of consultation for local guides and porters was similar to the price of a cup of tea. The sign announced some medicines were available without consultation, so those who'd run out of aspirin didn't have to suffer or to trudge back to Namche to replenish their supplies. But among the items listed there were a couple I couldn't work out. They were that of home visit (day) and home visit (night). It was going to be a bit of a bind for the doctors to come and pay me a house call in Scotland but I took their number anyway; it can be murder to book an appointment with my local GP.

I took a step inside where a doctor was explaining the use of some medication at great length to a lady in the reception-cum-waiting room-cum-gift shop. After he'd finished with her, she'd without doubt have nothing to report in her *Diaries* for the rest of her trip, or life, for that matter. At a gap in the doctor's explanation, the lady, who was from Alaska, took her opportunity to chronicle the stomach cramping that had been causing her discomfort for the last week or so. Unchristianly, I couldn't help but think, 'Come on, lady, it's only a bit of diarrhoea. By the time you've finished moaning about it, you could've been at Base Camp by now, get on with it'; but she made the mistake of pausing for breath. It let the doctor back in to drive the conversation.

I knew I was taciturn by nature but, even so, it had always impressed me, by comparison with the average Brit, how much our American cousins could talk; less impressed that, under any sort of analysis, all those words usually amounted to saying nothing much at all. I'd often wondered why the good folks at the Bristol Royal Infirmary hadn't come up with a chart to explain the degrees of this, too. I have often wondered whether this ability to spout comes from everything being available as a service in the US. There's a lot to talk about because of so many options to discuss and, at the same time, no need ever to spend time actually doing anything.

On one of my first trips to the States, I was astonished to find there was a *bona fide* business offering a service to re-grip tennis rackets, and that not in Los Angeles, but in a small college town in Alabama. In the UK, if you needed to fix your racket, you'd go to the shop, buy some tape, spend 10 minutes wrapping it around the handle and job done. In Auburn, you'd call up 1-800-GETA-GRIP. Three minutes later someone would be at your house to pull out a set of callipers to calibrate the length of your index finger for one of the 300 varieties of tape on offer, regrip the handle, run it in for you in with a quick game of doubles and gift wrap it with paper appropriate to the season. And the entire thing would be accompanied by incessant conversation.

'So, ma'am, I have the McEnroe-Borg orange pekoe retro grip on special or we're doing a two-for-one on the Agassi hyper-absorbent macro tape in either pecan or macadamia. What can I get you?'

'Gee, like, so what's the best?'

'Well, with the McEnroe-Borg, you get, like, a 50 per cent improvement in your sweat vector adherence.'

'Gee, that's like almost half!'

'Yeah, it will improve your game by a factor of three.'

'Really? I guess I'll take it, then, you must take credit, right?'

'Sure thing, but I think we can do better than that! Ma'am, if you take up the 1-800-GETA-GRIP loyalty card, I can offer you the McEnroe-Borg at a 20 per cent discount and throw in a Serena-Venus linoleum headband in camera obscura free of charge!'

'Gee, that sounds great.'

'Fantastic, now, would you like that wrapped in the French Open '78 *Le Figaro* paper or the authentic imported Wimbledon strawberry box?'

I could hear the doctor and the Alaskan lady were two such conversational heavyweights who were engaged in a slugging match going to last the full 15 rounds of verbosity. The Alaskan lady had jabbed her way through a thesaurus worth of words and the doctor had hit back with a verbatim reading of clinical anatomy. It didn't sound like he was going to stop with his explanation anytime soon, so after browsing the T-shirts and other items for sale, I stepped back outside.

Another petitioner was waiting patiently by the sculpture and he told me he thought he'd slipped a disc further up the mountain. The contest inside finished and, as the lady from Anchorage exited the practice, she threw one last defiant paragraph back into the waiting room before leaving, defeated. The man with the suspected slipped disc entered. I was expecting a bit of a wait, but the newly-crowned champion popped his head out the door. He was dressed in a blue HRA fleece, red cap, khaki walking trousers and sturdy boots.

"Hi, can I help you?" he asked.

"Yes please, but I've a bit of an unusual request."

"Don't worry, here at the HRA we're used to unusual requests."

"It's not what you think."

"Well, I'm not sure what I think, but I'll know better once I have a look at you."

"Thanks, but I don't need a consultation. I've a friend back home who worked here ages ago, back in the Eighties. She showed me some slides before I came to Nepal and asked me to stop by and get some pictures, so when I get home she could have a look and see how the place had changed since her day. Would it be possible, please, to come inside and take some photos?"

"Sure. You can take some pictures right here now. I can't let you take any pictures of anything sensitive or any in-flight consultation or anything like that, but if you want to take a picture of where I see patients, that's no problem. Give me a minute for my colleague to finish up and I'll tidy up and you can come in."

"Thank you very much. Sorry to be a pain." A few minutes later the patient passed me and confirmed he had a slipped disc; I asked him what he was going to do.

"Painkillers," was all he mumbled before he hobbled off, back crooked to his left. I was ushered into a spotless consultation room that was basic, but not too far removed from the ones I was used to in the UK, thinking perhaps that said something about NHS funding.

I took my photographs and stepped back outside where the American doctor had now been joined by another. They were from the USA and Scotland respectively. I thought it ironic the shorter, ginger one, called Alistair, was from the States and the taller, dark-bearded one named Raymond was from Edinburgh.

"I worked in Edinburgh until recently, you might know it? It was in Corstophine, in the same complex as the Ladywell Road medical centre."

"Yes, I know it, are you based in Edinburgh, then?" replied Raymond.

"Glasgow."

"That's a bit of a commute."

"Yeah, it was a pain, especially by the airport turn-off. Listen, thanks very much, gents, for letting me take the pictures, I'm sure my friend will get a kick out of them."

"No problem, it was a pleasure," said Alistair.

"Could I be cheeky, though, and ask you for one more thing, please?"

"I know ye are fae Glesger, big man, but I cannae help ye, we dinnae stock jellies here." Raymond put on the Weegie ned accent.

"Ha-ha, it's not that. My friend has, shall I say, moved on from general practice and now spends most of her days sticking needles into the faces of middle-aged ladies to get rid of wrinkles."

"Yes?"

"So, I've made a sign here and it would be cool if you could stand with it beside your sign that says all the things the HRA offers and let me get a picture." I showed them my artwork and the doctors struck a pose in front of the HRA service list, holding up my sign that read:

'WE DON'T DO BOTOX'

"Thanks fellas. Hopefully, that should get a smile, probably not from one of her recent patients, mind!"

"No problem. I hope so. So, are you on your way up or down?" enquired Alistair.

"Down, I was at EBC the day before yesterday."

"Cool, are you trekking alone?"

"Yeah."

"First time in Nepal?"

"No, third time, the last time I was here was 10 years ago. I trekked the Annapurna Circuit."

"Oh cool, I did that earlier in the year. Was the road there then?"

"Not on the Manang side, but on the other side it was pretty much there to Kagbeni."

"It's all road now, man, you can drive to Manang."

"No way! Shit, that was the best bit."

"Yeah, I wish I'd seen it back then. How did you find it, trekking alone?"

"It's been great, but really tough. The traverses across the hills from Shivalaya were hard going but the last couple of days before Base Camp were the worst. At Lobouche I was beginning to think I was past it and was about to give up at one point."

"Yeah, we all get that, but you made it right, age is just a number, man."

"Yeah, but it's a number that tells you that you're feckin' old sometimes!" But secretly, I now didn't believe my own response and I realised, with a warm satisfaction, I had to agree with him.

"Ha-ha, that's such bullshit, man, take it from me, I'm a doctor! Did you say you trekked from Shivalaya? I fancy walking out that way."

"Yeah, I think I enjoyed the lower valleys more than here. From Cheplung, it seems a bit more done by numbers, if you know what I mean. Down there, there are fewer trekkers, so you get the lodges almost to yourself and you have a chance to speak to the local people. Here it seems a bit less relaxed. It's not unfriendly, just more transactional."

"Yes, I've found the same," Alistair concurred. "Because the aid post needs to be manned all the time, we have to trek solo as well and I've found trekking in other parts of Nepal where it's commercial to be the same. I think it's a lot to do with the groups, especially the larger ones – the lodges' focus is on them because it's where the money is. The groups can also be pretty self-contained, they don't mix with each other most of the time and as an independent you can struggle to get a look-in."

"I hear that they can push it a bit too hard for some trekkers as well. I know I'd have hated going in a group because I'm so slow walking. Do you get a lot of people from the groups coming in with AMS because of that? I've been watching the helicopters going in and out this morning."

"Nah, the helicopters don't stop here for AMS patients. They take them to Lukla or Kathmandu."

"Really? What are the helicopters doing, then?"

"They're dropping off and picking up rich folks, who want to take a few pictures here, and then they fly them up to Kala Pattar to take some more from there."

"Wow, I didn't know that sort of tourism went on here! Do you still get a lot of AMS victims here, then? My friend showed me some slides of a Sherpa guy who was being recompressed with oxygen in a yellow bag thing they used for that."

"The Gamow bag. We still have the original compressor for that here. Come and have a look," offered Raymond, and he took me to see a cylinder stuffed into a stone storage annex.

We chatted some more about life in the village, what they'd done in their three-month assignments, what they were going to do at the end of it, what they did back home and other miscellany. Not only were they good sports, but they were also engaging characters. During the conversation, I failed to even come close to out-wording Alistair – he'd been only gently sparring with the lady from Anchorage – and so, content in the knowledge I would never be a contender, I bade them thanks and hoisted my pack to get back on the trail.

The path descended to the bridge over the milky river immediately after the last building in the village. There were several winding braids from which to choose, some of which were slippery cliffside strolls that brought on thoughts of a quick turnaround to the HRA with a fractured leg or worse. I was soon over the bridge and ascending towards Pheriche La as Raymond had described it. But the cough was upon me again as I took the first 100 steps or so upwards.

The trail seemed more exposed travelling in this direction and I could only put it down to the subconscious effect of driving on the left. The lane nearest the edge would be the side of the road on which I'd travel in the car, so felt more perilous. I was panting by the time I reached the cairn and prayer flags at the pass. I was delighted I hadn't needed to rest but was also confused the terrain was unfamiliar. As the trail broadened out, I realised I'd taken a much lower route to the bridge on my ascent; here, the route cut above well-kept stone-walled fields and herders' huts.

I reached a yellow Sagarmatha national park sign indicating I was at Huduwa, a touch under 4,000 metres and had 14 kilometres or a seven-hour walk to Namche. Lukla was 33 kilometres or 16 hours and, as it was mostly downhill, it didn't seem too bad a pace, even for me.

The day had warmed up under the blue sky and I stripped to my fleece again. A stray dog took a liking to me – perhaps it was my freshly scrubbed aroma – and followed 10 paces behind, hoping for a jettisoned titbit. A little further on, a white flagpole stood 10 metres tall, its flag wrapped tightly to the mast as a tour group of eight came winding their way up from below, neckerchiefs pulled nose-high to a person. Their pace seemed slow compared to mine but I knew they were making good time by the rhythmic click-clacking of their poles. The dog watched them pass and fell in line to follow 10 paces behind their last member, this his daily routine.

The path broadened further beyond some two-tone Sanskrit-painted boulders and I met the solitary lodge set on the wide plain at Orsho. It was a setting over which I could see the cavalry of the Mongol horde rampaging in full flight. I now understood how the lone galloper had ended up charging through Shomare to such disdain – it would be difficult to rein in, literally, the excitement of a ride down this valley.

It was too early for lunch but, when I stopped in Shomare, the restaurant was packed. It was the same place where I'd eaten on my way up. As I'd acquired the taste up-state, I started with a small pot of hot mango juice while waiting for the clock to move towards 11.30. My companions were largely quartets who were keeping the waitress busy with orders for multiple courses, but there was one man of a similar age to myself who sat alone at the end table. He was the one person I'd seen on the trail who'd managed to keep their attire and visage dustless.

He had a myriad of chrome cylinders into which he popped a variety of tools and other implements, the purpose of which I couldn't discern. After settling his bill, he folded a military-precision map, flung his pack onto his athletic frame and strode out the door. I thought him possibly a field geologist with years of experience in the Himalaya or, more likely, an MI5 agent on a top-secret mission to expose the supervillain's lair underneath Pheriche. That silver statue was the nosecone of a ballistic missile aimed at the Houses of Parliament. Deciding I was hallucinating again due to low blood sugar, I ordered my statutory noodle soup, this time with chicken.

Moderately sane again after the excellent noodles, I set off towards Pangboche. The trail at the village's edge was as sodden and slippery as it had been on the way up. Sliding down the muddy stream was more worrisome than a fall upwards had been on the ascent. I was grateful to reach the dry, beaten earth further down; it was a life-ending drop to the left.

Grey clouds rolled in above Pangboche as I walked along the corniche atop the Imja Khola, my subconscious left-hand drive syndrome kicking in again, and I was happy to reach the dzho-jam that was the village. There were dozens of trekkers checking into their accommodation for the night when I passed through, each scrambling to secure the best room. I considered it curious adjacent to the WC seemed to constitute prime real estate. Given my age, I could see the attraction of a short trip in the middle of the night, but that had to be weighed against the potential odour; two doors down would be where I'd pay top dollar.

I was soon at the brightly painted gate again, down the expertly constructed staircase and across the suspension bridge. On the far side, I was delighted to find the construction crew had completed their work. I leaned up against the freshly chiselled rock buttress to watch a train of long-haired ponies plod by up the new pavement, thinking it strange they had blue plastic jerry-cans strapped to their sides rather than the usual red gas canisters. A triangular sign, straight from *The Highway Code* and reading 'Rock falling', had been planted above the revetment. It must have taken a brave workman to paint it.

The construction drew me into the forest once more. I thought that, if all the trails were as well made as this one, the trek would have been nowhere near as alarming, but it would lose something in character. I didn't especially like the exposed sections but would reflect, with some satisfaction, I'd made it past them – but not until I was sitting safely and comfortably at home, flicking through the photographs.

I passed the huge mani and, on this side, the nunnery invited, in French, visitors to come inside and tour the gompa. My timing was way off for the ceremony, so I didn't dally. Soon afterwards, at a building site which implied it was going to end up as a luxury hotel, I saw the wooden sign which told me I was at my targeted destination for the day. The guidebook had indicated that, from Pheriche, it would be a two-and-a-half-hour trek to Debuche and, four-and-a-half hours after leaving, I'd arrived.

Debuche to Namche Bazaar

R ivendell was well named for its setting, sitting as it did within the forest above the raging Imja Khola, taking on an ethereal appearance in the afternoon's low cloud. I'd chosen to stay the night on my ascent, wanting to see if its elven theme ran through to prosthetic pointy ears and Kardashian-forced, straight-hair toupees for the staff.

The lodge was unusual in that it was set at right angles to the trail, its size befitting an elvish king. Entry to the main building's two stone storeys was via a porch squatting beneath a wall of windows. Its left wing was a single floor, its right two and upon which the second storey's stone had been clad with painted yellow boards. One thing was certain – in reviewing the place's aspect, Elrond was keen on natural light and his designer had done a fine job for him in accomplishing maximal illumination.

I swept under the banners declaring the house fealty, a flag in a pattern of Croatian check and the kingdom of Lavazza, and into the lobby but there was no-one there to greet me, which struck me as odd because I was sure my hosts should've heard me coming.

'And they say that you breathe so loud they could shoot you in the dark'

Even if it wasn't quite dark in the vestibule, it was positively gloomy. The porch gate had swung shut. To my left and right, led Legolas arrow-straight corridors, all natural light reserved for beyond the well-crafted doors they served. Ahead, a stair rose upwards in the murk and led me to the greeting of an elvish merchant of middle years in human terms, hardly a sapling for her kind.

"Namaste." She greeted me in the tongue of Quenya.

"Namaste, do you have quarters for a weary questor?" I responded in my most formal Mannish.

"Follow me." She glided down the stair and took me to my chamber. Its opulence was in keeping with my expectations following my exterior survey; the memory foam mattresses of the twin divans were loaded with a luxuriance of eiderdown duvets and pillows. The crushed velvet curtains were pulled back to afford a view of the grey mist now swirling in a spritely dance outside the double glazing. It was by far the comeliest of chambers with which I'd been presented on my quest. The token coin requested befitted that of an honoured ally, not a mere traveller.

"I'll take it," I confirmed and my host nodded gracefully before bidding me follow to refresh myself. The privy was a Gondor Style accompanied by dual washbasins. It was of such a superlative standard that, if she had offered it first as my accommodation, I'd have been satisfied to make it my quarters for the night.

"The feasting will start at six," Lady Galadriel told me sonorously. I returned to my chamber to brush up on my fay etiquette, hoping the evening's banquet was going to be entertaining. My impression from Peter Jackson's interpretation of Tolkien's books was that, apart from Legolas, who'd go down the pub for a barrel or two of dwarfish ale with his mate Gimli, elves were a humourless bunch who spent all their time straightening their hair. As I was polishing the last button of my cloak, I spied the last three quarters of a horse sticking out from the porch to my right. I paused for a moment to wonder whether a wounded Aragorn was being tended by Arwen in the dining hall. I straightened my helm and headed up to see.

The great hall was spacious and in keeping with the lodge's unmatched quality. A wood burner took pride of place in its centre and a roaring fire was being stoked by a group of travellers huddled around as I walked in. My companions were a group of four young ladies regaled in the livery of the grand duchy of Patagonia, a straggly-bearded merchant of ancient origin and a mage who was slave to his tabletop of wondrous magical devices. I took a small pot of lemonish nectar and mulled over what to eat.

"So, where are we exactly, then, Sue?" The query was posed in an estuarine accent.

"Oi dawn't knaw, Jen."

"What about you, Sal, do you knaw where we are?"

"I fink we're in Debuche."

"Where's that, then?"

"'Ere on the map, see."

"Naw, I mean on the trek, Sal, 'ow far 'ave we got to gaow?"

"I dawn't knaw, Jen. Wait till Tenzink gets 'ere. We can ask 'im."

"Where are we goin' tomorraw on the map, is it 'ere, Sal? I fink Tenzink said Pangbochy or Pherichy or somefink. There's another place 'ere, Sal, Dingbochy. What's that like?"

"You're right to think you're in Debuche, ladies. I think tomorrow you'll be heading for Pheriche, by the sounds of it." It was an Irish accent that interjected, softly clipped, its intonation a Dave Allen or Richard Harris.

"Awkay, fanks. Where are you from, Aeyerland?"

"Yes, Dublin."

"Where are you goin' to tomorraw? Pheriche, same as us, then?"

"I'm heading to Dingboche, god willing, and with the help of my wonderful guide," answered the merchant.

"Tenzink's a good guide as well, inne Sal?"

"Yer, 'e's great. 'E should be 'ere soon, shuddene? 'Ow 'ave you found all the walkin'? We didn't fink it would be *this* much each day when we signed up for it."

"I'm finding it hard, but at my age that isn't a surprise."

"'Ow old are you, then?"

"Can you guess?"

"I fink about 50, what about you, Sal?"

"Yer, 'bout the same."

"I'm 67 years old, ladies. Born in Dublin's fair city in 1952 ..." Michael, such was his name, was off, his blarney dial turned to 11, recounting his life story from poor north Dublin boy to comfortable prosperity in a seaside villa in Sandycove. He'd evidently had a full life, but I could tell by their vacant expressions the girls were bored after five minutes of his rambling.

"So, we've found it 'ard as well, Michael. Do you fink tomorraw is as 'ard as gettin' 'ere from Namchoy or easier?" Jen asked.

"Oi, oi, Nam-a-choy." The rest of the girls chipped in.

"I think it will be harder from now on," opined the mage, who'd lifted his head from the blue light. His accent was a precise French, his 'h' at the start of his word slightly more emphasised than it needed but otherwise executing perfect diction.

"You've got a lot of computers there, my friend, that's a lot for your porter to be carrying up," observed the craic dealer.

"I have no porteur, I am carrying them up myself. I am worried that it is too much," he remarked as a Nepali man in Patagonia and beanie trooped in. I wondered if the mage was also from Nice.

"I'm glad we've Tenzink 'ere and our porters. Tenzink, where are we goin' tomorraw?"

"We are going to Dingboche. I need to take your o-two levels now, give me finger please." Tenzing had pulled out a space-age device and slipped it on Jen's finger where it beeped in acknowledgement.

"Very good. No problem." He repeated the examination across his charges.

"Very good, all o-two reading in range. We can make Dingboche tomorrow, no problem."

"Let's see what your readin' is, Tenzink?" Tenzing complied, showing them his own measurement.

"Is that real? What are you Tenzink, a blinkin' goldfish? Dawn't you 'ave to breathe?" exclaimed Sal and he laughed in response, then suggested they play *Uno*. I'd kept quiet through the conversation, not wanting to spoil what was ahead of them with any 'I've done it' pearls of wisdom. That seemed like it would only end in condescension and that didn't seem right, so I kept my counsel.

I couldn't resist the Rivendell special, which was Lembas bread cleverly marketed as an olive pizza. Cleverley marketed because the olive was just that – a single specimen. The pizza was scrumptious but I was left disappointed by the shortfall of olives; it was a flavour I hadn't known I'd missed so much.

Michael had worn himself out with his life story and had retired. In a non-malign way, I hoped he'd need to pay a visit to the HRA, thinking ringside seats at the Michael-Alistair fight would be worth paying for. The French hacker had also returned to the privacy of his room, presumably to instigate some sort of run on bitcoin or socially influence the next US presidential election. I didn't want to barge into Tenzing and the girls' game, so decided to turn in myself.

Brego's hindquarters were still sticking out of the porch when I returned to my room. I thought the welcome mat would be grazed bare when I passed back over it in the morning. I read for a while and chose the music for the evening, my lullaby starting at track two of *Situation: Critical* by Ultra Naté. An hour later, I was ready for sleep; it was 9pm.

My plans for a restful night were soon interrupted by a resurgent cough. It became so annoying I nipped out to the Gondor Style and recycled a discarded bottle into my spittoon for the evening. It was well used throughout the night and I didn't so much wake to as wait for dawn. Before breakfast, I was almost disappointed to manage only one Type Four for the *Diaries;* the Gondor Style was so agreeable it seemed a shame not to spend more time in there.

The hall was empty when I arrived apart from my host. I selected the Italian breakfast which consisted of an omelette, toast with what Galadriel told me was Dingboche-sourced, home-made sea-buckthorn jam and a milk Lavazza. The jam was tremendous, better than the juice from the same berry, simultaneously tart and sweet.

A muscular young man entered the restaurant, his throat swathed in a camouflage-netting scarf above an olive drab jacket. He removed his soft hat and crumpled it between fists, holding it to his chest like a southern Baptist repentant in front of his minister.

"Could I trouble y'all to hey've some breakfast, ma'am?" He also chose a special from the à la carte and sidled up to my table.

"Need some comp'ny?"

"Yeah, park yourself. Sounds like you're from the south, you from Louisiana?"

"Good gueyess. Alabama. Name's Bill."

"Lee. I was in a place called Auburn, visiting a friend, years ago. Are they still big on their college football down there?"

"Auburn? That ain't far from where i'z from, but they'z the biiiiig rivals, man. I just graduyated from Alabama. We iz playin' em soon, it's the biggest match o' the sayeson. Where's home for you, buddy?"

"Glasgow, it's a big city in the west of Scotland."

"I'z been theh'yar, man. I walked that West Highland Way couple years back. It was great, I looove Scotlan', man. So green, so purdy."

"No way?! You'd have started about two miles from my house. I did it last autumn with my son and we left from our front door, pretty much. I agree, it's a great trek."

"Glasgow, man? How d'y'all deal weeth livin' theh'yar? I read me a repor' thayt said Glasgow is the murder capital of Europe, man, you not scayrred all tha tahm?"

"I've read something like that as well but it's complete rub ... trash. There are some rough parts of town but, overall, it's not a place where you feel threatened. We don't have guns, either, so if something bad is going to happen, it's going to be with a knife. It's not like the US where folks can pull an Uzi on you."

"Yeah, Alabama's crazy, man. Ev'ry redneck got 'em self a pump-action shotgun. I'z aginst everyone havin' a gun, but things iz so bad at tha moment, I got me a pistol at home jus' to keep maeself sayef."

"But isn't that the problem? Everyone fears everyone, so everyone buys a gun to get the first shot in, and it perpetuates itself?"

"Yeah, I giss so. Problem is, that's how it iz in the US, you'z gotta stay safe, man. Look after y'self."

"So, do you think that's okay? Or do you figure something should be done about it?"

"Well, for one thang, I ain't for gittin' rid o' all guns, man, but I'z for gun control, that's gotta be the way. I don't see how some redneck asshole needs him a machine gun or goddam air-to-air missil to keep his ass safe. I'd get rid o' all that stuff and keep it to what y'all can have is jus' huntin' rifles an' pistols. Tha's enough. You gotta tighten up on the peymits, too. I theyenk the two-week rule is a gawd un, no way some crazy should be gittin' himself a gun at Walmart like he's buyin' po-taty cheeps."

"Well, I guess you know best what would work in America. I know it's written in your constitution that you've the right to bear arms, just in case our Limey-asses decide to come and reclaim the colonies from you. I know it's a different culture to ours, but all I can say is it's nice not to have to worry about being accidentally shot when I'm out for a few beers in town."

"Yeah, but y'all know we don't worry none, either. Iz just part of things, we don't notice it ayhs a problem *at all.*"

Bill was solo trekking the Three Passes, heading to Dingboche that day. He had recently completed his postgraduate studies and was well travelled, his thing long-distance trekking. Our chat flitted across all sorts of topics. I found his opinions thought-provoking on just about everything, meaning we carried on long after we'd finished our breakfasts. I wished I'd met him earlier – he'd have been tremendous company– but it was time for him to make tracks.

After our goodbyes, I returned to my room and packed my gear. Brego was nowhere to be seen beneath the magnificent view the window framed towards Everest, Lhotse and Ama Dablam, all nestling their snowy heads in the arms of the blue sky that lit the wooded valley below. Keen to get going, I returned to pay my bill.

While I'd been chatting with Bill, a ladies' coffee morning had assembled and dissipated in the hall, leaving Galadriel on her own.

She invited me to join her in the remnants of a small pot before I left for the day. We chatted about where I'd been; at the mention of where I'd stayed in Lobouche, she enquired how Sangmu was doing. She was unsurprised by her rude health. The pot finished, she presented me with a souvenir necklace from which a phial of shining liquid dangled, and warned me there were some nasty spiders down valley, somewhere in the vicinity of Churkha, apparently.

Outside, I passed the horse, which was untethered and looking lost, abandoned as it was in the courtyard, and started the gentle climb through the rhododendrons to Tengboche. After a couple of minutes, my chest was protesting the climb wasn't so gentle at all. I guessed it was due to the infection – I was bringing up phlegm every few metres. Until this point, my lungs had always cleared within a few minutes of starting to walk, but whatever was clogging my breathing this morning was stubborn about giving way.

My head-down coughing gave me plenty of opportunity to take in the tracks on the trail. It appeared someone had been riding a mountain bike down to Rivendell. I thought that might have explained the apparent redundancy of Brego, the horse now old tech.

I'd soon spluttered my way back out of the woods, past the bakery and up to the monastery. The silent monk was in his usual place, placing the day's bets for his colleagues who were still busy whitewashing the chorten. I wondered if their job was modelled on the Forth Road Bridge operation; once the painting completed one circuit, it was time to go round again in the opposite direction.

At the lip of the drop to the trail to Phunki Thenga, I could see it was no mountain bike that had caused those tyre tracks. A contraption was slung beneath a pole supported by two track-suited porters in the manner of one of those old-fashioned cartoon depictions of an unfortunate explorer on his way to the cannibal cooking pot. The machine was a black metal seated chariot, with steering and braking available for the four mountain bike wheels. A tubular roll bar ran along each side and joined metal stations that coalesced into a metal handle at the rear, its construction reminiscent of an Iditarod dog sled. Another porter had a lady strapped to his back and there was an entourage of half a dozen other people following behind.

The porters unlashed the chariot from the pole and knotted the ropes around the frame's rear. Once they were satisfied with their work, they beckoned to the other porter and the lady was deposited carefully into the seat. She donned a helmet and sunglasses and strapped herself in; her porter placed himself on the back frame and gripped the handle, while the two other porters took the strain on the hawsers. The lady was going to go for a ride down to Debuche.

Except she had other ideas. Like a paratrooper dropping from the open door of a plane, one second the chariot was there and the next it wasn't. 'Unbelievable! She's going for a ride down the trail to Phunki!' I thought. The silent monk was so shocked by the spectacle he stopped talking on his phone. As I stood there in astonishment, my thinking moved on: this lady would be labelled 'disabled' in the West but by even contemplating such a feat, she couldn't have been anything further from that description. I'd realised it took determination to trek the gorge's exposed flank, but to hurtle down the same trail on four wheels – that would take real guts.

I peered over the path's edge and she was careening down at lightning speed in a cloud of dust. The brakemen flailed behind, ropes strained and trying to dig their training shoes into the dirt. The entourage filed over the lip, which was oddly evocative of lemmings, and jogged down the trail to catch up. I wanted to see how machine and driver had coped with the initial cornering, or more precisely be in position for rubber-necking the inevitable carnage of bent metal, so followed swiftly behind.

But the lady was an expert driver. I soon caught her up where the trail effectively became a series of short jumps down a cliff; the chariot was intact and being bound to the pole for further porterage, the driver already lashed to her carrier and down trail.

I managed to pass them but was overtaken myself by a Nepali lady carrying a box slung from her back. Swaddled in the middle and seesawing from side to side was an infant no more than six months old. The lady moved like a mountain goat, leaping between the rocks at each switchback, and seemed unconcerned by the bassinette's wild motioning. What did get her goat was the young porter who deigned to catch her up playing Nepali Death Metal at full blast as he skipped downhill. As he neared, he was shot a mother's look that said, wake the baby and you'll wake up to a smell of burning. He passed in silence but, as his head bobbed below the next change of direction, I heard him fire up the music again, safe in the knowledge she couldn't catch him.

As I reached the police checkpoint at the bottom of the hill, my knees were complaining bitterly about the punishment they'd received. The Montego Bay policeman looked at my papers in the same relaxed manner as he had on the way up, and made the same joke about my trekking speed. I thought, 'He's here every day, folks.'

I crossed over the river to the restaurants, the idea to take some lunch, but I'd timed it poorly. The place was thrumming with a bawdiness that belonged more at the Munich Oktoberfest's opening ceremony. I was impressed a high proportion of the clientele were enjoying a long glass of beer or two in the sun; after all, I like the odd ale now and again myself. But the rowdiness spoke of more than that. I wondered what had caused the need to party here, at midday; the restaurants were at the bottom of a ravine and getting out in either direction was a stiff climb. I wished good luck with that to anyone with a bellyful of Gorkha, but it wasn't for me.

I managed to find a seat at the end of a table indoors in a shack furthermost from the bridge. It seemed to be some sort of Mecca for trekkers who were searching out cortisone injections. Inside lay broken remains of walkers, all intently staring at their kneecaps as if wishing it was going to bring their ligaments back. In contrast to the atmosphere outside, the interior was determinedly downbeat. I was deterred from taking lunch by the combined soup-slurping of a table of Japanese ladies opposite and a beer-wielding Australian (is that a tautology?) who kept sticking his head through the open door, insistent on trying to lift the mood with cries of "Who wants a schooner, guys?"

I decided just to take tea and use a chocolate bar to keep me going until the next stop. I was going to miss my noodle soup, but the place was not conducive to dallying. A broad man stood up in his Tour de France cycling outfit, paid his bill and left. I nibbled my Sneakers bar, drank my tea and followed him soon after. The afternoon's climb was likely to be the trip's last significant ascent and I hadn't been looking forward to it. It was a beautiful walk up through the forest but, after the descent's punishment of my joints, it proved difficult to get my legs into a rhythm. My chest had become irritated again and after 10 minutes of climbing, I sat at the trailside coughing up green phlegm.

"I 'ave lost mon bonnet," declared the Tour de France guy heading back downhill, keen to maximise the advertising revenue he was sure to recoup from the exposure of Ibis Budget to the Nepali market. I trudged up in 50-step mode. Unfortunately, it was 50 steps to a heaving, rattling rasp rather than recovery of breath. The Tour de France had made it back to me before I'd reached the top of the ascent. He was *sans bonnet* but sanguine about his loss when I enquired; I don't think I'd ever seen a better Gallic shrug.

The trail flattened out among the switchbacks in the trees. A lady in a neckerchief pulled over to me as I sat trying to recover my breathing at the side of the path.

"Look, look. Same as you." She swung around, pointing at her bag, where beneath a Malaysian flag swung a cuddly, one-eyed rabbit. He was the Rabbid's pirate cousin, relishing the spoils of his ill-gotten gains from raiding the straits of Malacca.

"Where did you get?"

"It's from my daughter."

"Good, good. We take picture of animals together." I was happy to allow the Rabbid to expand his fame to Kuala Lumpur and we took some pictures. We walked together, rodents happily swinging, until the lodge at Kyangjuma where my noodle soup addiction needed to be sated. Evilly, I chose the Malaysian spiced rabbit broth Ra-Ra style. My Rabbid lives not far from the Highlands, and there can be only one!

"How long is it to Namche from here?" I asked the owner, more making conversation than interested. I knew it wasn't far.

"One-and-a-half, maybe two hours for you." His response was instantly deflating; I reckoned I'd covered the majority of the distance and was appreciating the prospect of a quick bite before the final run-in to Namche. My memory was that the section from Namche to Phunki hadn't taken much longer than that on the way up, but then again, I'd been elated at the sight of Everest for the first time. I began to doubt my recall and mulled over stopping for the day.

It dawned on me that was what the owner wanted, it was his way of drumming up some business. I couldn't blame him as Kyangjuma was another place to which the guidebooks gave short shrift. It was a shame because the views from the village were spectacular. I finished my belated lunch and, just in case he wasn't fibbing about the distance, scoffed another Sneakers for good measure before setting off.

The restraining wall of the local kennels must have been breached as I was tracked by a pack of Rottweiler-Husky crossbreeds in steppe hunting formation for the next half-hour. They were the only dogs I saw on the entire trip, apart from the beggar that had chased me at Pheriche La, which weren't basking in the sun in a form of prone coma. But I was glad when a Pony Express rider galloped through their midst, as they were becoming worrisome. The horse split the pack, seeming to dishearten them. I was thankful they looked far less threatening as they turned tail to head back to Kyangjuma.

The trail was becoming increasingly occupied from the opposite direction by groups of trekkers all sporting the same green, emblazoned T-shirt. I must have crossed somewhere between 50 and 100 people in the same uniform. From the passing snippets of conversation, I garnered they were on a cultural exchange and liked to discuss comparative theology. I wondered if they were on a pilgrimage to the Tengboche monastery to compare the relative tenets of their creeds and how they celebrated them. If so, I hoped the mass of people included a brass section and their tubas were packed on a dzho on the way up – that euphonium thingy was going to take some out-blasting.

I rounded the bend with the chorten and was soon on the flat where the locals burnt their rubbish to see the amphitheatre of Namche spread out below. In the mist, through the pine trees and in less of a hurry, its aspect was far more pleasing than I'd given it credit for on the ascent.

I remembered the guidebook had recommended a place in town where Jimmy Carter had once stayed. Excited by the prospect of staying in the same bed, I determined to take the presidential suite. Unless, of course, the Great Twitter Wotsit had recently been in residence. I reckoned Nepali mattress dry cleaning techniques didn't lend themselves to the removal of fake tan-tinged pee stains.

I ignored the first set of steps down to the village, thinking there would be more nearer my destination. It was a miscalculation as I ended up circling the entire gallery, entering the settlement on its far side and traipsing back into the centre. After a couple of rejections from places that were full, including the one recommended, I found a lodge that would take me. The guidebook had indicated that, from Debuche, it would be a four-and-a-half-hour trek to Namche Bazaar; six-and-a-half hours after leaving, I'd arrived.

Namche Bazaar to Monjo

T he lodge was the Shangri-La, my host a jolly Sherpa lady. My quarters were reached by a rickety, bare pine staircase that in Amsterdam would've been referred to as *De Trap*. I'd always thought that, for reasons of ease of pronunciation over the years, the Dutch had lost the 'ath' conjunction between the words. This trap was evidently of a Low Countries design; it had the same bound-feet width stairs that cater so well for the average Dutchman's size 15 clogs. In this place, the various hooks inserted in unobtrusive spots notionally there to allow the festooning of the staircase with scooters, rusty bicycles and photographs of mum's best *bitterballen* only served to snare and tear at my backpack.

The room was built into the hillside, the window affording a marvellous view of Namche's drainage system. The only bedding was economically provided by a single cot. I was going to move on and try elsewhere but was swayed to take the room by the host's convivial manner and her bathroom reveal. It was as if Jiri's exemplar of all sunken Victorian WCs had been transported to the wee corner of the lodge. A sign on the door advised sunglasses were recommended to combat the glare from the glazed tiles and gleaming porcelain.

I dropped my bag, indicated I'd like some tea and followed the lady as I was bid. We abseiled down to ground level and she led me across the alley to the 'Shangri La Annex'. To my mind, this resembled a Victorian railway station waiting room or an actual Great Western Railway carriage. Inside, lined up beneath the windows, were two rows of tables in polished black wood. The sheen said my host could've constituted the entire market for Sagbanda's annual beeswax crop. She checked me in formally at the counter, handed me a menu and stood expectantly, eyes gleaming.

"I'll have a small pot lemon tea, please, and ..." My eyes scanned a list of snack options on the menu that would've graced the best Bilbao Pintxo bar. I wasn't hungry, but she knew she had me, most likely in the same way she cornered everyone, and I'd take one of the items. I'd scoffed a couple of Sneakers bars during the day so thought I might as well continue the junk food theme with a plate of poppadum; after all, I'd been tightening my belt more and more as the trip had advanced, so didn't have to worry too much about losing the cut definition of my abs.

She was delighted with my choice and retired to the kitchen as I looked for a seat. The carriage wasn't installed with those helpful LCD indicators above the seats that tell West Coast Main Line passengers a place is reserved between Carlisle and Wigan North Western, even though it always seems unoccupied until Stafford. I reverted to my British rail etiquette.

"Excuse me, is this seat taken?" The carriage was empty apart from the young man towards whom I'd directed my enquiry.

"No ... huck, heh, gurrrrarhhh, huck." His reply was more guttural than a Prussian drill sergeant.

"You don't sound too good, mate, are you ill?"

"Yes, I 'ave ze bad cough."

"I have the same, not as bad as you though, by the sounds of it. Are you on your way up or down?"

"I was on ze way oop with my farrzheur, but I 'ave to come down from Dingboche. I 'ave cough and problem with ze toilette. My farrzheur, 'e go to Base Camp. I meet 'im 'ere when 'e finish."

"That's a shame. Still, I guess you got to see Everest. I've been a bit sick as well. Are you taking anything for your cough?"

"Yes, I go to Namche pharmacy. I 'ave all drug. If you want antibiotic, Diamox, Imodium, Ibuprofen, anything you want, I 'ave all." I was tempted to ask for an ounce of weed just to exercise his claim.

"I'm okay at the moment, thanks. When is your dad due back?"

"Tomorrow, or ze day afteur."

"How long have you been here already?"

"Five day."

"That's tough, being sick on your own, here. What do you do in Namche for five days?"

"Watch movie on iPad and eat pizza." My own cough seemed to break out in sympathy with our conversation and our host looked on at us with doleful eyes as she presented me with my poppadum. They weren't the plate-sized, dry crumbly crisps found in UK curry houses, more of a dustbin lid, their surfaces glistening with hot oil. They were delicious, but I was a little disappointed I hadn't been presented with a bowl of raw onions, sauce of Carolina Reaper chillies and pink yoghurt to accompany them.

I compared notes with the French drug dealer on all manner of sputum and phlegm before we conducted a stimulating discourse on the applicability of the classification index of the Bristol Chart, concluding some additional sub-categorisations would be helpful. What we thought of as a pleasant little chat meant the late afternoon slipped towards dinner time. The carriage filled up and we tried to change subjects but found, after our initial limerence based on a mutual love of all things bodily dysfunctional, we didn't have much left to say to each other. In the stony silence, I ordered a yak and chips as break-up comfort food and we agreed to stay in touch as friends.

Our new companions were a group of newly retired Australians, who were on day two of their trek, and a pair of Japanese couples of a similar age. The Australians were complaining with Aydin-level enthusiasm about their headaches, aching knee joints, sore shoulders and blistered feet. They were clearly loving every minute.

My dinner arrived, a thick dark steak smothered in onion gravy, chunky chips cooked crispy on the outside, fluffy on the inside and a medley of assorted steamed vegetables. Vegetables! There were peas, diced carrots and chopped green beans – I hadn't seen such an array, even in Kathmandu. It was scrumptious. I asked the smiling lady for mustard to complement the last morsel of meat but my description of a small container of hot yellow paste was met with the offer of the nearest comparable option: a jar of Marmite.

The Japanese folks' soups had arrived and a choir of harmonised slurping began. I finished my dinner, anxious to take my leave before the sound drove me mad. I exited into the ginnel and chewed over whether to keep the promise I'd made to myself for a raucous night out at the Irish boozer. The increase in my coughing caused by the cold air of outside put paid to that. It would have to be the next time I passed by, I thought, adding an unspoken 'Sorry Ed'. I broke out the carabiners, and after a couple of well-executed bat-hanging moves was back in my room, my raucous night to be spent Kindling. I finished *Gnomon*, thinking its dystopian premise novel but finding there were too many cul-de-sac diversions from what it was trying to say. It led me nicely to my musical choice for the evening and I flicked the Nano to start at track two of *Bush* by Snoop Dogg. An hour later, I was ready for sleep; it was 10.30pm.

I knew better than to expect an early night in the village that never sleeps, but reckoned 10.30 was about right to tuck myself in. I'd stowed my headphones and my sleeping bag had reached that level of toasty perfection optimal for dozing off when my descent into the land of nod was halted by a banging from next door. The occupant was unpacking. The door went to and fro several times and I could hear the brushing of teeth and flushing of the toilet. All fair enough, I thought, as I closed my eyes again and drifted off.

A cot's creak was followed by an extended groan that announced great pleasure at finding the bed. The walls in the Shangri-La were thinner than a dragonfly's wings, so I appreciated my neighbour had now settled in and wouldn't disturb me further. A minute later, another groan followed, coinciding with a muted thumping noise. The question arose in my mind: 'The person behind that partition isn't doing what I think they're doing, are they?'

There was more thumping, a final groan of relief that indicated a summit had been reached and silence. In my shock, I was left thinking how had he got the energy left to perform such an act and hoping he wasn't going to use any of the tissue paper making up our adjoining wall to clean up. Perturbed, I closed my eyes again, this time disturbed by the start of the gentleman's post-self-coital snoring.

My night's attempted repose went downhill from there. The coughing intensifying to compete with the volume of my sibilating companion, and so I had a fitful night at best. I was ashamed to have to empty a full spittoon into the gleaming conveniences, sneaking out to do so at the crack of dawn. I took the opportunity to record a Type Three in the *Diaries* while I was there.

My hostess was an early riser and the carriage was glinting pristine, ready for service when I tried my luck at breakfast. Stomach better, I couldn't resist the beans on toast option with a milk coffee to wash it down. Given the yak dinner's excellence, I was expecting something akin to a tin of Heinz's best over thick, crusty farmhouse bread. The two playing cards of grey staleness and a side saucer of beans were an immense disappointment. I took solace in my cup of coffee, which was Seattle standard.

An Italian couple entered with their guide. He ordered a couple of pastries and short coffees for them before taking a tea from the kitchen for himself. They had stridden in with the easy confidence in their appearance for which Italians are famed, positively owning the revealing spandex look. They were all muscular, tanned limbs, whitened teeth and moussed hair behind designer headbands, their accessories completed by expensively fashionable sunglasses and matching watches. It was hard to tell, but I might have spotted the Dolce and Gabbana brand logo on their walking poles. They appeared to have spent all night perfecting their outfits and being groomed for a Fendi fashion photoshoot, but only stayed long enough to wolf down their breakfast, presumably needing an hour's touch-up in make-up before starting the day.

I spoke with their guide, who was counting through bricks of cash, and I thought the models must command a top-dollar day rate. He was taking them to Gokyo via Thame and told me Namche was the last place to withdraw money, so he was making sure they had enough for the entire circuit. He'd learned his Italian from three years in Milan, studying and working as part of the Nepali diaspora, which I was coming to understand spread far and wide beyond the UK and India. The Italians were now outside, keen to be on their way, so I wished them good luck on their trek, and they bade me farewell.

As I was finishing my coffee, I was joined by Monsieur Le Pousseur. Keen for a reconciliation, he offered me a value pack of Imodium, but we both knew it was much too late for that. Next was Aspirin, which I also declined. My cough, which had been persistent throughout breakfast, had grown worse during this exchange and our host, evidently unsettled by our Western infirmities, chose to act. She brought a tub of something shiny and vaguely tangerine coloured from the kitchen and placed it on the table.

"Rub, rub," she insisted.

"Honest, that wasn't me last night, madam, it was the bloke next door."

"Rub on chest." She indicated I should take a scoop and apply it to my sternum.

"What is it?"

"Nepali medicine. Help breathe. Help with cough."

"What's in it? What's it made of?"

"Nepal!"

"Okay, well, if there's that much in it, I'll give it a go," I said and took a scoop of the Nepali Vicks, massaging it in where she'd indicated. It was effective from the get-go in clearing my nasal passages but failed to do much for my hack. I thought it best to be on my way, so settled up and wheezed my way up the trap to my room, passing a sheepish-looking man on his way to the bathroom. I gathered I'd collared my neighbour.

In the alleyway, the morning was chilly. I opted to see the town's lower part I'd missed on the way up. It was in the sunshine so the footing would benefit from being less icy. The route took me by The World's Highest Irish Pub which advertised 'Hot Honey Whiskey', 'Hot Chocolate Baileys' and the less appealing 'Donkey Piss' as specials. I especially liked the description of the Guinness: 'We have beer colder than your ex-girlfriend's heart'.

Steps took me down the side of the huge water-driven prayer wheels which dominated this part of the village. I wondered, as there was only one path, how the rules of passing with the mane on the left would work for ascending trekkers. The mane's construction was impressive, an entire stream channelled through a concrete chute to provide the power.

I passed a bright orange tent, fake window included, that advertised a 'Carry me back pickup service'. It offered backpack porterage and I thought I understood the offer of 'Carry me up', but not the other way around. Despite my coughing, I wasn't going to give up the pack I'd carried all the way up to Gorak for the last couple of days of the trek. I'd passed by the lotus lily pond, beautifully maintained chorten and was back at the police checkpoint on the village outskirts before I knew it. I felt a little short-changed the officer wasn't interested in mocking my speed and that he stamped my papers dispassionately.

The path's icy crusting turned into muddy rivulets as the sun rose. It was a marvellous day for the descent, and I had the bonus of the trail to myself. I dropped into a meditative state as I loped down the hillside among the fragrant trees, the chirruping birdsong back in this part of the forest.

I reached the steep drop to the suspension bridge. A porter of about 30 was labouring up, digging his T-bar shaped crutch into the ground ahead with gritted-teeth determination. No wonder, I thought. My noodle-loving gluttony must have cleaned out supplies further up the hill. It appeared stocks were being replenished in part by the 19 boxes of Ra-Ra produce I counted strapped to his back. If that weren't enough, a brand-new microwave in which to cook them was strapped to his spine as the base support for the cartons.

I reached the bridge in 90 minutes without much in the way of incident. My knees ached and I'd slipped once, causing the need to invoke the bottom slide technique for a few metres, but I was unperturbed by the mishap. There was a hold-up at the bridge for a train of dzhos, carrying blue parcels of trekking gear, to cross from the opposite direction and for a group of trekkers, on their way up, to record the moment in 1,000 phone images. I was steeling myself for an unencumbered dash across the bridge when a group of five Asian students rushed by me onto the centre of the span, their major subject acrobatics by the way they assembled themselves in a pyramid for a grelfie on the swaying traverse.

I was glad, and slightly envious of their confidence, when they were safely across, but my own traipse across wasn't as bad as my mental picture had been. I was happily wheezing at the top of the stone staircase before anyone else could use the bridge.

The valley was warm as I reached it and I was back in a T-shirt for the first time for a while. I stopped at the same restaurant in Jorsale where I'd shared lunch with Heinrich's group and wondered, sadly, what had become of them. The last time we'd met was at Tengboche. They were doubtless on their way home to Germany by now. I sat on the terrace and tried to order a noodle soup in their honour, but the owner wasn't keen to serve me. Were my table manners really that bad on my last visit?

"Group coming." The restaurateur was concerned my solitary presence was going to mess up his arrangements for a group of a dozen on their way up. In a way, I thought this summed up one of the major differences between the trek from Shivalaya to Thado Koshi and the one from there to Base Camp. In the lower part of the trip, I reckoned any lodge owner faced with this challenge would've pulled a chair out of thin air and insisted I join the larger party. Here the groups were viewed as sacrosanct, a cash cow not to be baited by any disturbance.

"No problem, I'll just take my noodles inside." He seemed happy with the compromise. I'd appreciated the tour guides would phone ahead and give the lodges an ETA for their parties but, even so, the exactness of the calculation of the group's pace was impressive. They arrived a matter of minutes later. The owner busied himself outside, helping the guide to make them comfortable and gearing up for a bumper set of profits from the afternoon's first sitting. As it was, though, he needn't have bothered moving on the one scraggly, beardy trekker as the midday sun was not to some of the group's liking.

"Can I sit here?" asked an Australian lady of around my age.

"Of course, no problem. Are you on your way up to Base Camp?"

"Yer. This is day two for us. We flew into Lukla yesterday and stayed in a place called Phakding."

"Well, your guide has chosen a good place to stop for lunch. I stopped here on the way up and the food was good. It's a bit of a climb to Namche so I'd have something substantial."

"Do ya think they'd do me a steak sandwich? I'm dying for one."

"I'm not sure, maybe they'll have something made from yak."

"Yak. Those furry things? I don't fancy that. Jenna, can ya bring me a menu? Jenna here's moiy daughter." She pointed to herself of 30 years past.

"Is your group all together, all family?"

"Almost, we're mostly school friends. See the couple at the end of that table? That's Natalie and Shane. They're celebrating their 25-year anniversary with this trip. I was in the same class as Nat, like most of the other girls."

"A trip to Base Camp is some way of celebrating!"

"Yer, Nat told us Shane-o had always wanted to do it. They told us and the Flemings over a few beers what they were doing and then Dean-o said he fancied doing it as well. So Jan, that's Mrs Fleming, Dean-o's wife said that he was a fat bastard and could never do it, which meant then that he was *defo* gonna do it. He insisted she had to come along to witness it and she said she wasn't coming unless I came along and it just kinda snowballed from there."

"Well, I hope you all enjoy it," I said as Jenna returned with the menu.

"Thanks, Jenna. Mmm, no steak sandwich? Don't fancy much on here. What do you have?"

"Noodle soup, usually."

"Jenna, see if Shane-o can get a beef noodle soup for me?"

"Okay, mum." Jenna returned to the sun terrace where Shane-o was applying his sunblock. Five minutes later, he came inside. I was impressed by his Test cricket application of zinc oxide – it meant his overall appearance was a good approximation of Merv Hughes meets Adam Ant.

"No beef here, Sheel-zo. You can have chicken, though." Sheel-zo nodded.

"How ya goin', mate?"

"All good, mate." My own noodles came and I self-consciously started eating, trying my best not to slurp.

Shane-o's shape was typical of the group; to a person they looked overfed on a lifetime of steak sandwiches. On my way up, I'd have presumed they were too out of shape for all of them to make it to Base Camp, but I knew better now from seeing how well the Welsh group had coped. I hoped Sheel-zo's group had plenty of whatever the Aussie brand equivalent of Fox's Glacier Mints was, thinking it was most likely 'Fox-o's'.

My wheezing came back as I finished my lunch. I considered it best not to dally with Sheel-zo much longer, lest I pass something on to her. So I wished them good luck with their trek. The lunch break had done me no good, my pack weighing a lot heavier as I re-hoisted it. My coughing intensified. It took me several minutes and half the LifeStraw to get moving. By the time I was climbing past the huge Sanskrit-painted boulders at the Sagarmatha park entrance my progress was half a dozen steps followed by a coughing fit.

At the park entrance, I waited behind three pensionable Italian men. They were at the opposite end of the sartorial elegance spectrum from the morning's Italians, their outfits consisting of a peaked cap above lime green string vests and 1980s-style short shorts. I thought they'd fit in well at the dancing in Pheriche.

The army guards waved me on, not interested in my papers. I made my way out through the checkpoint bustle and spied a lodge, the Shangri-La. It was only 1.30pm but I was feeling rotten. I couldn't ignore the chance the food might be as good as the namesake I'd left that morning, so called it a day. The guidebook had only indicated it would be a six-hour trek from Namche Bazaar to Lukla; there was no mention of the time to Monjo because it was deemed too near to the latter. I estimated the hoverboard-using author would put it at three. Four-and-a-half hours after leaving, I'd arrived.

Monjo to Thado Koshi

My latest Shangri-La was approached across a sun terrace that delivered a heaven-sent view across a valley that shimmered in the early afternoon's heat haze. My host was another smiley Sherpa lady, her demeanour quietly declaring her both a jolly granny and family matriarch. She wasn't to be crossed by anyone except any snot-nosed rug-rat, who could get away with anything as long as they called up the appropriate teary eye and full-wrap hug at any reprimand.

I wheezed my way past the door curtain and across a concrete floor to a pine staircase bolted on to the lodge's exterior wall, thinking either Prince Vultan commissioned the original design or the building's original inhabitants were Olympic-level pole vaulters.

I was spared such athletics in reaching the bedroom area, which was restricted to six boxy chambers. Granny Vultan indicated I could take my pick, so I chose a sunny corner room and dropped my gear. It was the basic set-up with twin cots, each surmounted with what I'd come to think of as mid-range foam mattresses. The window, framed in bare pine, provided the same view as the terrace, but I wasn't able to enjoy it as my gaze was focused on the concrete floor. The wheeze had turned into an extended episode of chest-burning coughing. It was a full 30 minutes before I could rouse myself to return downstairs to take some tea. It didn't alleviate my symptoms. Much to my shame, I purchased a small bottle of water to craft into a spittoon before returning upstairs to rest for the rest of the afternoon.

Snug in my sleeping bag, I chose *The Three-Body Problem* by Cixin Liu as my next reading and spent some time at the Puzzlepad. It wasn't the optimal use of my time in the valley that could have given the teahouse its name – there were other walks to try in the area – but it was the best I could produce.

A little dispirited, I made my way to the dining area for something to eat as the sun was dropping beneath the valley sides. The room's harsh concrete floor clashed with the flock wallpaper of flowers masterfully papered around all four walls, while an L-shape of tables was set out for guests. The area also served Granny Vultan's family. Her extended clan was sitting around a circular table, chatting and eating, the focus of everyone's attention a recent addition.

They seemed to be obeying a universal of human nature that, in a family group, a baby cannot ever be examined at eye level; a hoist to the skies in dramatic Lion King fashion is always required. What might we be expecting to see – a tail, perhaps? This might be necessary in the Fens of East Anglia but, in most places, would seem redundant. The nipper who was being subjected to this indignity bore it blithely. His elders confirmed a furry appendage was absent and the father was, indeed, the man in the group, not some passing lothario from King's Lynn with some satisfied nodding.

The convivial atmosphere lifted my spirits considerably and Granny V left the child with her mother, pootling over to attend to my needs. The baby was her grandson of four months old; his name was Nordchauby, as best I could make out. That was fantastic – 'chubby' should be appended to the name of all babies, in my opinion. I ordered a garlic soup as a starter and saw there were tuna momos on the menu, so added those on top.

My coughing intensified and I drained the LifeStraw to keep it dampened down. To the door's left was a kitchen cabin catering for the culinary needs of both the family and guests. As I entered to ask for water, I saw Daughter V was busy making the dumplings from scratch. I was keen to see how the lady made them so asked if I could observe. It didn't seem that difficult but whenever I'd tried to make dumplings in the past they either came out with the consistency of a crown green bowl or had crumbled into a white slurry. I was looking for a secret ingredient or technique that would banish my doughy-concrete balls into history. It turned out to be something mundane. Once the dough was made, the trick was to ball it up and cover it with a cloth in a deep dish for about half an hour. After the family secret was relinquished, I was shooed away by Granny V, lest I splutter on the rest of the food, and told to come back when beckoned.

Another family member entered the diner with a young child and they made their way across to the far side of the room where benches were laid out against the wall. The man unrolled a sleeping bag, laid it out on the bench, whipped his boots off and snuggled halfway down into the bag. Daughter V brought him a small pot and the young child emptied the contents of her Paddington backpack onto the table. Pens and pencils were heaped to one side and the young lady started work on a book she spread out before her. A finger darted across its surface, pointing back and forth.

"Po-ta-to."

"O-n-ion."

"Ca-rrot."

The half-bag man nodded, each page-turn recital of words met by a chuckle of encouragement and a hinging at the waist that said, 'Come on, next one now'. She moved onto the next chapter, her vocabulary perfect, but to my ears with the pronunciation of someone who was being taught by a non-native speaker, the stress on the syllables not in the right place. She moved on to grammar and started to struggle.

"The mouse eated the c'eese."

"The bird eated the bread." The man was still chuckling away, but he was shaking his head. He signalled he'd like me to come over.

"Is this your daughter?"

"Yes." He stroked her hair gently, his face mostly a wide grin.

"Her English is brilliant, how old is she?"

"She is six years old."

"Wow, only six. Her English is incredible, I wish I could speak a language as well as she can. What age do they start teaching English to children here?"

"From the start of school. It is important to speak good English here for the tourist business."

"Yes, and lots of other languages, I've learned. I've met Nepali guides who speak French, Italian and Japanese. All sorts of languages."

"It is necessary to know one more language to earn good money as a guide. For these languages there are special schools in Kathmandu."

"Yes."

"Can you help my daughter with her homework?"

"Sure." We went through the foodstuffs again and revisited the mouse and cheese. She was a gifted child; she understood the change to 'ate' straight away and from there was faultless until the end of the book.

The text was a Western one, full of scenes of multicultural families preparing food in urban domesticity. I wondered if her dad was quizzed by his daughter over why the scenes in the book looked different to her day-to-day reality, all designer kitchens with spanking new white goods rather than the open fire I'd seen in the cabin.

My garlic soup was ready, so I returned to my table. As soon as the girl spotted I'd finished my first starter, she skipped over with her book to my table and we went through her exercise again. We were back on page four when we were interrupted by Daughter V who wanted to show me the momo dough was ready and how she was going to make the filling.

She had minutely chopped cabbage and onions and mixed them with a tin of tuna. A dollop was placed in the dumpling's centre and pinched into the shape of a Cornish pastie. She shooed me back to my table while she completed making a tray-full.

The girl was waiting for the resumption of my avuncular duties and we cracked on with completing the book. My order of half a dozen momos arrived and the rest of the tray was shared with the family. The momos were superb, crispy but not too heavy, and the simple filling was delicious beyond its ingredients. They were also so filling I had no need to order a main course.

I waited for my pupil to return but her father had decided she'd overdosed on English for the evening. She needed to concentrate on something else, possibly maths. The family had polished off the momos, Daughter V cleared the plates and Granny V brought out a steaming cauldron of rice followed by a huge pot of lentils.

This was the signal for the suspension of homework and the father and daughter joined the rest of their kin at the table. I didn't feel comfortable being an intimate spectator at the family meal; this felt a more private occasion than where I'd been a guest and invited to the hearth at Goyem. The folks weren't in the slightest perturbed by my presence, but I thought it better to leave them to enjoy their dinner and not bother them with my spluttering. I returned to my book and, before bed, some music. My choice was to start at track 10 of disc 2 of *Greatest Hits* by 2Pac. Two hours later, I was ready for sleep; it was 10pm.

If the phlegm orchestra's brass section had been warming up and cleaning their tubes at dinner time, overnight I was treated to the full symphony. I had no rest until six in the morning and went to record a Type Four in the *Diaries*. There was no sink in the lavatory, and I didn't want to wake anyone by asking for the kitchen cabin to be opened, so I washed my hands in the cistern water.

I returned to bed and fell fast asleep. I awoke at eight refreshed and made my way down to a late breakfast. I ordered an apple porridge and milk coffee and was delighted when it was delivered, the porridge coming with real chunks of stewed apple. I was also surprised to find I had another trekker as a companion for breakfast.

"You sound very sick. I heard your cough all through the night."

"I'm sorry if I kept you up. It seems to have gotten worse over the last couple of days."

"That is okay. It sounds bad. Have you seen a doctor?"

"Not yet, possibly in Lukla."

"So, you are on your way down?"

"Yes, I fly out in a couple of days. What about yourself?"

"I am on my way to Namche today. I am going to Gokyo and then Base Camp."

"I was at Base Camp a few days ago, it's pretty cool to see it. Are you trekking on your own, then?"

"Yes. I always travel alone."

"You're brave to do so, I think. How have you found that as a woman? Have you had any trouble?"

"I walked in from Salleri and at some places I felt uncomfortable with the way some local men looked at me. I am used to hiking alone so I don't notice it much anymore if someone is staring at me, but there it was in your face. In some places I was worried something bad might happen."

"I think it's pretty safe on the whole but there was that case a few years ago of the girl who went missing in Langtang, I think she was Belgian. It sounded pretty gruesome, what happened to her."

"Yes. I think as long as you are careful and don't put yourself in a dangerous situation, then it is okay. Here is no problem because there are so many people, but in the Salleri region it is different. There are not so many trekkers so sometimes you pass some guys on the trek and you wonder what they are thinking. But it's not so bad, I'd worse looks on the Camino."

"Ah, I walked some of the Camino a couple of years ago. From Leon to Santiago. I loved it, especially Galicia. It's a bit different to this, though, isn't it?"

"Yes. The first time I did it, I walked from Saint-Jean-Pied-de-Port to Cabo Finisterre on the Camino Francés."

"First time? How many times have you walked it?"

"Two. At the end of the first time I liked it so much I sold my apartment in Berlin and just keep walking. The second time I walked from Lisbon along the coast to Santiago and then along the coast of Spain to France. Now I have come to Nepal to walk."

"So, what's your plan after here?"

"I don't know, but I am just going to keep walking until I have no more money. I will see where I am then."

"Wow, so you're pretty much a nomad now, a full-time traveller?"

"Yes. In Dusseldorf, I did my business examinations and then moved to Berlin for my job in a bank. I was working in a big office with hundreds of other people, my job business administration, but I did not like it. I thought there must be more to life than emails, Excel spreadsheets and some wine with friends at the weekend so I decided to see what the Camino was like. I liked it so much that when I got back to Germany I decided to do walking full-time. I am still young – if I walk for five years I will then only be 30 and I can go back to the fun of filling in spreadsheets."

"Yes. I'm sure you won't regret it. I did a bit of travelling in my 20s and it was some of the best times of my life. I admire your bravery in selling your apartment. It takes some courage to have no security to go back to."

"Ya, but I think of it differently. Now I have nothing to worry about in Germany, apart from my parents. If my mother has a problem, I can fly to see her in a few days. They know not to call unless there is a serious problem, so now I think of myself as free."

"Yes, if your travels don't work out or you get fed up being on the road you can always go back, Germany will still be there." Her name was Gabi. We chatted some more about our common experiences from the Camino and other treks she had planned. She was planning on spending a lot of time in New Zealand, hoping to find some work there, so we talked about the South Island vineyards and the Abel Tasman trek. But it was time to head out for the day, so we gathered our gear, paid our bills and parted company on the sun terrace, she off to her next adventure, me on my way home.

The late start meant the valley was already warmed and, after a dozen spluttering steps down the village stairs, I stopped to remove my fleece. I started my stroll and could tell almost immediately the day was going to be difficult – every few steps had become a coughing fit. The way was level, but it was slow progress.

I passed raised beds of herbs maturing in the sun. The beds resembled four-poster cots, possibly discarded from the tea lodges. Cross poles provided an elevated perimeter, for which I couldn't discern the purpose. My first thought was to keep birds away but my second they were an ideal perch for a hungry snow pigeon to rest on.

A little further on, I was struck by a notice for the 'Himalayan Plantation Programme'. Its text recounted that a student had set up the programme a couple of years earlier to grow native trees locally and take them into the Sagarmatha national park, as well as the adjoining buffer zone, to plant them in the jungle. I wondered if some plants in the raised beds weren't herbs but destined to form the future canopy of the forest in the hills around.

My coughing became a little less intense and I gathered a modicum of speed, soon stuck behind a trio of gabbling grannies. They were part of a train of British trekkers who were raising money for a breast cancer charity. Their conversation was about folks back home, more reminiscent of the solidification of their blue rinses under the hairdresser's driers than their trek along the Dudh Kosi valley. As I trudged along in their slipstream, I learned in all its glorious detail of the long-past scandal of a distant relative from Essex. Shame on you, Kevin from Braintree, you cheating philanderer, on how you mistreated our Lizzie. If I ever catch up with you, it won't be your brain I hang in the tree!

Eventually, the ladies realised the heavy breathing coming from over their shoulder wasn't some Craghoppers-clad voyeur overexcited by Gloria's salacious descriptions of Kev's pants-down exploits, but rather a wheezing trekker wanting to overtake. Soon after passing them, I came across the sign at the waterfall that told me again it was four hours to Namche and four hours to Lukla, depending upon how fast you walked. How much I appreciated the wisdom in that now. It was too early, even for me, to take a cheeky cup of tea, so I strolled on.

"Hey, you look tired. Would you like a coconut cookie?"

"Ah, Amos! Noach! How are you doing?" They were doing simply fine. They had been joined by three girls of their age who were all exceptionally attractive.

We came up to a boulder protruding from the cliff and, as if to emphasise his virility, Amos skipped up it and levered the ladies up to sit beside him. Noach wasn't to be outdone and scrambled up beside them. I knew I was outdone but maintained my dignity.

"Come on, guys, give an old man a hand, will you?" I was offered a wrist and pulled myself up; my reward was a handful of coconut cookies. Where did Amos get them all from, I wondered? His inexhaustible appetite for them seemed in equilibrium with an inexhaustible supply. I was grateful to take some off his hands, as were the ladies. They were from Chicago, taking a year out to backpack across the globe, Nepal their first stop after Europe.

"So where are Yisrael and the rest of the guys?" I asked.

"Two of the guys got AMS above Lobouche and the girls were going slowly, so we split up. We think they abandoned the trek." Noach shattered my impression of the Defence Force with that synopsis; I thought they'd have stuck together no matter what, after seeing how they'd performed on the rescue.

"Are you still planning on walking out or have you changed your mind and flying from Lukla?"

"Walk and then jeep from Salleri," Noach replied.

"I'm sure you'll have no problem with that after the Three Passes. Did Amos tell you about the rescue at Lobouche?" I asked the girls. He hadn't, so we sat on the boulder until the story was told and Amos's cookies were gone. He put the empty packet back into his pocket, presumably to be refilled by some alchemic spell before the next village, and it was time to move on. The youths jumped off the boulder and down the trail to leave me to scrape down on my behind and trudge after them.

The Himalayan Sherpa Hospital announced itself as a joint venture between the Nepali and German governments and it was still under construction. It was an impressive structure that looked mostly complete to me; all that seemed left to do was the entrance way's cobbling, which was well under way when I passed. My leisurely pace brought me to Herman Helmers before lunchtime. But I couldn't resist the temptation of a slice of wedding cake so dropped my gear on the grassy terrace and wandered inside to order.

The interior had the tangy smell of freshly ground beans. Before me, a deep glass counter displayed an impressive array of rich gateaux, cheesecakes and pastries. Each of the more luxuriant cakes had already been started on. I placed an order for a chicken burger and flat white, reckoning to see later what I fancied for dessert. Outside were a pair of Russian couples and I saw the reason for the impression made on the confectionery inside – they seemed to have taken at least one slice from each cake inside and were forking them down in an orgy of cream-filling consumption.

I averted my gaze and watched the schoolchildren traipsing in their blue jumpers and red satchels back uphill, wondering whether they were headed home for lunch or it was a half day. My burger justified its price and the coffee was excellent. I was disappointed I had no space left for the home-made *apfelstrudel* or chocolate cake the waiter was insistent I tried. I dallied for a couple of hours watching the world go by, but even then, I was still replete, so thought it time to make tracks.

The checkpoint at Tok Tok wasn't interested in my papers on the descent. A man from London in T-shirt, black jeans and trainers asked me how many more checkpoints there were and how many more permits he needed. I thought he needed to worry more about his apparel than where he was going.

My rest in the sun had done me some good up to the checkpoint, but afterwards I started to struggle again. My steps were laboured when I entered Phakding to come across Monsieur Le Pousseur and his father. They were drinking beer on the artificial grass at the restaurant on the main thoroughfare through the village. Le Pousseur was his same friendly self, but his father was not. He must have still been upset about his missing bonnet.

I left them to their *pressions* and trudged on, passed by Amos and his gang further on. They were dhal baat-fuelled and left me for dead but I think the Chicago girls were secretly glad for a bit of respite and stopped to chat. We walked together for a while, but I couldn't keep up for wheezing and so I was relieved when the Hilton's familiar faux brick outline came into view. I estimated the guidebook would've indicated Thado Koshi would be a two-and-a-half-hour trek from Monjo; five-and-a-half hours after leaving, I'd arrived.

Thado Koshi to Lukla

The improvement work on the Hilton was progressing as I arrived; a new porch and replacement frame were being fitted. I needed to squeeze past a workman who was hammering nails into the lintel to enter the lodge. There was nobody at the counter, so I knocked on the kitchen door and the lady who'd interviewed me previously rose from her secret hiding place behind a large tureen. She came over to see what I was making such a commotion about, not dropping a stitch in the baby socks she was knitting.

"Namaste. You stay here before. You want your things?" She pointed to the cupboard under the stairs. I faced a dilemma. On the one hand, I could make off with the fine booty of Aydin's manicuring equipment and live the rest of my days in unbridled, toe-pruning bliss; or on the other, I could do the decent thing and confess the stash under the stairs wasn't mine. It was a tough decision for a Scouser.

"Namaste. That is my friend Aydin's stuff, not mine. I'm just looking for a room, please."

"No problem. You go same room." She waved me to climb up to the second storey and take my usual accommodations. I dropped my gear and returned to the counter, fancying a small pot and some time on the terrace. With its sunny aspect and incredible view of Kusum Kangguru, it was a wonderful place to watch the world go by. I also wanted to avoid disturbing the lady too much more in the fabrication of her bootees.

"You're having a lot of work done," I observed.

"Yes. But it go very slow. Worker man like too much tongba. Drunk all time," she replied as she put the water on to boil.

"Oh dear, that's not good."

"He finish now." It wasn't much after two and I thought, even by British workie standards, it was still a bit early to knock off.

The porch work wasn't complete, and his tools and ladder stood there prepared for the resumption of labour. I squeezed by and took a seat outside, expecting to hear nails being battered into the woodwork soon.

The world was in full flow on the path beneath the terrace, countless donkey and dzho trains passing by. I wondered why the donkeys were going in both directions but the dzhos only ever seemed to go upwards. Groups of greenhorn trekkers strode purposefully towards Phakding and crossed dusty veterans slouching towards Lukla. A Pony Express rider panicked them all as he spurred on his steed down the steep slope that curved around the base of the terrace. Schoolchildren came down the hill in groups of threes and fours, giggling as they swung their satchels. It was a busy scene but, at the same time, I found it all remarkably peaceful.

The tea did my chest some good. The afternoon sedately plodded on and, after I'd drained the pot, I returned upstairs to gather the Kindle to read for a while on the terrace. As I summited the stairs, I noticed the door leading from the balcony back into the hillside was open. Intrigued by what lay beyond, I went for a nosey and discovered the porch work wasn't going to progress any further that day. Asleep on a woodpile was the carpenter, snoring with the irregular rasp of a spirit-induced stupor.

I considered how the proprietors put up with his drinking, whether he could've been the type of good friend or relative who'll be forgiven whatever their faults, or possibly that he was being paid in mash liquor. He looked comfortable enough, so I left him to his nap and spent the rest of the afternoon at my reading, first on the terrace, later in my room.

I clambered down to the diner for dinner shortly after darkness had fallen. I sat opposite a pair of silver surfers engrossed by something on an iPad as they supped on their soup. I must have been staring as the more whiskered man caught my eye and ventured a greeting.

"Where are you going?"

"I'm heading to Lukla tomorrow and then back to Kathmandu. What are you guys watching?"

"We heff made a film about our trek. We are watching what we did today."

"That sounds fun. Where were you trekking today?"

"We came from Paiya."

"Ah, so you started at Jiri or Shivalaya?"

"Yes. We are doing the Three Passes trek and then we will also go to Annapurna. We will do the Annapurna Circuit and then Annapurna Sanctuary treks."

"That sounds pretty full on."

"Yes, at my age I need to do as much as possible in this season. I am 78, so I do not heff many years left to live."

"Aw, come on. If you can walk all those trails at 78, then I reckon you'll live to at least 100. You look in really good shape, how do you stay so fit?"

"I live not far from Graz, in a small village in the mountains. I am retired, so I walk every day."

"That'll do it. Can I see your film?"

"Yes, of course." He showed me their footage. It was filmed from a head camera and I suppose would have souvenir value for them but I found it tedious. I'd trekked the trail they'd filmed but, by the way they'd captured it, I couldn't correlate anything on the screen with anything in my memory, apart from the shaking.

What they'd managed with the dubbing and soundtrack by dinner time was a different matter, though. I was impressed that, even without seeing what was presented frame by frame, a casual observer could've been forgiven for thinking they were watching a Germanic Die Hard set to thrash metal. The old man told me he was going to post the movie on YouTube at Namche so his friends could share. I hoped the guys from the Graz legion weren't expecting too much, unless of course they were into Megadeath in that part of Styria.

Having finished the movie, the man proceeded in the best tradition of technical bores to follow his film's explanation by a lecture on how best to record trekking action. This was followed by a detailed walkthrough of the camera's specification and, when that was exhausted, he proceeded with another lecture on how best to trek. I knew I wasn't the most graceful or efficient of trekkers but my being on the way down from Base Camp seemed to count for nothing in his eyes. I couldn't get a word in edgeways to let him know I'd also trekked the Annapurna Circuit and at least participate in some form of conversation, so was thankful my garlic soup arrived and I could escape his tedious oration for a while.

As my main course of tuna sandwich and chips arrived, which I was informed wasn't good trekking food, apparently, because the fries are only empty carbohydrates, and to my consternation, tuna from a tin isn't fresh, the front door burst open and smacked into the ladder. A shocked young Nepali man, who was carrying a microwave on his back, and young trekker porting a vacuum cleaner bustled through into the diner, steadying the ladder as they passed.

Both men disappeared into the kitchen area and dropped their loads. The Nepali man headed up the stairs and the trekker took a seat in an alcove by the kitchen door. The matriarch brought him some tea before, to my amazement, they conversed in fluent Nepali. It was clear that he was part of the family.

Eager to avoid another hours haranguing by the Austrian Spielberg, I made a sharp exit at the end of my dinner and retired to my room for some more reading and music. My choice was to start *Revolución de Amor* by Maná at track two and, an hour later, I was ready for sleep. It was 10pm.

I managed some rest in between coughing fits throughout the night, my last around five, and by the time I'd fallen asleep again, the dawn was showing. I awoke again, having in the end slept late, and felt moderately refreshed; there was nothing of note to record in the *Diaries* and so I headed downstairs for breakfast.

I chose toast with apple jam, if for no other reason than I'd no idea what to expect of the conserve, and a milk coffee to drink. There was no sign of the Graz Film Club. I presumed they were busy taking alternate shots of their boots and the sky on the way to Namche, so I was left alone with the proprietor. The jam approximated a compote and, once the strangeness of its texture on toast was overcome, it was delicious. Well fed, I retired upstairs, gathered my gear and returned to pay my bill.

"You are going to Lukla? Going home?" asked the proprietor's husband. He'd been in and out of the place during my two stays at the Hilton but I'd noticed he liked to keep a low profile.

"Yes."

"Fly tomorrow?"

"The day after."

"Then you have a lot of time. Take some tea with me."

"Why not?" I dropped my bag and sat down. My host nipped to the kitchen and returned with a small pot and two cups.

"How long to Lukla, do you think?"

"For me, two hour. For you, maybe three."

"Did the guys I saw last night go to Lukla to get the new microwave and hoover?"

"Yes."

"Your son? And the other guy, is he staying with you?"

"Yes, my son. Yes. Gérard stay with us, second time he live with us. He came last year from France to climb mountain and stayed in house one month. He climb other mountain this year and stay."

"I saw him in the kitchen with your wife. He speaks Nepali?"

"Yes. He speak Nepali all time with family."

"That's impressive, to learn Nepali in a couple of months."

"We are good teacher! He wake up, speak Nepali all day, eat dhal baat, go to bed, dream in Nepali."

"Are all your family here?"

"Yes."

"Do you live here all year round?"

"No. I have another lodge in Pangboche. We go there to live for three month but I am selling Pangboche lodge."

"Why? Is business not so good there?"

"Yes, not good business. Here, I have land, below lodge over there I grow tomato and vegetable. Food in kitchen come from garden but in Pangboche impossible to grow vegetable. More work, less money."

"I think I saw at Dingboche that they were growing vegetables under a covered tunnel."

"I never see this."

"So, is business here good compared to Pangboche?"

"Business not so good here also."

"Why is that?"

"Group trekker and trekker guidebook never stop Thado Koshi. All trekker from Lukla stay in Phakding first night. Now also problem with porter, there are too many donkey. In past, lot of porter stay in Thado Koshi, not so many porter now so business go down."

"So, if you don't mind me asking, how do you make the lodge work, make enough money?"

"Some trekker from Jiri, some from Salleri. So, I make some money and I also money from Japan."

"Japan?"

"Yes. I work in Japan for four year."

"Really, doing what?"

"In hotel. I make good money. Ten-dollar one hour. Buy land for Thado Koshi lodge. Now I make lodge better. More room, hot s'ower. Grow fresh vegetable, fresh fruit. I make eco-lodge, more people come for this."

"I hope so." And I did – it seemed a pity everyone stayed in the same lodges in the same villages along the way, an extra half-hour here or there in this part of the valley amounting to nothing. We chatted about his aspirations for the lodge until a none-the-worse-for-wear carpenter came into the room wanting to start banging, so I took my leave.

This was it, then – the last day's trekking. It started down the cobbles from the lodge to the river and back up the far side. By the time I'd crossed the suspension bridge strung across a landslip on the valley side, I was motoring. I passed the downhill-racing chariot, slung between its two labouring porters at Cheplung, motored past a Scandinavian couple who were struggling along a small incline and reached the junction with of the Shivalaya trail.

The route was marked with a yellow sign beneath a terrace planter of marigolds. I was sad not to be returning via that route, maybe to try the Pikey peak route out from Junbesi or some other adventure, while at the same time happy I was only a couple of hours from completing the trek. At least I'd a little more new scenery to see before I finished. I headed up the staircase towards Lukla following a lonesome porter labouring with his load of logs.

The trail to Lukla was being cleared further on. Either side of the path, folks were hacking at the forest with machetes to remove overhanging foliage. Beyond, the trail ascended and a group fresh off the plane trooped towards me. A pair of Russian ladies were heading my way behind a Vladimir Putin lookalike and his bodyguard. I thought the ladies at best unprepared for the trek in their leather jackets, blue jeans and sporting faux trekking boots with high heels. The only things redder than their lipstick were Vladimir's cheeks; he was struggling already.

They were followed by a bucket hat-wearing Asian fellow who couldn't seem to work out the alternation needed between his walking poles to effect forward motion and an overexcited Britisher who, I could tell, was going to annoy the rest of the group by gabbling all the way up. Unless, of course, he met with an unfortunate accident involving the Asian man's walking pole, which would naturally have had nothing to do with Vladimir's bodyguard.

I passed the construction of a new lodge where the builders considered it amusing to throw half-used bricks down at each other and passing trekkers, and then I was at the start of a village delimited by a gate-cum-chorten. I strolled along the beaten earth, concrete bridge, cobblestones and flagstones for a few minutes into an increasingly urban scene. The guidebook indicated Lukla would be a two-and-a-half-hour trek from Thado Koshi and, three hours after leaving, I'd arrived.

Lukla to Samjhana Street

T he Hiker's Inn was unlike any lodge I'd stayed in before, with perhaps the exception of the Kamala. Its location befitted its urban setting, in what would most accurately be described as a multi-storey shopping centre. It sat directly above the local branch of the Siddhartha Bank. I hoped I'd secure a room directly above the premises as I'd hatched a dastardly plan to pay for my entire trip in one fell swoop, a plot involving chiselling through the concrete floor into the vault. I'd realised the true purpose of Aydin's stash of 'nail clippers' at Thado Koshi.

The inn was up a ligament-busting spiral of stairs that, on any other day, would've been purely sadistic but here, at the start of a trek or at the end, was merely inconvenient. Above a floor that seemed entirely dedicated to technicolour portraits of hipster hairstyles way beyond my follicular ability to achieve, and 180 flights further up, lay the entrance to the inn.

The inn was decidedly upmarket compared to anything I'd stayed in on the trek. I gauged that, at a push, on one of the many days Lukla Airport was closed due to the weather, the reception-cum-diner could offer a Dornier-sized hangar for additional parking.

Newly painted, papered or stencilled motifs of Tibetan deities decorated the area's support beams. Its counter was a curve of frosted glass that fronted a wall-mounted cabinet overflowing with high-end whiskies. A shelf displayed neatly stacked china cups and saucers and a variety of sauces that reinforced the impression of superiority; there were the usual chilli, tomato and brown and also a never-before-seen-in-Nepal bottle of Worcestershire. Topping even that were the dull yellows of English and Dijon mustards!

The charcoal-grey floor tiles had been antiseptically mopped and, as if to emphasise the general atmosphere of purity, the tables sported a bottle of hand disinfectant in addition to the usual salt and pepper shakers. I looked down at the dusty footprints I'd spread across the foyer, abashed in the same way as my nine-year-old self would've been after traipsing through my grandmother's kitchen after a particularly successful afternoon of puddle rolling with the Afghan hound. I was half-expecting a receptionist in black tie or evening gown but, instead, she was a small teenage lady garbed in jeans and fleece.

"Namaste. Do you have a room, please?"

"Yes, sir, of course, what tariff would that be at?" 'Tariff?' I mused. 'This place *is* ritzy'. I prepared myself for a hill-sharking in the subtle manner of a central Edinburgh hotel more reliant on its name than inherent quality.

'Seventeen pounds 50 for a pot of tea?'

'Yes, sir.' Her equivalent would offer a gentle apology in a Morningside accent.

'And £20 for the scones?'

'Yes, sir, and you should also note the surcharge for the clotted cream, £3 a teaspoon.'

'Hang on, you charge extra for the cream on the Devon cream tea?'

'Yes, sir, the cream is optional.'

'Optional?'

'Of course, sir, along with the jam. You'll note the additional levy for that. Two pounds a spreading.'

'So, that comes to 45 quid for tea and scones?'

'Yes sir, per person of course.'

'Ninety quid?!'

'To which we've also added the 15 per cent service charge for your convenience, sir.'

'Eh?'

'And, if sir would like to add something in terms of a gratuity for your waiting staff, that would be most appreciated'. And you always do, embarrassed not to.

'That's marvellous, sir, I'll just add the nuisance of the 20 per cent Value Added Tax Her Britannic Majesty's Revenue and Customs insist we enforce. Now, how would you like to pay, sir? Twenty-five-year capital repayment mortgage? Alternatively, I can recommend the lax security across the road if you need to pay via the proceeds of a small post-office heist?'

Inevitably, you sweat through the charges exceeding your credit card limit and swear a stern vow never to darken the place's doors ever again. A promise broken the next time a recently arrived blue-rinsed relative needs impressing and treating to the sights.

"Err ... what tariffs do you have?"

"Private bathroom or shared?" My head was in a spin: 'Private? Bathroom?' This was a novel combination of connected words and so I had to see it.

"Private, please." The rest of my selections for the options went by in a blur.

"Very well, sir."

"Could I see the room, please?" The young lady showed me to my quarters, and I struggled to contain myself at the sight of the en-suite. A chrome dual-control shower was built into the tiles and there was a modern gleaming Western Style and washbasin. It would be advertised by Glasgow estate agents as a state-of-the-art wet room, by those in London as a spacious apartment with a minor damp problem.

I couldn't resist my own bathroom, whatever the price – which was more than reasonable for the decadence on offer – and so agreed the 'twin en suite, airport view, breakfast with milk coffee included, complimentary Wi-fi and phone charge' tariff. As it was lunchtime, I decided to take my Pig-Pen-like dust cloud back into the diner for something to eat.

The receptionist already having experienced my sullied apparel first-hand, I expected treatment by a team of bio-hazard technicians or at least to pass through some kind of portable car wash on my re-entry to the dining room. Instead, I was ushered to a corner which presumably doubled as the village decontamination zone.

I'd a few hundred metres to go to the airport but, to all intents and purposes, had finished the trek. It was time to celebrate with a slap-up meal and I thought: 'Noodle soup it is, then!' There were also several exotic items on the menu. Feeling adventurous, I opted to give the chicken sizzler and banana lassi a go.

"Good choice, the sizzler is great," advised a balding man who was slightly younger than me and sitting in the opposite corner wrapped in a puffer jacket.

"Thanks. Anything else I should try while I'm here? I have today and tomorrow."

"Yeah. All the sizzlers are great, and I love the breakfast here. I think I've tried everything since I've been here." His belly didn't look big enough for him to be that much of a glutton, but I knew from personal experience those puffer jackets could hide a lot of sins.

"How long have you been here?"

"Four days in Lukla, three days here."

"How come?"

"I got AMS at Gokyo. I had to be helivaced down to the hospital here. I spent a day in there and then afterwards recovered here."

"So, the AMS was pretty serious, then?" My questioning was ever Paxmanesque.

"Yeah. It was an emergency helivac. I'd a day in what passes for ER here. The doc said I'm recovered from that but had secondary pneumonia and I'm now on antibiotics to deal with it."

"But if you had pneumonia, shouldn't you be in hospital for that still?"

"Back in the US, yeah, but I think the inside of this place is cleaner than there. I discharged myself and am taking the tablets. I go see the doc every day."

"And so far, so good, I hope?"

"Yeah."

"So, are you stuck waiting for a flight back to Kathmandu?"

"I'm waiting for my friend; she'll be here maybe today or tomorrow. We'll fly out together after that. This is a good place to be, I could've ended up somewhere far worse, but I'm bored of Lukla. A day is enough in this town, four days will drive you nuts."

My new friend was from Seattle. We talked about his trek before my two courses arrived together. I was glad to start on the noodle soup as the sizzler more than lived up to its name; it gave me some time for the plate of chicken to cool to something below the temperature of Erta Ale on midsummer's day and for mastery of the use of cutlery while sporting asbestos gloves.

The food was suitably fitting for a celebration – it was the best I'd experienced on the trek. Replete and embarrassed at my state of dishevelment, I decided I'd make best use of my en-suite. I'd spend a large proportion of the rest of the afternoon under its purifying jets, don the least pungent of my clothes and go for a stroll through Lukla.

I decided to ask the inn for some truthful feedback on whether there was the faintest possibility my walking gear could be laundered to an acceptable standard or would be best served by local cremation.

On my return to the reception, I was pleased to find the local laundresses were up for the challenge.

My dreams of a sudsy afternoon were dashed almost as soon as I'd stripped for the shower. The best either faucet could muster was a shuddering of pipes and a coughed-up dribble of water. It confirmed to my mind a shower is usually best served if the water is turned on. A short, minimum-vestment, barefoot visit back to reception secured the receptionist's services who confirmed I wasn't mistaken in my shower control technique and, indeed, there was no water coming out. She undertook a quick return journey herself. On her second attempt back in the bathroom, the shower burst into life and we parted company, both delighted I could flush the noxious grime accumulated since Pheriche down the drain.

Alas, I had to return to reception 10 minutes later to hint it would be preferable if some form of water heating were activated before I proceeded further. Another visit was made to the en-suite to confirm I wasn't mistaken in my assessment the water's temperature could be improved upon if it failed to pool immediately into an ice rink on the shower floor. Assessment verified, the young lady nipped back upstairs.

I was now in something of a quandary: to strip down and hope to catch some hot water should it be forthcoming, or wait for further instruction. In the end, I hedged my bets and stood in the shower in my underpants, testing the jet at regular intervals and, when I say regular intervals, I mean every three seconds. Thirty minutes later, the receptionist returned, understandably averted her eyes, and told me to be quick about my washing. The shower was solar powered, and I had 10 minutes to scrub myself down before the power gave out. Spurred on by this deadline, the next nine-and-a-half minutes were the most efficient and enjoyable shower I'd ever had.

Scrubbed pink, I was reluctant to don what passed for the 'cleanest' threads from my wardrobe, but there was nothing for it. The soap's freshness only served to emphasise the pong of dried sweat from my clothing. I figured a stroll in the mid-afternoon air might freshen things up.

The guidebook had advised that, after the sleepy villages on the trek from Shivalaya, Lukla would be a culture shock – a bustling metropolis choked with a Los Angeles freeway level of traffic – but my impression wasn't that at all. The principal thoroughfare was deserted apart from several dogs. They mostly looked like they were auditioning for a part in a public information film about the effects of a nuclear strike. Only nearer the airport were things busier, a policeman seemingly gauging interest in the formation of a local aeroplane spotters club by counting every passer-by with a clacker counter.

The airport failed to live up to the fearsome impression I'd built up in my mind's eye, founded on its reputation as the world's most dangerous. I'd read in Alexa Johnston's excellent biography of Hillary the foundations for the runway had been flattened by the dancing of the 100-strong Sherpa construction crew. Hillary apparently only managed to persuade them to get their boogie on after copious amounts of chang. Unfortunately for Sir Edmund, *X-Factor India* hadn't made it to Lukla by 1964. The stomping had only achieved a gradient of one in 10, which in my imagination was almost vertical for an airstrip. At one end of its half-kilometre length lay a 300-metre drop; at the other a cliff most well suited to arrest any forward-motioning aircraft.

It didn't seem that awful in the afternoon's golden light. Yes, the tarmac did seem to lead abruptly to nowhere at the far cliff edge. It undoubtedly made take-off a bit hairy, but I could see there was a control tower so the controller could let you know where your crash wreckage was going to be spread. For landing, there was a broad apron onto which you could handbrake turn your De Havilland if you were in danger of fragmenting the fuselage on the uphill crag. The hospital was pretty much in the terminal, so I wondered what all the fuss was about. I also couldn't help but contrast the whole imagined air of terror at the airport with the placidly ruminating cows in the fields either side of the runway. They were possibly the least energised plane spotters I'd seen, although perhaps, on second thoughts, not.

So at that moment I perceived the most obvious danger from leaving Lukla was to the waistline. The terminal was hemmed in by bakeries, the German one a proud independent, not of the Herman chain. I didn't fancy a *strudel* and there wasn't much going on in terms of take-off or landings, so I turned around and started the short walk back to the inn.

I felt obliged to stop at the 'Scottish Pub.' A friend had visited a couple of years earlier and so I knew it had been renamed from 'The

Highlander'. Presumably, this was because the Lukla village council had got fed up with all the decapitated heads rolling around in the alley behind the place. Beyond a saltire daubed with faded sharpie marks, the only legible one being 'Hairy bawbag of Kala Pattar', the sign indicated the pub was downstairs.

Unusually for a Scottish boozer at three in the afternoon, it was closed. Further Glaswegian inauthenticity was lent to the place by the lack of clientele queuing around the corner to get in. There was nothing much else to see in town bar a surfeit of trekking gear shops, for which I'd no use, so I decided to return to my luxury accommodation and spend what was left of the afternoon at my Kindle.

In the expectation of a repeat of the fine-dining experience I'd enjoyed at lunchtime, I returned to the diner for dinner. My friend from Seattle hadn't moved since I left him for my city tour. I sat down in my designated decontamination zone and spied the flatscreen on a wall that had escaped my notice on my previous visit.

"What day is it today?"

"Sunday."

"I wonder if they'll have the Crystal Palace-Liverpool game on?" The young lady had been replaced by an older one, a person in a state of perpetual motion with nowhere to go. I asked her if it was possible to see the English football. She guided me through the wonders to be seen on the 500 channels beamed in via the satellite dish at the top of the complex. Unfortunately, most of these delights seemed to involve Bollywood musicals and dubbed American cop shows; the nearest we ventured to Selhurst Park was an ESPN sports recap of college-level netball. It was hardly Premier League, but preferable to watching Everton.

This led to a conversation in which my new friend claimed Seattle had a football team. Seattle Sounders, apparently, with Portland Timbers being their major rivals. I was explaining to him that in England, timber is sometimes used as slang for overweight and perhaps the name didn't suggest the most athletic of rivals when the door swung open. A tiny Asian lady in a bucket hat flopped over the threshold. This was his friend, although from their greeting it was obvious their friendship took the shape of a rather heightened form of physical camaraderie. With that, any hopes of further discussion on the relative merits of the MLS were dropped.

I ordered the pork chops, for the same reason I had when encountering any other piggy menu item on the trek – I'd still yet to see a porker in the vicinity. They were as excellent as the chicken sizzler, with the bonus of sharing the exact same sauce. A few additional people entered the dining room, but the place was so slow as to be incongruous with the perpetual motion lady's movements. She zipped across the floor to ask everyone on entering what time their flight was and whether she needed to confirm it for them. The couple from Seattle had broken the seal on a bottle of single malt. It didn't look like I was going to find any further company for the evening, so I retired to my room.

I was disappointed the satellite version of the football had been a dead loss, but reasoned I could still listen to it on the radio. The Wifi worked well and I could download a plethora of radio across the internet apps to sample a taste of home. Radio Five Live was my preferred station, but I was denied by the BBC's policy of not allowing access from overseas. I considered it scandalous that, as a licence fee payer, I'd be denied a service I'd already paid for. It was even more scandalous the engineers at the BBC would've been smart enough to block any access via a UK IP address obtained from a dodgy freeware VPN service. Not that I'd attempted to try this for an hour or so, of course.

No other UK-based site seemed to offer any commentary in real time. I gave up and read for a while instead before moving on to my musical selection for the evening which was *By the Way* by The Red Hot Chili Peppers, starting at track 10. An hour later, I was ready for sleep; it was 10.30pm.

My first night in Lukla betrayed it didn't have much of a party scene. The cough had returned on placing my head on the pillow but hadn't lasted long and my sleep, although fitful, had been undisturbed by music. It no doubt helped the inn was some distance from the rebranded Highlander. I'd avoided the clash of swords and, more importantly, Christopher Lambert's attempt at an Eilean Donan accent.

My stomach was also settled. I decided to discontinue the *Diaries,* reckoning if anything exceptional happened over the next 24 hours I could easily remember the day's entry. Breakfast was the American Continental. It included sunny-side-up eggs, terribly tasty hash browns and bacon. The toast was thick and crunchy, and the milk coffee would've graced any New York diner.

With the trekking around unappealing due to the chest infection I had a day to kill in Lukla. I decided to go and see what was happening at the airport, thinking I was sure that was the exact same phrase plane spotters use when they grab their civil aircraft recognition handbooks and head out for the day. By the time I arrived, I'd missed all the action and all that was left of the morning's spectacle was to observe the cargo hold of a Dornier being unloaded. Diverting as that was, I was feeling fidgety three minutes later and in need of some further stimulation.

The bovines were marginally more exciting. But I could tell there were only so many cud-chewing revolutions allowed before a bull becomes aware of your voyeurism. Uncomfortable eye contact would follow, during which the animal would express some form of annoyance at your presence or interest of a sexual nature. Either way, I thought, the bull is preparing to charge to do some damage to one end of your anatomy or another; I was keen to avoid a physical restructuring of any sort and so moved on back through Lukla.

I visited every store in a vain attempt to buy some Strepsils and kill some more time. I hadn't developed a sore throat yet, but it was the only thing I could think of I might need and you could never tell when Aydin might show up. I strolled back to the chorten-cum-gate. There wasn't much happening there, either – there were no Strepsils to be found and the dogs hadn't moved from their positions of the previous day – so there was nothing for it but to retire to the inn and take up residence on the roof terrace to read and get some sun. It was 10.15am.

I lunched alone on noodle soup and read some more post-lunch. I spied what could have been a pair of my underpants being gathered from a line below, although positive identification was difficult due to the lack of swarming flies. I went downstairs to gather my laundry. There followed a mystery of a missing T-shirt only solved when the house sleuth found that a local youth was parading around in it at the sleazy end of town.

On the T-shirt's return, the perpetual motion lady asked me what time my flight was and, on being informed it was 9.30am, she sped off out of the hotel. Half an hour later, she returned, pleased to have secured me a seat on the 6am departure but failing to notice I wasn't too happy with her actions. Call me ungrateful, but with my Airport Dad tendencies, that meant having to have gone to my bed two hours before our conversation and risen to get to the airport on time at approximately the same moment she'd left the building.

Dinner was a tenderloin steak with a remarkably similar sauce to the chicken sizzler and pork chops, eaten in a diner noticeably quieter. The evening's highlight came when I tried to be a fancy-pants and pay by credit card. I thought this was in keeping with the air of the place, but it was evidently a first. There was a machine, but the perpetual motion lady was unaware which buttons she should press, and what I should press in what order, to complete the transaction. She became frustrated and called the bank manager from the branch below. He dutifully made a house call and explained the simple procedure. This involved the keying in of such a precise sequence of passcodes I was surprised a silo hatch failed to open up in the dining room. The perpetual motion lady promised to remember the codes for next time. She took down the 'All major credit cards accepted' sign straight after the bank manager had left.

The entertainment for the evening over and three-and-a-half hours late for bed, I retired to my room. I categorically did not get frustrated again by trying to gain access to the BBC radio stream through nefarious means for two hours, before giving up to listen to music. My selection that would run through to the time to get up for my plane was *B.B. King & Friends: 80,* playing from start to finish, and an hour later I was ready for sleep; it was 11pm.

I was already awake by the time my early-morning alarm knock on the door came. I'd tried to sleep but Airport Dad is never denied. My breakfast was toast with jam and milk tea, finished within milliseconds of being delivered. I was going to be sharing the flight with a Kiwi man. He didn't seem in any rush to place his order. I tried not to show my anxiety – the flight was due to leave at six, but it was 5.15 already and we had a five-minute walk to the terminal so I knew, in my heart of hearts, we were bound to miss the plane.

After what seemed like hours, the Kiwi eventually placed an order and the perpetual motion lady served him his black tea and dry toast an aeon later. He took his time over finishing his breakfast and so, eventually, we left into the dark at 5.18. If our host had seemed sprightly inside the inn, this was nothing to her speed outside. There must have been a genetic relationship with Usain Bloat; we were at the terminal in three minutes flat.

The Lukla we passed through was curious at this hour; the signs of the lodges, Scottish pub and restaurants an unexpected illuminated neon. A store owner was sweeping away the dust from the start of the main shopping precinct with a witch's broom. I thought that a pointless and thankless task, especially with the state of that filthy Kiwi's boots.

We were guided to the check-in area where our papers were confirmed as being on the 9.30 flight, but we could get on the 6am flight if we felt like it. The weigh-in of our bags was evidently the procedure's most important element as the scales measured to the microgram. The security check was limited to a policeman asking me to confirm my luggage didn't contain any explosives. Having done so, my bag was handed to a random stranger who seemed to be passing by but who, presumably, was in charge of the next stage of its journey.

I followed the Kiwi down through further security which consisted of a metal detector that was uncommonly gentlemanly at this early hour, not seeming to want to beep any of the ladies who were carrying their mobile phones through. I took this as a sign and forgot to place my own phone in the tray at the side. I was waved through, the guard telling me it was fine if I swore that was all the metal I had on me. Little did he know what I'd stashed down my trousers after the daring heist of the Siddhartha's safe deposit boxes.

Reassured by the airtight measures undertaken for my protection, I found myself in the waiting room. I was delighted, after Amos' news, to see Chava and Esther had made it safely down from Gokyo. It was much too early for buoyant conversation, but we chatted quietly about their trip for a while. The two Canadian rescuers were also taking the same flight and, if I was still half-asleep, they were positively comatose. I think there was a flicker of recognition in one of their eyes when I said hello but not much more than that.

At 6.30, I was getting worried we'd be delayed as there was no plane to board. A little later, an aircraft swept out of the sky and hit the tarmac at the runway's edge. Its engines screamed as it rattled towards the wall running beneath the crag. I thought it beyond the laws of physics for the plane to have slowed so much that, at the junction with the apron, it was able to swing into its allocated parking spot at such a leisurely pace. I couldn't see an anvil attached to a rope slung by a coyote from the plane's rear door, so had to put it down to the pilot's skill.

We watched the porters unload the Dornier, every nook and cranny filled with boxes of Ra-Ra noodles. I hadn't realised my addiction had cleaned out the entire Khumbu but was thankful to see the next group of trekkers wouldn't be denied their pleasure. What were potentially our bags were loaded and it was time to board.

Once I've checked in and successfully navigated security, Airport Dad vanishes and is replaced with Placid Pop. I've never understood the need to be the first to attain one's seat, but that was evidently not the case for my fellow passengers. The ensuing rush to the Dornier after the doors were opened resembled something more suited to the announcement of a special deal on toasters at a Black Friday sale than boarding a plane before 7am at Lukla Airport. Anxious not to spoil my average trek speed or reputation for cool, I brought up the rear. I wondered whether the person who stencilled the numbers onto the tarmac was an overly keen Jack Bauer fan or simply wanted to give the pilot warning of the number of seconds left to get the plane airborne before the drop to a metallic grave at the runway's end.

I was last on the plane, surprised to be greeted by the air stewardess's namaste. It wasn't the namaste that shocked me, rather that any cabin crew was needed on a plane which was primarily concerned with its weight distribution, didn't serve drinks and had no toilet in which any ambitious trekker couples might celebrate their completion of the Three Passes. Most passengers would be able to work out the seat belt and brace position for themselves, apart from the Junbesi Austrians, of course, who'd need Suman and Ved to do it all for them.

I felt for the lady; she tried her best to convince everyone they'd be best using their whistle should the Dornier find itself 2,000 kilometres off course and plummeting towards the Indian Ocean, but nobody seemed the faintest bit interested. There was the anticipatory hubbub of the excitement at the start of a school trip and plenty of selfies being taken, but not much heed given to the stewardess.

Looking around, I was the only passenger who appeared concerned. It wasn't so much the plane's aspect worried me – it had two wings and they looked moderately well bolted in place – it was the smell. The aroma of fuel that had been overpowering on entering the cabin hadn't abated; if anything, it seemed stronger since the door had been closed. I hoped nothing was leaking and looked out on to the wing, anxiously trying to spot a telltale jet of fuel spurting from the engine.

The plane taxied off the apron and out towards the cliff wall. It turned to face in the direction of the precipice before the pilot gunned the engines. We were catapulted forward as he took off the handbrake at a whiplash-inducing rate of knots.

"Hooooleeeeeeeee shiiiiiiiiiiiitt." I broke my cool with uncharacteristic coarseness. We were airborne, with the Dudh Kosi below us and a crowd of proximate mountains on either side. Glaciers crawled down from snowy summits to meet verdant forests below. Despite my unease at the oily secretions coming from the engine, I couldn't help but revel in how spectacular it all was.

"Sorry for my language, that was a bit of a take-off." My neighbour was an Asian lady who hadn't looked up from her electronics throughout.

"Yes, the pilot has to decide whether to go for it or not," interjected a bulbous man sat in the front row. "He revs up to max rpm then lets go. It's do or die whether he has enough torque by the end of the runway. This plane has enough oomph to be airborne by the end of the tarmac but until recently the pilot was basically throwing the plane into thin air and crossing his fingers that he had enough power in the engines to climb out of the valley before he hit the bottom. It used to be more exciting then."

"It's not exciting, dear, like everything on this trip." My neighbour responded, her head still in her screen.

"Amy enjoyed it, didn't you, dear?" The man was talking to a girl of around 10 who was sitting next to him.

"Yes, daddy."

"Amy may have enjoyed it, but I didn't."

"That's a shame, did you have a problem with altitude or something else?" I asked, hoping to ease tensions.

"No, I hate trekking. I have one leg shorter than the other so cannot walk far, and yet he makes me come and walk uphill all the time."

"Oh, well, I can understand that, then, it doesn't sound fun, especially on tough days like the walk to Namche."

"We got a helicopter to Namche, so that was no problem," she responded.

"Oh, well, then, at least you cut that bit out. The flat bit is okay after Namche, but there are some tough bits on the climb to Tengboche and then again at the top by Base Camp."

"We got a helicopter from Namche to Kala Pattar, so that was no problem either," she replied.

"Did you get a helicopter back as well?"

"Yes, back to Lukla. I'll be glad when we get back to Singapore. It's too cold here. The food isn't good."

I wasn't sure what to say to that. I wasn't going to disallow her an opinion but it was so different to mine, despite the difficulties, and so instead I stared out the window into the clouds that had enveloped the plane, wondering why she'd bothered coming at all. But the answer to that was easy – it was because Amy had been persuaded by her dad it was a good idea.

The plane broke out over green, low hills dotted with shrines and I wondered if we were passing over the route from Shivalaya. We banked out of the narrow ravines and were soon over the broad central valley. The green gave way to browns. The browns formed into buildings and motorways of traffic. Kathmandu was a culture shock after the tranquillity of the mountains. Gazing upon the polluted bustle, I was almost not relieved to touch down.

The unloading of bags was a dangerous self-service affair only surpassed in its peril by an Asian man who seemed intent on having the top of his bucket hat sliced through while filming the spin down of the plane's propeller.

Chava and Esther negotiated an incredible deal on a taxi – at one stage I imagined they'd arranged a lease-back arrangement with the driver where he'd pay them the car's value over 25 years for the privilege of transporting us into the city – and we cab-shared into town. We parted company at Tridevi Marg, and I wound my way through the alleyways of a barely awake Thamel to my hotel. The guidebook gave no indication of how long it would take to reach Thamel from Lukla; four hours after leaving, I'd arrived.

Samjhana Street to Tribhuvan

The very idea of staying at the Acme Hotel was irresistible to my sensibilities, approached as it was via a tunnel painted on a wall. In reality, a shoulder-width alleyway led to its walled garden. It wound behind stores hawking all manner of authentic souvenirs. I passed stacked pallets of logogram-stencilled cartons of incense boxes along the way.

The reception had an old-fashioned charm set in its alcove, brass key fobs protruding from pigeonholes. I'd emailed the hotel from Lukla and received only a *pro forma* response so was anxious my reservation mightn't be confirmed, but I needn't have worried – the night porter was expecting me.

I checked in, thinking it strange the reception didn't also serve as the diner. The porter showed me to a twin corner room with a garden view. I dropped my gear, contemplating what to do next. Ten o'clock in the morning was too early to head out for a life-affirming celebratory beer and I didn't feel much like sightseeing. So I did what all conquerors of EBC do in such circumstances – went to bed for a nap.

My timing on awakening was perfect. The sun was firmly over the yard-arm and the seven hours that had passed since breakfast meant it was time for lunch. I made it the 50 metres to the Northfield Café without too much incident. I was understandably offered a shave and a haircut and, when I declined, a proposal of an 'all the way' massage, whatever that was.

It was strange being back in the oasis of the café. I wanted to shout out 'Look at me, I've done it' to the less weather-beaten clientele, harbouring an image of them crowding around to lap up every word of my riveting high-altitude stories. Instead, I took a table alone and ordered a random mint cocktail, one of the Northfield's fine burgers and chunky chips. The waiter managed a cursory, professional enquiry of 'Enjoy trek?', but that was as far as it got in fulfilling my need to share.

I headed a few doors down to the office of one of the white-water rafting outfits. A highlight from my trip 10 years earlier was rafting the Bhote Koshi river with them. An enduring memory was having to hurl myself from a stone embankment into the raft as the pilot fought to maintain its position against the raging spate. It got more exciting from there. The guidebook stated two-day trips went on Tuesdays and Thursdays. It was Monday, so my plan had worked out. The American lady, who was new, was unaware of the Bhote Koshi trip and called her boss, who trotted into the office.

"Bhote Koshi. We don't raft that anymore since they built the dam."

"You're kidding?"

"No, there is not enough water to raft. We do a trip to the Kali Gandaki." The boss tried his best with the other trips he had on offer, but they didn't fit with my timetable for the flight out. The rafting was to be an indulgence for completing the trek and I was looking forward to it, so it was an enormous disappointment to find it no longer ran. I tried to see the positive in supposing that somersaulting around in a watery rubber tube wasn't going to be the best treatment for my chest infection. But it wouldn't wash and so, crestfallen, I mulled over my remaining options for the rest of my time in Nepal.

The options of a short trek into the foothills or taking a scenic flight seemed unappealing. I could return to the Northfield in the hope of growing an entourage of drinking buddies to regale with my witty repartee, or more likely, find another lonely old guy waiting for their plane with whom to drown my sorrows, but that wasn't much to my liking either.

The idea of being bent into lots of unnatural positions by a nubile, crop-topped young lady *was* more to my liking, it was only the yoga would get in the way. I could retire to Freak Street and spend a few lateral days at the genuine opium den experience but I hadn't brought my violin or dressing gown. Souvenir shopping would be a matter of entering one of the myriad of emporia cluttering the Thamel streets and asking for one of everything, so wouldn't take long. Taking up the street hawker's generous offer of an 'all the way' would take even less. And so, against my better judgement, in the end I decided there was nothing for it – I had to go cultural.

The literature would have you believe Kathmandu is a medieval city preserved in aspic, a treasure trove of Nepali-Tibetan culture. It's something akin to saying all there is to London is Buckingham Palace and St Paul's Cathedral, that Edinburgh is only the castle. Come to think of it, Edinburgh is a bad example. I knew Kathmandu had some amazing sights to see, but dotted across a metropolis trying to drag itself up by its bootstraps from the worst of its squalor. The result is pockets of exquisite tranquillity and beauty amid urban mayhem. Call me perverse, but I like this about the place.

One minute you're at an intersection where a rolling pollution meter informs passers-by they're inhaling 114 Ugs per cubic metre, and the next you're in a leafy garden surrounded by orange-robed monks. But the good news was Kathmandu's sights were all within walking distance. If I was bothering with the advice from my guidebook, I'd have learned they were all within a four-minute stroll of Thamel. For more leisurely walkers, I estimated a 90-minute radius would cover it. That would include the 10 minutes needed at each kerbside to pluck up the courage to dash across.

My first excursion was to Durbar Square, which I'd had the great fortune to visit before the earthquake. This was a place that lived up to the billing of exotic ancient citadel. It was a shame to see it on its knees. But £10 to wander around and idly stare at piles of bricks was brazen, even by Tate Gallery standards. Especially since in the UK, it's traditional that people pay you to stand around idly looking at piles of bricks, or at least it was whenever I'd a summer job.

I followed that up with a stroll to the Kathmandu National Museum, situated over the Bagmati river and up a long hill beyond an army camp. It was diverting in the kind of way that insists you should examine every label on each exhibit in case you miss something exceptional, but at the end find you haven't. The metalwork exhibits from the Kathmandu valley made it worthwhile. But the kids from the multitude of school trips seemed to find me more of a fascinating old relic than the ornate brass work, judging by the number grelfies requested.

I returned to Thamel and treated myself to the superb, eponymous pizza at the Fire and Ice restaurant. The evening clientele were all well-heeled Nepalis celebrating birthdays, so I felt out of place and headed back towards the Northfield to trawl for some action. Apart from buying some company from my insistent hawker friend, it didn't look like there was going to be anyone with whom I could hang out, so I repaired to the Acme. The hotel was far enough from the Purple Haze to allow for the enjoyment of music. I kicked off John Mellencamp's *The Lonesome Jubilee* track five. An hour later, I was ready for sleep; it was 10pm.

After an excellent breakfast of fried eggs and sausage, Pashupatinath was my next destination. The temple complex is a UNESCO World Heritage Site, billed as one of the world's religious wonders. But to my mind, it failed to live up to that kind of expectation. The architecture of the complex, the murals and the burning ghats were diverting for a while but I'd have liked to have been allowed to see inside some of the temples. I understood that, as a non-Hindu, seeing any more than the golden cow's hindquarters was forbidden, but thought there must be some other points of interest for prospective tourists. The entire purlieu was generally filthy, with discarded offerings of marigolds, plastic bags, cigarette packets, bottles and other detritus. I found the market serving the pilgrims with all sorts of religious paraphernalia at the foot of the hill of more interest. The items for sale ranged from marigold necklaces to soft-focus daguerreotypes of Hindu gods.

I continued my tour with a visit to Boudhanath where the contrast to Pashupatinath couldn't have been more marked. Despite its popularity, once inside the pristine circular complex, there was a perceptible air of relaxation and tranquillity. As a result, I spent lunch and the rest of the afternoon there, watching the monks complete their circuits. The atmosphere helped with my cough so I strolled back to Thamel for dinner in good spirits.

I took some passable momos in a backstreet place off Chaksibari Marg for no other reason than they looked like they needed a customer. I hadn't bumped into anyone I'd met in the mountains and didn't fancy a night on a bar stool, so returned to my reading again. The pre-bedtime musical selection was *Raise Vibration* by Lenny Kravitz, starting at track two. An hour later I was ready for sleep; it was 10.30pm.

The next morning, I repeated my breakfast order and, well fortified, left to visit the Narayanhiti Palace Museum. This was the Nepali royal family's residence until their demise. I was not expecting much from the palace's modernist frontage – it reminded me of Holy Name Church in Fazakerley, Liverpool – but, to my delight, found this a gem of a place.

To my mind, the snapshot in time and the palace's opulence gave an incredible insight into the excesses of absolute monarchy. How many writing rooms, offices and bureaus does anyone really need? But I loved it, especially the conga past the crown jewels. There was a poignancy in the bullet holes in the walls where the dynasty came to an end in 2001.

Heading towards Narsingh Chowk, the Ug meter was showing 123 when I passed. I ambled back towards Thamel, looking out for where the caveman convention was being held, knowing there was a good chance of a top-end mammoth steak to kick start the Paleo diet I'd planned when I got home. My cough returned in the haze of particulates. So, I dedicated the rest of the day to my interpretation of what, I believe, ladies call 'shopping'.

'How can I help you, sir?'

'Can I have one of those, some of those and a few of those, please?'

'Certainly, sir, and may I suggest you also take some of these?'

'Yeah, okay.'

'These are also exceptionally good value, sir; I am sure your loved ones will be grateful to receive some of these, will you take them?'

'Yeah, okay.' And so on, until the average male is grateful the most helpful merchant gentleman has relieved him of the totality of his paper money.

After depositing my hoard of souvenirs in the Acme, I headed out for dinner. My last meal in Nepal would an upmarket dhal baat thali. I reasoned I wouldn't be eating rice and lentils again for a while. No-one else seemed to have the same idea and the place dedicated to such offerings was empty. This meant a lack of company again, and so, after dodging the hopeful pimp, I returned to the Acme for a repeat of my previous evening's entertainment. Musically, I rounded off my trip to Nepal with *Follow Me* by Yerba Buena, starting at track nine. An hour later I was ready for sleep; it was 11.30pm.

Airport Dad mode kicked in for my next-day mid-afternoon flight and so I took my breakfast shortly after midnight. My plan for the early morning was to do some last-minute 'shopping' for a pashmina shawl. I had approval of its colour and texture from *'TOO YOUNG'* via video call. Afterwards, I'd grab a cab to the airport. This plan allowed an Airport Dad level of contingency to cater for unpredictable events like traffic jams, a national strike or Godzilla rampaging through the Central Business District chewing up taxis. As I returned from breakfast to ready myself for the 'shopping' expedition, I noticed the door of the room next to mine was ajar.

"Hi Aydin."

"Hi Lee."

"That's a bit of a coincidence, you being in the room next to me. How are you doing?"

"Not bad, although I've lost way too much weight. What do you think?" He showed me the gap between his belly button and where his belt could stretch to.

"Yeah, that's a lot. Me too. I looked in the mirror when I got here and think I had the start of a six-pack; well, it was more like a six-barrel, but what's in a word?"

"You look okay, but look at me, I'm too skinny. I'm going to Chitwan this morning and I'm worried if I catch anything that gives me a gip tummy, I haven't got any reserves of fat to keep me going."

"Are you going to take anything for that?" I couldn't resist.

"No, I couldn't possibly." And he didn't let me down.

"Oh well, I'd recommend you feed yourself up at the Fire and Ice, then, they do a great pizza. Did you ever get your travellers' cheques changed, by the way? The Fire and Ice is next to a bank and they may change them there for you."

"Oh yes, I got them changed yesterday here in Kathmandu. It was a bit of a hassle, they had to call regional headquarters in India to sort it, but it only took five hours in the end."

"Cool, I admire your persistence. I have to get a pashmina shawl and then I'm heading off to the airport. See you for a cup of tea before I go?"

"Yeah. See you soon." I returned after a delay at the pashmina shop – the approved colour was no longer on sale – and so that was the last I saw of Aydin. His Bus-station Dad gene must have decided a threshold had been exceeded and he'd set off to Chitwan. I was sad I'd missed him and not only because I'd wanted to get a real good look at those nail clippers. Like almost everyone else I'd met on the trek, he'd helped me immensely along the way. Without the hospitality of the villagers, friendliness of the heroic porters and generosity of knickerless *fräuleins* I'd have never made it. Missing out on the chance to share a small pot while grouching one last time about it all brought home that I'd reached the end of my trip.

A wave of conflicting emotions swept over me. On one hand, I was returning home to my family. Unlike in Thamel, I'd have a captive audience to bore with my trekking stories. Well, for the car journey from the airport, at least.

I'd have an opportunity to put together an EBC playlist from the first song I'd listened to each night along the way. It would remind me of what I was feeling in that sleeping bag before lights out, so to speak. That came with a bonus the kids might, to their horror, cue it on the Sonos at Nunthala dawn chorus volume. Even better if they had friends around. I could introduce them to *Budi*.

I had a chance to break out from the niche research field of backpacker bar dynamics and advance my scientific career further. The 'raw' data in the *Diaries* would provide the input for a new high intensity weight-loss theory. The nine kilos I'd shed would be the supporting evidence. I only hoped I could make my submission to *Nature* before the Gingembre Twins. There was no way I could compete with their dietary findings from Dughla.

The techniques I'd learned in Chhimbu would come in handy if I decided to open a *raksi* distillery. My first premium batch, aimed at the East London market, could be branded as 'Kenja Dynamite'. Failing all that, I could apply for *The Great British Bake Off*. My 'Sneakers Pie' would guarantee me a Star Baker accolade.

But on the other hand, there was another adventure to be had, with the Rabbid not far away. I was sure Usain Bloat could whisk us away to the Manaslu Circuit or Mustang. I still had the business card for the 'Gates of Forbidden Kingdom Tea House and Trekking Lodge'. There was a sense of a missed opportunity in not heading that way. But the people along the Old Way to Everest Base Camp had taught me I *could* go again. Slowly slowly. So I knew, to paraphrase KTM, I'd be back.

First, I'd enjoy Christmas at home. I'd float the idea of turkey Ra-Ra noodle soup as this year's dinner. So I packed my bag, strolled to Thamel Marg and hailed a cab. The guidebook hadn't indicated how much time it would take to reach Tribhuvan International Airport from Thamel. Thirty minutes after leaving, I'd arrived.